'People must be prosecuted without fear or favour . . . anywhere where there is criminality, there must be accountability.'

JULIUS MALEMA[1]

MALEMA

Money. Power. Patronage.

MICAH REDDY

PAULI VAN WYK

Tafelberg

Front cover photograph: Gianluigi Guercia/AFP
Back cover photograph: Gallo Images/Frennie Shivambu
Cover design: Nudge Studio
Page design: Marthie Steenkamp
Editing: Riaan de Villiers
Proofreading: Riaan Wolmarans and Tracey Hawthorne
Indexing: Anna Tanneberger

Originally printed in South Africa
ISBN: 978-0-624-09082-3 (First edition, second impression 2025)

LSiPOD: 978-0-624-09616-0 (First edition, first impression 2025)

Epub: 978-0-624-09176-9

Contents

Timeline

1997 • Julius Malema elected chair of Cosas in Limpopo.

2001 • Elected president of Cosas (aged 20), starts spending time in
Johannesburg.

2003 • Elected ANC Youth League secretary in Limpopo.

2005 • First company directorship of Ever Roaring Investment.

• SARS first stumbles upon the name of Julius Malema in
Project Dunlop Roller Bearing, an unrelated organised-crime
investigation into Martin Wingate-Pearse.

2006 • First child, Ratanang, is born.

• Buys a house in Flora Park, Polokwane, for R1 million.

2007 • Registers the Ratanang Family Trust.

• Malema plays a crucial role in Jacob Zuma's victory at the ANC's
Polokwane elective conference.

2008 • Elected president of the ANC Youth League in April. Moves to
Johannesburg and rents property in Silvela Road, Sandton.

• ANC increasingly concerned about Malema's unruly behaviour.

• Cassel Mathale appointed as MEC for roads and transport,
Limpopo.

2009 • SARS instructs its Significant Case Unit to help Malema become
tax compliant.

Malema pays R3,6 million for the Silvela Road house he had rented, later tears it down and starts building his 'playboy mansion'.

Lesiba Gwangwa instructs his auditor to register Malema as a director of SGL Engineering Projects with 70% shareholding in the company. Six months later, On-Point Engineers fraudulently wins the bid to run the Limpopo department of roads and transport's Project Management Unit (PMU).

2010　After several failed attempts to help Malema become tax compliant, SARS instructs its Financial Investigations Unit to verify Malema's tax debts and launches Project Caesar.

ANC brings initial charges against Malema in April in a sign of growing frustration towards him from within the party.

Malema's benefactors buy him the farm Palmietfontein outside Polokwane for R1 million.

Ratanang Family Trust receives large cash payments from On-Point. The trust becomes an official shareholder in On-Point.

Cleared by the Public Protector of wrongdoing relating to tenders awarded to SGL Engineering Projects despite incomplete or missing tender documents of most municipalities investigated.

Malema and Gwangwa become the only directors of On-Point.

2011　Hawks start investigating Malema in relation to On-Point.

Malema's benefactors buy him the farm Schuilkraal outside Polokwane.

Ratanang Family Trust registered for tax for the first time, following numerous requests by SARS to do so.

In July, *City Press* reveals 'Malema's secret fund' and names the Ratanang Family Trust bankrolling him.

Suspended by the ANC.

2012　Expelled from the ANC.

SARS launches a tax inquiry into Gwangwa and raises assessments against Malema because he did not make full and frank disclosures.

Public Protector finds Limpopo roads department fraudulently awarded On-Point the PMU tender.

Malema appears in the Polokwane Regional Court on charges of fraud, corruption and money laundering.

2013 The NPA's Asset Forfeiture Unit attaches the Schuilkraal farm and later auctions it off.

Malema's properties in Sandton and Polokwane are seized to partly settle his R16 million tax debt.

The EFF is launched on 26 July at Uncle Tom's Hall, Soweto.

SARS succeeds with final preservation order for Malema's assets.

2014 SARS receives a provisional sequestration order against Malema, who requests a compromise agreement.

In a damning report released in March, Public Protector finds Jacob Zuma 'benefited unduly' from state-funded upgrades to his Nkandla homestead and should repay some of the costs. The EFF starts its 'pay back the money' campaign.

EFF wins over 6% of the national vote in the May elections and becomes the third-largest party in parliament.

Marries Mantoa Matlala in Polokwane.

2015 Sequestration case heard in the High Court in June – SARS withdraws the case without explanation.

Judge orders fraud and money-laundering charges against Malema in the On-Point case to be struck off because of lengthy delays.

2016 EFF wins landmark case in the Constitutional Court, which ruled in March that Zuma had breached the Constitution by failing to implement the Public Protector's Nkandla report.

Days before the August local government elections, Thulani Majola, whose company was improperly appointed to the multibillion-rand Giyani Water Project, starts paying Malema's front company Santaclara.

EFF wins 8% of the vote in the local elections, giving it a foothold in the metros.

2017 The first R5 million in VBS loot paid to Sgameka Projects not long after Tshifhiwa Matodzi allegedly met Malema and Floyd Shivambu.

2018 Zuma resigns in February. Cyril Ramaphosa becomes president.

In July, businessman Hendrick Kganyago begins paying Malema and Marshall Dlamini's front companies in apparent connection with the corrupt Tshwane fuel tender. By August the following year, Kganyago paid over R15 million to Mahuna, Santaclara, and DMM Media.

Afrirent starts paying Malema in July, around the time crucial decisions are made in the Johannesburg fleet tender. In October, Afrirent wins the R1,2-billion contract.

2019 EFF wins over 10% in the national election, cementing its place as the third-largest party.

2021 Malema meets former president Zuma at his Nkandla homestead for tea in February, in a sign of a rapprochement between the two leaders.

2023 MK Party formed.

2024 Zuma's MK Party gets 14,5% in the May national elections, displacing the EFF as the third-largest party. EFF support down to 9,5%. ANC loses its majority.

Defections from the EFF. Shivambu, the most senior EFF member to resign, joins the MK Party as secretary-general in August.

Unsuccessful attempts to forge an EFF–MK Party alliance. Malema labels the MK Party the EFF's 'biggest enemy'.

2025 Shivambu resigns from the MK Party.

Prologue

THIS IS NOT a biography of Julius Malema. After many unflattering articles about the Economic Freedom Fighters (EFF) and its leadership, the party banned the organisations we have written for – the amaBhungane Centre for Investigative Journalism and *Daily Maverick* – from covering its events.

The EFF labelled us 'agents of Stratcom' (the secret propaganda apparatus of the security police under apartheid) and 'enemies of the revolution', and Malema declared the party would no longer respond to questions from amaBhungane or *Daily Maverick*.

'Let them write any nonsense they want to write about us,' he proclaimed at a media conference in 2019.

Neither of us has interviewed Malema in any depth, and those who remain close to him refuse to speak to us. So, while we have gained many insights into his life, we have not set out to write an authoritative account of the man himself and his mercurial ways. But we do have a story to tell about his relationship with money and power, and what it means for South African politics.

Over the years, we have gathered plenty of information about his financial schemes and the moneyed people around him. This book, then, is not so much about him as his interlinked political and financial network. Put differently, it shows how Malema has leveraged his growing political power and influence to accumulate resources and build patronage networks, which he has then used to consolidate his political stronghold.

In the process, we hope to tell a broader story about the relationship between money and politics in post-apartheid South Africa – about the stealthy and insidious ways in which money courses through the political world; its corrosive effects on politics more generally; and how supposedly radical politicians have exploited popular grievances about poverty and deprivation to accumulate money and power.

Malema's maximalist politics took shape during his time in the African National Congress (ANC) Youth League but found their purest expression in the EFF, the party he founded in 2013 after being expelled from the ANC. Implicitly, and at times explicitly, he rejects the idea of the nonracial national community envisioned in the Constitution and seems to view the state merely as a pile of resources to which he and his camp of followers can lay claim.

Corrupt politicians are hardly unique in South Africa, where a new class of 'tenderpreneurs' has scrambled to benefit from preferential access to state procurement worth about R1,25 trillion a year. But Malema's political trajectory – and the volume of information we have about him – provides a particularly vivid insight into the toxic and often corrupt nexus between money and power in South Africa.

Throughout his relatively short but meteoric political career, he has proven to be a consummate political entrepreneur, using his growing political power to channel state resources to his allies and to extract rents from them in return, as we believe this book shows. He came to embody a particular brand of provincial clientelism that thrived under the radar while national scandals grabbed the headlines.

Several factors combined to turn provinces like Limpopo into swamps of corruption. These included the incorporation of the Bantustans, where the apartheid government let corruption fester; the post-apartheid restructuring of the civil service and procurement regimes; and the influence of an ANC that put party loyalty first and was quick to close ranks and protect corrupt cadres. It was from these turbid waters that Malema emerged onto the national stage, with his political clout backed by an impressive provincial patronage network, as we will see.

From early on in his career, his every step was marked by controversy. Before the dust had settled on one scandal he'd be careening into the next. But despite this and the media attention lavished on Malema, his financial machinations and the intricate details of how they worked aren't all that well known. After he turned into an anti-Zuma crusader, his earlier misdeeds (especially those related to the On-Point Engineers scandal, explored in Chapter 6) were forgiven by many and to a large extent forgotten; to many, he was temporarily rehabilitated. Then Zuma fell, and Malema was implicated in new corruption scandals, notably the collapse of VBS Mutual Bank.

Amid growing 'state-capture fatigue', the details of Malema's sleaze went unnoticed by many. To those who believed the whole political system was in any case rigged and corrupt, and who saw Malema as a political saviour – a Robin Hood in red overalls, robbing the rich to fund the revolution – the details mattered even less or could be easily explained away.

Absurdly, this has allowed Malema to present himself as an anti-corruption crusader. In February 2024, at the EFF's election-manifesto launch in Durban, he declared that an EFF government would not tolerate corruption, adding that the families of government officials who drove 'expensive German machines' should ask them where the money had come from. His own 'expensive machines' were not mentioned. Any journalist willing to question the source of his wealth or refer to his involvement in a range of scandals is swiftly labelled a 'Stratcom agent'.

Malema's political career has been funded by opportunistic business-people who have backed him with the possible expectation of benefiting financially via public procurement.

Many of those who have invested in him have seen hearty returns, while Malema's lifestyle appears to have far outstripped his parliamentary salary. At R125 000 a month (in 2025), his salary would not come close to paying for his burgeoning property portfolio or the designer suits, expensive watches and luxury vehicles to which he has become accustomed.

While amassing a personal fortune, Malema has also used a vast amount of cash to simultaneously fuel a growing political machine – one highly personalised in the figure of its commander-in-chief. Entrenching itself in the metros from 2016 onwards, the EFF appears to have ensured that donors were rewarded with tenders (even as the party's election manifesto demanded an end to the tender system) and pliant officials were promoted. It made seats in legislatures and political sinecures available to its allies, including disgraced officials and politicians, while members who brought in cash and resources were rapidly bumped up the hierarchy.

Meanwhile, Malema and other senior leaders allegedly harnessed the EFF's political muscle for private gain – in Limpopo, when EFF 'ground forces' were accused of acting as private enforcers working to protect Malema's personal interests; when EFF leaders appeared to abuse their public positions to protect the interests of a waterworks contractor who was paying Malema; or when the kingpin of the VBS fraud – on his own account – 'gratified' Malema and Floyd Shivambu on the apparent understanding that they would rein in the party's criticism of the bank.

The story of Malema's response to the death of his friend and bene-factor Matome Hlabioa illustrates the extent to which the party has been moulded around private interests. Hlabioa, a businessman closely asso-ciated with both Malema and former Limpopo premier Cassel Mathale, died of cancer in May 2015. While he was in hospital, Malema offered his wife, Marubini, a seat in parliament, essentially so that she could get access to government medical aid.[2]

She had no political experience and declined the offer, but it shows how Malema views the EFF as his own fiefdom – a vehicle for dispensing patronage. A seat in parliament, with a salary of R1 million and various perks, became a means of honouring his personal obligations to the widow of his deceased friend.

Like those of its leader, the EFF's finances are opaque. Its lavish spectacles and ability to fill stadiums with bussed-in supporters suggest a party flush with money from big donations. But the EFF's name is conspicuously absent in the mandatory disclosures under the Political Party Funding Act (2018), which came into operation in April 2021. It has said it relies on donations below the R100 000 threshold for disclosure, and Malema has publicly said that EFF donors should give less than that amount to keep their donations secret.

In the first year the law came into effect, the EFF, the third-largest party by voter share, disclosed only R3 148 176 of donations in cash and in kind. In the 2022/23 financial year, it only disclosed the sources of two donations, of R150 000 and R202 600 in kind, in contrast with the ANC's R51 million, roughly R54 million for the DA and ActionSA's R26 million. EFF sources consistently tell us that the party's finances are murky, that even the party treasurers have little grasp of cash flows and that members who ask too many questions are treated with suspicion.

Yet despite his contempt for rules and regulations – or perhaps because of it – South Africa's young democracy has served Malema well. His party's unruliness adds to its appeal among a citizenry brimming with resentment over the slow pace of change under democracy. Simultaneously, his party has exercised disproportionate power as a kingmaker and de facto coalition partner in the metros, portending a future of fractured and chaotic coalition politics at national level. It is an environment to which Malema's opportunistic brand of politics is perfectly suited, and it has enabled the EFF to extract a great deal with relatively limited support.

So far, the justice system has failed to catch up with Malema. In South Africa, that system can at times be impenetrable to those on the outside. But we hope that the insights we have gleaned, together with the work of other journalists in exposing the systemic failings, politicisation, and deliberate undermining of key institutions, will go some way to explaining the failure to hold Malema accountable so far.

The National Prosecuting Authority (NPA), which was gutted during the Zuma years, is still recovering. The state remains hamstrung in investigating and prosecuting political corruption and complex financial crime. Politically compromised officials – often deployed under Zuma – weigh down the few pockets of efficiency that remain, while Cyril Ramaphosa's inaction – notably his attempts to placate and reconcile warring factions in the ANC – allows the problem to fester.

In 2019, the president appointed Malema's powerful ally Cassel Mathale as deputy minister of police, and one of the main VBS suspects, Danny Msiza, spearheaded Ramaphosa's 2022 ANC re-election campaign in Limpopo.

The permanently embattled National Director of Public Prosecutions, Shamila Batohi, does not miss an opportunity to declare that the NPA is making more progress in combating corruption and reversing state capture than is generally known, yet its court victories are too few and the setbacks too frequent to instil public confidence in her institution.

Thus far, Malema has not only remained relatively unscathed politically but also managed what the last ANC spinoff, the Congress of the People

(COPE), failed to do – build a viable and lasting political offshoot from the party of liberation. At the EFF's lavish 10-year anniversary celebrations in July 2023, Malema told a stadium packed with red T-shirts and berets that 'the baby that was born in 2013' was nothing like COPE, the breakaway party which won 30 seats in the National Assembly in 2009. Following a leadership dispute, however, COPE was left with only three seats after the 2014 election, and failed to secure a single seat in 2024. 'We are not COPE. We are a generation that our ancestors have been waiting for; we are a generation that has inherited the struggle of our liberators,' he proclaimed.

With the rise of the EFF, Malema defied those who were ready to write his political obituary. Riding the growing wave of anti-Zuma sentiment and capitalising on the misery and anger of millions of South Africans consigned to poverty and unemployment, the EFF began to look like a serious radical challenger to the ANC.

Malema has always sown chaos for his own advantage, and his power as the head of the EFF has rested partly on his ability to exploit the ANC's internal divisions, as he did when Zuma led the party. When Ramaphosa replaced Zuma and the possibility of a clampdown on corruption and patronage loomed, a rapprochement between Malema and Zuma soon followed. Malema saw Zuma and his so-called Radical Economic Transformation faction as a way to undermine Ramaphosa and his allies, especially the constitutionalists seeking to clean up and revive the ANC and the state.

In three decades of democracy, most South Africans had pinned their hopes on the party that liberated them. At a more material level, many saw their interests as bound to the ANC in its domination of the state and as the source of jobs, resources and welfare, which undergirded the party's power.

The biggest threat to the ANC, however, came from within as its support was eroded by infighting, corruption and the arrogance of politicians who thought they were untouchable. But, with Ramaphosa's slow consolidation of power, factionalism was largely contained for the time being and the party was shorn of its most venal and parasitic elements. Although the ANC's slow descent continued and the internal balance of power remained delicate, it was brought back from the brink of an outright implosion. This undercut Malema's influence within his former political home, but worse was to come. The near-fatal blow to the EFF was the formation of Zuma's uMkhonto we Sizwe (MK) Party and its stunning rise in the 2024 national elections. As voting season approached, Malema at times let slip that he feared all was not well in the EFF, but few foresaw just how well Zuma's new party would do and the extent to which it would displace the EFF. As the latter haemorrhaged senior members who defected to the MK Party, its electoral prospects dimmed.

Politically, Malema is in trouble. Additionally, his legal woes have not gone away, and old scandals could come back to haunt him. The danger – as Zuma has shown so graphically – is what one powerful man's desperate effort to cling to power and avoid accountability can cost the country and its democracy. The EFF and the MK Party are at loggerheads, kept apart by two antagonistic egos. But it is conceivable that they may be thrust together by circumstance and united by a shared enmity towards the constitutional order.

Above all, Malema is a survivor; one way or another, he will not quietly walk off the public stage. Among numerous other factors, he may not be able to afford it.

We will return to all of these themes in the chapters that follow. But first, we need to trace the origins of Malema's money and power.

Micah Reddy and Pauli van Wyk

PART ONE
An Early Start

CHAPTER 1

The business of politics

THULANI MAJOLA HAS made it. Suavely dressed, with a shaven head, neatly cropped beard and perennial grin, he has the confidence of a man who knows exactly what he wants in life and, with the help of the right connections, knows just how to get it. A member of the new elite in good standing, Majola flaunts his money – the powder-blue Bentley parked outside the offices of his engineering consulting firm, LTE Consulting, in upmarket Sandton, north of Johannesburg, loudly advertises his success as a businessman.

The boardroom features the customary range of expensive single malts – essential tools of the trade for the schmoozing classes. Nor is Majola shy about his political leanings. The LTE corridors are a hall of fame of Africa's oldest liberation movement, with framed pencil sketches of ANC icons from its 100-year history lining the walls.

It's a sign of the source of Majola's wealth – something he is a little less showy about, and one reason he and LTE have been plagued by controversy. The company operates almost entirely in the public sector. And doing business with the government requires a willingness to navigate tricky political waters. For much of Majola's career at the head of his firm, this has meant cosying up to the ANC. He has been a major donor, dishing out millions to the party over the years. He has also received many lucrative government tenders.

The extent to which these two things are mere happenstance – and the concept of political donations in general – goes to the heart of the toxic nexus between business and politics in South Africa.

In recent times, as the political landscape has fragmented and the ANC's power has waned, succeeding in the ruthless marketplace at the crossroads of business and politics has required a chameleon-like ability to change colour, or to play different sides. In Majola's case, the evidence set out in this book suggests that he sought to 'diversify' his political portfolio by supporting a rising new force, the EFF, led by Julius Malema.

Speaking to us at his office in late 2020, Majola responds to questions about payments he made to EFF-linked entities with nonchalance. Why did he transfer R200 000 to a company later revealed to be closely linked to Malema? It was just an innocent donation, he claims.

Did he know anything about the company? Not really; the CEO approached him, claiming he needed T-shirts for a 'political campaign'. Majola asked no questions about the company or the campaign. He forked out the R200 000, and that was that.

Any other donations to this company? 'Not that I know of.'

But, as we will see, Majola's answers don't quite square with the picture that later emerged. The evidence shows that Santaclara Trading, a company used for Malema's benefit but fronted by a young DJ called Jimmy Matlebyane from Malema's circle, received millions of rand from LTE in numerous payments over an extended period.

Like many other emerging black-owned companies, LTE has taken advantage of the government's policies of black economic empowerment (BEE), aimed at redressing the economic inequalities created by colonialism and particularly apartheid.

When it came to power, the ANC viewed 'deracialising business ownership and control' as an important component of the Redistribution and Development Programme, the party's post-apartheid development blueprint. And, in 1997, a Green Paper on Public Sector Procurement Reform called for affirmative-action measures in government procurement processes.

In the early years of democracy, government focused on encouraging black shareholding of large businesses, mostly through voluntary 'BEE deals'. White-owned corporations seeking to gain the favour of the ANC government and ensure the survival of South African capitalism were keen to usher selected ANC figures into the ranks of the business elite. Black uber-capitalists began to emerge who essentially owed their wealth to the ANC, some having been 'deployed' by the party to the private sector. A few – like the current president, Cyril Ramaphosa, who moved back and forth through the revolving doors of politics and big business; his billionaire brother-in-law, Patrice Motsepe; and former Gauteng premier Tokyo Sexwale – became spectacularly wealthy.

The insurance giant Sanlam – previously a corporate flagship of Afrikaner nationalism – drove the formation of New Africa Investments Limited, while Anglo American was another enthusiastic early adopter of BEE deals, helping to spawn Johnnic Communications. Ramaphosa was involved in both of these ventures.[3] Through such politically tinged empowerment deals, the ANC gained a foothold in the gilded boardrooms of Sandton.

Many black consortiums involved in such empowerment deals, however, lacked capital and relied on highly leveraged financing arrangements, leaving them vulnerable to market fluctuations. The Johannesburg Stock Exchange (JSE) crash in 1997 led to the unravelling of some deals and an overall contraction of the black-owned share of the JSE. Meanwhile, BEE was pursued in other areas, including through skills development and employment equity, but was applied piecemeal. BEE increasingly drew criticism for enriching a small elite and failing to change the lives of the majority. In response, the early 2000s saw moves to codify BEE in law and policy.

Already in 1998, amid growing dissatisfaction, the Black Business Council appointed Ramaphosa to head a commission of inquiry into BEE. It defined BEE more broadly as an effort to 'substantially and equitably transfer and confer the ownership, management and control of South Africa's financial and economic resources to the majority of its citizens'. It proposed the adoption of focused BEE legislation and an integrated national strategy on BEE.

The year 2000 brought the adoption of the Preferential Procurement Policy Framework Act, which – as its name suggests – was meant to give disadvantaged groups preferential access to state procurement. This opened the door to the 'tenderpreneurs' – businesspeople who concentrated on winning government tenders for goods and services they were often not equipped to deliver, sometimes in collusion with corrupt politicians or government officials, and often at grossly inflated prices. The spectre of tender fraud began to haunt governance.

This was followed by a series of BEE charters in specific industries, which gained regulatory status. The Broad-Based Black Economic Empowerment (BBBEE) Act was passed in 2003 and came into force in 2004. It was aimed at broadening and deepening BEE, including by changing the racial composition of companies. BEE was further bureaucratised by the adoption of codes of good practice complementing the Act, which set out standard criteria for measuring compliance with BBBEE indicators on a scorecard. In the main, this dispensation still exists today.

In the meantime, beneath the respectable veneer of the BEE framework, the ANC's tenure in government had become inextricably linked to corruption and the siphoning of state funds. This occurred on various levels, from the upper echelons of national government down to the capillaries of local government, and most of it centred on procurement, sometimes involving enormous sums of money. The consistent expectation was that the beneficiaries of corruption would channel funds back to the ANC.

The multibillion-dollar arms deal in the late 1990s – often called the ruling party's 'original sin' – set the tone for decades of graft. It remains in the headlines to this day, with former president Jacob Zuma and the French arms company Thales standing trial on corruption charges that were reinstated in 2018.

In August 2021, Zuma's lawyers reportedly wrote to the ANC requesting financial statements and records of donations from German and French defence-industry firms, intending to show that the ANC, not Zuma, was the true beneficiary of the arms deal. The letter pointed to investigations conducted by German authorities that 'reveal that the ANC received a significant financial donation from the German corvette ship builders just after the awarding of the four corvette ship contracts by the South African government to the German corvette consortium'.[4]

Another major scandal was Oilgate, which saw millions of rand intended for oil condensate diverted from the state-owned petrol company

PetroSA to the ANC via a politically connected empowerment company. The money was paid to the ANC months before the 2004 elections.

In 2006, the existence of Chancellor House, a front company for the ANC, was revealed. In theory, it was meant to serve as the ANC's 'investment arm'. In practice, it served as a conduit to government for companies seeking anything from mining rights to tenders. This included the Japanese company Hitachi, which won a contract to supply steam generators to the state-owned power utility Eskom for a massive power project. For a sweetheart price, Hitachi gave Chancellor House a stake in the consortium that would do the bulk of the work. At the time, ANC cadre Valli Moosa was the Eskom chairman, and he presided over crucial board meetings where the tender was discussed.[5]

Neither Hitachi nor Chancellor House and the ANC faced any local consequences. It fell to US regulators to hold Hitachi to account. Faced with an investigation by the US Securities and Exchange Commission, the multinational reached a $19-million (R266-million) settlement with US authorities in 2015. Although Hitachi did not have to admit to wrongdoing, it was also not allowed to deny that it had sought to buy political influence through Chancellor House.[6]

Another money spinner for the ANC, as amaBhungane reported in recent years, is United Manganese of Kalahari (UMK), a joint venture in mining between the Russian oligarch Viktor Vekselberg and Chancellor House.[7] Alongside Batho Batho – 'a trust with ANC roots'[8] – Chancellor House and the Russian joint venture are the party's biggest and most reliable funders.

The Political Party Funding Act, which came into effect in 2021, required parties to disclose all donations received above R100 000, whether in cash or kind, to the Electoral Commission of South Africa on a quarterly basis. This amount is cumulative and must be declared immediately when the total value reaches R100 000. Parties may not receive donations above R15 million a year from a single donor, may not receive donations from foreign governments and agencies (except for training and policy development), and may not receive donations from any government department or state-owned entity.

In that financial year, an analysis by amaBhungane found that the hugely lucrative UMK effectively donated above the limit by splitting funds up through different related companies. Thus Chancellor House donated the maximum amount of R15 million to the ANC, but an additional R2,5 million came from Majestic Silver Trading 40 (MST) – a 'politically connected South African consortium' through which Chancellor House held its stake in UMK. UMK, 51% owned by MST, donated a further R5 million.[9] By this logic, the triple contribution would raise the potential annual donation from the UMK structure to R45 million, being R15 million from each of Chancellor House, UMK and MST.

Yet another stain on the ANC's reputation was its cosy relationship with Bosasa, a company that gained notoriety in the 2000s over suspicious prison-management contracts. It collapsed in 2019 amid sensational allegations of sleaze before the Zondo Commission of Inquiry into State Capture, along with claims that bribes were handed out like 'Monopoly money' – but not before it had raked in billions of rand from the state. Prior to its implosion, Bosasa had been a reliable financial backer of the ANC.

Corruption and malfeasance in the ANC perhaps reached a crescendo with the wholesale capture of the state by Zuma's allies, the infamous Gupta family and their cronies – which also forced a reckoning within the party. Public institutions were taken over and repurposed for private gain, with billions of rand siphoned out of state-owned companies and channelled to secret bank accounts abroad. The criminal justice system was hamstrung and packed with loyalists to protect Zuma and his business allies.

Meanwhile, the ANC Youth League (ANCYL), in which Julius Malema cut his political teeth, had turned into a training ground for the murky high-level business deals its parent body was making. The league's foray into the business world began as far back as 1997, with the establishment of the National Youth Trade and Investments Corporation. It soon started going after government contracts and was part of a consortium that tendered to build juvenile prisons in Mpumalanga. The bid was derailed amid an outcry from opposition parties after a member of the parliamentary correctional services portfolio committee disclosed his conflicting interest in the company.

A later ANCYL investment arm, Lembede Investments, had ties to the controversial mining magnate Brett Kebble. A forensic audit of Lembede, conducted during Malema's league presidency, found that hundreds of millions of rand linked to questionable deals were unaccounted for. Investigators recommended that the league's former leadership – alleged to have enriched themselves using the Lembede name – be questioned about the missing millions, but the new leaders showed no willingness to pursue their predecessors.

These are just some of the major corruption stains on the ANC's record in government, and they partly account for the party's economic heft. Its symbiotic relationship with the new BEE elite paying their tithes to the party, its deployment of cadres and the influence it wielded over state contracts all contributed to making the ANC 'by far, the best-resourced party in South Africa'.[10]

Flawed systems of governance have worsened the problem of corruption. In the post-apartheid era, procurement was devolved to many different state entities, each managing contracts with private suppliers and service providers. This chimed with trends in pro-market reforms and public management theory, which held that outsourcing and a greater role for the private sector would be more efficient and flexible – but it also aligned with the ANC's goal of nurturing a new black bourgeoisie.

Whereas in the past state contracts had mostly gone to large, established white-owned firms, procurement was now leveraged to support previously disadvantaged companies. But whereas tenders under apartheid had favoured bulk supply, they were now increasingly 'unbundled' and broken up into smaller portions to give more new entrants a share of the pie. This led to a dizzying array of contracts and contracting entities at various levels of government, and meant that there was 'very little visibility of all these transactions', as the minister of finance at the time, Pravin Gordhan, remarked in 2013.[11]

Although nominally prohibited from involvement in procurement and tender decisions, politicians retained broad discretion over the appointments of public servants. Political influence over procurement then flowed through loyal or beholden officials.

The ANC's objectives were always clear: to replace apartheid-era holdovers in the civil service with its own members, and to exert political control over an administration it deemed hostile to transformation.[12] A strategy document adopted at the ANC's December 2012 national conference held in Mangaung in the Free State stated openly: 'In order for it to exercise its vanguard role, the ANC puts a high premium on the involvement of its cadres in all centres of power. This includes the presence of ANC members and supporters in state institutions.'[13]

The placement of ANC cadres and sympathisers in the state bureaucracy and state-owned entities was overseen by its deployment committees, the first of which was established at a national level in 1998 and headed by Zuma – deputy president of the ANC at the time – with local and regional committees formed afterwards. By packing the public service with loyalists, the ANC fused itself to the state, from the top and down to the local level, where accountability was weakest. Politically connected companies could now tap vast reservoirs of wealth in the form of procurement budgets – with a portion of the cash ultimately reverting to the ANC. Clientelism and corruption flourished, and the flow of illicit funds enriched cadres while strengthening the party's patronage machine.

The ANC was not entirely blind to the corrosive effects of its policies. As a discussion paper from 1999 noted: 'Being a member of the ANC today is perceived as opening up possibilities of material and social advancement, either in the form of public or civil service positions or opportunities for enrichment through government economic empowerment programmes.'[14] The gravy train steamed ahead.

As Malema's star was rising, the days of the great private-sector empowerment deals were over. The BEE barons had amassed obscene wealth, but they had also cornered the market. There were only so many emerging black capitalists that blue-chip companies were willing to accommodate; now, state procurement was the mainstay of emerging businesses, and barriers to entry tended to be low.

But the scramble for tenders was often fiercely competitive, drawing in minor entrepreneurs and corporates alike – many of whom were prepared to pay politicians for a leg up. With lax rules on party funding and weak, compromised institutions, illicit money coursed through South

African politics, reaching unprecedented heights under Zuma's infamous presidency, which lasted for almost a decade, from 2009 to 2018. He had entered office trailed by major corruption scandals and amassed many more during his two terms, from the misuse of public funds to upgrade his Nkandla homestead to dubious dealings with the Gupta family.

Tender rigging and procurement fraud ran rampant as a host of government officials, politicians, middlemen and 'tenderpreneurs' colluded to siphon money from state coffers.[15] Under the cynical rallying cry of 'radical economic transformation', Zuma became the talisman for a range of kleptocratic interests.

Malema was elected president of the ANCYL in April 2008. Like Zuma, he flourished in the not-quite-legal and sometimes outright illicit economy where politics and business blended seamlessly. Asked by his biographer, Fiona Forde, whether he was more of a businessman than a politician, Malema responded with a rhetorical question: 'Do the two have to be mutually exclusive?' He added: 'I'm a good deal broker. That's what I am.'

He was indeed a deal broker in a party riven with sleaze, and by the time he was expelled from the ANC in 2012, he was already facing serious corruption-related charges. But despite the cloud hanging over him, he salvaged his political career. In 2013, he founded the EFF on a pro-poor ticket, seeking to capitalise on growing disillusionment with the ANC, particularly among jobless and disenchanted young people. Less than a year later, the new party won a respectable 6,35 percent of the vote in its first general election, gaining 25 seats in a parliament dominated by the ANC. His return from the political wilderness and the rise of his new party caught the eye of businesspeople eager to shore up influence, and brought a steady flow of payments to both him and the EFF.

One of these businesspeople was Thulani Majola. His first known payment to Malema was made on 28 July 2016, when R500 000 popped into the account of Santaclara, the company fronted by the young DJ. That was just days before the five-yearly municipal elections, which would be a major test of the EFF's staying power. The party won 8 percent of the vote, giving it more than 750 councillors in local municipalities across the country.

Meanwhile, the ANC's share of the vote declined by 8 percentage points – from 61,9 percent in 2011 to 53,9 percent. Even more painfully, the party lost control of three big metros, namely Johannesburg, Tshwane and Nelson Mandela Bay – a blow that threatened to disrupt its patronage networks. Before 2016, ANC politicians had an iron grip on the metros outside the Western Cape – and their budgets. Now, power and patronage in the urban centres were up for grabs.

The EFF was suddenly thrust into the role of kingmaker in both the capital city and the economic heart of the country. While the shaky new coalitions under the DA in Tshwane and Johannesburg did not formally include Malema's party, they relied on EFF cooperation and voting power to stay afloat. Staying out of formal coalitions was a shrewd political calculation on the EFF's part, allowing the young party access to the levers of power without taking on the risks and responsibilities of incumbency.

The party's newfound clout and ability to swing metro politics pulled emerging business owners into Malema's orbit. The evidence shows that Majola was just one among numerous others who made significant donations to Malema and his party. Whether these payments were merely donations by civic-minded entrepreneurs, or whether there was something more sinister at play, are questions that will be explored in this book.

CHAPTER 2

The boy from Seshego

I**N THE RUN-UP** to the 2021 local government elections, a massive billboard loomed over the highway at the entrance of the township of Seshego, outside Polokwane. It showed the EFF commander-in-chief's grinning face accompanied by bold yellow writing: 'Land and jobs *manje*! Vote EFF Nov 2021!' EFF posters were plastered all over bus stops in the area. This was Fortress Malema, and the son of Seshego was an unstoppable force.

Much had changed since Polokwane was known as Pietersburg. Back then, it was not the sort of place that nurtured hope among its black residents. The city was a bastion of Afrikaner conservatism, and the Pietersburg region had been the only part of the country to reject President FW de Klerk's whites-only referendum of 1992 on whether to continue his proposed reforms. In March 1994, with the country's first democratic elections approaching and representatives of the ANC and other liberation movements sitting with their white counterparts to discuss the amalgamation of Seshego with Pietersburg, members of the neo-fascist Afrikaner Weerstandsbeweging tried to obstruct the proceedings.[16] Malema was 14 years old at the time.

Founded in 1886, the same year as Johannesburg, Pietersburg was a genuine frontier settlement – a tiny outpost for displaced Boers on the fringes of their nascent state. Gold and land attracted white settlers, while malaria and conflicts with local Venda and Pedi communities pushed them away. For the first half of the 1900s, Pietersburg remained an unremarkable white provincial town serving as an agricultural hub for nearby farms, but it began to transform after the 1948 ascent to power of the National Party and the beginning of formal apartheid.

The post-World War Two boom years saw rapid urbanisation of a kind that haunted apartheid's ideologues and legislators. People of different races were drawn to Pietersburg, with many poorer arrivals squeezing into densely packed suburbs and slums that defied colonial colour bars. It was an affront to apartheid's architects. To a regime obsessed with sex and purity, uncontrolled urbanisation was synonymous with race-mixing and miscegenation. The towns and cities at risk of becoming incubators of racial vice needed strict regulation. In the 1950s and 1960s apartheid lawmakers resorted to a barrage of legal measures to unscramble the racial Rubik's Cube and keep South Africa's races apart.[17]

Like countless others, Malema's grandfather, Johannes Malema, was caught up in these waves of urbanisation when he moved roughly 60 kilometres from an impoverished rural settlement to Pietersburg.

In the 1960s, as apartheid social engineering gathered momentum, the Malemas and thousands of other black residents were forced to move to the newly established township of Seshego, 13 kilometres outside Pietersburg. Hoping to quell resistance to the removals, the authorities offered shack owners their own small brick houses in the new township.

The Malemas moved into one of these houses in Zone 1, an area so poor that it was called 'Masakaneng', named after the jute sacks that the new residents used to cover their windows.[18] The Malema family was among the poorest of the poor, living in a place designed to keep them out of sight. Their tiny home could barely contain their growing family. They had nine children – eight daughters and a son – and a new generation of grandchildren soon followed.

The early 1970s brought a major rupture when Johannes left his wife Sarah for another woman. As a labourer, his income had been modest and intermittent, but Sarah was now left to manage the impoverished family alone. Her daughter Florah found employment as a domestic worker in the Indian neighbourhood of Nirvana, but she had health issues and could not carry on working after a vicious epileptic seizure. In her early twenties, Florah gave birth to a daughter, but the girl died as a toddler. Some years later, on 3 March 1981, she had Julius Sello Malema.

Fiona Forde, Malema's biographer, describes the 'deep love' Malema developed for the two women who raised him: 'His grandmother understood him, and she would always stand by him, through thick and thin, both as a young boy and in later life. And while he and his mother didn't always see eye to eye, least of all on his hot-headed outlook on life, she was his number one and he hers.'[19]

The Malema household was the centre of a large extended family – aunts, uncles and cousins. 'There was a time when the household numbers would swell to a dozen and more,' writes Forde. The family had to build shacks in the yard to house everyone.

Some of those extended family members would later be roped into Malema's burgeoning business network. But in his early years, he led the typical life of a young black boy growing up in an impoverished township. He learnt to hustle from an early age, sometimes just to feed himself. Forde describes him as 'knocking at the doors of neighbours and future comrades at meal times'.

Just a few years earlier, the shock waves of the 1976 student uprising in Soweto had hit Pietersburg and surrounding areas, where schooling more or less ground to a halt. The University of the North – founded for black students in the 1950s, 40 kilometres east of Pietersburg – became a hotbed of protests. It was here, in July 1969, that Steve Biko was elected president at the inaugural conference of the South African Students' Organisation.[20] Forty-six years later, on 16 June 2015, the EFF founded its student wing, the EFF Student Command, on the same campus.

In the 1980s and early 1990s, townships were ablaze. The ANC's armed wing, uMkhonto we Sizwe (MK), stepped up attacks inside the country, states of emergency were declared and large parts of South Africa were rendered ungovernable by mass protests. The ANC and the United Democratic Front (UDF) were at war with the impis of the Zulu nationalist Inkatha Freedom Party (IFP), which was secretly backed by the state, and the security forces were storming through black communities. The anti-apartheid movement found willing recruits in politicised youths, often unemployed or out of school, and in the 'com-tsotsis' – young men and boys who traversed a life of gangsterism and crime but who also served as enthusiastic shock troops in the township unrest. Malema spent his formative years in this volatile setting, where politics offered an attractive path amid an otherwise bleak future.

He claims that, at a young age, he was given paramilitary training – something some of Forde's sources scoffed at. Regardless, he was clearly drawn to politics early on – he says he joined the Masupatsela, an ANC youth brigade, at the age of nine. Older comrades who mentored him describe an energetic young activist doing political odd jobs, putting up posters and helping out at events.

While still in primary school, he became a member of the Congress of South African Students (Cosas), the feeder organisation for the ANCYL. By the time the ANC assumed power in 1994, he was old enough to join the youth league, which had been revived three years earlier. Brash and bold, he slid easily into the role of student politician.

Forde paints a picture of a young man who seemed to relish confrontations with teachers and other authority figures. Soon, he was making a name for himself as a champion of student causes in Seshego. In 1997, three years into the 'new South Africa', he took a step up when he was elected provincial chairperson of Cosas in Limpopo. In his new role, he locked horns with the MEC of education, Joe Phaahla, whom he accused of being a 'contraception to transformation'.[21] Malema remained unfazed by attempts to silence him, including a threat by Phaahla to sue him.

In 2000, the year before he matriculated from Mohlakaneng High School in Seshego at the age of 21, Malema made a bid for the presidency of Cosas. He had broad support, including from outgoing president Lebogang Maile, but faced a strong opponent in Kenny Morolong. A tumultuous elective conference saw violence break out between the rival factions, while Morolong was suspended following rape allegations that surfaced at a critical moment. Morolong denied the rape and nothing came of it. Winnie Madikizela-Mandela, then-president of the ANC Women's League, was eventually called in to calm things down, and she decided to disband the conference. When it resumed the following year, Morolong had been hounded out of Cosas and Malema's path to the presidency was clear.

Malema was now in charge of 300 000 students, each paying a R5 annual membership fee – a significant financial responsibility. His increased prominence – heightened by his combative style – brought increased public scrutiny. 'Cosas leader was a "real dunce" at school', read one particularly unforgiving headline. The article went on: 'He is leading pupils, but his schooling track record hardly qualifies him as a role model.'[22] Years later, his official matric results were circulated publicly, with his 'G' for standard-grade woodwork eliciting the most mockery. He brushed the criticism aside, saying he'd had little time for studying as he was entirely preoccupied with politics.

Malema was spending a lot more time in Johannesburg. After his election as Cosas president, he rented a flat in Hillbrow, not far from Luthuli House, the ANC's headquarters. And, with Seshego a more than three-hour drive away, he even attended some classes at a school in Soweto.

With Malema at its helm, Cosas made headlines for its rowdy protests. In May 2002 – after he matriculated but before his term as Cosas head was up – the organisation provoked public outrage when students rampaged through the streets of Johannesburg, looting and vandalising businesses, ostensibly in protest against a directive of the Gauteng department of education that schools should close their gates during teaching hours for safety reasons.[23]

The unruliness prompted concern among ANC luminaries. The student wing was supposed to be a conveyor belt for future leaders of the party. Former Cosas presidents blamed the poor discipline on a lack of guidance from the ANC, despite the national leadership of Cosas being housed in Luthuli House. The minister of education at the time, Kader Asmal, suggested that Cosas be depoliticised. Malema, having eventually matriculated, was studying at Unisa at the time.

While members of the public and some party elders were put off by Malema's confrontational approach, many of his peers admired him as a brave and radical young leader. He refused to be domesticated by an ANC leadership that they regarded as staid, aloof and unrevolutionary. As Malema rose through the political ranks, their frustration with the 'conservatism' of the Mbeki presidency grew. The Cosas leader was increasingly seen as the embodiment of the unbridled spirit and political energy of young people. In 2003, when his tenure ended, he was elected secretary of the ANCYL in Limpopo.

At this early stage of his career, Malema was already mixing business and politics, with a specific focus on government contracts. In his interviews with Forde, he was candid about his involvement in government tenders when he was still in high school. 'Malema and his friends competed against the teachers to provide the school uniforms for the few hundred learners, and the teenagers won the bid,' writes Forde.

Malema teamed up with the future ANC heavyweight Pule Mabe, then a budding journalist. He told Forde that Mabe was the driving force behind their tender successes, and he was just 'helping out'. Among these successes was a deal to coordinate entertainment at the inauguration of the mayor of the Waterberg District Municipality in Limpopo. They also won a tender to supply branded water bottles to Lepelle Northern Water – the state-owned utility that would come to play a central role in the Giyani water scandal.

The deals of Malema's early years were relatively modest, but they grew more ambitious as his political ascent continued. The young boy from Seshego was on his way to becoming a power broker in Limpopo.

CHAPTER 3

SARS comes sniffing

JULIUS MALEMA'S EARLIEST recorded salary is a monthly paycheque from April 2004 for R12 500,[24] before tax, for serving as the ANCYL secretary in Limpopo. He was, however, already supplementing his income from political jobs with money from outside sources and business ventures, and his total income for that year was almost R80 000 more.[25] We know this because much of Malema's financial history is laid bare in publicly available court records that have been filed in the various legal battles in which Malema had to try and fend off the taxman over the years. Around this time, Malema rekindled a childhood friendship with local businessman Lesiba Gwangwa, a move that would have a major bearing on his future. According to Fiona Forde, they bumped into each other at the home of Matome Sathekge, a housing developer and business associate of Cassel Mathale's, the ANC provincial secretary in Limpopo at the time.

At a time when Malema was often seen in T-shirts, shorts and sandals, Gwangwa was smartly dressed and wore a ready smile. He had registered his company, Segwalo Consulting Engineers CC, trading as SGL Consulting Engineers, in 2002 and was hungry for business opportunities. As reported by Forde, Sathekge allegedly told Gwangwa that Malema could steer some tenders their way. In return, the youth leader would apparently get a cut, payable in cash to family and friends.

Speaking to Forde, Sathekge denied that he had arranged any such meeting, and Gwangwa denied any impropriety. While Malema did not deny that a meeting had taken place or that it had resulted in a working relationship with Gwangwa, he described the discussions differently.

'What was central in me being introduced to these young chaps was for them to help the Youth League. SGL was donating money to the Youth League programme,' he told Forde. However, the resultant cash flows – dealt with later – seem to tell a different story.

Malema also tried to establish his own businesses, with mixed success. Operating in a world for which he was ill-equipped, income tax also became an issue. The ANC was notoriously lax about registering its employees with the South African Revenue Service (SARS), sources say, so Malema and others were not registered and no tax was deducted from their incomes. Nor did the 23-year-old Malema pay tax on his additional income. These early mistakes established a pattern that would persist for many years. When SARS eventually caught up with him eight years later, Malema explained that the April 2004 paycheque was the first he had ever received.[26] At the time, he had 'accepted that the ANC would pay all the necessary taxes'[27]. He had no formal business training, and his knowledge of tax matters was 'extremely limited'. He repeated this story to the media, painting a picture of an eager but naive young businessman who just wanted to get on in a brave new world.

It was easy for investigators to sympathise with Malema. At the time, SARS had adopted a policy to help the president, judges and politicians to be tax compliant. According to SARS insiders, two commissioners, Oupa Magashule and Ivan Pillay, initially asked investigative teams to go easy on Malema and give him a helping hand. Consider the context, their argument went, of the young gun from Seshego who had grown up in disadvantaged circumstances that had compromised his education, and was now struggling to improve his life and navigate a complex tax system. If he needed guidance and support, SARS would assist, they decided. Over time, however, Malema's attitude changed their minds.

From about 2004, Malema became a shareholder in and director of a raft of companies that mostly depended on the state for business. He also began to receive large sums from wealthy benefactors, which he was not keen to advertise.

In 2004, Malema and his cousin Ronny acquired the shelf company Blue Nightingale Trading 61. Two years later, Malema was its sole director. Scarcely a year after starting up, Blue Nightingale managed to grab a slice of a R200-million Limpopo government contract for medical waste management. The winning consortium, Tshumisano, had a youth empowerment component with a three percent stake. The consortium partners awarded this to Blue Nightingale, incorrectly believing that it was owned by the ANCYL and allegedly unaware that Malema had become its sole director.[28]

Although Malema denied having received payouts linked to the waste-management tender, documents suggest that he received about R260 000 from Tshumisano Waste Management around March 2006. In his defence, Malema explained that he had become a director long after the tender had been awarded.[29] This would not have precluded him holding an ownership stake before and long after the tender machinations, as Forde pointed out. Malema denied his involvement at the time.

However, awarding the tender to Tshumisano was seriously irregular. In 2007, after a rival bidder cried foul, the Supreme Court of Appeal (SCA) found that the provincial department of health and social development's handling of the tender did not meet the standards of 'fair, equitable, transparent, competitive and cost-effective' procurement.[30] There were indications that department officials were willing to iron out defects in Tshumisano's tender after it had already been awarded. The bid was also eight times the cost of its rival. The SCA set aside the award. Undeterred, the health department simply reinstated the contract with Tshumisano.

Malema's other listings as a director included Ever Roaring Investment, Nkgape Mining Investments and 101 Junjus Trading. 'Junjus' is a nickname coined by Malema's friend and erstwhile mentor Pule Mabe. These businesses seemed to have varying levels of success, but none of them shot the lights out. Ultimately, in the documents available to us, we could find no trace of direct payments from Blue Nightingale, Nkgape Mining, Ever Roaring or Junjus Trading to Malema's personal bank accounts.

When Forde asked Malema about this era and the companies linked to him, he responded by saying there was a point when he registered companies in his name 'and tried to do some jobs and was not successful, and the companies became dormant'. Yet, when SARS launched its investigation, it found that Malema's income continued to outpace his salary.

In the 2006 tax year, the total cash deposited into his account rose marginally to R223 096, compared with R215 800 in 2005.[31] While the increase was not substantial, two related points are noteworthy. First, Malema failed to declare any of this income to SARS, and when later compelled to do so – a matter we will discuss further in this book – he significantly underreported it. Second, the name of Selby Manthata, a businessman from Tzaneen, appeared for the first time alongside a R10 000 deposit into one of Malema's bank accounts.[32] This marked the start of a long-standing relationship that, as court records would later reveal, contributed significantly to Malema's eventual wealth.

The bulk of the extra cash in his bank account was deposited by Malema himself, his cousin Ronny and his ally George Raphela, who would later follow him to the EFF. Malema explained these cash deposits to SARS a decade later as donations from unnamed 'political supporters'.[33]

Malema told Forde that, around 2005, he had been frozen out of government and its financial perks when he found himself on the wrong side of a provincial party divide. He was loyal to Cassel Mathale, who was at loggerheads with the province's premier, Sello Moloto. 'You know, we were suffering financially at that time, and the government was not so available to me. I was not so powerful then,' he remarked. But circumstances were about to shift in his favour.

Gwangwa, now Malema's business partner, started winning tenders, including a job to build a R2,1-million taxi rank in Ga-Masemola, south of Polokwane. His company, SGL Consulting Engineers, subcontracted the construction to Malema's company Ever Roaring, as well as Moloko Business Enterprises. Moloko was owned by Mathews Mathabatha, who was also a partner in Ever Roaring[34]. The project – reportedly characterised by delays and shoddy workmanship – missed its construction deadline of August 2007 and was finally completed by another company in October 2009.[35]

In the meantime, shifts in the political sands would cascade into Limpopo as well. In 2007, the feud between President Thabo Mbeki and Jacob Zuma, whom Mbeki had fired as his deputy president in 2005 over corruption allegations, came to a head. At the time, Malema was a staunch Zuma supporter, while Moloto backed Mbeki.

When Zuma was tried for rape in 2006, Malema joined in the virulent attacks on his accuser, the daughter of one of Zuma's comrades in exile. In one particularly chauvinistic speech, Malema said she had clearly 'enjoyed' sex with Zuma. 'When a woman didn't enjoy it, she leaves early in the morning. Those who had a nice time will wait until the sun comes out, request breakfast and ask for taxi money,' he proclaimed. Malema would later be fined R50 000 by the Equality Court over his remarks.

Zuma was still deputy president of the ANC, and his eventual acquittal on the rape charges cleared the way for him to challenge Mbeki for the ANC presidency at the party's elective conference in Polokwane in 2007. Various state institutions, particularly intelligence agencies and the criminal justice system, were influenced to fight this factional battle.

The fact that power was seeping away from Mbeki seemed to bode well for Malema, politically and as a businessman. In the 2007 tax year his income more than doubled to R539 854.[36]

The year 2006 also saw the birth of Malema's first child, Ratanang, from his relationship with a woman from Seshego, Maropeng Ramohlale.

On 25 October 2007, days after the boy's first birthday, Malema founded the Ratanang Family Trust with an opening deposit of R100, with Ratanang as the sole beneficiary and Malema the only trustee. The trust deed stipulated that all capital and income should be used to benefit Ratanang, and that the trustee should 'refrain from managing the trust property to their own advantage'.

At that time, the flash and cash swirling around the young ANC politician became obvious, while the media and SARS were prodding Malema about paying his taxes. This was unwelcome, so one of his funders, an open-handed businessman, suggested that he use a trust as a means of protection. Never blind to the potential of a scheme, Malema took to the idea with alacrity. The trust's importance as a hideout would grow along with Malema's financial muscle. But it didn't take long for journalists and authorities to cotton on.

In an interview with Forde three years later, Malema insisted that the trust was a charitable vehicle with 'people from outside the family as trustees', and that it had earned him no wealth. He also claimed it was tax compliant, 'because to buy properties, you have to have a tax certificate and pay tax on property as well. So there is no problem there.' He repeated the same thing to journalists, saying 'Ratanang [Trust] has declared its taxes since inception without failure'[37].

None of these claims was true. By the start of 2011, the trust had not even been registered with SARS.[38] As an olive branch to the tiresome taxman, Malema's auditors registered it in February that year. By then, more than three years after the formation of the trust, millions of rand had washed through the accounts.

However, the trust was still not tax compliant, and despite the stipulations in its deed, Malema used it to fund his lifestyle and become extremely wealthy. Charity sucked on the hind teat. A few thousand rand were paid to legitimate charitable causes, and no independent trustees were ever registered. The trust, SARS found, was a mere 'conduit' and an 'alter ego' for Malema 'to receive funds'.[39]

Even if the money flowing through the trust was used for charity, it would *still* have contravened the trust deed, which clearly stipulated that the capital and income should be used only for the benefit of Ratanang. Tellingly, Malema would not allow Forde to look at the trust's financial statements. 'He has a good laugh to himself when I ask to see the finances,' she writes.

Rather naively, Malema seemed to believe that the trust would be more private than his personal account. 'Nobody will see the financials of the trust,' he told Forde. But this was wishful thinking.

CHAPTER 4

More power, more money

IN THE RUN-UP to the ANC's fateful Polokwane elective conference
in December 2007, Jacob Zuma had few supporters as fervent as Julius
Malema. The ANCYL's leader in Limpopo played a prominent role in
Zuma's campaign to unseat Thabo Mbeki as ANC president, publicly
proclaiming that he was prepared to die – and to kill – for Zuma.

Although the battle for the ANC leadership dominated the headlines,
one of the items on the undercard was almost as momentous: a proposal
to disband the Directorate of Special Operations (DSO), or Scorpions,
a specialised investigations and prosecutions unit of the NPA formed
during Mbeki's presidency to investigate and prosecute high-level crimes,
including corruption. Among others, the Scorpions had investigated the
arms deal and several high-ranking ANC politicians like Jackie Selebi,
Tony Yengeni and Zuma. These politicians also included another Malema
benefactor, Thaba Mufamadi, businessman-turned-finance-MEC in
Limpopo and later a member of two parliamentary finance committees.
Unsurprisingly, the plan to kill off the elite crime-fighting unit found
broad support within the ruling party, especially among those in the
Scorpions' crosshairs, and from Malema.

At the time, Mufamadi featured in a Scorpions investigation into a
pensions and social grants scandal,[40] and he later came under scrutiny
because his company, in which Malema's ally Cassel Mathale was also
involved, was embroiled in a questionable lease deal housing the Department of Home Affairs.[41] Years later, Malema admitted to SARS that
Mufamadi was one in a long list of 'donors'.[42]

This is supported by bank statements showing what appears to be a strategic flow of cash to Malema from ANC-linked individuals days before the elective conference. Our records show that on 23 November 2007 Mufamadi transferred R6 000 to Malema's personal Absa account.[43] Two weeks later, on 8 December 2007, the Limpopo businessman Collins Foromo, Malema's one-time driver, made a cash deposit of R5 500 into the same account.

Foromo's rise as an entrepreneur mirrored Malema's political ascent, and it is clear from social media that he developed a taste for Lamborghini supercars and Patck Philippe watches. He has been a constant in Malema's life, apart from a falling-out in 2014 that apparently resulted in Malema not inviting him to his wedding in December of that year.

From as early as the days of On-Point Engineers – the company that received taxpayers' money from the Limpopo department of roads and transport in a scam which the NPA and the Public Protector later described as criminal and corrupt, as discussed in Chapter 6 – journalists linked Foromo to Malema's ecosystem as a benefactor and possible conduit. According to the *Mail & Guardian*, Malema allegedly handed the then-provincial MEC for education, Dickson Masemola, a list of his preferred recipients for the department's tenders.[44] Sources claimed the list included Foromo and his then-girlfriend, two of Malema's cousins, and two allies in the provincial ANCYL.

In another instance, around 2011 Foromo was paid almost R1 million for 'fixing potholes' that apparently never existed.[45] Foromo confirmed the payment and service but denied he was a friend of Malema's. 'He's my leader. He's not my friend. And if they thought I used to drive him in 2004, 2005 and 2006, it's because I had a car,' he said.

Foromo's denials stand in stark contrast to information from our sources in law enforcement, who maintain that he remains instrumental in Malema's financial interests. Corroborating this, an additional three independent sources revealed that for the past five years Malema enjoyed 'full use' of a sprawling, three-storey house in Waterkloof Heights, Pretoria, which deed documents show belongs to Foromo's family trust. The trust bought the 2 266-square-metre estate, initially featuring a modest house, in September 2017. There was no bond recorded against the property. Soon after the purchase, the original house was knocked down, and over time, a large mansion with two subterranean floors took shape. A neighbour said that construction appeared to progress slowly and recounted that when he and a friend – someone who knew the builders who were on site – passed by the property, they were told that it was 'Malema's house'.

A second source, a friend of Malema's, said he attended a 'lockdown party' that Malema hosted at the Waterkloof house during the Covid-19 pandemic. It was 'one of the most beautiful properties I have been to', the source claimed, adding that one of the underground levels has been turned into a club equipped with expensive music equipment and speakers.

The payments made by Mufamadi and Foromo in 2007, although relatively small, came just before the ANC's Polokwane conference, held from 16 to 20 December, where Malema and his supporters in the ANCYL took on the role of kingmakers. In the end, the hodgepodge alliances that formed around Zuma – many stemming from disaffection with Mbeki rather than any real love for his rival – resulted in a roughly 60–40 voting split in favour of the challenger. Having been ousted as ANC president, Mbeki was a lame-duck national president from that moment on.

The resolution calling for the disbandment of the Scorpions was easily adopted under the 'caretaker presidency' of Kgalema Motlanthe, backed by Zuma's supporters, including Malema – a decision that haunts South Africa to this day.

Malema had backed the winning horse in Polokwane, and his political trajectory continued upward. A few months later, he was elected national president of the ANCYL, in circumstances just as controversial as his election as Cosas president in 2001.

The ANCYL was split into two factions ahead of its elective conference – one backing Malema, the other backing its national organiser, Saki Mofokeng. The first group was led by the outgoing president, Fikile Mbalula, and the latter was backed by its secretary general, Sihle Zikalala. Both groups backed Zuma, but the second believed Mofokeng was more experienced and articulate.

Mufamadi again paid Malema, this time just under R40 000, in the months leading up to the conference, held in Bloemfontein on 7 April 2008. (He eventually also helped Malema to buy a house in Polokwane.)[46]

At the conference, accusations of vote-rigging were flung around like banknotes in a tumble dryer. Some of the placards at the conference read: 'Even with all the money flying around, Saki will still win' and 'RIP Julius, try after getting matric'.

In the end, Malema pipped Mofokeng by a narrow margin. Seven provincial representatives on the electoral commission insisted that voting had not been free and fair, and spoke of intimidation. Chaos ensued, with chairs hurled at Mbalula. Although Malema claimed victory, with his supporters carrying him shoulder-high to the podium to make his inaugural speech, the conference was postponed without the election result being confirmed. That only happened at a special congress the following month, after Mofokeng had conceded defeat and moved on to the business world.

The sword finally fell on Mbeki in September 2008, when the ANC recalled him as president following a controversial finding by High Court Judge Christopher Nicholson that he had interfered with the NPA and the Scorpions to ensure Zuma's prosecution for corruption, fraud and tax evasion. Nicholson canned the prosecution of Zuma on charges including racketeering, corruption, money laundering, fraud and tax evasion. Stunningly, the judge also expressed his opinion on issues that were never before the court, like criticising Mbeki's dismissal of Zuma as deputy president in 2005 and his decision to stand for a third term as ANC president.

Four months later, a full Appeal Court bench wrote a scathing critique of Nicholson, basically saying he had exceeded the limits of his powers based on his personal feelings, that his 'findings' on ANC politics were 'gratuitous'[47] and that he had 'overstepped the limits of his authority'. They then overturned the judgment. For Mbeki, the Scorpions and the country, it was too late. By then, the ANC deputy president, Kgalema Motlanthe, had taken over the presidency, an office he would hold until the following year's general election.

Politically and on the business front, Malema's future beckoned. Now leader of the ANCYL, he secretly received a 70 percent stake from Gwangwa in the second iteration of SGL, a company called SGL

Engineering Projects. In June 2011, in the run-up to his bid for a second term as ANCYL president, Malema's critics would bemoan the 'SGL-isation of politics', a reference to the company's perceived role in keeping Malema in power.[48] Power attracts money, as Malema's bank statements from that time attest.

In the 2009 tax year, which spanned most of Malema's first year as ANCYL president with a monthly salary of no more than R40 000, his estimated taxable income nearly doubled to about R810 000 for the year.[49] When later pressed to declare his annual income, he pegged it at R365 371. This total included at least R10 000 in contributions from Mufamadi and several untraced cash deposits, some as large as R100 000. SARS struggled to determine the source of these funds, particularly as Malema's story kept changing.

Journalists also began to ask questions about the changes in his lifestyle.

Following his election, Malema moved to Johannesburg to be close to the heart of politics. He signed a lease for a house in the upmarket suburb of Sandton, in Silvela Road, at R18 000 a month. Malema liked the property; by mid-2009, he had decided to buy it. He would repeat this modus operandi often in the future.

First, he 'raised money', as he described it to Forde, to pay a year's rent upfront. The property cost R3,6 million. The Ratanang Family Trust paid R2 million in cash towards the Silvela Road property, and Malema eventually told SARS that the money had been donated by his associates Mufamadi, David Mabilu, Thulani Nkuna, Ali Boshielo and Selby Manthata.[50] SARS, however, treated it as income, given the apparent business relationships between Malema and his donors.

Most of the money for the property was channelled through the Ratanang trust. Besides Malema's deposit of R100 to open the account, the first payment into the account was R50 000 in cash, deposited in April 2009 by the Limpopo-based company Selby Construction.[51] Manthata, the founder of the company, had been a benefactor of Malema's for at least four years before starting to channel money to the trust. At first, the amounts had been relatively modest, ranging between R1 000 and R10 000. But they would soon grow significantly.

Like Manthata, Boshielo's business interests were primarily in Limpopo, in a range of sectors, including construction, mining, catering and medical waste removal. Boshielo made headlines in 2010 when a printing company in which he held a stake – alongside the ANCYL's investment vehicle, the South African Youth Development Trust – secured a lucrative printing contract from the Limpopo government[52].

Boshielo also served as a director of the ANCYL's Lembede Investment Holdings, alongside Lonwabo Sambudla. Lembede was intended to be part of a network of companies reportedly acting as fronts for the youth league, but it eventually went bust.[53] Malema told a journalist from *City Press* that he would close down Lembede. Sambudla did not respond to requests for comment at the time.

In 2012, when SARS summoned Boshielo to a tax inquiry investigating Gwangwa's network, he admitted to investigators that he had given money to Malema and would continue to do so because he believed in Malema's cause. However, during the inquiry, SARS highlighted several inconsistencies in Boshielo's testimony and concluded that the 'objective circumstances indicate that these payments were not made out of liberality or generosity. Something was expected in return.'[54]

Meanwhile, Mabilu was also emerging as a connected Limpopo businessman. The property developer, through his Vharanani Group, made substantial cash payments to the Ratanang Family Trust, according to SARS court documents. Some of these funds were ultimately used for the Silvela Road property, SARS found. When journalists got wind of some of this, Mabilu – who famously hosted a purple-clad Malema at his wedding celebration in Mauritius in 2011 – declined to answer their questions.[55]

To supplement the cash payment for the Silvela Road property, Malema applied to Absa for a R1,5-million home loan, which was granted and soon settled. On a salary of less than R40 000 a month, he could not have afforded the instalments. Exactly who helped him to gain and settle the bond remains unclear.

Around the same time in 2011, he knocked down the house in Silvela Road and started building a R16-million multistorey mansion, nicknamed his 'bachelor's pad' by journalists, complete with an underground panic room and a party deck.[56] His friends again footed the bill – in this instance, mainly On-Point and related companies, our records show.

When questioned by journalists about the origins of his apparent wealth, Malema reacted angrily, saying everyone should butt out of his so-called private affairs. He made all sorts of claims, including that he earned enough to pay for all of it and that his tax affairs were in order. These untrue but widely published claims got the attention of SARS, our sources say. Far from being a private matter, much of the funding for the construction work at the Silvela Road property came straight from On-Point – a company that, during this period, made most of its money from an unlawful scheme involving public funds from Limpopo's department of roads and transport. The public had every right to know.

From around 2008, different SARS units had adopted a lenient approach, repeatedly trying to guide Malema towards tax compliance and warning him to get his affairs in order. Instead of cooperating, he gradually began diverting funds from his personal accounts to the Ratanang Family Trust and got his friends and benefactors to pay his bills, including those associated with the Silvela Road property.

By 2009, SARS's enforcement units was scrutinising his acquisition of the Silvela Road property in particular.[57] Their investigators took a dim view of his strategy of having his bills paid for him. They saw these payments mostly as undeclared income – particularly, they argued, because Malema and his friends appeared to have engaged in a business relationship. For example, the investigators found that Manthata and Boshielo were business partners who directly paid large sums to the conveyancer, architect and builders associated with the property. Despite what Malema might have believed at the time, SARS was able to scrutinise the Ratanang Family Trust's financial records and noted that the names of some of his friends appeared next to large sums in the trust's bank statements. Investigators didn't buy the story that Malema's 'friends' had showered him with large sums of cash because they ran out of ways to improve their own lifestyles and wanted him to have a nice life, too. Instead, SARS found 'significant evidence' of business relationships between Malema and Gwangwa, Manthata and Boshielo in particular.[58]

For these reasons, and despite Malema's protestations describing the cash as donations, dividends and gifts, SARS later classified the more than R8 million spent on the Silvela Road property as taxable income (more about this in Chapter 11).

Manthata started his construction business in 2001[59], around the time when the province expected an infrastructure funding injection from the national government. He and his brother, Makgetsi Manthata, seemed to be ahead of the curve, thanks in large part to the former's friendship and business relationship with future Limpopo premier Cassel Mathale.[60] Through Mathale, the charismatic Selby reportedly became a close associate of Malema's.

The Manthatas – whose companies were involved in building roads and Reconstruction and Development Programme houses – were netting tenders worth millions of rand at the time.[61] Businesses linked to the Manthatas directly benefited from the On-Point deal, for example. (Selby would later convince a court that he could not have known about the misdeeds that preceded the millions he received from the Limpopo department of roads and transport.[62] But more of that to come.)

The exact origin of Selby Manthata's wealth may well be up for debate, but what is undeniable is that his initially modest 'donations' to Malema ballooned to regular payments ranging between R50 000 and R300 000. Between April 2009 and December 2010, he paid between R2 million and R3,5 million in cash into the Ratanang trust. When SARS investigators later asked Malema about these cash deposits, he said Manthata had given him money out of goodwill and philanthropy. Belatedly, Manthata also filed donor declarations to SARS, describing his relationship with Malema as 'friend'. All in, our records show that the Ratanang trust received north of R10,5 million between April 2009 and December 2011. Of this, Gwangwa's group of companies appears to have paid about R5 million, Manthata's companies about R3,5 million, Mabilu R300 000 and Boshielo and another friend of Malema's, Sthembiso Steve Bosch, each at least R200 000.

Like the others, Bosch is a Limpopo businessman who has in the past been linked to Malema, Cassel Mathale and state contracts. He claimed to have co-founded the first ANCYL branch in what was then Pietersburg in 1995, serving for a period as its treasurer-general.[63]

The balance of the funds flowing into the Ratanang trust consisted of small cash payments from various and sometimes untraceable donors.

'Private political-party and politician funding is a tricky horse to ride,' Malema's legal and financial advisers wrote to SARS in July 2012, seeking to explain that all these deposits really were political donations and that the Ratanang trust was not 'merely a conduit' for questionable payoffs.

The 48-page letter also contains an account by Malema of his own life, specifically regarding his relationship with money. He said he had become involved in ANC and student politics around 1990, when he was about nine years old. His family had little money, but his mother, a domestic worker, and his pensioner grandmother raised him as best they could. The letter paints a picture of Malema's popularity gaining traction over time because he was one of the masses and fought for their cause as much as he did for his own. He held no reverence for power, not even the ANC's.

By the late 1990s, he wrote, he was a provincial Cosas leader, and students and people believed in him and his work to such an extent that 'numerous businesspersons and political leaders' financially supported him 'through donations in order to execute our mandate'. His first salaried income came from his work as ANCYL provincial secretary in Limpopo around 2003. His need for money then increased when he had to relocate to Johannesburg. 'Therefore, donations from politicians and/or businesspersons have been part of my upbringing.'

It is an argument that Malema later repeated in court papers, arguing that 'donations' to politicians previously excluded from the economic system were normal practice.[64] 'I was the beneficiary of gifts and donations over the years, and I have been maintained by them,' he said in 2015,[65] adding that the donations were 'relatively humble' and below the limits for declaration to SARS. Donors were often unknown to him, and though some were wealthy, most were 'ordinary citizens of modest means'.

By 2012, Malema said, his profile was rising: 'It stands uncontroverted' that he was counted among the most recognisable politicians in the country, if not on the continent. In his capacity as a politician, he was required to travel 'extensively'. When he needed funding for his political activities, 'amounts of cash would be deposited by political supporters or comrades' into his account. He couldn't remember who most of these donors were. What is certain, Malema argued, is that the donations were given to him out of 'pure liberty or disinterested benevolence', and the donors were not motivated by 'self-interest or the expectation of a quid pro quo of some kind'.[66]

'In late 2009,' Malema wrote to SARS, 'I was informed by SARS that I had not submitted tax returns [on his ANC salary] for the years 2006, 2007 and 2008. I was unaware that I had to submit tax returns as I assumed that my taxes were settled by [the ANC] and paid directly to SARS . . . as soon as I became aware that I had not complied with the submission of my tax returns, I instructed my advisors to prepare and submit returns . . .'

After Malema's battles with Zuma turned toxic, his court papers reflected an additional, somewhat changed, perspective. Between 2012 and 2015, he repeatedly argued, he had become 'embroiled in disputes with the state president . . . as well as with various members of the ANC regime', and that 'I verily believe that I am subject to serious government abuse as the result of me falling out with president Jacob Zuma'.[67] Malema then claimed his fellow countrymen believed he was 'persecuted by the president, and others, with the aim to destroy [his] credibility as a leader'.

In his words, he began to argue that the authorities were on his back because Zuma and the ANC had unleashed them. Over the years, he had 'collected donations' in order to 'defend' himself against what he described as campaigns against him. People donated happily, Malema said, whenever he 'became a target for financial humiliation by certain members of the ANC regime'.

SARS didn't buy the story about the disinterest of Malema's benefactors. According to sources within SARS, Malema also ignored many warnings to get his tax affairs in order, despite his claims that he had acted immediately. Some of this is supported by the voluminous court papers filed between Malema and SARS.

The Directorate for Priority Crime Investigation also began investigating Malema in 2011. Nicknamed the Hawks, the directorate was established in 2008 to replace the disbanded Scorpions, to investigate organised, economic and other serious crime. Amid the Hawks and SARS investigation, Malema's claims of using the money for his political work collapsed.[68] A bank card linked to the Ratanang Family Trust had paid for clothing from Guess, Louis Vuitton and Armani, a stay at the luxury Twelve Apostles Hotel and Spa in Cape Town, and liquor from PicardiRebel.[69] Seven cheques were cashed for a total of R310 000 at the men's boutique Vigano. From 2009 to 2010, the trust also paid R250 000 into Malema's personal bank account. Its largest expenses related to his expanding property portfolio, including his Silvela Road bachelor's pad. The bulk of the 'donations' from 'benevolent' donors seem to have been used to fuel his lifestyle. The authorities took a dim view, arguing that the money was illicit income.

Malema's argument about charity expenses also didn't hold up. Small amounts for the construction of a Baptist church in Seshego, a house for the Olympic athlete Caster Semenya, wheelchairs and 'Seshego House' (no further description provided), as well as other unspecified cash payments, were the sole charitable expenses to be found. Possibly due to legal advice, it appears that Malema never tried to argue that any of these trust expenses were for the benefit of his son.

Perhaps sensing trouble, particularly after SARS and journalists started asking questions, he amended the trust deed in May 2010. The changes ensured that 'any other beneficiary nominated by the trustee from time to time', not just Ratanang, could share in the spoils. Malema, as the sole trustee, could not lawfully nominate himself as a beneficiary. He remedied this by appointing his grandmother, Sarah Mathebu Malema, as the second trustee.

Today, trusts are highly regulated to combat abuse of their benefits, particularly by placing distance between trustees and the assets held in the trust. The core rules that define a trust can be counted on one hand.[70] First, a trustee owes a fiduciary duty to the beneficiaries of a trust. It means the trust must be administered in good faith and in the best interests of the beneficiaries. The second requires a complete separation between the assets in the trust and the assets of the trustees, to protect beneficiaries from the insolvency, divorce or death of a trustee. It also means, crucially, that trustees may not manage or use the assets in the trust as if they were their own. The third speaks to continuity of assets in a principle referred to as subrogation. Simplified, it means that when a property held by a trust is sold, the proceeds remain under the control of the trust. The last rule dictates that a trustee runs a type of 'office' when handling the affairs of a trust.

Malema seems to have contravened all these rules in his management of the trust. There was no separation between his assets and those of the trust. The Silvela Road bachelor's pad is a clear example. The house was partly funded with money that flowed through the trust, but the property was registered in Malema's name. Cash from the trust was used to buy property, clothes, food and liquor for his personal benefit.

It is hard to say whether Ratanang really did derive any benefit from the trust that bore his name. His school fees, as well as the child support paid to his mother, Maropeng, appear to have come mostly from Malema's Mazimbu Investment Trust. This account appears to have mainly received income from a taxi business and some small-scale farming in Limpopo, a limited extract of the trust's bank accounts show.[71]

During the 2013 court battle between SARS and Malema, centred on his sequestration, SARS investigators argued that the Ratanang trust's expenses did not align with the description of a 'family trust'.[72] 'The trust reflects a large number of deposits, a significant amount of which were in cash and the majority of such was spent on [Malema's] personal expenses . . . It is contended that the trust was merely used as a conduit for [Malema] to receive funds and was in actual fact the alter ego of [Malema],' SARS investigators argued. But more was to come.

PART TWO
In the Red

CHAPTER 5

The Limpopo kingpin

FROM 2009, Julius Malema – then still president of the ANCYL – found new ways to expand his political and business influence in Limpopo, notably by working with the ANC's provincial leader, Cassel Mathale. Malema had helped Jacob Zuma rise to power at the ANC's fateful elective conference in Polokwane in 2007, a politically expedient move that worked in his and Mathale's favour. The following year, Mathale became the chair of the ANC in Limpopo, and eventually the province's premier.

According to Fiona Forde, Malema was not cowed by the older and more experienced Mathale. As president of the ANCYL based in the ANC headquarters in Johannesburg, Malema wasn't a public office-bearer, but was nevertheless calling the shots across Limpopo, allegedly doing all the 'hiring and firing' in Mathale's government.[73]

As the two men shored up their political power, people whom journalists would soon link to the pair started getting their hands on tenders.

One of these involved the University of Limpopo, which had hosted the ANC's conference in Polokwane. The university's vice-chancellor, Nehemiah Mokgalong, was reportedly close to Mathale. Moreover, Kgalema Mohuba, the university's influential marketing and communications director, moved in the same business circles as Mathale and his wife, and had several business partners in common.[74]

In January 2011, the university awarded a lucrative three-year catering contract for its Medunsa campus to a company called Bohlaleng Foods. Its owner, Mandla Seopela, was a speechwriter for Mathale and reportedly a confidant of Malema's. He later helped to mobilise political support for Malema following the latter's expulsion from the ANC.

Soon after Seopela secured the contract, Collins Foromo – described as Malema's 'friend and former driver' – secured a R27,8-million contract to convert one of the university's gymnasiums into a laboratory. According to amaBhungane, which broke the story in 2012, the tender was part of a three-phase project valued at about R60 million. The contract raised questions within the university council, and prompted opposition parties to demand an investigation into procurement at the university.

A spokesperson for the DA insisted that Mokgalong and Mohuba should explain how the tenders had been awarded, adding that 'Malema's war-chest cannot be filled at the expense of the South African public'.[75] The chair of the IFP Youth Brigade, Mkhuleko Hlengwa, labelled the tenders 'nepotistic', and demanded a quick and thorough investigation.[76]

Malema denied these reports. In characteristic fashion, his spokesperson, Floyd Shivambu, saw fit to say: 'Whoever is trying to link us to any form of wrongdoing in tenders is being a fucking arsehole.'[77]

In mid-2011, the same year in which the university contracts were dished out, the Limpopo department of health gave contracts for supplying medical labels and forms to Tshepo Malema, Julius's cousin, and Nthabiseng Ntshangase, a business partner of Malema's associate Ali Boshielo. The *Mail & Guardian* claimed the provincial government had rushed through the tenders without following the required procedures.[78]

One source was quoted as saying the department had got three quotations for each contract, but the companies were all owned by the same people. 'So they chose one, and the money was released very quickly.' Mathale's office was also alleged to have ordered that the contracts be issued – a claim it denied. A whistleblower alleged that, among other things, the tenders were massively inflated.

When approached by journalists, a departmental spokesperson said the matter was being investigated. By then, the auditor-general had also launched an investigation. On top of this, Julius Malema was accused of having leaned on the department to pay up.

The department's chief financial officer, Friday Mushwana, reportedly told the *Mail & Guardian*: 'He [Julius Malema] phoned me on my cell when I was driving to Johannesburg and told me that there are young people who are complaining that the department is not paying . . . He said these young people need to be paid.'[79]

Staggeringly, according to this report, two zeroes were added to Tshepo Malema and Ntshangase's contracts to increase them from R450 000 to R45 million and from R260 000 to R26 million respectively. Although the younger Malema was not paid after the whistleblower's report had sparked investigations, Ntshangase received a payout for the smaller amount – weeks after news of the scandal had broken, and the payments had supposedly been frozen.[80]

When presented with claims that the premier's office had ordered the contracts to go ahead, Mathale's spokesperson responded by referring to formal government policy: 'The premier is not responsible for the awarding of contracts in government. Supply-chain management issues are governed by the Supply Chain Management Framework Act. All departments are guided by this legislation when they deal with procurement matters, and the premier does not play any role in this process.'[81]

Tshepo Malema told the *Mail & Guardian*: 'Yes, I have contracts. I am a young, growing businessman, and part of my work is not to respond to newspapers.'

For his part, Julius Malema denied that he had tried to pressure the department. 'I wouldn't call a person I do not know. I don't know him. I've never met him. I don't remember making a call to any person about payments.'[82]

Collins Foromo and Tshepo Malema cropped up again in another amaBhungane investigation into a school nutrition programme in Limpopo in 2012. Utilising a budget of R1,7 billion over two years, the department of education contracted hundreds of companies to deliver food to primary and secondary schools across the province's five districts – often learners' only regular daily meal.

AmaBhungane and the *Sunday Independent* uncovered widespread irregularities in the tender process, which was adjudicated in May 2011.[83] Journalists found that a coterie of Malema's friends and family members – Tshepo Malema and Foromo among them – had benefited from the dubious tenders. Malema had allegedly handed a list of favoured service providers to Dickson Masemola, the province's MEC for education – which the two men denied. Malema said that he had 'never sent any list to the department. Whoever says that I did, must produce that list and say, "At this time and at that place, Julius Malema gave the department this list." I don't even know anyone who deals with nutrition in the education department.'

Arandi Trading Enterprises, a company owned by Tshepo Malema, was given a chunk of the project. According to media calculations, it was worth between R4,6 million and R5,2 million over two years, to feed nearly 4 500 learners. His company was evaluated for the Capricorn district, which includes Polokwane and Seshego, but was also given work in the Vhembe district.[84]

Malema's bodyguard and security advisor Jabavu Oliphant got a R5-million slice of the pie, but according to amaBhungane, failed to deliver anything. Other important figures who got in on the feeding scheme and who would play an important role in Malema's network were his cousin Matsobane Phaleng, former ANCYL and later EFF member Jossey Buthane, and Malema's close associate Jacob Lebogo.

The auditor-general's annual audit of the department revealed multiple irregularities in the tender process, as did an unsuccessful court application by two businesspeople whose bids had not succeeded. Among other anomalies, some of the companies that had won contracts had only been registered the previous year and could therefore not have met the requirement to submit audited financial statements for the 2009/10 financial year. Some bidders who received high scores were not appointed, while some who scored low in the tender evaluation process, or who were not evaluated at all, were appointed instead.

The fate of the school feeding scheme, which was a disaster from the outset, mirrored the situation in the province at large, which was descending into a financial crisis. In December 2011, the national cabinet placed five Limpopo departments, including the department of education, under administration and ordered the introduction of severe cost-cutting measures. This decision followed the provincial administration's failure to pay its officials overtime. *City Press* also reported that the province had asked the minister of finance, Pravin Gordhan, for a bailout or advance of at least R700 million, as the banks would not lend it any more money.

In the meantime, Malema's own economic fortunes had risen in inverse proportion to those of his home province. Indeed, various 'benefactors' – mostly businessmen active in Limpopo – were paying him increasing amounts of money. Between 2005 and 2008, some of these payments were still as little as a few hundred rand. By 2010, they were rarely smaller than R20 000 and included amounts of R180 000, R140 000 and R250 000.

None of this was declared – in fact, Malema did not file tax returns at all, eventually forcing SARS to launch a formal probe and claim outstanding taxes going back to 2005.

In 2010 in particular, Malema's income exploded. SARS eventually calculated that his taxable income had risen from just over R810 000 the previous year to no less than R7,25 million – 795 percent higher than in 2009, and 3 264 percent higher than in 2005.

Malema was aware that his lifestyle was attracting attention from journalists and rival entrepreneurs in Limpopo. In an apparent attempt to put some distance between himself and the large sums of money, he increasingly used the Ratanang Family Trust as a vehicle for receiving 'donations'.

In May 2010, in an apparent attempt to ensure that income into the trust would not be regarded as personal, taxable income, Malema added his grandmother as a trustee, and changed the definition of bene-ficiaries. Added to this, he did still nothing to register the trust as a taxpaying entity. Following fruitless appeals, SARS eventually did so itself in February 2011.

According to SARS, in the 2011 tax year, Malema's taxable income amounted to at least R5,24 million, primarily paid into the Ratanang Family Trust but also paid on his behalf to third parties. He eventually underdeclared a taxable income of R885 204.

Payments into the trust in Malema's 'boom year' of 2010 included at least R100 000 from ANC heavyweight Tokyo Sexwale, via his company

Mvelaphanda Holdings.[85] Malema told SARS investigators it was a 'donation' for an ANC event. At the time, Sexwale had political aspirations and seemed to regard Malema as a valuable ally. When questioned by Forde, Malema denied that Sexwale had ever made donations to him or the trust, and said people were trying to discredit him by saying he had been bought by Sexwale.

By 2011, Malema's property portfolio was also growing. He owned a house in Flora Park in Polokwane that he had bought in 2006, as well as the house in Silvela Road, Johannesburg. Back in 2006, he had also made a quick buck on a property flip in Polokwane involving a 'friend', Matane Mphahlele. The property was sold by the municipality to Mphahlele for R222 000 in August of that year. It was only transferred into his name the following April, and then immediately transferred to Malema, all on the same day and at the original price. A few months later, Malema sold the property for over three times more.

Forde put it to Malema that it looked like Mphahlele had fronted for him so that he could avoid public scrutiny. He replied that Mphahlele had lacked sufficient funds to buy the property, so he had stepped in to buy it from him. Some of the proceeds from the sale went towards Malema's Flora Park property.

In a later twist to the story, Mphahlele claimed that his own lawyer had colluded with Malema, the head of the municipal department of housing Clifford Motsepe, and other municipal officials to transfer the property to Malema. He admitted that he had never paid for the property, but accused his lawyer of failing to facilitate the payment and failing to inform him that it had been registered in his name.[86]

Malema's associates also profited from a series of questionable property transactions during large-scale municipal property sales in Polokwane. In August 2011, Forde and the amaBhungane journalist Craig McKune wrote that a group of politicians and businessmen close to Malema and then-premier Mathale had been given privileged access to a municipal property sale in Polokwane.[87] These members of the province's 'inner circle' were alleged to have jumped the queue and bypassed a supposedly open public process. This allegation, brought to the *Mail & Guardian* by well-placed sources, was roundly denied by those involved. Nevertheless, it reported, deed records revealed a long list of connected individuals who had benefited from the sale.

This controversy went back to April 2009, just after Mathale had become premier. More than 100 residential plots in an affluent area called Ster Park – aptly nicknamed 'Tender Park' because it housed many wealthy, politically connected residents – were sold off by the municipality at bargain prices. The *Mail & Guardian* cited a source as saying, 'When the municipality is going to sell properties, there is normally very serious demand. The property is usually sold for much lower than the market price. Some people buy and sell at a higher price within a week.'

In several cases, prominent figures acquired property by using third parties as fronts. The municipality would transfer the property to that party, after which it would immediately be passed on to the actual buyer. The *Mail & Guardian* identified 15 such transactions. Among the apparent direct and indirect beneficiaries were Mathale and his business partner Selby Manthata; the ANCYL secretary in Limpopo, Jacob Lebogo; and Malema's benefactor and business partner Lesiba Gwangwa. At the time, in August 2011, Manthata and Gwangwa were already in the news because of the On-Point scandal.

Other businessmen seen to be close to Malema, including the property magnate David Mabilu, also got hold of plots. Previously, Mabilu had profited significantly from property deals involving the government, earning a quick R40 million from the questionable swaps and sales of state land. In 2008, he traded parcels of land bordering Seshego, which had been occupied by squatters, for municipal land – including a prime piece of land in an area linking Polokwane to Seshego. He then sold this and two neighbouring properties he had bought privately to the Limpopo department of local government and housing for R51 million – more than five times the amount he had effectively paid for them.

According to an amaBhungane report, he had basically made a killing 'buying land from one arm of government and selling it to another one'.[88] The person Mabilu negotiated with at the provincial department, senior general manager Ngoako Molokomme, attended Mabilu's lavish, multimillion-rand wedding in Mauritius in October 2011.[89] Also in attendance, and kitted out head-to-toe in purple – purple designer suit, matching shoes, and purple fedora – was Julius Malema.

At the time, Malema was driving around in a R1,2-million Range Rover 'lent' to him by the owner of MPPJ Property Development, Matome Hlabioa. In July 2011, *City Press* quoted Hlabioa as saying: 'He [had] been driving my cars long before he became president. If Julius wants something like a car, I give it to him. I own more than 10 cars. If you look at the car he is driving . . . it's cheapest car I own.' He denied that the loan was a quid pro quo for Malema's help in winning public tenders.[90]

In April 2011, the auditor-general raised questions about irregularities and poor record-keeping in connection with more than 100 provincial tenders, including three worth R60 million awarded to MPPJ for the construction of schools. By then, Hlabioa had scored provincial contracts worth more than R200 million.[91] In 2014, eNCA reporters visited a rural Limpopo school built by MPPJ and found it was derelict and vandalised. A government spokesperson said the school was not in use because of a contractual dispute with MPPJ that had been taken to court. The Limpopo government would not pay until it was satisfied with the work.[92]

Hlabioa died of cancer in 2015. By then, he had left the ANC and joined the EFF. Malema's address at his friend's funeral spoke of their mutual loyalty, but also of Hlabioa's value to Malema as a donor. He slammed the ANC for '[refusing] to give even a single comment on Matome Hlabioa's death just because he left the party to join the EFF', even though 'they are sitting in Frans Mohlala House', the ANC's glitzy provincial headquarters in Polokwane, which opened during Malema's tenure as ANCYL president and which, according to him, was funded by Hlabioa.

The crisis in Limpopo dented Mathale's political fortunes, but he survived. In December 2011 – the same month the cabinet deployed an emergency intervention team to Limpopo – he was re-elected as ANC chair in the province. He lost this position when, in the wake of the On-Point scandal, the ANC disbanded its provincial executive committee in March 2013. Several months later, the party also withdrew its support for Mathale's premiership, and he resigned from this position on 15 July 2013. He then joined the 'old boys' club' of disgraced politicians in the ANC's parliamentary benches. In February 2018, President Cyril Ramaphosa appointed him as deputy minister of small business development, and in May 2019 he became the deputy minister of police. He still held this post in mid-2025.

CHAPTER 6

All roads lead to Limpopo

IN SEPTEMBER 2009, the Limpopo government, then headed by Cassel Mathale, appointed Ntau Letebele as head of its department of roads and transport. It was a routine procedure, and attracted little attention.

Days into Letebele's term, an acting general manager sent him a memorandum stating that the department lacked capacity. The proposed remedy was to appoint a 'Project Management Unit' (PMU) that would assist internal staff.[93] Therefore, his approval was sought to engage a 'suitably qualified Project Management Unit' (in practice, an external contractor) for an initial period of three years.

The motivation for the memorandum was questionable. Until then, the construction and maintenance of roads had mostly been handled by the parastatal Roads Agency Limpopo. At the time, the agency was regarded as efficient, although critics said it favoured only a handful of companies.[94]

Letebele went along with the recommendation, and tender number PUDP394PMU was published on 11 September 2009, only 11 days after he had taken up his job. It required bidders to have extensive, proven experience in the design and construction of roads, traffic stations, weigh-bridges, intermodal facilities, cost centres and airport infrastructure. The unit would be mandated to initiate the planning, contracting for, and overseeing of roadworks by service providers. This included the provision of drawings, diagrams and designs for infrastructure upgrades. In all, 16 companies entered bids for this highly specialised appointment.

Then matters took an unexpected turn. One by one, seasoned firms with extensive experience of government contracts were eliminated in the early stages of the process, often for technical reasons such as incorrect paperwork. But the biggest shock still lay ahead. On 13 October 2009, On-Point Engineers – a previously unknown company – won the R52-million bid to run the PMU. The contract, which would stretch over three years with an option of renewal, was signed three days later. In contravention of national and provincial Treasury requirements, it had taken barely a month to complete the entire process.

On-Point did appear to have an excellent track record – on paper. In the bid documents, the company described itself as a 'multi-disciplinary' firm with 'international expertise' and a nine-year background in engineering work. Its BEE credentials were impeccable. Its tender application listed a large workforce with specialised skills and impressive CVs. The owner of On-Point, Lesiba Gwangwa, was well known in Limpopo, even though the company wasn't. He stated under oath that On-Point had an annual turnover of R2 million.

Almost none of this was true, the Public Protector would find later. When the tender was advertised, On-Point existed only in name[95] and had never been operational. It had not employed a single engineer or any other specialised employee. Some of the people listed in the bid documents had never been employed by or associated with On-Point. The company had no valid tax certificate or dedicated office space. Simply stated, it was a shell.

For reasons which (despite numerous probes into the matter) have never been adequately explained, the Limpopo department of roads and transport simply accepted On-Point's bid documents at face value. When the bid was evaluated, it scored exceptionally high on functionality.

A person who worked for Gwangwa at that time recounts how they were required to work into the early-morning hours 'to fill in bid forms, because [they] had to be submitted the next day'. This was actually unnecessary, the person said, because Gwangwa seemed to know that he would get the contract. 'He simply wanted everything to look legit. Gwangwa even wanted to insert my husband's name in the bid documents and list him as an engineer working for On-Point. I just said no.'

It also remains unexplained why Gwangwa was so sure he would win the tender. The fact that the Ratanang Family Trust was later given an indirect 50 percent stake in On-Point offered some clues.

Everything about On-Point was a mirage.[96] When Hawks investigators eventually interviewed the firms listed as references in the company's bid documents, it became clear that they had no relationship with On-Point and had not agreed to have their logos included in the tender submissions.

On-Point's chief financial officer, Malose Leolo, later admitted to forensic investigator Trevor White that he had only been appointed to the position after the firm had won the PMU tender. Gwangwa had attached Leolo's CV simply to bolster On-Point's bid documents and not because he was a real employee. Even after working at the company for a while, Leolo did not recognise most of the names on the list of employees attached to the bid documents. A number of these people said their CVs had been submitted without their consent or knowledge.

A timeline illustrates just how the company and the bid were assembled at the last minute. Bids for the PMU tender were due on 1 October 2009. On 7 August 2009, company documents show, one of Gwangwa's business partners, Kagisho Dichabe, was appointed a director of a five-month-old shelf company, Achir Shelf 8 (Pty) Ltd, which had never traded. On 31 August, a resolution was passed to change the name to On-Point Engineers (Pty) Ltd. A day later, Letebele became the new head of the department of roads and transport.

Gwangwa was appointed as director and CEO of On-Point on 16 September 2009. Seven days later, on 23 September, share certificates were issued to the Makatele Family Trust, Tshiamo Dichabe (brother of Gwangwa's partner Kagisho Dichabe), and Gwangwa's company Guilder Investments. Each entity then owned an equal share of On-Point. (A year later, just before On-Point started raking in the big bucks, Malema orchestrated the buyout of Dichabe and the Makatele Family Trust. The Ratanang Family Trust and Gwangwa Family Trust then each owned 50 percent of Guilder Investments, which wholly owned On-Point.)

On-Point's company address in Bendor, Polokwane – actually SGL's business address – was registered on 24 September. A certificate stating that the company was now named On-Point was issued the following day.

These events seem to show that Gwangwa had begun to prepare On-Point for the tender even before it was advertised, and before Letebele's appointment. Years later, the Public Protector, Advocate Thuli Madonsela, would state: 'That On-Point was given preferential treatment is without doubt. The unanswered questions are further compounded by the fact that evidence suggests that On-Point knew about and started preparing for the bid some time prior to September 2009.'[97]

On-Point's tax certificate was another key issue. A major feature of the public procurement system is that all companies bidding for government contracts have to produce a valid tax clearance certificate, issued by SARS. If they fail to do so, they are immediately disqualified. In this instance, the tax clearance certificate submitted belonged not to On-Point but to the shelf company Achir Shelf 8. Not even Letebele could ignore this glaring shortcoming.

So, on 7 October 2009, he sent Gwangwa the following letter: 'Please take note that you have submitted the tax clearance certificate of Achir Shelf 8 (Pty) Ltd. You have to submit the tax clearance certificate of On-Point Engineers (Pty) Ltd. Failure to submit the required document within two days after receipt of this notice . . . will disqualify you from further participation in this process.'

The next day, Gwangwa provided an extraordinary response: 'Kindly note that Achir shelf 8 [sic] (Pty) Ltd, Registration number 2009/007402/07 is a shelf company that On-Point Engineers (Pty) Ltd, registration number 2009/007402/07 bought and we had registered a name change from Achir Shelf 8 (Pty) Ltd to On-Point Engineers (Pty) Ltd which was approved by cipro [sic]. Further note that the Registration number on the tax clearance that we submitted is similar to the one of On-Point's registration number.'

This was not only patently invalid, but also amounted to an admission that On-Point was brand-new, had never traded, and lacked the capacity and expertise claimed in the bid documents.

On 9 October 2009, Gwangwa did send Letebele a tax clearance certificate in the name of On-Point. Gwangwa's accountant at the time, Seraj Ravat, remembers the panic over the certificate well. In a later affidavit to the Hawks,[98] Ravat stated that Gwangwa had telephoned him, saying that On-Point 'will be generating lots of money and that I should apply and retrieve a tax clearance certificate'. Gwangwa then phoned him repeatedly, stating that the certificate needed to be issued in the name of On-Point Engineers and not that of the original shelf company, Achir Shelf 8.

In the same week, Ravat's assistant paid multiple visits to the SARS offices in Randburg to obtain the certificate, which was finally issued to her on 9 October. Ravat informed Gwangwa, who said 'they do not have time to collect it in Pretoria but that I should SMS the tax clearance certificate number to him, and he will send someone to collect it at the SARS Randburg offices'.

Gwangwa's earlier admission about the shelf company should have disqualified the entire bid, but it had no effect on Letebele or the department's chief financial officer, Malehu Thindisa, who chaired the bid adjudication committee.

Three years later, Madonsela wrote that it was 'mind-boggling why the stark discrepancies between the bid document and the tax clearance certificate did not disqualify On-Point or present red flags regarding the possibility of tender fraud to those who dealt with the bid, particularly the head of department'. She found that, at the time of the bid, On-Point 'only existed on paper' and had no dedicated office space, while the entire workforce at SGL House did not add up to the headcount provided in the bid documents.

When interviewed by Madonsela, Gwangwa danced around awkwardly. First, he claimed the bid document included a 'profile' document on On-Point's composition and 'all the elements of the other companies that came together'. This was a fiction, because nothing that remotely substantiated the existence of a joint venture was submitted. Then Gwangwa tried to argue the 'nine years of experience' issue was a 'misunderstanding', as the bid documents had referred to the cumulative experience of the team. But even if that were true, the maths did not add up.

Later, he said he had made this mistake because English was not his first language, but eventually admitted that it might have been an 'oversight'. Explaining his signature on problematic documents, for example, Gwangwa said he sometimes just signed 'a pile of documents' without checking 'each and every one of them, because I rely on my staff'.

The Ratanang trust became an indirect shareholder in On-Point in August 2010. However, money from the On-Point contract started flowing to the trust and Malema much earlier. Specifically, the trust received the first of what would become regular monthly payments from the Guilder Investments Group of companies on 7 August 2009 – the same month in which the Polokwane businessmen blew life into Achir Shelf 8/On-Point. The R150 000 payment was described as 'Acb Credit Sundowns Property', a misspelling of Sandown. A payment of R50 000 with the same description followed less than a week later.

In August 2011, when it became impossible to deny the evidence presented in the media, Malema famously admitted to owning shares in On-Point through the Ratanang trust. 'We are shareholders as a family,' he told journalist Craig McKune.[99] He denied that he had played a role in directing any tenders to the company, saying, 'I just queue when the dividends are due.'[100]

On the same day in October 2009 when Letebele, on behalf of the Limpopo government, signed the expensive PMU contract with On-Point, the provincial government asked the company to provide working drawings, concept diagrams and detailed designs for eight of the projects it was meant to manage, largely involving access roads and pavements. Astoundingly, Letebele agreed to pay On-Point an additional R8,4 million even though the work required was included in the original contract. In a clear indication that On-Point did not have the required capacity, the work was farmed out to freelancers. On 31 October 2009, barely two weeks into the contract, On-Point submitted its first invoice, to the tune of R1,57 million. No meaningful work could have been done in two weeks to justify the payment,[101] but no one in the department asked any questions.

One early incident may explain why no one risked raising their voice. It involved the acting general manager for roads infrastructure, Saracen

Mojapelo. He had been a member of the bid adjudication committee and convenor of the bid evaluation committee that had recommended On-Point's appointment to Letebele.

On 13 November, less than a month after the signing of the contract, Mojapelo started raising concerns about On-Point's conduct.[102] The exact nature of his complaint is not known. However, the score sheets filled in during the evaluation of On-Point provide a clue. These show that Mojapelo scored On-Point 34 out of 70, while a Denel employee, Colbert Marobela, and Lesiba Kekana, an official in the provincial department of finance, awarded On-Point 53 and 50 points respectively. Marobela later told investigators that he had known Letebele since childhood. A department of roads and transport employee told them Marobela had attended Letebele's 40th birthday party in 2010.[103]

Both the Public Protector and PricewaterhouseCoopers (PwC) investigator Trevor White were puzzled by Marobela's appointment to the bid evaluation committee, as he lacked the required expertise. When White analysed the score sheets, he found that Marobela and Kekana had awarded On-Point the same points in various subcategories, which seemed to show that they had colluded in giving On-Point artificially high scores.[104] Both Marobela and Kekana denied knowing each other and any suggestion of collusion.

Whatever the reasons for Mojapelo's qualms, Letebele dealt with them by suspending him, 'pending investigations into alleged misconduct'. The media was told he had missed a deadline for issuing tender advertisements.

On 17 November 2009, Mojapelo lodged a complaint against Letebele in a letter to the then MEC for roads and transport, Pinky Kekana.[105] Kekana did not reply, and Mojapelo decided to resign and take early retirement. He was the only person on record within the Limpopo department of roads and transport who ever dared to raise concerns over On-Point.

In terms of its contract, On-Point was required to participate in the evaluation and appointment of all prospective service providers and to oversee their work. This is where the real shenanigans began, as the companies of family, friends and individuals sympathetic to Gwangwa and Malema gained access to a rich seam of government funds.

These included Malema's younger cousin Tshepo Malema, who – according to his friends – refers to himself as an 'entrepreneur' and 'man in black', a reference to his penchant for dressing in black. Despite his claims of being a property developer, insiders say he 'helps out' with Malema's business ventures.

From 2011 onwards, Tshepo's companies won tenders worth millions of rand, many from provincial departments in Limpopo, and some of them under questionable circumstances. In July 2011, for example, his company Arandi Trading Enterprises received a contract from a provincial bid evaluation committee weighted with On-Point staff for the supply of painting materials.[106] It was one of 250 companies that submitted bids. The committee disqualified 243 for 'non-compliance' with tender procedures, and seven remained. Arandi Trading then happened to submit the lowest bid and to snag the tender.

When interviewed by Madonsela, Letebele claimed that On-Point staff had served on the bid evaluation committee because of their specific expertise. By contrast, she found that, given the nature of the goods to be procured, very little, if any, specific expertise was required. When she asked for payments and invoices, Letebele claimed there was none because Arandi Trading had not yet been given any work. Based on the information she had, Madonsela eventually found the contracts awarded to Arandi Trading were 'improper' but 'not necessarily unlawful'.[107]

During this time, Tshepo Malema made various payments to his cousin and the Ratanang trust. When questioned by SARS, Julius explained that Tshepo (and his cousin Ronnie Malema) sometimes deposited cash received on his behalf from unknown donors supporting his work without expecting anything in return.[108] SARS eventually classified these payments as taxable income.

In 2012, Tshepo and Foromo were charged with fraud[109] relating to a R63-million tender to fill real and imaginary potholes in Limpopo. Little to no work was done. The NPA provisionally withdrew the case in 2013 due to insufficient evidence,[110] and nothing has come of it since.

Despite Tshepo's apparent good fortune and conspicuously affluent lifestyle, there is no record of him owning any property. He refers to himself as a 'property developer', and insiders say he 'helps out' with Malema's business ventures.

Steve Bosch, also a Malema benefactor, secured a number of contracts from the provincial department of roads and transport. Bosch had been a member and later provincial treasurer of the ANCYL. He is five years older than Malema and according to a mutual friend, a 'far more experienced businessman' – particularly when it came to benefiting from political connections.

Letebele signed off on two contracts with Bosch's company Sizani Build It and the contract with Tshepo Malema on a single day. When the Public Protector asked him for paperwork related to these and other contracts, he could not produce any. Given this, she could not make a finding about Bosch and Tshepo. However, tax records show that in July 2009 and February 2010, Sizani Build It paid a total of R200 000 into the account of the Ratanang Family Trust.[111] Malema told SARS these were donations.

Perhaps even more indicative of the symbiotic relationship between Bosch and Malema were payments to Aurelio Cimato, the architect who designed Malema's house in Silvela Road. In March and June 2011, shortly before the two tenders were awarded to Sizani Build It, Bosch made two payments to Cimato totalling R1,2 million,[112] to the benefit of 'J Malema'. This was first revealed by journalists from the *Sunday Times*, and later confirmed in SARS court documents. When the paper's reporters phoned Malema in August 2011 for an explanation, he swore at them and claimed he knew nothing about the payments.[113]

Bosch claimed that all the payments to the architect related to his own projects. However, he was stumped when journalists asked him why he had named Malema as the beneficiary, and why Sizani Build It had sent an SMS to Malema's phone to confirm the payments. Bosch first tried to deny the SMS confirmations before reportedly asking: 'Do you know how many Malemas are here in Polokwane and Botswana?'[114]

The only 'donation' Bosch did acknowledge was in the form of cash and building materials given to the Ratanang Family Trust in 2009 to build a Baptist church in Seshego in honour of Malema's mother. Today, there is no evidence of Bosch's contribution. Two large black plaques mounted on each side of the entrance state that the church was built by the Ratanang trust.

In April 2010, Letebele decided to establish a departmental database of prospective service providers for smaller contracts – a procedure sanctioned by the National Treasury. In principle, it was a good idea to create a list of potential service providers whose credentials, skills and experience had already been evaluated by a departmental panel. Whenever work needed to be done – upgrading a road, building a bridge or filling potholes – the department would have a list of approved service providers to choose from. This process would be more efficient, and save time and money. Letebele duly published a tender notice calling on local companies to apply for registration.

In practice, however, the scheme fell flat. The database did not automatically select a service provider suited to a particular job – this still had to be done manually. This opened the door to wholesale corruption. The database ended up being used to provide a sheen of legitimacy to On-Point's dealings with four companies in particular: Oceanside Trading, HL Matlala and Associates, Mpotseng Infrastructure and Baitseanape Consulting Engineers.[115] Later, Madonsela and White paid close attention to these contracts.

In 2010 and 2011, along with hundreds of other hopefuls, these companies applied to be added to the database. At that stage, On-Point was already functioning as the PMU, and it was well placed to influence the process.

Madonsela later found that On-Point was not meant to be involved in the evaluation of bids by prospective service providers.[116] Yet Letebele appointed two On-Point employees and one departmental employee to sit on the service provider review panel. The On-Point owners Lesiba Gwangwa and Kagisho Dichabe apparently wielded considerable influence over who was included in the database.

In 2012, when the National Treasury ordered its investigation into a R2-billion 'black hole' in Limpopo's finances, the legal and tax consultancy PwC was one of the firms roped in to boost the forensic capacity of the Hawks, and the prickly matter of On-Point soon crossed the desk of PwC partner Trevor White. The Ratanang Family Trust was a major beneficiary of the company, and when the Public Protector eventually made her recommendation – effectively to seize Gwangwa's and Malema's assets – the NPA enlisted White to prepare an affidavit supporting its court application to attach Schuilkraal, a 139-hectare cabbage farm located 12 kilometres north of Polokwane, bought by Gwama Properties but seemingly on behalf of Malema.[117]

The Hawks botched the issuing of subpoenas for bank statements, which meant that White had to rely on limited information. For example, he only had one set of annual financial statements for the Ratanang Family Trust, for the year ending February 2010.

White's contributions to the case were only partly successful. When in 2016 the NPA appealed against the acquittal of two of Malema's funders – Selby Manthata and his wife, Hellen Moreroa – on charges of fraud and corruption, two High Court judges severely criticised White, calling him a 'biased' and 'unreliable' witness. For this and other reasons, the appeal was turned down.[118] By contrast, in March 2013, White's report detailed that Schuilkraal was bought with the proceeds of crime for Malema's benefit. This enabled the NPA to attach the farm as a forfeited asset.[119]

White's analysis, the documents he studied and referred to, the Public Protector's report, and findings by SARS attached to court documents filled out a picture of how the On-Point scam operated. White found that Gwangwa and Dichabe had been particularly involved in the inclusion of certain companies on the service provider database.[120] For example, while examining the bid evaluation score sheets, White noticed what seemed to be obvious signs of collusion between the On-Point officials on the panel. They often awarded identical and unjustifiably high scores in five evaluation categories to certain, clearly preferred companies.

According to White, a red flag was that the third person on the panel – the one not employed by On-Point – scored them low to medium, while the two On-Point officials scored them high to highest. Also, both White's affidavit and the Public Protector's report shows that all the preferred companies were somehow linked to Gwangwa and, in some cases, indirectly to Malema.

As noted previously, the main preferred companies were Oceanside Trading, HL Matlala and Associates, Mpotseng Infrastructure and Baitseanape Consulting Engineers. Oceanside's sole member and sole owner was Hellen Moreroa, the wife of Selby Manthata. He was a signatory to Oceanside's bank account while Moreroa was not. By 2011 Manthata was one of Malema's largest funders. In March 2011, Oceanside paid R1 million to the conveyancing attorneys responsible for transferring the ownership of Schuilkraal to Gwama Properties.

According to the Public Protector's report, Hosea Matlala, the sole member of HL Matlala, had been a friend of Gwangwa's since school days.[121] The sole member of Mpotseng, Arthur Phetla, was a former director of On-Point. He was also a friend of Gwangwa's who knew him from high school. When questioned by Madonsela about his ties to the company, Phetla denied any knowledge of his On-Point directorship. He eventually complained to the Engineering Council of South Africa that he had never consented to being made a director of On-Point, but did not act on its advice to file charges of fraud against Gwangwa and On-Point.

Baitseanape's sole member, Ephraim Thipe, was not as close to Gwangwa as the other three. While he moved in the same circles as Gwangwa, they were not necessarily friends, and he received the fewest contracts among the four companies.

The fly-by-night nature of these four companies was another common feature. Besides departmental work, they did little or nothing.

According to Madonsela's report, Mpotseng Infrastructure was contracted to design and construct pavements in six municipalities, to the tune of R42 million. Phetla soon realised that Mpotseng Infrastructure did not have the capacity to do the design work, and asked Gwangwa for assistance. The designs were then completed by Qualis Consulting, at a cost of R1,6 million, but Phetla was dissatisfied with the work. As a result, the designs were finalised by Mpotseng, and Phetla declined to pay Qualis the full amount.

The sole director of Qualis at the time of the On-Point scam was Gwangwa's then fiancée, Salphy Mphahlele. Although she was not involved in the operations of Qualis or any of the Guilder Group companies, she received a monthly salary.[122]

Gwangwa was loath to have Qualis linked to him directly. Despite his 100 percent shareholding in the company, he made sure that his name did not appear on any publicly accessible documents, told his staff not to disclose its existence, and only became a signatory to the company's accounts well after its registration.

Others, such as Oceanside, appeared to be shells, with little operating capacity. The bid documents submitted during the selection process were augmented with CVs of individuals not employed by these firms, often without their knowledge. Freelancers were misrepresented as full-time staff to create the illusion of experience.

When questioned by journalists, Kekana the MEC, vehemently denied that On-Point employees had a say in which companies were appointed. She said the procurement processes were 'watertight', and if On-Point employees attended the meetings, it was only to 'render technical support'.[123] Evidently, this was far from the truth.

The most significant commonality among these four companies was their connection to Malema. A large chunk of the money paid by the department to Oceanside, Mpotseng and HL Matlala ultimately ended up with him. But although the money was flowing, trouble was brewing.

As part of the On-Point scheme, Gwangwa concocted a plan to fleece its co-conspirators.[124] It developed as follows: after On-Point had extracted a staggering R8,4 million from Letebele's department in exchange for designs and drawings for eight pavement projects, a carefully rigged tender procedure was launched. Gwangwa ensured that companies owned by his friends were registered on the service provider database and then appointed to work on the projects.

Next, On-Point provided the same drawings and designs it had previously submitted to the department to Oceanside, Mpotseng, HL Matlala and Baitseanape 'to review'. These four companies then resubmitted the same drawings – with little to no alterations, but under a different company name – to the department. In some cases, the replacement of the company logo was so badly done that the deletions were still visible.

Thanks to On-Point, which in its capacity as the PMU partially authorised the payments, the four companies were promptly paid. Oceanside was paid R6,2 million, Mpotseng R2,5 million, HL Matlala R4 million and Baitseanape R2,7 million. The department had been deceived – willingly or not – into paying On-Point R8,4 million, and then paying the four companies R15,4 million for essentially the same drawings. Without a single stone being laid, Letebele's eight pavement projects had already cost the department R23,8 million.

While the four companies were still counting their cash, Gwangwa came knocking. Despite them being owned and managed by friends and close acquaintances, he falsely told them the department had not paid On-Point for the designs, and that they had to do so. To this end, Gwangwa got his associates to sign secret memorandums of understanding (MoUs) which stated that these back-end deals were not to be disclosed to anyone – including the National Treasury. In an astounding move, Gwangwa then used the MoUs to claim anywhere between 40 percent and 95 percent of the fees the department had paid to these four companies.

The department of roads and transport paid On-Point R52 million for its job as PMU, and an additional R8,4 million for drawings that should have been produced under the original contract. Added to this, Gwangwa extracted further sums from his friends via the secret MoUs. Effectively, therefore, On-Point was paid three times for the same work. Madonsela later characterised these and other MoUs as 'corrupt back-to-back agreements' which ensured that On-Point bagged far more than its R52 million fee for serving as the PMU.

Ephraim Thipe was the only subcontractor to baulk at this. He initially agreed to the MoU with On-Point, but later refused to pay it anything. In contrast, the others – Oceanside, Mpotseng and HL Matlala – complied and paid over the amounts claimed by On-Point.

Gwangwa's predatory conduct clearly irked somebody enough that details of his underhand dealings were leaked to journalists. In August 2011, the *Mail & Guardian* and *Sunday Times* reported that On-Point had 'dangled tenders' in front of would-be contractors and then demanded to be made a silent partner while also taking a large cut once the contract had been awarded. Extensive media coverage linked Malema to the Ratanang Family Trust and On-Point. Malema could no longer deny his association with the trust, and tried in vain to present it as a charitable organisation from which he did not benefit.

He consistently claimed that he had never influenced tenders, that he was simply a shareholder in On-Point through the trust, and did not get involved in business operations. 'You are talking to the wrong person,' Malema told a journalist in early August 2011. 'Being a shareholder does not mean we know what is going on in the company. I am not involved in the running of the company, and I can't respond to what I don't know.'[125]

Malema attributed everything to Gwangwa, who was not a prominent politician. He had not been active in student politics, and had never played a visible role in the ANCYL or ANC. But several investigators, including Madonsela and White, later found that until 2012, Gwangwa's business existed almost solely because of government contracts, and that much of the proceeds went to the Ratanang Family Trust. Madonsela eventually found that the trust had 'benefited improperly from the unlawful, fraudu-lent and corrupt conduct of On-Point' and the 'maladministration' of the Limpopo roads and transport department.

When asked to explain the nature of his relationship with Malema, Gwangwa told Madonsela that they had grown up together, and were childhood friends. He went on to say that Malema was an 'intelligent and resourceful person' with many friends and acquaintances, and that his relations with business leaders 'across the globe' made him an invaluable asset. Similarly, he told a later tax inquiry that he had given Malema half the shares in Guilder Investments because he was well connected, and this would be 'good for business'.

He went on to say that Malema had 'contacts, leads, business leads', and confirmed that his business depended on tenders from the provincial government as well as municipalities in Limpopo. Gwangwa did not refer to his payments to Malema as 'donations'; instead, he insisted that they were made 'in anticipation of sharing profits'.

At the request of the Hawks, Gwangwa's former accountant, Seraj Ravat, later calculated that R106,7 million had flowed to On-Point in the 18 months between August 2010 and January 2012.[126] However, he did not have all the financial records.

As for Malema, we calculate that he received around R21,4 million in cash, assets and subsistence support from the On-Point scam alone. This amounts to just more than 40 percent of the original tender value of R51,9 million. This calculation does not include cash stuffed into envelopes, boxes and tog bags. One source in Gwangwa's office said she had to 'pack cash' into A3 envelopes about 30 times during the few years she worked at SGL House, and that Gwangwa's other employees did the same. The calculation also does not include money spent on petrol cards, or estimates of unknown services rendered and paid for.

If Malema and Gwangwa were the architects and ultimate benefi-ciaries of the On-Point scheme, Letebele was the mason who dug and laid its foundation. Yet he was never found guilty of wrongdoing by anyone other than the Public Protector. In her On-Point report, Madonsela found that the conduct of the department, specifically Letebele, and the bid evaluation and adjudication committees was 'unlawful, improper and constituted maladministration', and ordered Letebele to cancel the agreement with On-Point. (Effectively, this had already been done when the national government took over much of the provincial adminis-tration.) She also said the provincial government should investigate Letebele's conduct, and if necessary take disciplinary action against him.

Letebele resigned in 2013 after an internal investigation into the On-Point contract was announced. The department allowed him to leave, and his resignation effectively pre-empted any findings against him and those about whom he could testify. It also buried information on whether he had been pressured to act in On-Point's interests. In a familiar round of governmental musical chairs, he was then appointed CEO of Great North Transport, a subsidiary of the Limpopo Economic Development Agency.

In 2017, he was arrested and convicted, along with his son and an accomplice, for kidnapping and assault with grievous bodily harm following a horrifying incident that occurred around 21 December 2014.[127] The charges were linked to the abduction of three men who were suspected of burgling Letebele's business. They were taken to a farm, where they were badly beaten and locked in a storeroom. One of the victims died during the night. Letebele was sentenced to eight years in prison.

While there is no evidence directly implicating her, Pinky Kekana, the political head of the Limpopo department of roads and transport during the On-Point scandal, has survived and prospered. She was viewed as a political ally of Mathale and Malema, Mathale having appointed her to this portfolio in 2009.

The following year, Kekana was the subject of a complaint to the Public Protector by Thandi Moraka. At the ANCYL's provincial conference in Makhado, Moraka, the provincial deputy secretary of the League, and other provincial leaders were voted out and replaced by Malema's allies. The conference had descended into chaos, with Malema kicking out the supporters of his rival, popular chairperson Lehlogonolo Masoga, and police firing teargas at them. Malema wanted his relatively inexperienced ally, Jacob Lebogo, in the senior leadership, and he later expelled Masoga, whom he saw as a threat in his own stronghold of Limpopo.

Fleeing the conference in her car, Moraka was pulled over by a traffic officer attached to the department of roads and transport, acting on Kekana's instructions, and arrested. She was accused of stealing conference accreditation papers vital to confirming Lebogo as provincial secretary. The case of theft was later struck off the court roll, and Moraka asked the Public Protector to drop her complaint against Kekana, as she preferred that it be dealt with internally within the ANC. Nevertheless, the Public Protector pursued the case, eventually finding that Kekana had abused her powers for narrow political interests. She ordered Kekana to apologise and that the Premier take 'appropriate action' against her. Kekana did not apologise as instructed, and her office announced that it would take the report on legal review. It is unclear what became of that process. In 2011, her department was among those placed under administration by the national government.

In 2012, following the release of the Public Protector's On-Point report, the DA called on her to step down,[128] but she remained in her post. That December she was elected as the ANC's provincial treasurer. In March 2013, she was made MEC for economic development, environmental affairs and tourism. In July, Mathale's successor, Stan Mathabatha, announced a major reshuffle in which Kekana was one of eight MECs fired from the executive council.

Kekana was elected to the National Assembly, ranked 10th on the ANC's provincial party list, in 2014. The following year, she was elected to the national executive committee of the ANC Women's League. In December 2017, she was elected to the national executive committee of the ANC.

In February 2018, Ramaphosa appointed her as deputy minister of communications, and in August 2021 as deputy minister in the Presidency. In May 2024, she was re-elected. A month later, she was appointed deputy minister of public service and administration.

CHAPTER 7

The gathering storm

SHORTLY INTO ZUMA'S term as president, which began in 2009, the high-flying Malema began to run into trouble on two fronts. First, his political power base began to weaken. Less than three years after Jacob Zuma's victory at Polokwane in 2007, a rift had developed between him and the troublesome ANCYL leader. Malema's increasingly insolent attitude alienated many in the party hierarchy, and a series of missteps saw him facing disciplinary action.

One arose from his penchant for singing the controversial song 'Dubul' ibhunu' (Shoot/Kill the Boer), popularised in the 1990s by one of his idols, the former ANCYL leader and firebrand Peter Mokaba. Mokaba – whom Malema has described as a 'hero' and his 'mentor' – famously sang it at a memorial for Chris Hani in 1993, following the latter's assassination.

In 2002, Mokaba, then 43 years old, became ill and died. A crowd gathered outside Polokwane to mourn his passing spontaneously sang: 'Kill the Boer, kill the farmer!' The song then faded until its resurrection by Malema, and soon became a feature at ANCYL rallies, provoking condemnation from the Afrikaner lobby group AfriForum and other conservative whites.

In March 2010, in a case not involving Malema, a High Court judge banned the song, ruling that its lyrics amounted to hate speech and were therefore unconstitutional. The ANC hit back, describing the judgment as 'incompetent'. It argued that the words 'kill/shoot the Boer' were not meant literally and had to be seen in the context of the struggle against apartheid.

Just days later, the leader of the right-wing Afrikaner Weerstands-beweging (AWB), Eugène Terre'Blanche, was killed by two of his farm workers. Conservative South Africans were quick to draw a link between the song and the killing, claiming that the lyrics incited this sort of violence. Seeking to prevent a racial flare-up, the ANC top brass warned members in a statement to 'restrain themselves',[129] especially by singing songs that could be perceived as 'contributing to racial polarisation'. The statement did not mention the song by name but referred to it as 'the song that is hotly debated currently'.

A drawn-out controversy followed, and Malema continued to sing the song during a visit to Zimbabwe, and subsequently. (In 2025, the song gained international notoriety when the US president, Donald Trump, used it to bolster claims of 'white genocide' in South Africa.)

Malema's stance on Zimbabwean politics was even more embarrassing for the ANC. Publicly, Zuma had initially taken a firmer position against Zimbabwe's ruling Zanu-PF than his predecessor, Thabo Mbeki, whose policy of 'quiet diplomacy' had effectively condoned Zanu-PF's abuses. While the ANC and Zanu-PF had deep historical ties, the South African government was trying to broker a political settlement between Zanu-PF and the opposition Movement for Democratic Change (MDC). Zimbabwe's economy was in ruins, and the 2008 election that had returned Robert Mugabe to power was marred by violence and electoral fraud.

In April 2010, South Africa's image as diplomatic ombud was dealt a blow when Malema and a handful of Youth Leaguers visited Zimbabwe. Malema and his troupe went around the country on a 'study tour' to learn from Zimbabwe's nationalisation and indigenisation programmes, visiting mines and small-scale farms, attending a soccer match and meeting Mugabe himself.

The South Africans were lavishly entertained, and Malema received a fawning reception from Saviour Kasukuwere, Zimbabwe's minister for youth, indigenisation and employment, who likened the young politician to the prominent Zimbabwean leader Alfred Nikita Mangena, who was killed in his thirties during the country's war of independence.[130]

Malema and his comrades also made a stop at Donnington, the large commercial farm owned by Gideon Gono, the long-standing governor of the Zimbabwean Reserve Bank. In a statement after the trip, the ANCYL praised Gono – who had presided over the near-total collapse of the Zimbabwean economy – as an 'agricultural genius'. It also lauded the country's controversial land reform process as a 'courageous' move that would 'contribute a lot in durably empowering the people of Zimbabwe'.[131]

Following their return to South Africa, Malema arranged a media conference at Luthuli House, the ANC headquarters in Johannesburg. He restated his support for Zanu-PF and Mugabe, and slammed the MDC as a 'Mickey Mouse' party that worked from 'airconditioned offices in Sandton' instead of fighting its struggle in Zimbabwe. The BBC journalist Jonah Fisher interjected: 'You live in Sandton,' following which Malema lost his temper, and accused Fisher of undermining black people and exhibiting a 'white tendency'.

He then ordered security guards to 'remove this thing'. Fisher packed up his belongings and shook his head, saying, 'That's rubbish.' Malema shot back: 'Rubbish is what you have covered in that trouser . . . you are a small boy, you can't do anything! Go out! Bastard! Go out! You bloody agent!'

The episode made international news and provoked a strong rebuke from the ANC, which stated: 'The unfortunate outburst by Julius Malema did not only reflect negatively on him, but also reflected negatively on the ANCYL, the entire ANC family, our Alliance partners as well as South Africa in the eyes of the international community.' But Malema and the ANCYL dug in, saying that they would 'never be remorseful about disrespectful journalists'.

It was increasingly apparent that the ANC leadership would need to clip Malema's wings. Moreover, Zuma had personal reasons for doing so. He knew all too well how potent the ANCYL under Malema had been as a factional force within the ANC. They had helped him to victory at Polokwane, but he could not rely on the volatile young leader to support his re-election at the end of 2012. In a growing war within the ANC, new fronts were opening in the provinces where pro- and anti-Zuma factions struggled for control.

Then the opportunity arose to undermine Mathale and Malema in Limpopo by cutting away their webs of patronage. Under Mathale's administration, the province had descended into mismanagement and corruption. Unauthorised expenditure ballooned, and civil servants were at risk of not being paid. In December 2011 five provincial departments – education, public works, health, treasury and roads and transport – were placed under national management.

Zuma also tasked the minister of finance, Pravin Gordhan, with untangling the corruption in Limpopo. In January 2012, Gordhan stated that the province faced a potential funding shortfall of R2 billion, and accused unnamed people in Limpopo of attempting to 'sabotage' the Zuma government.[132] After uncovering some networks of corruption, he proceeded to shut them down.[133] One potential cash cow that was killed was a R900-million housing tender awarded to a string of companies owned by Julius Malema's allies or benefactors, including Matome Hlabioa, Collins Foromo and Selby Manthata.

This tender was awarded the day after Zuma had won his second term as ANC president at the Mangaung elective congress in December 2012, defeating deputy president Kgalema Motlanthe, who was backed by the ANCYL and ANC in Limpopo.[134]

Malema's political fortunes in the ANC had already dwindled dramatically, and after years of treading on the tiger's tail, he was clearly on a collision course with the party and its chief. In May 2010, he faced disciplinary charges over derogatory remarks made about Zuma. He was ordered to apologise, pay a R10 000 fine, and attend a political school as well as anger management classes.

In April 2011, the ANC brought renewed disciplinary charges against Malema and several other ANCYL office bearers – its bellicose spokesperson, Floyd Shivambu, deputy president Ronald Lamola, treasurer-general Pule Mabe, secretary-general Sindiso Magaqa and deputy secretary-general Kenetswe Mosenogi. They were due to appear before an ANC disciplinary committee at Luthuli House in August 2011, but the meeting was postponed when violence erupted in the Johannesburg city centre. ANCYL members and supporters threw rocks, bottles and bricks at journalists and police, and burnt ANC flags and T-shirts bearing Zuma's image.

The accused eventually appeared before the committee in August, and its decision was announced at Luthuli House on 10 November. Outside, a large metro police contingent was deployed, and two streets were cordoned off. While acquitted on charges of inciting hatred and racism, Malema was found guilty of undermining the party leadership, sowing division in the party and bringing it into disrepute. Accordingly, he was suspended from the ANC for a period of five years. He had two weeks to appeal against the decision. Should an appeal fail, he would need to vacate his position as ANCYL president.

Shivambu – whom the chair of the disciplinary committee, Derek Hanekom, described as 'defiant, arrogant and ill-disciplined' – was found guilty of prejudicing the reputation of the ANC for swearing at a journalist, and of accusing the party of 'associating with imperialists'. His membership was suspended for three years, and he was ordered to vacate his position. Magaqa was found guilty of bringing the party into disrepute and sentenced to an 18-month suspension, suspended in turn for three years. All the others were found guilty and received similar sentences.[135]

Malema did lodge an appeal. However, in a decision announced on 25 April 2012, an appeal committee chaired by Cyril Ramaphosa, then ANC deputy president, upheld the charges and expelled him from the party in which he had grown up. He had increasingly embarrassed the ruling party, and miscalculated by opposing Zuma's re-election as ANC president in 2012 and supporting Kgalema Motlanthe. He had also publicly turned against the ANC's alliance partners, the Congress of South African Trade Unions (Cosatu) and the South African Communist Party.

For now, he was out in the cold. But any sense of defeat hanging over him was outweighed by his unwavering self-belief and sense of invincibility. In May 2012, at his first press conference since his expulsion, he declared, 'My blood is black, green and gold. I will die in the ANC. I will stay and sleep here, outside the gate of the ANC. My umbilical cord was buried here in the ANC.'

Wearing an ANC Youth League beret and ANC-branded Mandela shirt, Malema sat between two close comrades, Shivambu and Magaqa. Initially, he charmed reporters with his usual wit and humour, but cut a strangely quixotic figure when he declared, with typical bombast, that he would return to lead the ANC. He emphatically rejected any suggestion that he would form a new political party, declaring: 'It has never crossed my mind. I will never do that.' Instead, he said, the battle would be fought within the 'broad church' of the ANC.

Trouble was brewing on another front as well. Newspaper reports were increasingly linking Malema to a group of companies in Limpopo managed by his childhood friend Lesiba Gwangwa. These included SGL Consulting Engineers and, later, On-Point Engineers. Politicians and others were demanding official probes into tender procedures as well as Malema's tax affairs.

In February 2010, a media storm broke over Malema's lifestyle and the sources of his apparent wealth. Three newspapers reported that Malema – then still the salaried president of the ANCYL – had benefited substantially from government tenders, most of them in Limpopo. Taken together, a legal newsletter wrote, the reports painted a picture of 'unrestrained excess and cronyism'.[136]

According to the *Sunday Times*, between 2007 and 2008, Malema was allegedly involved in more than 20 contracts each worth between R500 000 and R39 million, and one of his businesses, SGL Engineering Projects, had profited from more than R130 million in tenders in just two years. These included a tender from the Roads Agency Limpopo, headed by Sello Rasethaba, a close friend of Malema's who had been appointed in 2009 shortly after Cassel Mathale had become premier of Limpopo.

In a major story in *City Press* headlined 'Malema's R140m tender riches', Piet Rampedi and Dumisane Lubisi wrote that SGL Engineering Projects, which they described as 'Malema's engineering company', had won at least R140 million in tenders from Limpopo local governments over the previous two years.[137]

He had two homes – one in Flora Park and the one in Silvela Road – worth R45 million that were not mortgaged, a love of Breitling watches, 'which retail at R250 000 a pop', and lived a life of luxury. 'While he will not say how much he earns, his salary cannot cover his lifestyle – but revelations about his business interests may finally explain where he gets his millions,' the report said.

Meanwhile, the previous week, Zwelinzima Vavi, general secretary of Cosatu, had made a widely publicised call for cabinet ministers and senior government officials to undergo lifestyle audits as 'part of their commitment to transparency and clean governance'. He said it would be 'very interesting to establish how some officials could afford more than one mansion, holiday homes and expensive holidays'.

Vavi also said the government should enact a law to force politicians and government officials to choose whether they were servants of the public or in business to make a profit. 'They cannot be both at the same time. The spread of the capitalist culture of greed is threatening to undermine all the progress we have made since comrade Madiba walked to freedom 20 years ago.'[138]

Soon afterwards, Malema issued a statement saying that, following his election as president of the ANCYL in 2008, he had instructed his lawyers to process his resignations from all the companies he had been involved in while based in Limpopo. They assured him that this had been done, and he was no longer a director of any company.[139]

The ANCYL 'totally supported' the idea of lifestyle audits for public representatives, senior government officials and others, and that law enforcement institutions should be empowered to audit people who accumulated wealth 'in ways that could not be explained'. But this should happen to everyone, not selected individuals who were audited to satisfy 'narrow factional interests'.

Malema said his ANC salary was 'way above' R20 000, but he would not disclose the exact amount, because he claimed his contract with the party did not allow this. Contrary to media reports, his property was bonded, and he owned only one car. 'I have never engaged in any illegal tender-awarding process, as I have never occupied any position in government, both as a public representative or public servant.'

He attributed the allegations against him to 'those who own the means of production (particularly mine owners)' who wanted to prevent the ANCYL from advocating the nationalisation of mines, and those who though the ANC Youth League would not support their re-election. 'We will never fall into their trap and will be more determined to fight for a more radical ANC.'

Later the same day, journalists established that, along with Gwangwa, Malema was still listed as a director of SGL Engineering Projects and three other companies. When approached for comment, Malema's lawyer, Tumi Mokwena, said Malema had instructed him to terminate his directorships. 'This happened somewhere in 2008. He said he did not want to have an interest in any company any longer.' The fact that he was still listed as a director of SGL Engineering Projects would be investigated.[140]

When approached for comment, ANCYL spokesperson Floyd Shivambu said: 'He [Malema] gave the orders to the lawyers; whether the database was updated is not our problem.' He said he took exception to the fact that a journalist who did not attend the morning briefing had contacted him about the issue. 'You are out of order. Fuck you,' he said before putting down the phone.

On the same day, a COPE office-bearer in Limpopo lodged a complaint with the Public Protector over the awarding of tenders to SGL Engineering Projects by municipalities in Limpopo and North West.

On Sunday 28 February 2010, in a report in *City Press*, Rampedi wrote that Malema had lied when he told the media he held no shares in SGL Engineering Projects. In fact, he owned 70 percent of SGL and was registered as a director of the company.

At a local election rally later that day in Durban, Malema claimed Rampedi had faked his signature on the company registration form. (This claim was later disproven by the public protector Thuli Madonsela.) Addressing ANCYL members, he said: 'We will not be broken by newspapers. They must put my name to sell newspapers. The journalist faked my signature because they want to portray me as a bad person.'

City Press also ran a report headlined 'Juju's dodgy R27m bridges', telling the story of three multimillion-rand bridges and roads built by SGL Engineering Projects – 'Julius Malema's company in Limpopo' – which 'washed away within weeks of their completion'.[141]

Around the same time, Malema arrived at the EWN news studio in Sandton in a Range Rover without number plates for an interview with

Redi Direko (not yet Tlhabi).[142] During the interview, she bluntly told him he was 'waffling' to evade accountability, and suggested that he release a song called 'blaming everyone but yourself'. Malema was adamant that he had done nothing wrong, falsely denying any directorship of SGL Engineering Projects or any involvement with the companies reported to have won lucrative state contracts. If there was wrongdoing, 'let it be reported and investigated', he said.

Early the next month, on 2 March, Mokwena stated that the signature on the 'alleged' company registration form published in *City Press* was not Malema's, and that Malema was 'deeply disturbed' by suggestions that he had lied. Legal recourse was being considered.[143]

The national chair of AfriForum Youth lodged another complaint with the Public Protector over the awarding of tenders to SGL Engineering Projects.

The furore continued. The next Sunday, 7 March 2010, *City Press* reported that Malema had not submitted tax returns since his election as ANCYL president two years previously. None of his companies were tax-compliant, while Malema himself had never submitted any returns.

Triggered by the report, the leader of the Independent Democrats, Patricia de Lille, issued an explosive statement in which she said it was 'extremely likely' that Malema was 'stealing from the poor through tax evasion'.[144] A whistleblower had told her that neither Malema nor his businesses were tax compliant, which begged the question of how SGL Engineering Projects had managed to get Limpopo government contracts worth R140 million between 2007 and 2009.

'If these are the kinds of leaders we are grooming for the future,' she said, 'leaders that have different rules for themselves than the rest of us and who claim to be pro-poor when in fact they are ransacking the poor, then we are faced with a very bleak future.'

She added that she had submitted parliamentary questions to two ministers, asking them for details about the tax status of Malema's companies and whether they complied with tender requirements in respect of tax clearance certificates.[145]

In the midst of all of this, Malema hosted 'a birthday bash as lavish as the lifestyle that has focused attention on him', according to the

Sowetan.[146] When he turned 29 on 3 March 2010, he staged an event for more than 5 000 mostly elderly people in the Seshego Stadium outside Polokwane. Malema's grandmother Sarah cut the birthday cake, while the Limpopo premier, Cassel Mathale, stood at her side.

Guests included Jacob Zuma's aide Zizi Kodwa, the Limpopo MEC for roads and transport Soviet Lekganyane, and Limpopo businessman Tom Boya. The ANCYL provincial secretary, Jacob Lebogo, claimed the food was prepared by 'volunteer catering companies'. The event was enlivened by the musicians Rebecca Malope, Solly Moholo and Winnie Mashaba. The party then continued at the Mekete Lodge, a luxury lodge outside Polokwane then owned by Matome Hlabioa. Malema would take it over years later and refurbish it, partly with cash from VBS Mutual Bank.

Malema was constantly in the news, with his scheming providing endless fodder for investigative journalists. In response, he and the ANCYL fell back on the narrative that the country's 'white-controlled newsrooms' could not stomach the thought of a black person succeeding.

The Public Protector's first report on the awarding of tenders by municipalities in Limpopo and the North West was released on 16 August 2010, but did not produce any fireworks. It confirmed that Malema was a director of SGL Engineering Projects, but noted that only three tenders were awarded to it in the period under review.

Due to poor record-keeping, Madonsela could not determine whether one tender and five contracts awarded to SGL Engineering Projects had complied with the relevant procurement legislation and other prescripts. Regarding the others, the procurement processes generally complied with relevant legislation and regulations.

The work done by SGL Engineering Projects was generally of an acceptable quality and standard. Moreover, she had no evidence that contracts or tenders were awarded to the company as a result of friend-ships, favouritism, nepotism, political affiliations or any other form of improper interference. The Public Protector recommended that steps be taken to improve supply chain management regulations as well as record-keeping.[147]

However, based on complaints by local residents, and leaked documents that had not been at Madonsela's disposal, journalists continued to document corruption surrounding SGL Engineering Projects, as well as its alleged poor performance. According to communities in Limpopo, some jobs were not completed on time, some had to be redone (sometimes by other companies), and others – including taxi ranks, bridges and roads – were so poorly built that they collapsed after a few months.[148] A water reticulation system in Sekhukhune was reportedly so badly built that it cost many times the initial amount of the contract to rectify and complete.

On 10 July 2011, the *Sunday Times* reported that Malema was building a 'multimillion-rand fortress' after demolishing his R3,6-million Silvela Road home. The multistorey home would include a party deck and a secure basement where he could take refuge from attack.[149]

A week later, then-DA spokesperson Dianne Kohler-Barnard asked SARS to investigate Malema's finances. 'It is inconceivable that someone who claims to live on a R25 000 salary from one of the ANC bodies can get at bank loan for R16 million. One needs an investigation into where the money is coming from. If someone is handing out money to him, we need to know who it is.'[150]

Another exposé followed on Sunday 24 July 2011. After months of investigative work, *City Press* journalists Adriaan Basson and Piet Rampedi wrote a story headlined 'Malema's secret fund' in which they revealed the existence of the Ratanang Family Trust. The trust was registered in 2008 soon after Malema had been elected as president of the ANCYL.

Two sources had told them Malema and his benefactors used the trust as a vehicle to fund his lifestyle. Thousands of rand were regularly deposited into the account. One source had told them that frequent deposits were being made from different banks, especially in Limpopo.

Another source, a businessman who moved in Malema's circle of friends and associates, told them he had deposited R200 000 into the trust's bank account after Malema had facilitated a government tender for his benefit. According to him, at least 20 other businesspeople he knew of were doing the same.

Before publishing the story, *City Press* asked Malema for comment. He immediately instructed his lawyers to apply for an urgent court order prohibiting the newspaper from publishing it. In the course of the application, Malema's legal team denied that he was involved in criminal activity. According to his advocate, Malema did not deny that money had been paid into the Ratanang Family Trust, but these were not bribes – 'he says the payments are contributions for this cause and that cause'.

The application was rejected with costs. Judge Colin Lamont said the public had a right to full disclosure about people in public positions, high-profile people and 'those who invite comment about themselves'. The questions posed to Malema were sufficiently clear and detailed, and should have been easy to answer.

On 5 August 2011, the *Mail & Guardian* reported that Malema was 'doling out state tenders to his pals' through a company part-owned by the Ratanang Family Trust. While he, On-Point and the department of roads and transport denied this, Malema had 'at least indirect influence' over who was awarded tenders from a three-year budget allocation of reportedly R4,6 billion.

Later that month, a spokesperson for the Hawks disclosed that it had launched an investigation into alleged fraud and corruption by Malema. 'We are looking into the [Ratanang Family] Trust, and whatever any avenues our investigation brings us to,' he stated. 'We will not be taking cues from the media in our investigation. We have our own ways of finding stuff out.'[151]

At that point, many people were tempted to write Malema off. A 2013 article in *New African*[152] magazine began with Malema telling the writer how his friends had deserted him in droves. It continued: 'With no professional qualification, he has reverted to farming cabbages on land he purchased during his tenure as President of the African National Congress Youth League.

'Even that farm is about to be taken away from him. What stands between him and penury are lawyers. However, lawyers and slot machines are synonymous. No coin means "no play".'

CHAPTER 8

The On-Point case rises and flounders

IN THE SECOND half of 2012, the On-Point scheme began to cave in on its perpetrators. On 10 October, the Public Protector, Thuli Madonsela, published her report titled *On the Point of Tenders* which laid bare much of the network of nepotism and corruption surrounding Lesiba Gwangwa's companies, including money that flowed to Julius Malema and the Ratanang Family Trust.

She found that the awarding of the PMU tender to On-Point by the Limpopo department of roads and transport had been 'unlawful and improper'. Determining whether anyone in the department was guilty of corruption would be left to the Hawks. However, she commented that it appeared to 'constitute the crime of fraud'.

The awarding of tenders to three service providers (the so-called back-to-back agreements) constituted corrupt practice. The awarding of tenders to two other companies was improper but not necessarily unlawful.

As one of two shareholders of Guilder Investments, the Ratanang Family Trust had benefited improperly from the 'unlawful, fraudulent and corrupt conduct' of On-Point and the maladministration of the department. The conduct of the department, specifically that of Letebele, was 'unlawful, improper and constituted maladministration'.

As noted before, Madonsela recommended that the contract with On-Point be cancelled, and legal proceedings instituted against it to recover 'improper financial benefits'. Both Gwangwa and On-Point should be blacklisted, and the Hawks should investigate the department, the bid committees and all recipients of contracts awarded with On-Point's participation. Letebele resigned before he could be disciplined, and most of Madonsela's recommendations were implemented only partially – or not at all. However, a month previously, in September 2012, Malema and his business associates had been served with warrants of arrest on charges of corruption, fraud and money laundering. There were various iterations of the charge sheets.[153] Eventually, those charged were Julius Malema; Lesiba Gwangwa; On-Point director Kagisho Dichabe; and Selby Manthata, his wife, Hellen Moreroa, and his brother Makgetsi. Four companies – Segwalo Consulting, On-Point Engineers, Gwama Properties and Oceanside Trading – were also cited.[154]

On Tuesday 25 September 2012, Gwangwa, Dichabe and the Manthatas appeared in the Limpopo Regional Court in Polokwane.[155] Police were present both inside and outside the court building. Several streets were cordoned off, and police helicopters circled the area. They were granted bail of R40 000 each.[156]

Malema appeared the next day on a single initial charge of money laundering. According to the charge sheet, he 'ought to have known' that he was benefiting from the proceeds of unlawful activities. He was granted bail of R10 000.

Supporters who had staged a night vigil sang and danced behind a razor-wire fence outside the court building. Addressing them through a loudspeaker, Malema said: 'I'm here because some people have taken a decision to conspire against me . . . I'm not corrupt and I do not engage in fraudulent activities . . . And today they have proved it, that they do not have a case of corruption against me, they do not have a case of fraud against me . . .'

Malema repeated his claim that Zuma was behind his prosecution, saying the ANC leader had sent investigators to arrest him for 'anything'. He called for Zuma to be removed as ANC president and also charged with corruption. He was 'unshaken' by the charges brought against him, and would continue the struggle for economic freedom.[157]

Shortly afterwards, the NPA charged Malema with 51 counts of fraud, money laundering and corruption-related offences 'in a pattern of wrongdoing that indicated racketeering'. The charge sheet alleged that Malema had played a leading role in the restructuring of On-Point's shareholding and that the discussions where he and Gwangwa became the sole shareholders of the company took place at Malema's house.

For reasons the NPA never adequately explained but ostensibly to make for a quicker prosecution, Manthata, his wife and brother, along with their company, Oceanside, were tried separately on charges of money laundering and corruption. One of the main issues was the R1 million that had found its way from the department of roads and transport to Oceanside, after which the Manthatas had made a part payment for Schuilkraal farm. The Manthatas argued that the R1 million was a legitimate loan, and that they had done nothing wrong.[158]

Less than two years later, in March 2014, the Manthatas were acquitted.[159] A jubilant Malema told his supporters that the charges against him should also be dropped. 'I have already said this is a political case – the more they proceed with it, the more they are going to get exposed.'[160]

The state appealed against the Manthatas' acquittal, and redeployed advocates Henry Nxumalo and Billy Moalosi. They had already been involved in the case in various ways and were seemingly well placed to argue the appeal.

The Manthatas' counsel was Advocate Laurence Hodes, SC – a highly experienced advocate with a formidable reputation. According to a former colleague, Nxumalo and Moalosi were 'like lambs to the slaughter'.

It was a bad time to be a prosecutor. The NPA was in flux, drained of experienced prosecutors, and worn down by political battles. The National Director of Public Prosecutions, Mxolisi Nxasana, was also new in his job, having succeeded an acting director, Nomgcobo Jiba. Before the end of the Manthata appeal, Nxasana was manoeuvred out of office by Zuma and his allies and replaced with Shaun Abrahams, whose apparent subservience to political influence and unwillingness to act decisively would earn him the nickname 'Shaun the Sheep'.[161]

'Bear in mind that Nxumalo and Moalosi would have received little to no assistance in terms of guidance,' their former colleague explained. 'They would not have been able – and should not have been expected – to put a complex commercial case together.' The source believed Nxumalo and Moalosi were effectively set up to fail, and their seniors offered little support.

The state's case was also undermined by the poor performance of its star witness, PwC director Trevor White, who had been commissioned by the NPA to produce a forensic report on the On-Point role players. White's report was flawed, and Hodes took him to the cleaners. The state relied fully on the report White had compiled before the cases were separated, and no new forensic report explaining the case against Manthata, Moreroa and Oceanside was submitted. This omission seemed to cost the state the case.

In January 2016, the two High Court judges who heard the appeal delivered a withering judgment.[162] According to them, White was biased and the evidence 'full of lacunae'. The presentation of the evidence was unstructured, and the trial was conducted in a 'haphazard fashion'.

Hodes had readily admitted that 'what had taken place when the tender to the third respondent was awarded raises eyebrows, to put it mildly. Clearly, the pieces of a jigsaw puzzle are present, but the appellant failed to build the jigsaw. One can see that a case could perhaps be made out, but the appellant failed to join the dots.'

Moreover, the appellant did not call key witnesses, such as the head of the department, members of the bid adjudication committee, or Gwangwa, the CEO of On-Point. Although it was apparent that the tender process was tainted by many irregularities, with 'clear conflicts of interest and a nexus between the main players', the state had failed to prove its case beyond a reasonable doubt. The appeal was dismissed.

In August that year, the case against Malema, Gwangwa and Dichabe was struck off the roll, after the state had asked for yet another postponement because Dichabe claimed to be sick and was hospitalised. The trial judge, Billy Mothle, said three years - from 2012 to 2015 – was 'too long for a person to have a sword hanging over his head'.[163] Because the accused had not pleaded, the state could decide to reinstate the case, but for now they were free to go. Malema smiled and embraced his counsel, Advocate Mike Hellens SC.

The charges were never revived. The NPA seemed to have slumped into inaction, partly due to the internal leadership conflict caused by

Zuma. In the next decade, issues such as the On-Point scam and the origins of Malema's wealth faded. Much of this amnesia resulted from Malema's political campaign against Zuma, whom he positioned as public enemy number one. It was a goal opposition parties (and much of the general public) could unite around: getting rid of a president who was willing to wreck state institutions in order to shield himself and his cronies.

Malema suddenly seemed less menacing. Many people were willing to overlook his faults and foibles in the interests of getting rid of the most immediate threat to good governance and democracy, namely Zuma. Given Malema's ability to ignite popular anger, other opposition politicians began to view him as a potent weapon in a shared cause. As the ANC slid morally, Malema and the new party he had founded in 2013 – clad in red overalls, and chanting 'Pay back the money!' – took on an increasingly righteous hue.

But Malema's escape continued to irk many. In March 2018, the lobby group AfriForum established a private prosecutions office, staffed by Advocate Gerrie Nel. Before joining AfriForum, Nel was a leading prosecutor at the NPA assigned to particularly difficult cases. A former wrestler, he took the same approach and energy into the courtroom, earning him the nickname 'Bulldog'. Nel in full cry, peering over tiny spectacles, became a familiar sight on television screens. He soon sent the NPA a letter demanding that the prosecution of Malema in the On-Point matter be reinstated, failing which AfriForum would launch a private prosecution.

At the time, the appointment of Shaun Abrahams as National Director of Public Prosecutions was being challenged. So, a full 20 months elapsed before Advocate George Baloyi, acting director of public prosecutions in Gauteng, informed AfriForum in November 2019 that the NPA intended to 'arraign' On-Point, Gwangwa, Dichabe and Thomas Rasethaba. (Rasethaba, an early shareholder in On-Point, was not prosecuted in 2012.)

Baloyi said they would be charged with fraud for misrepresenting the capabilities of On-Point to the Limpopo department of roads and transport. Gwangwa and On-Point would also be charged with another three counts of fraud relating to his dealings with his business partners.

Oddly absent were the many corruption and money-laundering charges – as well as Malema.

Stating that he had declined to prosecute Malema 'at this stage', Baloyi continued: 'After the finalisation of the trial in this matter, the record of the proceedings and any credibility findings [sic] that the court might have made during the trial as well as the report of the prosecutor who conducted the trial will be perused to determine whether a criminal prosecution should be instituted against Mr Julius Malema.'

In a seemingly placatory move, he added that a separate investigation would be launched into Malema's administration of the Ratanang Family Trust, and a decision would then follow. Baloyi promised that the Gwangwa matter would be 'enrolled in the High Court in due course'. This has never happened.

In December 2019, Nel replied caustically: 'In the hope that the decision merely exhibits a lack of understanding of the law, the facts or the practical implementation of a prosecution, we have respectfully decided to enlighten you with our view.

'Our intention is to ensure that justice is done and that the principle of equality before the law is upheld. The failure to prosecute Mr Malema not only creates a perception that he is sheltered from prosecution but [also] entrenches the belief in society that the NPA cannot purge itself from the practice of selective prosecution.'

Nel pointed out that Malema had been gifted the 50 percent shareholding in Guilder businesses, and that the payments for Schuilkraal suggested money laundering. As a result, it seemed as if the NPA had deliberately avoided implicating Malema, and its decision to charge Gwangwa but not Malema was 'irrational'.

Nel continued: 'It reminds one of the NPA's failure to prosecute Mr Zuma together with Mr Schaik on charges of corruption at the time. The NPA must certainly have learnt its lesson [from] the devastating consequences of a delayed prosecution.'

This must have stung, because the next letter from the NPA was not from Baloyi but from his boss. In April 2021, the deputy director of national prosecution, Advocate Rodney de Kock, confirmed Baloyi's decision.

Startlingly, De Kock revealed that the prosecutions team had already thought in 2014 that there was insufficient evidence to prosecute Malema on charges of fraud or money laundering. This was almost a year before the charges against him were dropped. Some time in 2016, a new prosecution team reviewed the case and came to the same conclusion. This decision was confirmed by a high-level panel of senior management. Following Nel's appeals, a senior state advocate had undertaken yet another review, coming to the same conclusion. The reason for the lack of evidence, De Kock wrote, was that the core allegations against Malema had not been investigated.

This eye-popping admission suggests that the NPA might have jumped the gun when it instituted the initial charges. It was simply unprepared – a recurring problem in high-profile corruption cases. Parliament has dwelt on this matter for years, highlighting the poor quality of investigations by the police and the Hawks.[164]

Since then, Nel has written multiple letters to the NPA – few of which have been dignified with a reply. In May 2023, De Kock (now deceased) did write that the Hawks and the NPA had 'prioritised the finalisation of the outstanding issues' in the case of *State v Malema and Others*. Nothing has happened since.

It is difficult to say what would have come of the main On-Point case had it gone to trial in 2015. As noted earlier, Malema, Gwangwa and Dichabe were initially charged with 55 counts of fraud, money laundering and corruption, which the NPA said formed a pattern of racketeering.[165] Malema was meant to answer to 51 of these charges, including allegations that he was involved in the unlawful awarding of the R52-million contract to On-Point as well as its fraudulent misrepresentations. As far as we know, only Dichabe and Gwangwa could be tied to the tender documents submitted to the department.

There were a number of departmental officials on the witness list, and one or more could have testified that Malema had leaned on the department. But no such evidence emerged in public, and the state probably did not have it. Without it, it would have been difficult to prove Malema's guilt.

But the pattern observed in Malema's life over the span of three years – a fleet of cars bought and serviced, the purchase of two farms, a house in Sandton, payments to his staff, chartered jets and millions of rand pouring into the Ratanang Family Trust – might have been awkward to explain.

According to a confidential source, one of the problems about prosecuting Malema is the High Court's criticism of Trevor White and sections of one of his forensic reports. Returning him to the witness box would again expose the state to an obvious broadside.

However, in March 2013, the NPA's own Asset Forfeiture Unit, led by Advocate Willie Hofmeyr, won a court order to attach and sell Schuilkraal farm, based on the same facts as well as a report from White.[166] The state had used another legal team to argue that Schuilkraal had been bought with the proceeds of crime – and won. While White was criticised, the facts went largely uncontested.

Given this, some analysts believe a reinstated case may succeed. Gwangwa's former financial manager, Nicolette Honeycomb, would have much to contribute. When the SARS tax inquiry started, she drafted an affidavit that laid bare much of the workings at the heart of the On-Point network, as well as recurrent payments to Malema. She never testified, because Malema's case never went to trial and she wasn't called as a witness in the Manthata case, so her reputation is still intact, and her potential evidence unheard.

The meticulous records reflected in her affidavit include diary entries, invoices, bank statements and eyewitness accounts. The Asset Forfeiture Unit also used the information in her affidavit to attach Schuilkraal. More of that in Chapter 10. First, we need to deal with the state agency that came closest to destroying Malema and ending his political career.

CHAPTER 9

Project Caesar

THE FULL STORY of how Julius Malema ended up in SARS's cross-hairs starts long before his opulent lifestyle first made headlines. In fact, it begins in 1997, when the drug trafficker Nelson Pablo Yester-Garrido, linked to Pablo Escobar's Colombian drug operations, fled to South Africa.[167] US authorities were on his trail after they had gotten wind that he was planning to purchase a Russian submarine for cocaine smuggling.[168]

In 2002, South African police arrested Yester-Garrido in Johannesburg on an Interpol warrant. He was driving a Mercedes-Benz owned by a Martin Wingate-Pearse and carried forged identity documents, including one in Wingate-Pearse's name. Wingate-Pearse was a businessman, selling imported and branded coats and jackets. As SARS investigator Johann van Loggerenberg explains in *Tobacco Wars*,[169] imported clothing was often disguised as packing material for large goods like furniture, circumventing import duties and the apartheid clothing embargo.

In 2004, police asked SARS to support its Project Chaser, an undercover operation targeting an international syndicate linked to Yester-Garrido.[170] (Sixteen years later, in 2020, Yester-Garrido, then 63, pleaded guilty in the US state of Florida to conspiracy to distribute a large amount of high-grade marijuana and was sentenced to five years imprisonment.)[171] As crime often functions within an ecosystem, when SARS got involved, its investigators started looking into the entire network around Yester-Garrido and Wingate-Pearse. This is how they were led to Adriano Mazzotti, Wingate-Pearse's brother-in-law, and drug dealer

Glenn Agliotti, who often met with Yester-Garrido[172]. When journalists in 2007 asked Mazzotti and Wingate-Pearse about Yester-Garrido, they claimed they knew him only under his pseudonym of 'Lamas', and that they were unaware that he was a fugitive.[173]

SARS launched its own Project Dunlop Roller Bearing, conducting a massive search-and-seizure operation in April 2005. About 250 SARS officials, some accompanied by sniffer dogs, searched 26 business entities linked to 11 people, including Wingate-Pearse, Mazzotti and Agliotti. No drugs were found, but according to SARS official Ronel van Wyk in her 2018 affidavit to a SARS commission of inquiry,[174] 230 tons of contraband and second-hand clothing were confiscated. Investigators also seized 200 000 pages of documents, which supported SARS's renewed tax claims.

When journalists asked about the raid in 2007, Mazzotti told the *Mail & Guardian*: 'Yes, there were raids, there was a police investigation. Nothing untoward was ever found, and in particular nothing relating to drugs . . . We've always conducted our business in a legal manner.'[175]

Yet Mazzotti's business Carnilinx, in which Wingate-Pearse, Kyle Phillips and Mo Sayed are his business partners, wasn't always compliant with tax and customs legislation. Carnilinx used what Van Loggerenberg describes in *Tobacco Wars* as 'ghost exports'[176] – a complex set of actions designed to make it look as if goods had been exported when they had not, thereby reducing the tax payable. In a mea culpa affidavit[177] Mazzotti gave to SARS, dated 6 May 2014, under the heading 'The unlawful conduct', Mazzotti confessed: 'Carnilinx accepts that it acquired tobacco unlawfully and wrongfully . . .' No records were kept of cigarette manufacturing, concealing entire transactions – 'this was deliberate so as to avoid any detection,' he stated. He also admitted that the company received R8 million in cash that was not recorded in its books and that it paid no excise duties, concluding: 'We accept we did wrong.'

A substantial amount of the cash, Mazzotti said, 'was used by [himself, Phillips and Sayed] as company expenses engaging in expensive dinners, entertaining businesspeople, politicians and other people [whom] we considered would be useful in advancing the business of Carnilinx. In retrospect, this was not only improper conduct but immoral.' Mazzotti later claimed that he had been pressured by SARS into writing the affidavit.

Among those receiving Carnilinx cash was one Julius Malema. When questioned, Mazzotti's staff told investigators Malema was 'an ANC Youth League guy' and 'a friend of Mazzotti's'. Malema knew Wingate-Pearse, too, and when the latter died in 2022, Malema slipped into the Rosebank Catholic Church from a side entrance to attend his memorial service.[178]

SARS then scrutinised Malema's own finances. While companies linked to him were receiving money from government entities, he had not filed any personal tax returns. The Malema name was not widely known at the time, and his income wasn't big enough to warrant sustained attention. As SARS became more insistent over the years, Malema fobbed them off with a series of ever-changing explanations. Eventually, by 2009, SARS assigned its Significant Case Unit to help Malema become tax-compliant.

This effort had an interesting history. In the 1990s and early 2000s, SARS adopted a sympathetic attitude towards recalcitrant or defaulting taxpayers. During apartheid, tax avoidance had become a form of civil disobedience, lending it a degree of legitimacy. As the democratic state sought to foster a new black middle class, SARS approached emerging black businesspeople and higher earners with caution. While its managers remained committed to bringing all non-compliant taxpayers into the fold, they favoured the carrot over the stick.

At the time, it was not uncommon for naive politicians to appoint consultants to deal with their taxes, only to discover later that they were not tax-compliant. One source recalls that Malema's explanations were so convincing that some SARS officials initially suspected he might have been the victim of a scam.

By March 2010, however, SARS officials realised that their concilia-tory approach had failed. Malema had yet to file a single tax return, or to register the Ratanang Family Trust as a tax-paying entity. Public events might have accelerated the shift in SARS's approach. On 3 March 2010, Patricia de Lille, leader of the Independent Democrats, launched her public attack on Malema, saying it was 'extremely likely' that, due to tax evasion, he was stealing from the poor.

A week later, Malema told students at the University of Johannesburg that, if he failed to pay taxes, the minister of finance, Pravin Gordhan, had a right to take everything in his bank account and give it to the poor. 'If I do not pay taxes, I am asking to get arrested,' he said. He added that he lived a life of poverty. 'I don't read about it – I know what poverty looks like,' he said after reportedly arriving at the university in a white Range Rover. He also said De Lille should get her facts right, referring to her in derogatory terms.[179]

After this, no one at SARS still thought that patience and kindness would resolve the matter. Cross-referencing their findings with media reports about Malema's connections, SARS officials began to realise that they were not looking at someone with messy tax affairs who had merely forgotten to cross some t's and dot some i's.

The result was a formal tax probe dubbed Project Caesar, aimed at investigating Malema's tax affairs as well as the entire financial eco-system around him. The Financial Investigations Unit began its work in April 2010, and what it found was stunning. The money pouring into Malema's personal and trust accounts came from companies and business-people who had won tenders, some of them breathtakingly large, from the provincial and municipal governments in Limpopo. A key figure in this network was Lesiba Gwangwa.

Malema continued to provide different explanations for the money flowing into his accounts. Initially, he claimed the payments were dona-tions from 'anonymous donors'. Once some of these alleged donors were identified, his legal team conceded that the word 'donations' had been 'liberally and sometimes, in our view, incorrectly used'. Eventually, Malema argued that some of the payments were donations, while others were shareholders' dividends which were therefore exempt from tax.

SARS took a dim view of these explanations, particularly regarding the monthly 'dividends' of R100 000 Malema received from Gwangwa. During later court proceedings, investigators stated that Malema had failed for years to register both himself and the Ratanang Family Trust for tax purposes, and had submitted inaccurate information to SARS for the tax years 2005 to 2011.

In 2012, SARS assessed total unpaid taxes for the years 2005 to 2011 at R16 million, inclusive of penalties and interest.[180] Yet SARS investigators suspected that the full extent of Malema's taxable income had not yet been established. In April 2012, SARS also launched a formal tax investigation into Gwangwa's finances and tax affairs.

A search-and-seizure operation at SGL House and an affidavit by Gwangwa's financial manager, Nicolette Honeycomb, revealed that, besides the payments into Malema's bank accounts, Gwangwa had also bought Malema's cars, paid his bodyguards and other employees; bought and serviced his vehicles; helped to buy his properties; covered his travel expenses; and paid his legal fees. Added to this, Malema's bodyguards frequently collected boxes and envelopes stuffed with cash from Gwangwa's Polokwane office. As a result, towards the end of 2012, SARS increased Malema's tax bill to more than R18 million.

In the meantime, the collection process was already under way. Malema had until early September to settle the initial tax bill of some R16 million. When he failed to make a payment, SARS obtained a warrant of execution against his assets.

The sheriff of the court attached the contents of Malema's home in Flora Park, Polokwane, and his rental home in Sandown. Malema was in the Sandown house when the sheriff came knocking. Mysteriously, not many luxury items landed up on the attachment lists. In Polokwane, the sheriff listed items with an estimated resale value of R32 200, including couches and chairs, tables and beds, CD players, DVDs and speakers. At the Sandown house, the sheriff wrote up couches and rugs, umbrellas and paintings, amplifiers and televisions to the value of R45 100.

Possibly due to concerns that Malema could have been 'dissipating' his assets, SARS asked the court to appoint the now-deceased insolvency practitioner Cloete Murray as curator bonis. Murray took control of the Polokwane house, which was later sold.

In February 2014, SARS won a provisional sequestration order. This had far-reaching implications for Malema – not only financially but also politically. At that time, he was due to become an EFF MP. In terms of the Constitution, he could not take up his seat in parliament if he was sequestrated.

Meanwhile, two years before, parliament had passed an amendment to the Tax Administration Act that allowed struggling taxpayers to make an offer of settlement. This was subject to various conditions, notably that they made 'full and frank disclosures' of their financial affairs. They also had to submit a three-year projection of income. Settlement offers would then be considered by a committee.

The amendment came at an opportune time for Malema. The provisional sequestration order had demonstrated that he could not foot his tax bill. He made two settlement offers, the second of which was accepted and signed in May 2014. While it was meant to be confidential, it was leaked to the media – and it soon became clear why Malema had tried to keep it from becoming public knowledge.

He acknowledged that he had farmed on a small scale on Schuilkraal, managed a taxi business in Limpopo with three cheap cars, and leased out his sound system to party-goers. However, the farming stopped when the NPA sold off Schuilkraal in mid-2013, the cars were 'scrapped', and the sound system was attached when SARS sold off his household assets in the same year. None of this income had been declared, but he promised to do so.

By then, Malema had accepted SARS's calculation that his tax debt for the years 2005 to 2011 was R18,2 million. He offered to pay them R7,26 million. This amount would come from a number of sources. Just more than R3 million was reserved in trust and managed by Murray after a number of Malema's assets, including his properties in Polokwane, had been sold. (This excluded a 3,4-hectare smallholding at Palmietfontein, southwest of Polokwane, which Malema claimed was worth only R250 000.)

Another R1 million would be 'loaned' to Malema by Kyle Phillips, one of Adriano Mazzotti's business partners. Whether Malema ever paid back the money is unclear. He first claimed it would be 'donated' by Renier Martin, Mazzotti's bookkeeper. Months later, when it became evident that the payment was not made by Martin but by Phillips, investigators concluded that Malema had failed to make full and frank disclosures. As a result, SARS later argued that Malema had reneged on his agreement.

Another R3 million would be paid in six monthly instalments of R500 000 each – mostly from the newly established Julius Sello Malema Trust, which had always been cloaked in secrecy. Malema simply claimed that it was a vehicle for financial support from some of his supporters. Instead, it emerged, in part supported by trust documents, he himself had instigated the trust. Malema and Shivambu had asked a prominent EFF member, Mandisa Mashego, to chair and manage the trust as one of five trustees. (She later resigned from the party after tensions developed between her and Malema.) The last R180 000 of the settlement amount was meant to be paid in monthly instalments of R30 000.

Startlingly, Malema also confessed that he had pocketed the proceeds from the sales of EFF regalia. The money was 'deposited into my bank accounts for my subsistence', he stated. It added up to least R140 000 in the first few months of the EFF's existence, marked in his SARS agreement as 'proceeds from merchandise sales'.

The EFF, Malema said, 'also deposits irregular stipends for travel and subsistence whenever needed'. He added that, if much of his parliamentary salary were used to repay the tax debt, he would 'continue to earn a living through sales of merchandise and possible stipends from the EFF'.

Malema's alleged dipping into EFF money, as well as competition over positions, fed into the party's first significant revolt. In February 2015, nine months after Malema had signed his settlement deal with SARS, EFF members Andile Mngxitama, Khanyisile Litchfield-Tshabalala, Mpho Ramakatsa and Lucky Twala were suspended for, among other things, bringing the organisation into disrepute, publicly criticising the leadership and conducting unauthorised press interviews.

According to an EFF member who later left the party, the revolt was largely driven by personal grievances, including members being left off the parliamentary list. Their fraud and embezzlement allegations against Malema were a convenient means of hitting back. Two months later, in April 2015, the EFF's chief financial officer in the Gauteng legislature, Wiekus Kotze, accused Malema and Floyd Shivambu of financial malfeasance.

Kotze was an oddity – a moustachioed Afrikaner in a radical black nationalist party.[181] Previously, he had briefly been involved in Mamphela

Ramphele's Agang. Before that, he had been a political organiser for the ANC for several years. He grew up in a farming community outside Hartbeespoort Dam, where his parents were said to have sheltered political fugitives during apartheid. He was sycophantic in his praise for the EFF and its leader. 'I joined EFF when it was not fashionable for an Afrikaner to join EFF!! I am still here and I am going nowhere!! I love EFF and CIC Malema!!' he tweeted on 24 November 2014.[182]

Six months later, in April 2015, the one-sided love affair was over. Sitting next to a fuming Kenny Kunene, also a former EFF member who would remain prominent in politics, at a media conference, Kotze claimed he had been suspended in November 2014 because he knew about Malema's swindling of the EFF.[183] Kotze said he had opened a case of financial mismanagement against Malema. The EFF retaliated by laying charges related to financial irregularities against Kotze. Neither case went anywhere.

In terms of the settlement agreement with SARS, Malema's estate would remain under provisional sequestration until his tax debt had been paid off. If he failed to comply with the deal, SARS would finalise the sequestration. Additionally, he would 'refrain in future from making negative, unfounded or false public comments or statements concerning SARS's.

Malema also agreed to release a media statement, which read in part: 'I accept that I did not attend to my tax affairs in the manner that I was required to by law in the past, and in certain instances, I left my financial affairs in the hands of others without making sure that my obligations were complied with . . .

'I accepted and acted on advice from persons which, in hindsight, I should not have. It is so that at times I was very frustrated with the process and I may have said things publicly that reflected negatively on the reputation of SARS and some of its officials. Where I may have made public utterances that may have suggested bias or wrongdoing on the side of SARS, I unreservedly apologise.'

However, the truce did not last – the agreement disintegrated six months later, in November 2014. The R1-million 'donation' was found not to have come from Martin, while SARS argued that Malema had failed to declare one of his houses as an asset, and regular payments had not been made as stipulated.

After March 2013, SARS re-examined Malema's 2012 cash flows and tax declarations. This revealed that he had received at least R13,8 million in 'income' in the 2012 tax year alone – an extraordinary sum, equal to his total 'income' for the previous two years combined. However, he had only declared an income of R927 200.[184] When SARS pressed him for an explanation, warning him of further penalties, he simply did not reply.

About 60 percent of the R13,8 million had come from Lesiba Gwangwa, and the rest from Selby Manthata, Ali Boshielo and Steve Bosch. SARS found that the largest chunk – R5,58 million – had gone towards the building of Malema's mansion in Silvela Road. Gwangwa had also paid almost R80 000 in legal costs when Malema tried to prevent *City Press* from publishing its story about the Ratanang Family Trust. The application was rejected with costs.

In March 2015, SARS abandoned its compromise agreement with Malema and applied for the sequestration order against him to be made final. By this stage, he had already paid SARS R7,2 million. However, SARS argued that his breach of the agreement rendered all previous payments null and void, and presented him with an updated tax bill totalling R32,9 million.

Around this time, unrelated political machinations were unfurling within SARS. In September 2014, Jacob Zuma's new SARS man Tom Moyane was parachuted into the revenue service. At the time, SARS investigators' probes into the Gupta family, a number of KwaZulu-Natal businessmen and Zuma's son Edward were well under way. Moyane's destructive reign was minutely detailed four years later before the Commission of Inquiry into SARS, instituted by President Cyril Ramaphosa and chaired by Judge Robert Nugent.

The later Commission of Inquiry into State Capture, chaired by Judge Raymond Zondo, heard even more about Moyane's reign when the erstwhile finance minister Nhlanhla Nene suggested that Malema and the EFF had a vested interest in shielding Moyane from scrutiny. Nene wanted Zondo to investigate SARS and Moyane for stopping certain investigations, including a probe of Adriano Mazzotti.[185]

Zondo eventually found that SARS offered 'one of the clearest demonstrations of state capture as observed in other state-owned entities and state institutions', and that Zuma and Moyane had played key roles in this process. He recommended that prosecutions be considered for the awarding of contracts to the controversial Bain consultancy firm, which had worked hand in glove with Moyane, and that the latter should be charged with perjury for providing false information to parliament.

Sources in the National Treasury and the Hawks told us that Moyane had also meddled in their investigation into Malema and allegedly made sweeping changes to the SARS investigation teams probing the Malema case.

The application for Malema's final sequestration was heard in the Gauteng High Court in Pretoria on Monday 1 June 2015. It was a pivotal day for Malema and his new party. If the sequestration went through, he could not return to parliament.

Hundreds of EFF supporters gathered outside the court, and police cordoned off the road with barbed wire, 'nyalas and rubber bullets ready'. One supporter said if the case went against Malema, Pretoria would be 'in chaos'.[186] Some wore T-shirts saying '#SARSMustFall' and held banners which claimed SARS had become a political tool.

Nic Maritz, advocate for SARS, told the court the parties had entered into a conditional compromise agreement in terms of which Malema's tax debt had been brought down to R7,2 million. However, Malema had not been honest about the sources used to settle his debt, which led to SARS cancelling the agreement. Besides this, Maritz said, Malema also owed an additional R13,5 million for the 2011 and 2012 tax years. He argued that once Malema had been sequestrated, SARS would be able to recover the outstanding taxes.

A sceptical Judge Gregory Wright questioned Maritz about the reasons for SARS's application. From the court record, it appears the judge doubted the likelihood of SARS successfully claiming the unpaid taxes amid a sequestration process.

After the lunch break, to everyone's surprise, Maritz told the court that SARS had decided to withdraw the application to sequestrate Malema. He did not offer any reasons, saying only that it was a 'sensitive matter'. EFF leaders and supporters in the packed court cheered and applauded.

Outside the court, supporters thronged around Malema. Addressing them from an EFF-branded truck, he continued to claim that the failed sequestration order was politically motivated. Without offering any evidence, Malema claimed that the ANC was using SARS to attack the EFF leadership because it had no other response to the growth of the party.[187] At the same time, he called on his supporters not to demand the fall of SARS. 'We are going to need the SARS, and therefore don't destroy the institutions you have built which could contribute to the sustainability of our democracy.'[188]

On 3 June, SARS said in a media statement that it had made its decision after weighing up issues raised by the judge – most significantly, that SARS had several legal instruments available to it to recover Malema's outstanding tax debt. It also considered the fact that the Julius Sello Malema Trust had started to comply with its tax obligations.

A further consideration was that Malema had withdrawn an application for an order declaring that SARS was bound by the compromise agreement. SARS was therefore not bound by the agreement, and the court had also not ruled on the matter. As a result, SARS could now take further steps to recover the outstanding taxes.

Wrangling between Malema and SARS continued, and Malema eventually reinstated his application for a declaratory order. In a judgment delivered on 29 April 2016, Judge J Jansen said the 'crisp issue' was whether, due to alleged non-disclosures and misstatements by the applicant, SARS was no longer bound by the agreement, as provided for the Tax Administration Act. This was a factual issue that the court could not determine on the basis of the affidavits, and therefore the matter was referred to trial.[189] But this, it seems, never happened.

Despite the flurry of court cases, the outcome of the tax war between Malema and SARS remains murky. In essence, he owed SARS R16,2 million in arrear taxes for the 2005–11 tax years. An updated assessment increased this amount to R18,2 million. SARS then settled for an amount of R7,2 million, which Malema eventually managed to pay. This meant that SARS had written off R11 million.

Malema owed an additional R13,5 million for the 2011 and 2012 tax years, which was also in arrears. Whether this was ever paid also remains unclear. Sources suggest that it fell by the wayside when Tom Moyane took over at SARS and the R7,2 million tax bill was settled – by whom, exactly, remains unclear. No further tax issues involving Malema are on public record.

The 2012 inquiry probed 15 suspected breaches of the Value-Added Tax Act and Income Tax Act by Gwangwa and 18 of his companies, some of which still included Malema as an indirect stakeholder through the Ratanang Family Trust. In May that year, Gwangwa applied to the High Court to have the inquiry set aside. In an opposing affidavit, the SARS senior investigator argued that Gwangwa's application was 'an attempt to delay or frustrate the SARS investigation and specifically an attempt to prevent SARS from carrying out its duties'.[190] In August, the High Court ordered Gwangwa to testify at the tax inquiry.

Little more is known about Gwangwa's tax affairs. Apparently, SARS eventually assessed Gwangwa's outstanding tax at R50 million, which remained unpaid. SARS then obtained a court order to appoint a curator bonis over Gwangwa and his business entities. The curator sold some assets, and the proceeds were paid towards the tax debt. Whether SARS then wrote off the remainder is unknown.

Today, Gwangwa has his own website, featuring suave self-portraits and a description of himself as a 'pan-African senior executive, engineer and strategic leader', with 'vast experience in engineering design and planning, commodity mining, and process chemicals sectors, both as an executive and non-executive'.

A section titled 'My Experiences' includes Segwalo Consulting Engineers and Qualis Consulting, the company he was once reluctant to associate with, but the Guilder Group, SGL Engineering Projects and On-Point are not mentioned. He is still the sole director of the erstwhile On-Point, which changed its name to Mungu House.

The following table reflects Malema's tax affairs from 2005 to 2012, showing his income declared to SARS, SARS's eventual calculations of his actual income, and the amount by which his income had been underdeclared.

	Income declared to SARS	Actual income	Undeclared income
2005	R0,00	R215 800,00	R215 800,00
2006	R183 096,00	R223 096,00	R40 000,00
2007	R465 274,00	R539 854,00	R74 580,00
2008	R347 691,00	R491 113,93	R143 422,93
2009	R365 371,00	R810 939,88	R445 568,88
2010	R597 560,00	R7 260 169,44	R6 662 609,44
2011	R885 204,00	R5 247 573,91	R4 362 369,91
2012	R927 200,00	R13 868 334,00	R12 941 134,01

CHAPTER 10

Two key witnesses

TWO UNLIKELY PEOPLE played a vital – and, until now, largely unknown – role in the On-Point saga. The first was Nicolette Honeycomb, who worked at Lesiba Gwangwa's Guilder Group of companies as finance and human resources manager. The second was Seraj Ravat, the Guilder Group's accountant.

In April 2012, SARS launched a formal probe into Gwangwa's business network. On 7 May, Honeycomb received a notification to attend the inquiry by the end of the month. As she told us in an interview, she decided to 'reveal everything' after having 'a helluva argument with Lesiba on the day before I was to attend the inquiry'.

Asked about that argument more than a decade later, she could not quite recall what it was about, but she remembered that she experienced Gwangwa as threatening. 'I took it very badly, because my children and I were living in the same security complex as Gwangwa. He wasn't direct, but there was a definite threat.' Honeycomb was a single parent.

Around the same time, one of her colleagues fell victim to a violent home invasion. There was no evidence that the incident was related to the drama playing out at SGL House, but she was spooked.

'I told Lesiba I couldn't work like that,' she told us, 'and I resigned on the spot. The day after I testified at the inquiry, my office was locked and I had to pack my things. He told me he couldn't have someone in my position work a month's notice.'

But Gwangwa's precautionary measures had come too late. Honeycomb had already mirrored her hard drive. She also had her diary and was later, at SARS's insistence, allowed to access many invoices and supporting documents. On 11 July 2012, she signed her affidavit to SARS.

This 32-page document, plus lengthy appendices, remains one of the most explosive sources of evidence in the On-Point saga. Honeycomb has never been publicly identified, and most of the details in the affidavit have never been published until now.[191]

Ravat, the accountant, was also called to testify at the SARS inquiry, and agreed to draft an affidavit. Like Honeycomb, he has not previously been identified, and much of his affidavit has not been published before. Taken together, they provide a vivid picture of how the Guilder Group was managed, and the raft of payments made by various entities in the group to Julius Malema.

Honeycomb is a rosy-cheeked Afrikaans-speaking woman, hailing from Vanderbijlpark. After obtaining her matric at Hoërskool Driehoek, she left the Vaal Triangle to study accounting at the University of Pretoria. She was adventurous and always looking for new horizons, which is how she wound up in Polokwane.

Initially, she worked as a financial manager and accounts administrator for various companies in the agricultural, retail and construction sectors. In January 2011, she was appointed as finance and human resources manager at the Guilder Group.

Back then, Honeycomb wore her dark brown hair in a bob that reached her shoulders. She had left her job in the construction industry after receiving treatment for burnout, having worked 16-hour days while caring for two small children on her own. Keeping up with the news was not a priority, so she walked into SGL House with no prior knowledge of the clouds hanging over the company.

She was diligent and attentive to detail. Every time Gwangwa gave her an instruction, she wrote it down in her big, round handwriting in an A4-sized diary and ensured that it got done – a habit that would result in her entering witness protection two years later. In her diary, Honeycomb referred to her employer as 'Mr. G'. Everyone else was referred to by their first names – including Malema, who appears as 'Julius'.

Within weeks, Honeycomb had effectively become Gwangwa's right-hand person, and as such began to attend to Malema's finances as well. In

February 2011, a month after her appointment, she negotiated employment contracts for Malema's bodyguards. Around the same time, she processed several payments to the Johannesburg firm Cimato Moroldo Architects for sketches of Malema's projected mansion in Sandton.

Gwangwa told her to make all payments towards Malema's building project from his lesser-known companies Mminathoko Infrastructure and Qualis Consulting. As a result, Honeycomb asked the architects to change their invoices. According to her, Gwangwa used these two companies for payments he didn't want to be traced back to SGL House. He particularly wanted to keep Qualis a secret.

Honeycomb met Malema twice, and they did not converse on either occasion. The first time was when Honeycomb took coffee to a wendy house behind SGL House, where Malema and Gwangwa were locked in a confidential discussion.

The second was towards the end of 2011. Gwangwa had asked Honeycomb to withdraw cash, put it in an envelope, and meet him at a construction site in the Polokwane suburb of Welgelegen, where he was having a house built. By then, she was used to the large amounts of cash swirling around her employer. When he arrived, she walked towards his vehicle and handed him the envelope. Next to Gwangwa, in the passenger seat, was Malema.

By early 2012, separate state investigations into Malema's network had started to converge. In February, Trevor White and PwC's probe into corruption at the Limpopo department of roads and transport was extended to include payments to On-Point. In May, PwC gave the National Treasury a status report with findings on On-Point, and the firm's mandate was extended to support the Hawks investigation into tenders awarded to Gwangwa's companies. In June, just two months after SARS had launched a tax inquiry into his business network, the Public Protector summoned Gwangwa to testify about his involvement in On-Point, state tenders and Malema's financial affairs.

The Hawks also jumped into gear. From mid-2012 onwards, Hawks investigators began to approach Guilder Group staff, asking to meet them in secret. Most were unwilling to stick out their necks. One employee told us she had to meet a Hawks investigator in an abandoned building on the outskirts of Polokwane, and was given a burner phone. She was spooked by the whole process, and it got worse during the inquiry. 'Lesiba was there, so I had to speak carefully because I did not want to lose my job. Nicolette [Honeycomb] told everything as it was, and she was fired on the same day.'

Honeycomb's affidavit tells the rest of the story. Besides the explosive allegations about Gwangwa and Malema, it provides a fascinating insight into how On-Point operated behind the scenes – including machinations by Gwangwa to prevent investigators from gaining access to sensitive information.

On 7 May 2012, Honeycomb wrote, she received a notice to attend an income tax inquiry to be held at the end of that month.

She set to work to copy the hard drive of her computer and handed it to a SARS attorney. When she testified at the inquiry, investigators were interested in 'very specific documents', which they required copies of. Returning to SGL House on 30 May, Honeycomb saw that she had been locked out of her office. She had resigned earlier that week and Gwangwa made it immediately effective. SARS's attorneys intervened, strong-arming Gwangwa into letting Honeycomb remove 12 lever arch files with invoices and lists of invoices, spanning the time of her employment. She was also allowed her personal diaries and notebooks. All of these were handed to the SARS attorneys.

SARS instructed Honeycomb to bring a copy of the email correspondence between Gwangwa, herself and Ravat, but her computer was no longer in her office and she had no access to it. Gwangwa had already handed a compact disc with all the emails to SARS. She wrote: 'I had the opportunity to peruse the emails on the compact disc . . . and I confirm that a large volume of the emails between Mr Gwangwa, Mr Ravat and myself are not contained thereon.'

Honeycomb's affidavit explained the structure of Gwangwa's Guilder Group – which consisted of nine companies, including On-Point and SGL Engineering. The employees of one entity would often do work allocated to another entity 'without any financial implication', despite Gwangwa's attempts at keeping their operations separate. She added: 'To the best of my knowledge, no invoices were issued between the various entities for services tendered by employees of another [sic] entities within the Group.'

Gwangwa's companies mainly worked on tenders awarded by the Independent Development Trust, municipalities in Limpopo, the Limpopo departments of housing and roads and transport, and the Roads Agency Limpopo. Sometimes, Honeycomb had to issue the companies' invoices, except for On-Point's, which were issued at the PMU at the department of roads and transport. She did however receive copies of some of the paperwork. Honeycomb was also tasked with making payments from the companies' bank accounts. She used to compile lists of invoices due for payment and Gwangwa, in turn, would pick which invoices had to be settled. Honeycomb then loaded the payments and Gwangwa authorised the transactions. These invoices Honeycomb kept in lever arch files – all of which she attached to her affidavit.

In an explosive section titled 'The financial relationship between Guilder Group and Malema', Honeycomb listed payments the Guilder Group entities made for Malema's benefit. These included security guards as well as various domestic employees; numerous motor vehicles, used by Malema, his bodyguards and employees in Johannesburg as well as Polokwane; vehicle maintenance, tyres and petrol; and vehicle rentals.

Next came Cimato Moroldo Architects, which designed Malema's house in Sandton; more than R986 418 towards the transfer of Schuil-kraal farm; electricity accounts for Schuilkraal; clothing to the value of about R100 000; holiday accommodation; travel expenses, including domestic flights on chartered planes and international travel; and services and furniture for Malema's house. Added to this were large payments to the attorneys retained to get Malema out of trouble with SARS, and other legal fees, including those emanating from his failed attempt to gag *City Press*.

And then there was the cash. Gwangwa asked Honeycomb to write out cheques from different accounts in favour of various employees which they would have to cash. Cheques up to R10 000 were used for petty cash, but some amounts were far larger.

Gwangwa asked her, for example, in August 2011 to cash a cheque from SGL Consulting to herself to the value of R15 000 and bring the

money to him. In September and October, she cashed two cheques for
R50 000 each and deposited the total of R100 000 into the account of
the Ratanang Family Trust. She then described the incident at Welgelegen
when she handed Gwangwa a large amount of cash while Malema sat
next to him in the vehicle.

A section in the affidavit titled 'The financial affairs of the Guilder
Group and Mr Gwangwa' brought more startling information. In terms
of the PMU tender, Honeycomb wrote, On-Point assisted the department of roads and transport to issue, adjudicate and manage tenders. It
had an office at the department and its invoices to the department were
generated there. She filed copies.

However, Gwangwa sometimes asked her to issue invoices on behalf
of the Guilder Group. When these were issued in the name of On-Point,
they were not issued to the department but to other private entities,
such as Mpotseng Infrastructure. Some of those invoices related to the
'back-to-back' agreements and MoUs entered into between these entities
and On-Point.

Honeycomb also attached to her affidavit a schedule and Gwangwa's
handwritten notes about the profit share between On-Point and the
entity it had entered into the secret MoUs with.

Gwangwa instructed her to issue an invoice in the name of Segwalo
to Mr Dada of Dada's Hardware in the amount of R1,14 million. 'To my
knowledge,' she wrote, 'there were no services rendered or work done by
Segwalo in respect of this invoice.'

When, during 2011, the first media reports linked Malema to On-
Point, Gwangwa believed someone at the SGL head office had leaked
the information to the press. In August, he asked Honeycomb to remove
all the computers from the offices on a Sunday morning, and take them
to her home. Gwangwa then arranged for the computers to be collected
from her home, and she never saw them again. The following Monday,
Gwangwa 'feigned absolute ignorance' about the disappearance of the
computers, and asked her to do the same. She arranged for the delivery
of new computers.

Not long after, Gwangwa told her that people were going to visit the
office and she had to ensure that three employees were there until they

arrived. Three men arrived and requested an interview with the three employees. Soon afterwards, all three resigned and left the group.

During the same period, Gwangwa asked her to remove all files and documents relating to entities other than On-Point, Mminathoko, Segwalo, and SGL from his office as well as hers. He specifically told her that he did not want third parties to link him to Qualis. He also asked her to remove the file containing all the secret MoUs. She packed all the documentation into boxes, and Gwangwa arranged for their removal. When employees required information or documents from these files, Gwangwa would arrange for them to be available.

Gwangwa also covered his personal expenses from company funds, Honeycomb wrote. Cash from the businesses maintained his vehicles, for example. He owned a Porsche, Audi TT and a Golf 6. When invoices were issued to Gwangwa or the Gwangwa Family Trust, they were paid by one of the entities, and Gwangwa would instruct her to ask for an invoice to be issued to the said entity.

Gwangwa further paid his fiancée, Salphy Mphahlele, listed as the sole director of Qualis, a monthly salary, although she did not render any services to Qualis or any of the entities in the Guilder Group.

In another example of Gwangwa's scheming, Honeycomb described how he used to pay the school fees for the child of his contact person at FNB from On-Point.

About Malema, Gwangwa mostly appeared tight lipped. One of the few times he discussed his friend with Honeycomb, was when he told her that Malema was a shareholder and that all dividends paid to him were therefore justifiable. Honeycomb diligently made a note of this in her diary. This was days before SARS sent out its shock notice of a tax inquiry and Gwangwa might have felt the heat. His instruction to Honeycomb to renumber all the company invoices from number 1 upwards was another indication that he might have been pre-empting an investigation.

On at least two occasions, she had to 'pack cash into the top of a [typing] paper box and cover it in such a way that it would not look like cash,' Honeycomb wrote. At other times, the cash was simply stuffed in envelopes.

Like Honeycomb, Seraj Ravat worked at the heart of the Guilder Group. Many potential witnesses were unwilling to commit themselves, but Ravat was one of the few who, despite knowing it could land him in trouble with his client, agreed to draft an affidavit.

In the affidavit, dated 15 May 2012, he said he was introduced to Gwangwa in June 2007, and began to provide Gwangwa's then wife, Sally Phala, with accounting services for her close corporation. Later that year, Gwangwa started transferring more of his own accounting work from KPMG to Ravat.

In 2008, Gwangwa asked him to register a new close corporation, SGL Engineering Projects. In August of that year, Gwangwa asked Ravat to come to Polokwane to take over the accounting of Segwalo Consulting Engineers. In October, Gwangwa phoned Ravat and asked if he knew Julius Malema. Ravat, who followed the news, knew that Malema had been elected president of the ANCYL just a few months earlier at a chaotic conference in Mangaung. Malema apparently needed a bank loan, and Gwangwa told Ravat to 'urgently' draft an appeasing letter to Malema's bank, along with a payslip stating that Malema worked at Mminathoko Infrastructure and earned R20 000 a month. Ravat obliged, even though he knew Malema was not employed at Mminathoko Infrastructure.

SGL Engineering Projects was initially dormant, but in April 2009 Gwangwa asked Ravat to convert it from a close corporation into a private company and to add Malema as a director, with a shareholding of 70 percent. Ravat did not do this himself, but handed it to a 'helper' outside the offices of the Department of Trade and Industry (DTI). The signatures of the directors and shareholders were copied, and judging by the handwriting, all the signatures were made by the same person. This was probably done at the DTI offices.

Towards the end of 2008, Gwangwa told him that he was separating from his wife and had asked a lawyer to create a trust named the Gwangwa Family Trust. He instructed Ravat to make the trust the sole member of Segwalo Consulting Engineers and Mminathoko Infrastructure. The trust was duly registered.

In early October, Gwangwa asked him to apply for a tax clearance certificate in the name of On-Point Engineers 'and not the original shelf name which was Achir Shelf 8 (Pty) Ltd'. His assistant repeatedly went to the SARS office to try to obtain the certificate, which was finally issued on 9 October. The PMU contract was awarded to On-Point Engineers three days later, on 12 October 2009.

Toward the end of 2009, Gwangwa told him he needed a new attorney, and Ravat recommended Mpoyana Lazarus Ledwaba.

On 14 April 2010, Ravat, Gwangwa, and Ledwaba attended a meeting at Malema's house in Polokwane, held at Malema's request. This was the first time Ravat met Malema.

It signalled the start of Malema's efforts to get rid of some business partners before the big money started rolling in.

'Julius was very nice,' Ravat told us. 'You know, he'll treat you like royalty. It was the first time I went to his house in Flora Park. It was an average house, not a mansion at that stage.' When they got there, Malema was relaxing on the couch – he had just returned from Zimbabwe where he had met Robert Mugabe, and paintings and other items seemingly from Zimbabwe were hanging on the walls.

Ravat knew who Malema was – he had seen him on television, knew of his antics, and was therefore nervous. 'I never expected to meet somebody where you hear his screaming . . . and then he serves you with his own hands.' It was also the first time that Ravat heard the name Ratanang Family Trust, which, he wrote in his affidavit, he understood would be for Malema's benefit.

According to Ravat, Malema took control of the meeting, issuing instructions about the management and shareholding of the entities. Gwangwa listened.

Malema told them that he did not want a repeat of the media reports earlier in the year when he was a director of SGL Engineering Projects, and that Ledwaba needed to change some shareholdings with immediate effect.

Malema instructed that Guilder Investments should be owned equally by the Gwangwa Family Trust and the Ratanang Family Trust. In turn, Guilder Investments would own Qualis Health and Safety Consultants, Gwama Properties, and On-Point Engineers. Malema and Gwangwa agreed that SGL was still 'fresh in the media' and some assistance from the company was needed. This could perhaps be done later.

In May 2010, Gwangwa told Ravat that he was unhappy with the performance of On-Point's financial manager, Maleose Leolo, and that he wanted Ravat to take over this role. Leolo called Ravat a few days later to confirm his resignation, but would not give further details as to the reasons behind it.

Offering a possible clue to Leolo's gripe is Ravat's first task in replacing him. Ravat had to submit On-Point's VAT returns for the period ending April 2010. Gwangwa ordered him to lower the amount. 'I did not declare the VAT on a payment [On-Point] received on the 28th of December 2010, amounting to R2 681 866,31, due to On-Point not having received any income in January and February 2011,' he stated in his affidavit. Gwangwa had told Ravat he 'cannot afford that much' and that 'I should lower it'.

It was an eye-popping revelation considering that the company had received more than R60 million for drawings in eight projects and for its job as PMU for the Limpopo department of roads and transport between April 2010 and November 2011.

From our analysis, it appears that On-Point was in a perpetual cash crunch, primarily because of Gwangwa and Malema's spending. Ravat agreed with our assessment.

Malema demanded to be paid monthly 'dividends' of R100 000 between October 2009 and May 2012. The term 'dividends' is of course a misnomer. On-Point simply did not hold the retained earnings to pay out such a monthly sum.

Then there was Malema's expensive lifestyle. On-Point and associated companies covered the costs of his bodyguards and household staff, a fleet of cars and their upkeep, shopping sprees for designer clothes, property renovations and acquisitions, travel, electricity bills and a steady flow of brown envelopes stuffed with cash.

The second payment that Ravat did not declare for VAT was on 28 April 2011, for almost R2,9 million. This was due to On-Point paying R1 million towards 'Ratanang Farm', apparently a reference to Schuilkraal. The entire sum was recorded as a shareholder's loan to Guilder Investments. This VAT payment was due at the end of May 2011, but not enough funds were available to pay the full amount. Ravat repeatedly asked Gwangwa and Honeycomb to create a separate bank account for 14 percent of revenue, thereby making it easier to pay VAT, but this was never done.

'The non-declaration of income was only done on the instruction of Gwangwa since he did not have sufficient cash flow and needed tax clearances regularly to continue being awarded tenders. I resolved to pay the amounts when cash flow permits, but this has never happened until my resignation,' Ravat wrote in the affidavit. 'I never received benefit, in cash or otherwise' for withholding On-Point's VAT declarations, he stated.

Ravat's affidavit also provides insight into how Malema sidelined his partners just as On-Point was poised to rake in the big bucks. In September 2010, Gwangwa asked Ravat to prepare a valuation of On-Point Engineers, since he had to pay out the other two shareholders, Kagisho Dichabe and Thomas Rasethaba. Guilder Investments was to become a 100 percent shareholder in On-Point.

Ravat presented the shareholding in a meeting at Malema's Sandton home on 15 September 2010. This was the second time Ravat met Malema – and 'the man was even nicer', he recalled.

By then, On-Point was raking in millions of rand from the Limpopo department of roads and transport, as well as the companies awarded tenders by the PMU, and further steps were taken to rid themselves of their earlier partners, essentially by continuing the restructurings and buying them out.

Ravat's calculations came to R1 million to be paid to Dichabe and R420 000 to Rasethaba's Maketele Family Trust. Without looking at Ravat's presentation, Malema pegged the buyout at a total of R3 million each. 'Nobody present challenged this amount or asked how Mr JS Malema came to this figure,' Ravat said in his affidavit.

He later told us: 'I don't think Julius knows how to read [financial statements] . . . He put it to one side and said, "Three million! Is everybody happy?" No one said a word. He then added, "From On-Point, just pay them three million and they'd be happy."'

Malema wanted Dichabe and Rasethaba out because he 'wanted himself in . . . Soon after that meeting, the dividends started rolling to Malema. At the same meeting, he said, "Look, we are going to do dividends." So I told Gwangwa, you don't have money for tax. How are you going to pay out dividends? Gwangwa used to get his nerves up, because he said, "Julius is just spending, and I cannot handle this thing".'

Gwangwa and Malema's partners never did get the full payout. 'Part of the R3 million was paid out to be settling a 2007 Range Rover at the bank amounting to R516 692,20, and the rest to be transferred over eight months into the account of Kopania Engineers. To date I have only seen R946 209,07 out of the R3 million being paid so far,' Ravat wrote.

That was the least of Ravat's worries, though. In addition to the missing VAT declarations, he never submitted the 2011 annual financial statements for Gwangwa's companies to SARS – because the books made little sense.

A net profit of R10,2 million was calculated, but there was only R665 000 in On-Point's account; R1,26 million had been drawn from On-Point during the 2011 financial year (written up as owner 'drawings for personal use') and On-Point had paid R900 000 to the Ratanang Family Trust, described on the bank statements as 'dividends'.

Moreover, On-Point had paid more than R5,2 million towards property. Only R300 000 was for the Quinn Street property registered in the name of On-Point. The remainder went to properties effectively owned by Gwangwa and Malema. On-Point had also paid R1,7 million towards ANC Youth League costs such as conferences. Gwangwa instructed Ravat to change the description from 'ANC expenses' to 'strategic expenses'.

On 21 July 2011, when Gwangwa summoned Ravat and Ledwaba to a meeting at his offices in Polokwane, Ravat had reached a turning point. At the meeting, Gwangwa reviewed the draft financial statements for Guilder Investments, and asked Ravat to take over all tax matters for Malema and the Ratanang Family Trust. (SARS was hot on Malema's tail at the time.) Ravat declined, saying he did not have the resources to serve such a 'high-profile individual'.

Gwangwa forged on, asking him to join the Guilder Group full-time, and offering to compensate him for his entire fee list. 'It was at this point,' wrote Ravat, 'that I realised I did not want to continue working with Mr LC Gwangwa, but I could not bring myself to resign given that so much information was shared with me.'

Gwangwa shared his ideas for new business opportunities with Ravat, saying that he intended forming a new company that would bring in about R500 million 'through the National Department of Health'. Gwangwa then said Malema wanted feedback on how blind trusts worked. Ravat wrote: 'These statements made me feel sick in my stomach, and this is when I started suspecting Mr LC Gwangwa of serious wrongdoings.'

The same evening, Ledwaba phoned Ravat with bad news. Malema had called him: the media knew about the Ratanang Family Trust. The net was tightening around Malema.

On 5 August, Gwangwa and Ravat met in a car park at a shopping centre in Sandton to discuss the transfer of Schuilkraal farm in Limpopo to Gwama Properties. Gwangwa explained that the transfer to the Ratanang Family Trust had not gone through, and that he felt the farm should rather be registered under Gwama Properties, since the media had already reported on the Ratanang trust. He also said it had been a 'mistake' to deny the previous year that Malema was a shareholder of SGL while his name was still listed as a company director.

Soon after, Ledwaba asked Ravat to accompany him to a meeting at OR Tambo International Airport where Brian Kahn Attorneys – meant to assist Malema in sorting out his tax affairs – would be introduced to Malema. Gwangwa also attended. This was Ravat's third and last meeting with Malema.

'Mr [André] Bezuidenhout [an advocate retained by Kahn] spoke harshly to Mr JS Malema and said that if he does not shut his mouth and allow them to bring his affairs in order, he will go to jail. The meeting lasted under ten minutes.'

Years later, Ravat still spoke about this meeting in awed tones. 'Jeez, you should have seen that guy talk to Julius . . . He sat like a little puppy in that chair and said absolutely nothing. Julius just took it. JM said very little in that meeting. In fact, he was a mouse. He did not react. He just said, "Yes I will." '

After the lawyers had left, Malema instructed Gwangwa to make sure there was enough money in the accounts to pay them, and 'even estimated this at between R3,5 million and R5 million'.

Our data shows that from August 2011 to December 2011, R1,2 million was deposited into the account of Brian Kahn Attorneys from Segwalo Consulting Engineers, 'a corporation wholly owned by the Gwangwa Family Trust'. Technically, Malema owned no shares in Segwalo. Gwangwa footed Malema's bill.

And then there were the others. Gwangwa asked Ravat to sort out the personal tax of Matome Jacob Lebogo, who was the provincial secretary of the ANCYL. In November 2011, Lebogo came to see Ravat about his taxes for the previous five years. Gwangwa told Ravat to attend to this urgently, 'since he [Lebogo] is working with us'. Lebogo's Mercedes ML 4x4 was parked outside, and when Ravat later asked Lebogo – having been privy to his income – how he could afford an SUV, Lebogo said he 'sometimes received a little cash' from Gwangwa, and that he would 'support' Gwangwa's companies since he was giving back to the ANC Youth League.

On one occasion in December 2011, Lebogo appeared at Ravat's office with Tshepo Malema, and instructed him to sort out the latter's tax affairs as well. 'I did not act further and never saw or heard from Mr T Malema again.'

On 1 February 2012, 'after plucking up enough courage', Ravat told Gwangwa in writing that he was resigning, but Gwangwa insisted that he continue with his duties until a replacement could be found. Following this, Gwangwa twice appeared at his office without an appointment. 'He raised points that Mr JS Malema is very powerful and that I need to work with him until the investigations are over and also that black people cannot be rich without being suspected of wrongdoing.'

And then there was the attempted cover-up. Ravat was due to appear at the SARS inquiry on 25 April 2012. In the late afternoon of 24 April, he received a call from Ledwaba, who said he wanted to brief him about the inquiry and should meet him at the Royal Elephant Hotel in Centurion. He agreed. To his surprise, Gwangwa was there as well.

Ledwaba instructed him to answer questions in only three ways, namely 'yes', 'no', and 'I don't know'. He also said he need not be too concerned about the inquiry, and that SARS was 'only fishing'. Ledwaba also cautioned him not to mention their meeting at the inquiry. 'Just before excusing, Mr LC Gwangwa stated that he believes the SARS inquiry's objective was to make him turn against Julius, but that he cannot do that.'

At the end of the first day of the inquiry, on 25 April, Ledwaba told Ravat to wait for him in the car park, but he never arrived. Later that evening, Ledwaba phoned Ravat. He told him he was 'talking too much' and needed to 'work with him' (Ledwaba). The 'strange way' in which Ledwaba talked gave Ravat the feeling that Gwangwa was listening and that Ledwaba had been instructed to pressure him.

Ledwaba said that Ravat should meet him at his office in Pretoria the next morning before going into the inquiry. 'It was after this call that I decided . . . rather than answering questions and being interrogated, that I would approach the SARS officials and tell them what I know.'

Following the strange call from Ledwaba the previous evening, Ravat did not feel comfortable giving his testimony in front of Gwangwa and his legal team, and he asked for them to be removed. The only communication he received from Ledwaba after this were two SMS messages asking for his file on Lebogo.

On the evening of 10 May, he received a call from Gwangwa's personal assistant, Vicky Rene Bridger Yiangou, to tell him she had been subpoenaed, together with Honeycomb and two other Guilder employees. She also told him Gwangwa had said to her that he (Ravat) had 'put her in trouble' during the inquiry, and that she needed to give him (Gwangwa) all the emails Ravat had sent to their offices. When he told Yiangou that there was a 'suspicion' that the tenders awarded to Gwangwa's entities were fraudulent, 'she simply replied that she knew'.

In conclusion, Ravat wrote: 'My reasons for not approaching the authorities earlier were due to: a fear that I would be killed, beaten up or even framed if I spoke; I did not suspect the awarding of the tenders to Mr LS Gwangwa's entities was rigged until late last year after meeting Mr ML Lebogo; I really believed Mr JS Malema was untouchable.'

In December 2023, Ravat spoke to us in his home in Centurion, from behind the same desk he had bought 20 years previously when he started his accounting practice.

'Nicolette Honeycomb is a very soft person,' he said. 'They brought her in as financial manager because I said no. She really tried. But they did not want to work straight, they wanted to work crooked. So Gwangwa got really harsh with her.'

He also offered significant insight into his career path, in the context of the evolving post-apartheid economic landscape. In the mid-2000s, the 'Indian market' was saturated, and left no room to grow for an ambitious young accountant starting out on his own.

The mid-2000s also brought the rise of the 'tender boys', and he became involved with this growing community. It was an untapped market, and Gwangwa was his first big client.

One thing led to another, and in 2012 it all blew up. 'When I think back to this . . . it gives me horrors. It was really an ugly thing . . .'

Ravat acknowledged that he had made some 'serious mistakes' while working for On-Point. SARS, for example, had decided that investigators could not rely on any of the financial records and documents he created. Income was not fully declared, while VAT and tax calculations were muddled. Nevertheless, he eventually tried to do the right thing, and it cost him dearly, as it did Honeycomb. 'I resigned in that time from Gwangwa's business,' he told us. 'Everybody thought I was a hypocrite. It wasn't like that. When SARS came and knocked on my door . . . it was terrible.

'I went broke. I couldn't buy my family an ice-cream. It was that bad. It was that ugly. I had no money. I just kept answering questions from these people. The investigators made me think . . . as gullible as I was at that stage . . . [that] if you [testify and tell the truth] you will be okay. I couldn't bill. I couldn't work. I couldn't sleep at night.'

Honeycomb's candour also had far-reaching personal consequences. While under witness protection, she married the lawyer who represented her in the On-Point case. Given that she and her children had to keep moving from town to town and province to province, the marriage did not last. During the same period, she also lost her father. Soon after, Honeycomb decided she'd had enough of Polokwane, and of South Africa. She now teaches abroad, and has no plans to come back.

CHAPTER 11

Deals on wheels

THE TESTIMONIES OF Nicolette Honeycomb and Seraj Ravat paint a vivid picture of how Malema had accumulated his wealth, including numerous properties and a fleet of vehicles.

In 2008, when Malema was elected ANCYL leader, he moved to Johannesburg. Early the next year, he rented a three-bedroom house in Silvela Road in the Strathavon suburb of Sandton at R18 000 a month. He could not have afforded this on his ANC salary, and told his biographer, Fiona Forde, that he had raised the money for the rent and deposit from the businessman Pule Mabe and others. After two months, as mentioned before, he decided to buy the house.

Malema badgered the owner, Ken Hollingsworth, into selling him the property, which then had a book value of R2,9 million. Hollingsworth eventually agreed to a price of R3,6 million. Malema accepted and, in a transaction dated August 2009, bought the property, supported by a bank loan of R1,5 million.

The first sign of this acquisition in Malema's bank accounts was on 7 August 2009 when a company in Gwangwa's Guilder Group deposited an amount of R150 000 in the account of the Ratanang Family Trust, with 'Acb Credit Sundowns Property' given as the reference. Between this date and October 2010, SGL, On-Point, Segwalo and their affiliates paid R1 030 000 in 12 payments into the trust, all with variations of 'Sundowns Property' as references.

When SARS eventually investigated these transactions, Malema at first attributed much of the income to dividends from his shareholding in On-Point. However, On-Point did not yet exist in August 2009. The name of Achir Shelf 8 was only changed to On-Point on 25 September 2009, and the Limpopo department of roads and transport appointed On-Point as its PMU in October 2009. Malema later revised his account, describing the funds as dividends paid out to him as a shareholder in Guilder Investments. When SARS pointed out that the payments were too large and regular to be dividends, he again changed his tune, saying they were donations from Segwalo.[192]

In the end, SARS classified the deposits as taxable income. When investigators asked the conveyancer of the Silvela Road property for a statement of account, it showed that between September and October 2009, the Ratanang Family Trust had paid R1,5 million into the account.[193] Some of the money seemed to have come from the Gwangwa network and some from Selby Manthata. Additionally, Malema told SARS that Manthata and his friends Thaba Mufamadi, David Mabilu, Thulani Nkuna and Ali Boshielo had paid about R500 000 directly to the conveyancer.

Around the same time, in late 2009, Mabilu's company Vharanani Properties made two payments totalling R300 000 to the Ratanang Family Trust. The money was then moved to the conveyancer. The last payment into the conveyancer's account, of R105 000, was made on 18 December 2009 with the description 'IB Bank Payment Sundown [sic] Estate'.

How Malema paid off the R1,5-million bond on the Silvela Road property is not known. At any rate, he had the existing house demolished and instructed the Johannesburg-based Cimato Moroldo Architects to design a large and elaborate new house, which Independent Newspapers dubbed 'Malema's R16m playboy mansion'.[194] The plans included an elevator, an underground bunker, a cigar lounge, a wine cellar, a theatre and a 'techno room'. The outside features included a swimming pool and jacuzzi.

On 9 February 2011, Lesiba Gwangwa told Ravat and Honeycomb to have all payments linked to the building work invoiced to On-Point. Honeycomb duly noted these in her diary, copies of which eventually ended up at the SARS inquiry and in the Polokwane High Court. Between March and November 2011, according to her notes, On-Point staff paid a total of R1 642 080 in five instalments to Cimato Moroldo and another R135 000 to 'Eloien Creations', an interior design studio.[195]

In the course of the 2012 tax year (March 2011 to February 2012), SARS realised that its investigations had not halted the flow of questionable money to Malema – it had simply been diverted. Malema had allegedly instructed his benefactors to pay the architects directly. The work on the 'playboy mansion', for example, was boosted by R2,3 million between March and June 2011. Steve Bosch's company Sizani Build It paid R1,2 million to Cimato Moroldo.[196] Ali Boshielo's Bitline contributed R500 000, and Gwangwa's companies R600 000. On-Point Engineers, Mminathoko Infrastructure and Qualis Health and Safety collectively paid at least R2,8 million into Cimato Moroldo's account in favour of Kwandisa Construction.

SARS subpoenaed the architect firm's bank statements. In total, it had received at least R5,6 million from a number of wealthy businessmen towards funding Malema's mansion.

Malema's run-in with SARS came to a head well before the work was completed. In December 2013, the property – with only the concrete framework standing, and a huge basement dug out – was auctioned for R4 million.

By 2010, Malema had set his sights on another property – a 3,4-hectare smallholding at Palmietfontein, southwest of Polokwane. Between March and July 2010, six cash deposits totalling R998 001,53 were made into the account of the conveyancing attorneys. One payment was marked 'Tzaneen Ratanang', the rest 'cash' and 'direct deposit'. Who exactly made the payments is unclear. At one stage, Malema claimed they were 'donations' from Selby Manthata. In June that year, the property was registered to the Ratanang Family Trust.

SARS eventually traced at least R355 000 paid towards the renovations of the house at Palmietfontein between November 2011 and January 2012. Somehow this property escaped the sequestration, and it remains registered to the Ratanang Family Trust to this day.

Over the past years, Malema has allegedly poured millions into this property, spending much of it on security walls. Features include a basketball and tennis court, a 1 200-square-metre main house with a reinforced roof and walls for security purposes, a swimming pool, a 400-square-metre second house and a number of outbuildings and garages. According to local residents, Malema even arrives there in rented helicopters.

Another prominent property in the Malema saga was Schuilkraal, a 139,3-hectare farm outside Polokwane. Gwama Properties bought the property for R3,99 million in 2011. As noted earlier, Gwama Properties was wholly owned by the Guilder Investments Group, in which the Ratanang Family Trust held a 50 percent stake. In reality, Malema devised a convoluted scheme to cede R3,99 million from the Ratanang Family Trust to Gwama Properties, which then bought Schuilkraal on his behalf.

To fully understand the Schuilkraal acquisition, we need to trace the funds used to buy the farm back to their origins. Schuilkraal was paid for in four tranches. The first was a R1 million deposit, paid directly to the conveyancing attorneys by the company Oceanside, owned by Selby Manthata's partner, Hellen Moreroa. Oceanside was one of the beneficiaries of On-Point's tender heist at the Limpopo department of roads and transport. According to the affidavit by the PwC investigator Trevor White in the successful ex parte preservation application brought in terms of the Prevention of Organised Crime Act of 1998, the R1-million Nedbank cheque was signed by Manthata.[197]

The second payment for Schuilkraal appears to have originated with the department of roads and transport. Eight days after the department's last payment to Mpotseng Infrastructure (another player in the On-Point heist) for a R2,5-million contract, the company paid R1 million to On-Point. Five days later, On-Point passed on the same amount to Schuilkraal's conveyancing attorneys, with the description 'Ratanang Farm'.

The third payment, also from On-Point, again suggests that Malema was bleeding that company dry. On-Point had received many millions from its Limpopo contract, but by 20 June 2011 it had only just over R500 000 left in its bank account.[198] Gwangwa then moved R1 million from his company Segwalo to On-Point, a transaction labelled 'Trf Farm purchase'. Next he moved the R1 million – described as 'Ratanang Farm' – from On-Point to Schuilkraal's conveyancing attorneys.

The fourth and final payment of R986 418 towards Schuilkraal, according to Honeycomb's meticulous records, revealed that Malema's friend Ali Boshielo was also involved in the Schuilkraal transaction – and that Malema was pulling the strings, despite his attempts to distance himself from the transaction.

On 28 June 2011, the transferring attorneys sent Boshielo an email under the heading 'Balance Payable'.[199] It read:

TO: RATANANG TRUST
For attention: ALIE [sic] BOSHIELO
RE: TRANSFER – REMAINING EXT. FARM SCHUILKRAAL 623
We confirm that the outstanding amount payable to effect transfer of the property to Ratanang Trust is as follows:

Balance outstanding – purchase price (VAT included)	R950 000
Transfer costs – per statement attached herewith	R36 418
TOTAL PAYABLE	R986 418

Twenty-four minutes after receiving the email, Boshielo forwarded it without comment from his BlackBerry phone to Malema's ANC-linked email address. Less than two hours later, Malema forwarded the same email to Gwangwa, who passed it on to Honeycomb. On a printout, her handwritten notes jotted down Gwangwa's further instruction: 'Maureen Occupational rent end of Sept'. 'Maureen' was the person dealing with the Schuilkraal matter at the conveyancing attorney's offices.

On 8 July 2011, 10 days after the Schuilkraal email landed on Honeycomb's desk, Gwangwa's company Qualis Health and Safety made the fourth and last payment of R986 418 to the conveyancing attorneys. In his affidavit, White argued that this money came from the property developer David Mabilu, a friend of Malema's. Between 18 March and 6 July 2011, Mabilu's company paid R2,44 million to Qualis. It's not clear what this money was for but, considering the absence of personnel and skills at Qualis, it certainly raises some questions.

The businessman Arthur Phetla, the sole member of Mpotseng, told White that his company had also paid Qualis R1 million around the same time, triggered by 'several intimidating calls to the staff of Mpotseng' about payment.[200]

All the evidence – including Ravat's affidavit – suggests that Malema wanted to buy Schuilkraal via the Ratanang Family Trust. But on

21 July 2011, he received some unsettling news.[201] After circling the trust for about a year, *City Press* was on the brink of publishing a story revealing that Malema had a secret trust that was bankrolling his extravagant lifestyle,[202] including the purchase of various properties, and that the payments were kickbacks from various companies involved in illicit government contracts, notably in Limpopo.

Malema had to scramble to contain the fallout. Among other things, he was in the midst of sensitive talks with SARS. As reported previously, he first tried to prevent the newspaper from publishing the report, but his attempt failed, and the report ran on Sunday 24 July. Two days later, on Tuesday 26 July, Malema halted the Schuilkraal purchase and instructed the conveyancing attorneys to transfer the funds in their trust account held on behalf of the Ratanang Family Trust to Gwama Properties. This was a clever move, as the money would only move in the attorneys' accounts and leave no trace in the bank statements of either the Ratanang Family Trust or Gwama Properties. Two days later, on 28 July, Gwama Properties bought the farm, with Gwangwa signing the deed of sale. Malema had removed himself from the picture.

But the reprieve would not last. Honeycomb's diligent bookkeeping and SARS's prescient request for the conveyancing attorneys' records soon uncovered the truth about the Schuilkraal scheme.

As noted previously, in her report of 10 October 2012, the Public Protector recommended that the National Director of Public Prosecutions and the head of the NPA's Asset Forfeiture Unit should deal with the evidence of criminal offences 'in the appropriate manner'.[203] In November 2012, on the strength of Trevor White's affidavit, the NPA successfully applied to the High Court for a forfeiture order allowing it to seize Schuilkraal and sell it on behalf of the state.

In an affidavit, Advocate Willie Hofmeyr, head of the NPA's Asset Forfeiture Unit, argued that the money with which the property was bought 'was acquired as a result of fraud, theft, money laundering and/or corruption'.[204] On-Point had unlawfully received the PMU tender from the Limpopo department of roads and transport, caused the improper appointment of service providers like Mpotseng, entered into secret agreements with those service providers, and then received unlawful kickbacks which were funnelled back to Malema.

'Most of the payments received as a result of the said secret agreements were channelled through On-Point and other related entities to pay for the property,' Hofmeyr explained in an affidavit.

Schuilkraal was attached in early December 2012. At that time it had a thatched rondavel, a vehicle workshop, a storeroom, a swimming pool, three boreholes, a cattle-loading facility and another 'partially completed' structure with four bedrooms, a kitchen and a lounge.[205]

In January 2013, journalists photographed Malema on Schuilkraal between rows of healthy-looking cabbages and tomato plants.[206] By 10 June 2013, when Schuilkraal was auctioned off for R2,5 million, the cabbages and tomatoes had all gone to waste.

A few months later, in December 2013, Gauteng traffic police arrested Malema for driving at 215km/h in a 120km/h zone.[207] A court eventually ruled that the state could not prove the device used to record the speed was in good working order. But hard driving came at a cost. On-Point's bank statements and Honeycomb's records bore witness to repairs for various scrapes and bumps, along with other vehicle fixes.[208] One of Malema's bodyguards had filled in the paperwork for those incidents and dropped off the invoices at SGL House.

In early 2011, On-Point paid R54 790,85 for repairs to a Mercedes-Benz C63 AMG used by Malema. In August 2011, SGL Consulting Engineers paid R2 051 for a service; two months later, it paid R4 989,07 for mag-wheel repairs, balancing and alignment. Also in August, On-Point paid R27 263,29 for repairs to Malema's Mini Cooper.

Malema's bodyguards had the use of a Chevy Spark in Johannesburg and a Ford Focus and Volkswagen Polo Vivo in Polokwane. The vehicles were bought and kept by the Guilder Group. In early 2012, the Ford broke down and was towed from Polokwane to Pretoria. The same car cost On-Point R6 870,30 for a service. At one point, all of these vehicles were seemingly out of service. On-Point then simply rented vehicles for Malema and his bodyguards from Badiredi Travel and picked up the tab.

On 30 August 2012, Malema was loudly cheered when he climbed out of a luxury Mercedes-Benz Viano bus to meet striking mineworkers at the Aurora mine in Grootvlei, Springs.[209] The ANC had expelled Malema earlier that year. He was crafting a new, post-ANC image for himself, sporting a white shirt and black beret – a style of headgear that journalists at the time observed had become his trademark.

Malema seemingly wanted to upstage Jacob Zuma, who had promised but failed to help the desperate mineworkers. Zuma's nephew Khulubuse Zuma and former president Nelson Mandela's grandson Zondwa Mandela had stakes in the mine at the time. Malema's visit was one of his first major public appearances after being forced out of the ANC.

'We will make these mines ungovernable until the whites listen,' he told the cheering crowd. 'They must pay a decent wage – R12 500 a month as a basic wage for all . . . Zuma came to see if he could help you workers, but all he was doing is checking out business opportunities for his nephew. We thought it would be nice to be a black person after 1994, but it's gotten worse than apartheid . . . our leaders have lost their way . . .'

He was speaking just days after police had killed 34 striking mineworkers at Marikana mine in the North West. Tensions were high on the mines. 'We are happy that Malema is coming to address us because he is the man who can solve corruption in this place,' a miner, Wanina Siwaphi, told journalists. Grootvlei miners sang along with Malema: 'Phansi, Zuma, phansi [down with Zuma] . . . Phansi Zuma!'

In November that year, Malema visited residents of Lenasia extension 13 who were outraged that their homes, built on land meant for government housing, were being demolished. Floyd Shivambu and Sindiso Magaqa followed Malema out of the black Mercedes-Benz Viano. 'Where is our president now?' one homeless protester asked. 'Julius Malema is here. He is fighting for us.'

The Hawks and NPA later included the Mercedes-Benz Viano on the charge sheet against Gwangwa and Malema. Gwangwa's office staff had managed the acquisition of the vehicle for Malema in August 2011, yanking R834 179,98 out of the Guilder Group's purse.[210]

They had first shopped around for a cost-effective option, resulting in two quotes made out to Gwangwa and On-Point Engineers. Based on an offer to purchase signed at McCarthy Mercedes-Benz in Menlyn, On-Point had to foot the first payment of R209 000 on the Viano.

The second payment of R382 659 was made by Generic Core IT Solutions, a company owned by Jacob Lekalakala, one of the Gwangwa associates with whom he signed the secret MoU to obtain tenders and was then swindled.

'I personally deposited the cheque issued by Generic Core IT Solutions into the bank account of Mercedes-Benz,' Honeycomb told SARS. At the top of her diary on 2 August 2011, her neat, round handwriting recorded: 'Follow up cheque Genericcore Jacob', along with Lekalakala's cellphone numbers and 'R382 659' next to it.

Gwangwa's company Qualis Health and Safety paid the third and last instalment of R246 520,98 to the dealer.

From these accounts, it appears that the money used to pay for Malema's Viano first came from the Limpopo government. It moved through layers of seemingly legitimate companies, some steps removed from Malema, and the car was never registered in his name. Nevertheless, SARS attached the Viano in January 2013.

CHAPTER 12

Until Jesus comes

THOSE WHO PREDICTED that Julius Malema's expulsion from the ANC would end his political career were deeply mistaken. In 2013, he and his band of ANCYL exiles embarked on frenetic efforts to cobble together a new political party that would challenge the ruling ANC. Despite endless internal conflicts and controversies, and an increasingly scandal-plagued Jacob Zuma at its helm, the ANC still seemed impregnable, and it would take a serious onslaught to dent its political hegemony.

On 26 July 2013, more than 1 000 delegates from across the country gathered in Soweto. It was an auspicious date on the revolutionary calendar – on the same day in 1953, Fidel Castro's guerrillas had attacked the Moncada Barracks in Cuba, marking the beginning of the Cuban revolution. The modest Soweto venue, ironically named Uncle Tom's Hall, was less auspicious.

The delegates were to lay the foundations for a radical, pro-black and pro-poor party. With the formation of the Economic Freedom Fighters, Malema formally walked back his promise that he would never leave the ANC.

With national elections less than a year away, the EFF would have to engage 'in electoral warfare before it could crawl', as the political analyst Susan Booysen put it to describe the unsuccessful splinter party COPE.

Like COPE, the EFF was an offshoot of the ANC, and would need to compete for constituencies that were loyal to the latter. As the oldest liberation movement on the continent and the party that defeated apartheid, the ANC still had cachet in the eyes of the voting public. Its historical mission gave it legitimacy and a lasting emotional appeal among many voters, no matter how tarnished it had become in recent years.

On 15 March 2004, Zuma famously proclaimed that the ANC would rule 'until Jesus comes back', and repeated this often in the following years. COPE's disastrous history showed that breaking away from the ANC was a near-certain path to oblivion.

Though COPE was not the rupture some expected, it drew significant support at first – 7.4 percent of the vote in 2009, and more than the EFF achieved in its first election. But the party soon started imploding. Donors turned away in droves and many of COPE's members were reminded of an old ANC adage – 'it's cold outside the party' – and returned to the warmth of the ANC. By 2011, former defence minister Mosiuoa 'Terror' Lekota, and Mbazima Shilowa, who had been premier of Gauteng, were in court fighting over leadership of the party.

Shilowa eventually figured there was little to lose and some happiness to be gained from a life of aristocratic idleness in the Cape winelands, where his winery, Epicurean, makes premium Bordeaux blends. Lekota led a rump party into the 2011 local government elections, from which it walked out with a mere 2.3 percent of the vote, leading to media epitaphs like 'No Hope for Cope'. Whatever political charm Cope had going into 2009 had rapidly evaporated two years later.

Janus-faced Cope harked back to a glorious ANC past – its name an echo of the 1955 congress in Kliptown that adopted the Freedom Charter – but it never truly managed to stake claim to that history. It pretended to be the 'real ANC', washed of its sins and shorn of corrupt, opportunistic hangers-on, but it could never shake its image as a clique of bitter Mbeki-ites (even though Mbeki never publicly endorsed the party). At the same time, looking ahead, it groped for something new, never quite finding it. For the most part, its policies were well worn and stamped with trademarks from the ANC's time in power. It failed to offer a compelling vision and simply planned to do what the ANC in government had done, but better.

The story of COPE's decline was a dire warning to the EFF. The new party faced strong political headwinds, but there were signs that the landscape was changing. Rampant political corruption and government failure were increasingly viewed as symptomatic of the ruling party's decay, compounded during Zuma's term. While a black middle class had begun to flourish during the first two decades of ANC rule, many black people had been left behind, and the gap between rich and poor remained among the largest in the world. A quarter of the workforce was jobless, with almost three-quarters under 35 years old. This created fertile ground for a radical, charismatic leader like Malema, who could effectively tap into mass anger and frustration.

Even those who had done relatively well under the ANC were becoming disillusioned. Many members of an increasingly assertive middle class were fed up with the party's cadre deployment, perceived corruption and mishandling of the economy, and were less and less likely to identify with the ANC.

Unlike COPE, the EFF offered a coherent political programme rooted in the radical policies of the ANCYL. During his time as ANCYL president, Malema had sought to radicalise the ANC, emulating the rebellious Youth League of Tambo, Mandela and Sisulu. Dusting off the slogan 'Freedom in our lifetime', popularised in the 1940s, the league under Malema declared 2012 'the year of economic freedom in our lifetime'. According to Malema, this meant that the economic clauses of the Freedom Charter 'should be realised to the fullest'.[211] This simple and compelling message became the cornerstone of the league's political agenda. Major features of its political programme were radical land redistribution, the nationalisation of mines and a ban on labour brokering, all of which were carried over to the EFF.

Following Malema's expulsion from the ANC, it seemed likely that a significant chunk of the ANCYL's supposed 360 000 members would follow him out of the party, and the EFF would inherit the league's revolutionary mantle.[212]

Then came a dramatic turning point in South African politics. On 16 August 2012, police opened fire on striking mineworkers at Marikana in the North West, killing 34 and wounding many others. While the massacre shocked the nation, it could not have arrived at a more opportune time for Malema. It was an event he was uniquely positioned to exploit.

One news headline asked: 'Will Marikana resurrect Julius Malema?' The article quoted Malema's biographer, Fiona Forde, as saying: 'Marikana is a godsend for him, but it is also a wake-up call for the media and the public for writing him off following his expulsion from the ANC.'[213]

To many, the massacre was a grotesque display of the degree to which the ANC government had failed to transform economic relations, and how alienated the party had become from its support base. Harrowing scenes showing riot police armed with semi-automatic rifles mowing down mineworkers at point-blank range were endlessly replayed on television, reminiscent of the darkest years of apartheid.

Cyril Ramaphosa, soon to become ANC deputy president, was a board member of Lonmin, the company whose workers were striking, and it emerged that he had called on the police to act against the strikers.

While the ANC scrambled to contain the fallout, Malema was quick to act. Arriving on the scene two days later, he turned the event into the start of a campaign to foment a 'mining revolution' in which he visited mining communities across the country, challenging them to make the mines 'ungovernable'. In front of a crowd of striking miners who had gathered in the dry winter veld, he declared: 'President Zuma's government has murdered our people.'

Mining unrest spread, culminating in five months of industrial action on the platinum mines of North West province in 2014 – South Africa's longest wage strike. It was the ideal setting for the formation of a supposedly pro-poor, pro-black radical party.

Malema is an energetic campaigner and a compelling political frontman. His penchant for spectacle, his way of grabbing and swaying media attention, his ability to capture popular anger and distil it into powerful messages, and his youthful appeal made him the ideal candidate to mount a radical populist challenge to the ANC.

On 18 June 2014, opposition members of parliament (MPs) – including those in the the DA – applauded as Malema walked up to the speaker's podium, clad in the EFF's trademark red overalls, red beret and black gumboots, with his maiden speech in hand. Its theme was 'Economic freedom in our lifetime'. He was due to reply to Zuma's dull State of the Nation address the day before.

The EFF had won 6 percent of the vote in the May 2014 elections, and held 25 seats in the 400-seat legislature. At times, it sounded as if its MPs were occupying many more – their rowdy defiance energised a staid institution weighed down by 'decorum' and more than a decade of the ANC's overwhelming majority.

In grand fashion, Malema started by saying: 'We want to acknowledge and greet millions of South African workers. The poor, downtrodden and dejected masses of our people . . . our people mandated this movement, the EFF, to speak on behalf of the homeless, the landless, the domestic workers, security guards, farm workers, cleaners, waiters and waitresses, recipients of social grants, construction workers, the unemployed and poverty-stricken masses of our people who are forgotten by the ruling elite.'

He said that the EFF would not oppose the 'ANC they all remembered', but the 'ANC of Marthinus van Schalkwyk [the National Party leader who had crossed over to the ANC] and Cyril Ramaphosa'.

Next, he turned his attention to Zuma, who was watching the 33-year-old newcomer from his front bench, his mouth turned downwards in disapproval.

Tossing parliamentary etiquette aside, Malema addressed Zuma directly, saying: 'You no longer represent the hope of the hopeless masses of our people . . . Your speech yesterday was uninspiring and lacked a central theme . . . No one will remember what you said . . . You and your party should stop playing with semantics, especially when they relate to [the] radical economic agenda, because you lack courage and you have sold out the revolution.'

At that time, the media were increasingly focusing on state capture, and the EFF seemed to inject new energy into opposition politics when even diehard ANC members were becoming disenchanted with their party under Zuma. Capitalising on this promising setting, Malema positioned Zuma as public enemy number one.

In the two years since his expulsion from the ANC, he seemed to have stepped into a gap in the country's politics and capture a new political zeitgeist – one of growing disenchantment with the political status quo of post-apartheid South Africa. He was fully aware that the timing of his split from the ANC was propitious.

In his maiden speech he went on to say: 'The ANC is part of an elite pact that seeks to protect white monopoly capital and white minority privileges . . . This has led to the formation of the EFF, because there was a political vacuum, and nature does not allow the vacuum.'

The EFF packaged its message in simple slogans like 'Pay back the money!' and 'Zupta must fall!', as well as terms redolent of struggle history, such as 'white monopoly capital' and 'expropriation without compensation'. Even its name invoked the linkages in the 1955 Freedom Charter between political and economic freedom.

No one could whip up anger against Zuma as Malema could, and with each successive scandal, the president was handing his enemies the rope to hang him. In her March 2014 report *Secure in Comfort*, Public Protector Thuli Madonsela highlighted how R250 000 in state money had been spent on upgrades to Zuma's sprawling homestead at Nkandla in rural KwaZulu-Natal. Two years after his maiden speech, in the debate on the 2016 State of the Nation address, Malema tore into Zuma as follows: 'Zuma is no longer a president that deserves respect from anyone. He has stolen from us. He has collapsed the economy of South Africa. He has made this country a joke, and after that he has laughed at us . . . he is not our president. Zupta must fall!'

The EFF routinely heckled ANC leaders, interrupting debates and breaking parliamentary rules, eventually resulting in their being violently removed by security guards in the full glare of television cameras. It was the sort of performative politics Malema relished and, given that the president's credibility had been shredded, many looked on the EFF's antics with approval. Malema's popularity seemed to grow in inverse proportion to Zuma's, and with each passing day the president's grip on power seemed to wane.

After a sweeping and controversial cabinet reshuffle in March 2017, the country was rocked by the so-called Gupta Leaks, published by *Daily Maverick*, amaBhungane and others,[214] which exposed the inner workings of state capture. These revelations breathed new life into public protests against Zuma and his government, bringing together a host of opposition parties and movements. Malema marched arm in arm with Nqabayomzi Kwankwa from the United Democratic Movement (UDM) and Mmusi Maimane from the DA, demanding a secret ballot for a no-confidence vote against Zuma.

In December 2017, Ramaphosa won the race for ANC president, defeating Nkosazana Dlamini-Zuma, Zuma's former wife. Following pressure from his party, Zuma resigned as national president on 14 February 2018.

CHAPTER 13

The dash for cash

THE EFF'S POLITICAL theatrics were drawing attention, but besides the raw energy of its members, the party also needed money. Who were its funders? Among the early donors was Thulani Majola, the suave owner of LTE Consulting who, just days before the 2016 local government elections, had paid R500 000 to Santaclara, the company used for Malema's benefit and whose director was reported to be one of Malema's relatives.

We have been able to establish a very clear image of Majola's business activities over several years. Bank statements, affidavits, reports from the Public Protector, Special Investigating Unit and parliament, and reams of internal LTE documents including email correspondence and legal reports all paint a very detailed picture of the businessman and how he made money from the state.

By the time of Majola's payment, the EFF had passed its first electoral test, winning 6,35 percent of the vote two years before in the 2014 national elections. It was a promising result for a new party. Though COPE had performed better in its debut election in 2009, the EFF displaced COPE as the third-largest party in parliament and was the official opposition in two provinces: in Malema's bastion of Limpopo and in the North West, where it had campaigned vigorously in the wake of Marikana.

But the real test of whether it would be a flash in the pan or become a lasting political force lay in the 2016 local elections. And the party continued to grow, albeit modestly, gnawing away at the ANC's waning majority.

Majola had been playing the political field long before he sent the R500 000 to Malema. Before his link to the EFF was made public, his name had cropped up over the years in various media reports about state contracts awarded to LTE.

The company's fortunes appeared to be connected, at least in part, to the movements of ANC heavyweight Nomvula Mokonyane. Wherever she went, LTE seemed to score big government contracts. This began with Mokonyane's stint as Gauteng premier from 2009 to mid-2014, when LTE scooped up a R200-million housing project south of Johannesburg in Sweetwaters, Kanana Park. This sparked a falling-out between Majola and other LTE directors who were shocked to learn that LTE had been appointed for work they believed it did not have the capacity to perform.

According to Asogan Pillay, who founded the company at the end of the 1990s, Majola had been 'deployed' to LTE from the firm of an investor in the mid-2000s, when he was a young 'shining star'. The investor ended up parting ways with LTE, but Majola decided to stay on. 'He was a quick learner and worked very hard, sometimes 14, 15 or 16 hours a day. His eagerness to learn and his energy propelled him very quickly,' Pillay told us in an interview.

Unlike Majola, who had no political background when he joined the company, Pillay and other LTE leaders had always been aligned with the ANC. But Majola soon became a shrewd political operator, 'manoeuvring into various political relationships that benefited him'. He 'jumped' on LTE's political connections and 'took them to another level', Pillay recalled.

In 2014, Majola's relationship with other directors, including Pillay, began to sour over a controversial project at Sweetwaters. At the heart of the falling-out was Simbi Phiri, a Malawian businessman who had once done work for LTE after Pillay introduced him to the company. The two had been friends, and their children went to school together.

According to Pillay, Phiri had a reputation for being 'pushy and aggressive', which served LTE well when clients were reluctant to pay. But his insistence on getting his way became disruptive and began to alienate his colleagues. In a March 2014 email that surfaced later, an LTE employee wrote to the company's managers: 'The fact that Phiri has on several occasions contacted the team directly, and berates and threatens them with their livelihoods, is completely out of line. I accordingly request that his position be clarified and his behaviour curtailed.'

Phiri was ultimately encouraged to part ways with the company and start his own, which led to the formation of Khato Civils.

Phiri, a flamboyant figure, isn't afraid of the media spotlight. Over the years, his colourful business activities have provided fodder for journalists. In 2016, Botswanan authorities froze his and his companies' bank accounts for allegedly having failed to declare hundreds of thousands of US dollars brought across the border from South Africa. Phiri was cleared the following year, and the accounts were unfrozen.[215]

Meanwhile, he and his companies Khato Civils and South Zambezi courted controversy over a Malawian water pipeline project worth hundreds of millions of dollars that critics decried as a colossal waste. According to media reports, Khato Civils won the bid to construct the pipeline despite being the most expensive option at $200 million more than the second-highest bidder. Phiri's companies were allegedly not only responsible for procurement and construction but also prepared the feasibility studies for the project, leading to charges that he was both player and referee. One source told amaBhungane that the project had 'a built-in conflict of interest'.[216] A spokesperson for Phiri's companies denied the allegations, labelling them 'insinuations that are made with malicious intent'.[217]

Phiri, according to media reports, has admitted to funding political parties in South Africa and Malawi. After he invited a group of journalists on a junket to introduce them to the 'real' Mr Phiri, one glowing report quoted him as saying: 'We have supported political parties here in South Africa but I don't harbour political ambitions whatsoever. Let me tell you: you cannot do a project in an environment without knowing the technocrats, the politicians and the community. These are stakeholders and they are [on] different levels, we have to engage.'[218]

Phiri and Malema apparently got to know each other, and the latter would allegedly visit Phiri's house in Midrand, Gauteng. It is not clear when this happened, but a video circulating on social media in 2019 showed them sitting together in a plush lounge, drinking Malawian gin.

Like Phiri, Majola isn't coy about his political connections. In a group photograph taken at the 45th birthday party of then-Ekurhuleni mayor Mzwandile Masina, Majola, in a blue and black dinner jacket and bowtie, stands between Malema and the EFF's Mbuyiseni Ndlozi. Also in the picture is Masina and controversial ANC politician Tony Yengeni.

Phiri and Majola worked hand in glove on the Sweetwaters project. Much of what is known about this came from a memorandum prepared by law firm Bowmans after a preliminary 2014 investigation into the matter, which was ultimately canned. From 2009, long before the feud within LTE, the company operated as consulting engineers for the Gauteng department of human settlements, providing 'professional services and specialist studies' for the Sweetwaters development. But the scope of its work did not include construction. In 2014, Pillay and the LTE board learnt that Majola, then CEO of LTE, and Phiri, now owner of Khato Civils, had allegedly 'facilitated' a R200-million contract for the construction of a water and sewer reticulation project at Sweetwaters. LTE was given a provisional letter of appointment dated 13 February 2014, but two letters signed by Majola subcontracted most of the work – valued at about R175 million – to Phiri's company, Khato Civils.

Bizarrely, those two letters were dated 11 February – two days before the department's letter appointing LTE. Pillay, then executive chairman, was alarmed. So, too, was the board, which was presented with a fait accompli. They believed that the company lacked the capacity for construction, was lining itself up for failure and that the murky tender process posed significant reputational risks. 'I didn't know we'd been appointed to construct, let alone that we'd outsourced to Khato,' Pillay told us. 'Everything was handed over to Khato, and the funds were flowing.'

According to the Bowmans investigation, no formal tender process was followed for LTE's expanded work. Instead, the company was quietly appointed, allegedly relying on the same tender specifications it had helped the department to draft. The department insisted on proceeding with the contract on the grounds that it was a 'presidential priority'.

Within the company, there was a deep dispute over the deal. According to internal documents, some directors raised red flags about LTE's lack of capacity to undertake the work and the fact that it assumed all the legal and reputational risk while Khato reaped most of the reward. The scope of work was vague, and the necessary approvals had not been obtained. The whole thing, claimed Pillay, was a sham. For months, in a series of frantic emails, he and others had warned of the risks and the need to mitigate them.

Towards the end of the year, Pillay was trying, and failing, to pull LTE out of the contract altogether and cede it to Khato. He was so concerned that he commissioned the investigation by Bowmans law firm. The memo from the law firm is damning, listing a litany of irregularities and highlighting the same concerns that Pillay and other senior managers had about the tender.

In early 2015, Pillay handed over a dossier to the ANC's top six leadership documenting the irregularities he had witnessed at LTE. He felt there was not much more he could do. Frustrated, he walked away from the company and provided information to the Special Investigating Unit (SIU). Nothing appears to have come of this. He formed another consultancy called ETL, which stood for Ethical Technical Leadership – an apparent allusion to his views on the incumbent management of LTE and its ethical shortcomings. Soon afterwards, two of Pillay's closest colleagues followed him out the door, leaving LTE firmly under Majola's control. Majola now had the massive Sweetwaters contract in hand and was free to run the company his way.

The Sweetwaters project provided part of the template for a far greater scandal to come. LTE, as later investigations by the SIU and Public Protector would find, was improperly appointed to another major infrastructure project – also involving Mokonyane – and once again outsourced the construction work to Khato. But this time, the cost ran into billions of rand.

As his relationship with Pillay unravelled, Majola seems to have been eyeing Giyani in rural Limpopo. The ground for the Giyani water project was laid in 2009, after drought led to the declaration of a state of disaster in the region, which used to be part of the 'homeland' of Gazankulu.

Here, little change is visible from Gazankulu's days as a 'dumping ground' for Africans who had been forcibly removed from 'white' urban areas. Scattered across the otherwise empty scrubland and rust-coloured earth are little villages of huts and matchbox houses – in stark contrast with the lush plantations in the neighbouring farming district around Tzaneen, where tomatoes, avocados, mangoes and bananas are commercially farmed.

The declaration of disaster did nothing to improve residents' lives. They complained bitterly about taps running dry, having to drink polluted river water and the dilapidated state of the area's water infrastructure that had been built in the 1970s and neglected ever since. Newborns at Nkhensani Hospital, the main medical centre, were often sent home unbathed. In late 2014, with nothing having changed, two senior government figures visited again: Jacob Zuma and Nomvula Mokonyane, who was now minister of water and sanitation.

Mokonyane called an 'imbizo' in Giyani to address the crisis. According to *City Press*, citing three unnamed sources in the department, Majola attended the imbizo and 'it was a foregone conclusion' that LTE would be given the work to sort out Giyani's water woes.[219] The next day, a team of officials from national and local government as well as Lepelle Northern Water – the state-owned entity responsible for providing water and sanitation to numerous municipalities in the region – met LTE. Within days, Lepelle, which would implement the project to provide clean water to Giyani, appointed Majola's company to conduct 'emergency' infrastructural work over five years, valued at nearly R91 million.

The R91-million contract, however, became a ticket to something far more lucrative. LTE would be positioned to secure additional state work to the tune of billions of rand as a result of the initial emergency contract.

After its appointment to the Giyani project, LTE drafted a wide-ranging development plan, far greater in scope than the 'emergency' project, which effectively piled additional work onto the initial limited project. In subsequent investigations into the water project, Lepelle CEO Phineas Legodi and Carel Schmahl, the entity's general manager of operations, claimed that they were acting on a directive from Mokonyane's ministry. One document from August 2014, submitted by Schmahl and approved by Legodi, notes that the department recommended that Lepelle use LTE.

In September, just a month after the initial contract, Lepelle handed LTE an expanded project that had ballooned to around R2,2 billion, more than 24 times the size of the original contract. LTE was supposed to deliver a 'turnkey' solution and oversee the entire project from start to finish. This was revealed in a presentation the SIU made to parliament in November 2023.

Meanwhile, Majola had been preparing to involve his friend Phiri in the deal. LTE subcontracted most of the work to two of Phiri's companies: Khato Civils for construction and South Zambezi as a 'subconsultant'. Within a month of starting the expanded project, Khato invoiced Lepelle for more than R170 million. This amount was promptly paid – a staggering figure, considering that the initial R91-million LTE contract was intended to run over five years. A subsequent report by the Public Protector in 2020 found that the R170 million – claimed 'as advances and for measured work' – was exorbitant and that Lepelle 'should not have allowed this to occur'.[220] The same report noted that 'there was a clear lack of value for money as LTE/Khato was allowed to charge any rates that they wanted'.

By March 2016, the Giyani water project was already making the news. A headline in *City Press* on 14 March read, 'R170m and still no water'.[221] The article noted that, despite the millions sunk into the project, residents went without water for up to five days at a time, and some were forced to use water from nearby rivers.

Julius Malema was also starting to pay attention to Giyani. After all, this was his own political backyard, and a project of this size was unlikely to escape his notice. With local government elections set for August 2016, the EFF leader was campaigning in his stronghold province and the water crisis was among the issues on his political agenda. In March, he visited Nkhensani Hospital, where he told reporters: 'The people of Giyani have been complaining about water for a very long time. [. . .] And we heard that there's a company that has been given a contract for billions to come and give people water here. So, we wanted to see if that water has been delivered.'

Four months later, just before the municipal elections, this company – LTE – paid R500 000 to Malema. Majola deposited the funds into the account of Santaclara Trading, a front company used for Malema's benefit. Established in 2013, the same year the EFF was founded, the company was initially registered as Voorsprong Trading and Projects. Its sole director was Tebatso Kubus Malema, then 21 years old, who in company records listed his address as the same Seshego home where Julius grew up, and which remains the company's registered address. On 25 January 2015, the company was mentioned in a *City Press* report about a car allegedly bought for Malema with EFF party funds and registered under Voorsprong's name.

The EFF explained to the paper that licensing authorities had advised it that the vehicle could not be registered in the name of a political party. An EFF spokesperson was quoted as saying: 'This was not a secret, it was an over-the-counter transaction . . . this vehicle was bought by the EFF and registered with a proxy company.'

Soon after the company's founding, Tebatso Malema was replaced as director by another young man – one Phumi Jimmy Matlebyane, a Polokwane-based DJ known on social media as Jimmy-fire Malema. He regularly performs at Mekete Lodge, Malema's 'boutique' establishment located outside Polokwane. In a recent photograph, Malema was pictured spinning the decks alongside the boyish-faced Matlebyane.

Among Matlebyane's listed addresses is that of the same Sandown property Malema rented and later bought through his Munzhedzi Family Trust and which would feature in news reports about his suspicious financial transactions.

Santaclara was not just loosely connected to Malema through his associates. Rather, as we explain in this book, it was an extension of his own finances – a slush fund used for his personal benefit, and to a lesser extent to fund his political activities. From 2019 onwards, amaBhungane tried to establish the legal ownership of Santaclara as well as DMM Media (linked to senior EFF figure Marshall Dlamini) and Mahuna Investments. It did so by submitting COR24 forms (a form used to request access to information held by a company, as per section 26 of the Companies Act) to the three companies, to which they were legally obliged to respond. However, they simply refused to provide the information, despite complaints by amaBhungane to the Companies and Intellectual Property Commission, which is supposed to ensure compliance, and attempts by the Seshego sheriff to serve letters of demand at the companies' registered addresses.

Though amaBhungane could not obtain the share registers, the bank statements recording payments into and out of the Santaclara bank account show that Malema was in control of the account, and its credit card accompanied him inside and outside the country.

In October 2018, Malema travelled to the Rwandan capital of Kigali to attend the Pan-African Parliament convened under the theme 'Winning the fight against corruption: A sustainable path to Africa's transformation'. The Santaclara credit card went with him, paying for hotel meals, alcohol and a restaurant. Just before Malema jetted off to Rwanda, the card was used for R40 000 worth of purchases at high-end fashion stores in Sandton.

Months before that, in July, the card was used for transactions in East London, where Malema attended an event marking the EFF's fifth birthday. It was there, in front of a crowd of supporters at the Sisa Dukashe stadium, that Malema pointed a pistol and then an assault rifle to the sky and fired off what were allegedly live rounds. The firearms had been handed to him by his bodyguard, Adriaan Snyman.[222]

The Santaclara card fuelled Malema's lavish lifestyle, paying for clothes from stores like Louis Vuitton in Sandton City and hefty bills at liquor shops and nightclubs. In early July 2019, Malema and his wife Mantoa Matlala, whom he had married in 2014, enjoyed a weekend of opulence and haute couture at the Durban July horse race, which Malema has attended regularly over the years. He appeared at the race in a tailored grey suit, accompanied by his comrades Floyd Shivambu and Godrich Gardee. The day before, Santaclara had paid R33 450 for 'cooperate wear' – presumably a misspelling of 'corporate wear'. It also paid for groceries, liquor, fuel and a hotel in Ballito, just north of Durban.

The payment records include school fees and airtime for Malema's son, Ratanang; a gym membership and other subscriptions; insurance payments; and improvements to Malema's properties. They also cover his charitable endeavours, as payments marked 'old age taxis' and 'house donation' suggest, as do payments marked 'Matome's mom' – probably in support of the mother of his deceased friend, businessman Matome Hlabioa.

Some of the Santaclara money appears to have been funnelled to Malema's various business ventures. Payments described as 'Vilakazi' and 'Grand Azania' probably refer to the wine bar and restaurant that Malema set up with Shivambu on Vilakazi Street, Soweto, which later became Sud Restaurant. Grand Azania was the planned name for the establishment and also the name of the company used as a conduit for the flow of VBS funds to Shivambu, as explained later in Part Three. Santaclara also covered various expenses at the luxury Mekete Lodge, including furniture, event coordinators and sound systems.

Large incoming and outgoing transactions were also marked 'EFF' – attesting to the blurred boundaries between the party and its leader's personal interests. There were also regular payments of R50 000 or R100 000 into the account from an unknown source for 'consulting services'.

There were large cash deposits, too, including R80 000 broken up into five separate payments on the same day in March 2017. Information about that depositor also seems suspicious as the labels on the transactions were mostly variations of the same cellphone number – a possible attempt to obscure the identity of the sender.

Santaclara provided Malema with millions every year, vastly outstripping his parliamentary salary of just over R1 million. From mid-2018 to mid-2019, for instance, the Santaclara account received over R13 million. Much of this came from businesspeople and companies doing business with the state, like Thulani Majola and LTE.

The R500 000 that Majola paid to Santaclara on the eve of the 2016 elections was the first of many such payments. Just a month later, Santaclara's bank account pinged again with R300 000 from Majola.

Majola admitted to us that he had paid Santaclara, but only an amount of R200 000. That payment had been brought into the public domain by a *Sunday Times* story published in October 2019, titled 'Julius Malema's "slush fund" exposed'.[225] The newspaper had obtained a snippet of Santaclara's bank records and the article mentioned the R200 000 deposit from LTE Consulting, 'the company behind the controversial R2,2bn project to supply water to Limpopo'. When we put this to Majola, he claimed that Santaclara's CEO – whom he could not name and said he hadn't met – had solicited the money for T-shirts for some unspecified political campaign, and that he had no knowledge of the company's links to Malema and the EFF, nor did he care to know to which political campaign the cash was going. Regardless, it was only a fraction of his total payments to Santaclara, which amounted to more than R3 million between 2016 and 2019.

Majola was also dishing out donations on the other side of the political aisle, paying more than R14 million to various ANC structures, like the ANC in Gauteng and KwaZulu-Natal, in the same period. However, unlike the ANC payments he made, when Majola paid Santaclara he sent money directly to the EFF leader himself, not to his party. The Santaclara account, as we have said, was used for Malema's personal benefit, and this may well have been a strategy to keep Malema onside, especially in light of what was to play out later on.

Majola's company wasn't the only entity involved in the Giyani project that donated money to Malema. One little-known construction firm that was subcontracted to work on one of the pipelines also paid money to the EFF leader. In an online profile, its sole director, Nicholas Selamolela, is a member of the Lemba tribe, which, according to oral tradition, has Jewish roots, although most of its members identify as Christians. Malema has claimed to have Lemba roots but without providing details.

Selamolela is a leader of the South African Jewish Board of Deputies and, according to his biography on the board's website, he grew up in the Venda 'homeland', studied Judaism in Israel and has survived the vagaries of the business world by adhering to a simple philosophy: 'Share your gains with others.' He certainly seems to have extended this ideal to Malema, donating more than R1,7 million to the EFF leader over the course of the Giyani debacle.

As the project ground on through 2016, it churned up growing scandal and controversy. A steady stream of media reports cast LTE, Mokonyane and her department in a negative light. LTE's adverse media coverage was also not confined to the Giyani debacle. In July 2016, *City Press* labelled the massive Lesotho Highlands Water Project – the multibillion-rand development started under apartheid to provide water from Lesotho to Gauteng via a network of dams and tunnels – as 'Mokonyane's Watergate'. Again, LTE was at the heart of the controversy. The *City Press* article accused Majola of having 'met with Lesotho officials to demand tenders, freely dropping Mokonyane's name in the meetings'.[224]

The newspaper claimed that the director-general of Mokonyane's department had ordered a halt to the procurement without providing any reasons, and that both the South African and Lesotho governments had removed officials seen as obstacles to LTE's involvement and replaced them with more pliant ones. One such pliant official, according to the article, was Masupha Sole, a Lesotho bureaucrat who had served a prison sentence for receiving bribes from international companies in the late 1980s and early 1990s in connection with an earlier phase of the project.

On the South African side, the chief delegate to the bilateral commission set up to oversee the project, Zodwa Dlamini, was abruptly 'redeployed' – or effectively demoted – in late 2015, and she lodged a complaint with the Public Protector. A subsequent report shed little light on the decision to remove Dlamini, noting only that the minister had expressed 'concerns regarding issues of governance' under Dlamini and 'her failure to deal with issues relating to the Procurement Policy'.[225]

Responding to *City Press*, spokespersons for Mokonyane and the department denied the existence of an improper relationship between the minister and LTE or any other wrongdoing, saying the allegations were 'false, malicious, speculative and calculated to discredit and damage her good name'. They claimed there was an agreement to amend procurement policies to promote emerging black companies in South Africa and Lesotho.

In 2016, the Giyani project was heading into troubled waters. Reports claimed that the department was running out of money and there were payment backlogs.[226] A departmental spokesperson told reporters in November that cash-flow problems made it hard to keep projects like Giyani moving, adding that 'we believe each financial year [that] government will allocate us a certain amount to complete the project in stages'. Although the department later denied it was 'broke, as alleged'.

Contractors and subcontractors were becoming anxious, and the massive growth of the Giyani project meant that, for LTE, billions of rand were at stake. There were rumours that the National Treasury was investigating the beleaguered project. It was at this point that the EFF leadership appears to have sprung to action and started lobbying in LTE's interests. On 27 October, the party published a statement condemning what it understood to be a National Treasury decision to terminate the Giyani water project.

'The EFF strongly condemns the decision by the National Treasury,' the statement read, 'and accordingly, we have written letters to the office of the president, the minister of water and sanitation and the minister of finance respectively, demanding that the process to deliver water to the people of Giyani should not be discontinued.'[227]

EFF deputy president Floyd Shivambu wrote to finance minister Pravin Gordhan the same day, stating: 'It has come to our attention that National Treasury has written to Giyani municipality instructing that the project to deliver water to the people of Giyani should be terminated due to shortage of funds. We write to demand that the process to deliver water to the people of Giyani should not be discontinued because for a very long time, the people of Giyani have [been] promised water.'[228]

Malema soon turned his attention to Mokonyane, calling her eight times in December. Speaking at an ANC event in the Eastern Cape months later, Mokonyane said that Malema had kept insisting that Giyani service providers be paid. Those same companies, Mokonyane said, were also 'funding' the EFF leader.

Malema acknowledged calling her. 'Yes, I called her,' he told a journalist. 'It's not even a secret, because workers in Giyani had not been paid during December holidays, and they called us.' On 24 December, a day after the last of the barrage of phone calls to Mokonyane and just in time for Christmas, another R100 000 from Majola popped into the Santaclara account.

In the new year, Mokonyane's department admitted to falling behind on payments to contractors, and Khato moved workers off-site. Claiming it was owed over R250 000, the company launched legal action against the department, which it later withdrew. There was a growing rift between the contractors and the department, with the latter later claiming that payments on the Giyani project had been halted due to discrepancies between the work done and the amounts claimed by the contractors, which had to be verified by technical teams.

On 7 February 2017, Shivambu ratcheted up the pressure on Mokonyane. The EFF's second-in-command, and also its chief whip in

Boy Mamabolo Foundation
@BoyMamabolo

The 1998 Mohlakaneng High School LRC 🎓🎓
🎓

Above: A young Malema (front right) with his idol Peter Mokaba (centre), first president of the South African Youth Congress, which later became a re-established ANC Youth League. Mokaba profoundly shaped Malema's political views.

Left: Julius Malema's political aspirations became apparent while he was still at school. Here he is (sitting in the middle) with Boy Mamabolo (standing on the far right) during his student years at Mohlakaneng High School.

Above: Malema during his ANC days, celebrating his birthday with champagne, and with Jacob Zuma cutting the cake at the ANCYL's 66th anniversary. Malema proclaimed in public that he was prepared to die – and kill – for Zuma.

Above: Malema having drinks with self-confessed hitman Mikey Schultz (far left), businessman Adriano Mazzotti (second from left) and Mazzotti's business partners, Mohammadh Sayed (centre, with his arm around Malema), Kyle Phillips (second from right) and Martin Wingate-Pearse (right). It was when SARS investigated Mazzotti that it first stumbled upon the then little-known Malema name and discovered that he was not paying tax.

Above: Malema, his wife Mantoa, and EFF spokesperson Vuyani Pambo with Mazzotti in Ibiza, Spain, in 2022, at Mazzotti's daughter's wedding. Malema and his family also lived in Mazzotti's high-security compound in Hyde Park. According to Mazzotti, Mantoa rented the property at market price.

Above: Jossey Buthane, a former ANC regional leader and manager in Pinky Kekana's office when she was Limpopo MEC for roads and transport. A longtime Malema associate, Buthane later led the EFF in Limpopo. He allegedly tried to thwart community protests against Mazzotti and his associates' controversial chrome mine.

Above: Cassel Mathale, deputy minister of police, was the MEC of the Limpopo department of roads and transport and then the premier of Limpopo at the time of Malema's ascent. Mathale appointed Ntau Letebele as head of the Limpopo department of roads and transport. Eleven days after he took over, Letebele put out a tender for an external contractor to manage procurement, with dire results.

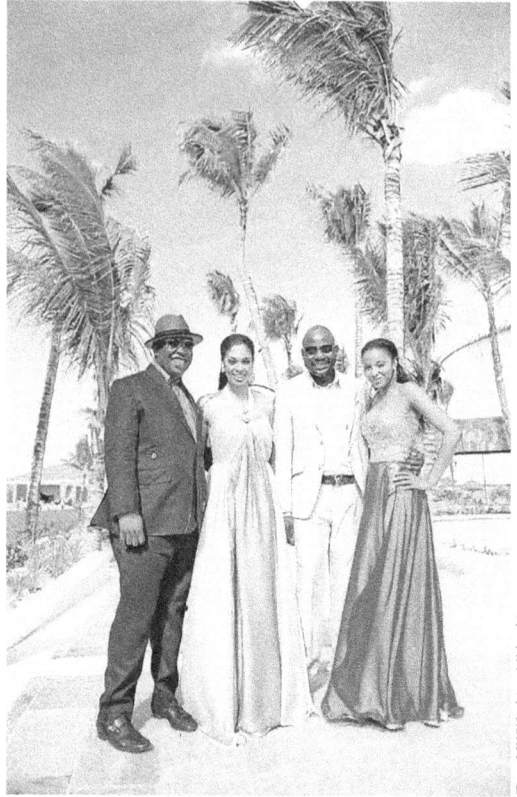

Right: Malema in a purple designer suit at David Mabilu's wedding in Mauritius. Limpopo property magnate Mabilu made a fortune in questionable state property transactions. He made substantial cash donations to Malema and helped pay for his mansion in Silvela Road, Sandton.

Below: Lesiba Gwangwa, Malema's partner in On-Point Engineers, in court in 2012 for fraud, corruption and money laundering. He was later acquitted of all the charges. Gwangwa paid millions of rand to Malema's Ratanang Family Trust and gave him 70% shareholding in one of his companies.

NH29

9/2/10 Gumboe – Drivers licence, Add Phone

Loan 1 month end of month R1500-00

- Aralio Aralio – Julius building house
  Onpoint
- Raffcel & R50K Ten Cash + Carry
  CNC Cash + carry
- Monthly report as soon as we have an acc. syst.

2012 Inq. date of receipt
BB

week 18
122-244 RSA, LESOTHO, NAMIBIA, ZIMBABWE: Worker's Day;
MALAWI, SWAZILAND, ZAMBIA: Labour Day

Public holiday

Tuesday

1 MAY

NH60

07.00 — Work from 10.00 – 13:20

07.30

08.00

08.30 Julius – shareholder. Dividenter justified

09.00 Jolon. spreadsheets

09.30 1. Inter company transactions
         Muith Quotes – negligegen

10.00

10.30 2. Invoice numbering – incorrect

11.00

Above: Nicolette Honeycomb, Gwangwa's financial manager, kept meticulous records. In diary entries she noted 'Aralio – Julius building house', a reference to the architect of Malema's Silvela Road mansion in Sandton, Aurelio Cimato, who was paid by Gwangwa. In a 2012 entry, she wrote 'Julius – shareholder Dividents [sic] justified' and then struck it through. Gwangwa, at pains to justify his payments to Malema, called them dividends, even though the company did not have the financial health to justify the R100 000 per month it paid Malema.

Right: Malema with his cousins Tshepo Malema (left) and Matsobane 'Tsubi' Phaleng (right). Their business endeavours seemed closely tied to Malema's political rise. Malema used a company ostensibly owned by Phaleng to channel millions of rand in questionable payments from government contractors and money looted from VBS to himself.

Below: Malema arrives at court in Polokwane in September 2012, charged with money laundering, fraud and corruption linked to the On-Point scandal. The case was later struck off the roll due to numerous delays. Even though the judge warned that the charges could be reinstated – and with untested witness testimony that could be used – the National Prosecuting Authority has shown no appetite for the case since.

tsubi_phaleng

♡ 146 ◯ 3 ⊽ ◻

Liked by **julius.malema.sello** and others
tsubi_phaleng Brothers
7 March 2021

Instagram

AFP Photo/Stephane De Sakutin

Lucky Nxumalo/City Press/Gallo Images/Getty Images

Gallo Images/OJ Koloti

Above: Malema on his Schuilkraal farm outside Seshego, Limpopo, bought for him by benefactors, including Gwangwa. At the last minute, when he realised he was under scrutiny, the farm was registered to a company one step removed from Malema. Despite these efforts, Schuilkraal was later attached and auctioned off by the National Prosecuting Authority.

Left: Nomvula Mokonyane was minister of water and sanitation when LTE scored the Giyani water tender. With the project mired in controversy and Mokonyane's department not paying contractors, Malema allegedly took up LTE's cause and 'harassed' her, insisting that LTE be paid. The company appeared to have found a new rainmaker in the EFF leader.

Daily Maverick/Israel Nkuna

Above: LTE, whose CEO donated large amounts to Malema, was appointed to provide 'emergency' water infrastructure to drought-stricken Giyani in a contract that ballooned to billions of rand and ended in failure. Parts of the parched region still remain without access to clean running water.

Twitter/X

Left: Thulani Majola, the CEO of LTE, at a birthday party for then Ekurhuleni mayor Mzwandile Masina in 2019. Majola stands between Malema and then EFF spokesperson Mbuyiseni Ndlozi. LTE made several large 'donations' to Malema.

Right: Simbi Phiri, the Malawian owner of Khato Civils, who worked closely with LTE in Giyani, benefiting from the controversial tender.

Gallo Images/Media24/Sizwe Sama Yende

tsubi_phaleng
The Best Minds

...

♡ 81   💬 1   ⧩

🔖

Liked by **julius.malema.sello** and **others**
15 May 2018

Above: Inside Mekete Lodge, Malema's luxury venue outside Polokwane known for its lavish late-night parties.

Left: Matsobane 'Tsubi' Phaleng poses with a Mekete Lodge vehicle.

Google Maps

Above: Malema's smallholding, Palmietfontein, paid for by one of his benefactors. The satellite image shows a view of the main house, the pool, smaller outbuildings, a tennis and basketball court, staff quarters and an open area where, according to neighbours, Malema sometimes arrives in a rented helicopter.

AFP Photo/Alexander Joe

Above: Mpho Ramakatsa (middle), effectively Malema's second in command as the EFF was starting out, was voted out at the first EFF elective conference and eventually kicked out of the party for criticising the leadership.

Above the photo credit reads: Ihsaan Haffejee/Anadolu Agency/Getty Images

Above: Despite his avowals of eternal support, Malema fell out with Zuma and blamed the then ANC leader for 'persecuting him' when he was charged with fraud. Malema demanded Zuma's resignation, and the EFF enthusiastically took part in the 'Zuma must go' protests in 2016.

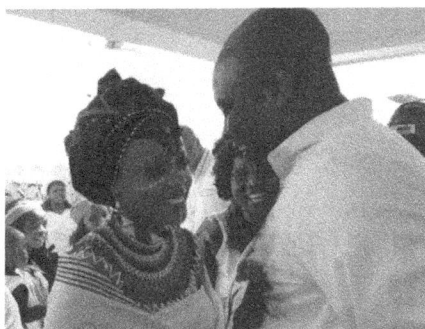

Twitter/X

Above: Floyd Shivambu lived large, but was perpetually short of cash. Shortly before his 2017 wedding to Siphesihle Pezi (pictured), he sent a WhatsApp message to Limpopo business tycoon Lawrence Mulaudzi: 'Please don't forget to activate that intervention. Am in great need.' He added the bank account details of Grand Azania.

Right: The EFF leadership socialising at the Eyadini Lounge in Durban. The Mahuna credit card was Malema's constant companion, and paid for not only his son's school fees, but for designer suits, renovations at Mekete Lodge, and the EFF's nights on the town. The card duly paid the bill at Eyadini.

mbuyisenindlozi
Eyadini Lounge

Liked by **motzn** and **2 886 others**

mbuyisenindlozi In @eyadiniloungenuz with the leadership for dinner... towards the EFF 4th Anniversary Celebration taking place in Durban on 29 July, 2017: Curries Fountain, DUT

View all 60 comments

10 July 2017

Instagram

Above: VBS Mutual Bank clients Nyawasedza Raphunga (left) and Margaret Chauke (right, clutching her bank book), whose life savings were stolen in the VBS fraud.

Right: This graphic, first published in *Daily Maverick*, shows how the Shivambus benefited from the VBS money.

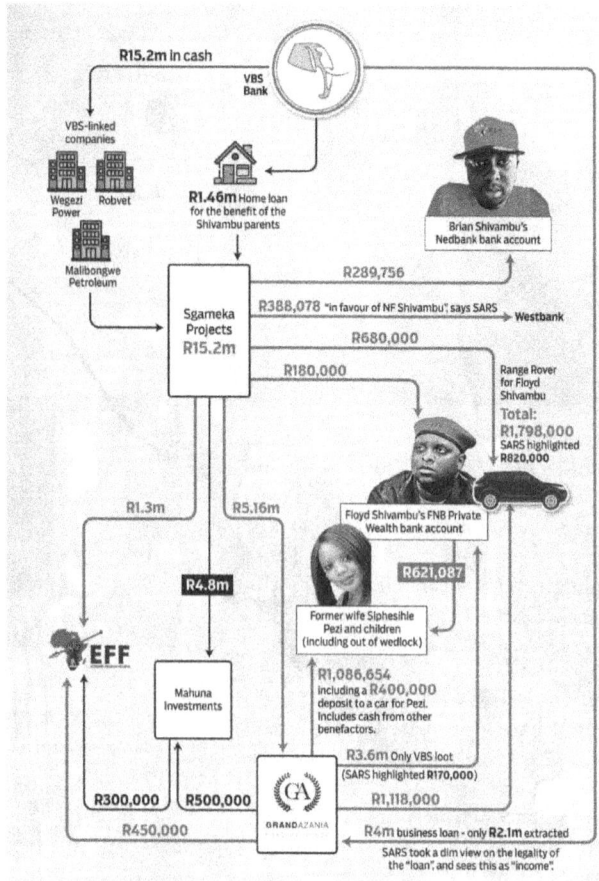

R15.2m in cash

VBS Bank

VBS-linked companies

Wegezi Power   Robvet

Malibongwe Petroleum

R1.46m Home loan for the benefit of the Shivambu parents

Brian Shivambu's Nedbank bank account

R289,756

Sgameka Projects R15.2m

R388,078 "in favour of NF Shivambu", says SARS → Westbank

R680,000

R180,000

Range Rover for Floyd Shivambu
Total: R1,798,000 SARS highlighted R820,000

R1.3m   R5.16m

Floyd Shivambu's FNB Private Wealth bank account

R4.8m

R621,087

Former wife Siphesihle Pezi and children (including out of wedlock)

EFF

Mahuna Investments

R1,086,654 including a R400,000 deposit to a car for Pezi. Includes cash from other benefactors.

R3.6m Only VBS loot (SARS highlighted R170,000)

GA GRANDAZANIA

R300,000   R500,000

R1,118,000

R450,000

R4m business loan - only R2.1m extracted
SARS took a dim view on the legality of the "loan", and sees this as "income".

Right: Malema was a regular at the Durban July. When he attended the event in 2017, the Mahuna bank card was used in Durban. Again, in 2018, the bank card went with him to the July. His other front company, Santaclara, paid for 'cooperate wear' (presumably corporate wear) as well as liquor and a hotel in Ballito. Here he is at the races with EFF leaders Godrich Gardee (right) and Floyd Shivambu in 2019.

Instagram

Left: Over R10m was paid into Mahuna Investments between 2017 and 2018. Of this, R5,3m consisted of illicit money from VBS bank. This list shows a few of the items Malema spent his slush fund's money on in 2017 and 2018.

THE SHOPPING LIST

2017 - 2018

CHECKERS HYPER	R 3 670
DURBAN JULY	R 569 270
EMPORIO ARMANI	R 3 650
FIREWORKS OVER THE 2018/19 NEW YEAR	R 50 000
GAME	R 16 921
GUCCI	R 67 800
INCREDIBLE CONNECTION	R 22 999
ISTORE	R 15 139
LACOSTE	R 15 760
LM TAILORED SUIT	R 415 087
LOUIS VUITTON	R 35 100
MATSOBANE PHALENG	R 254 000
MEKETE LODGE	R 1 790 000
PNP	R 28 839
SANDOWN HOUSE AND POOL	R 458 050
SCHOOL FEES	R 203 021
SKINS COSMETICS	R 34 695
SPITZ	R 6 765
WOOLWORTHS	R 7 232

TOTAL	**R 3,998,007**

Daily Maverick

Above: Tshifhiwa Matodzi, chair of VBS Mutual Bank. In a bombshell affidavit, Matodzi explained how Malema and Shivambu unlawfully benefited from the VBS fraud. Although he is currently serving a jail term, Malema and Shivambu have remained untouched.

Above: Thembinkosi Rawula, an EFF MP who spoke out against the party leader. He said that Malema 'admitted to [the] EFF taking VBS money to finance the revolution'. Malema sued him for defamation but lost the case.

Above: Herman Mashaba during his time as mayor of Johannesburg. Over his three-year tenure, which began in 2016, he went from being hated by the EFF to being dubbed the 'EFF mayor'.

Above: Malema and Marshall Dlamini at the EFF's second National People's Assembly at Nasrec in Johannesburg in 2019, where Dlamini was elected EFF secretary general. Dlamini remains one of Malema's closest loyalists and continues to play a key role in his financial network.

Above: Malema, Shivambu (right) and Dlamini (left) at a rally in Polokwane in 2024. Despite the EFF's electoral decline, Malema remains a vocal and unpredictable presence in South African politics.

Above: Shivambu announcing his departure from the EFF to join the uMkhonto weSizwe Party in August 2024, an affiliation that lasted less than a year.

parliament, circulated a letter to Mokonyane that he had signed. It was a sweeping personal attack on the minister, alleging without evidence that her supposed lover was the real power behind the ministry and controlling the department's payments – claims she denied. The letter zoomed in on the failure to pay service providers, asking whether the department was facing legal action for non-payment and, if so, why it was not paying.

The allegations aimed at Mokonyane stemmed, at least in part, from a submission by an anonymous whistleblower earlier that month to the SIU and the Hawks. However, the EFF was selective with the facts, and what it chose to omit was telling.

The whistleblower had complained that LTE and Khato were appointed 'without following due process', and said it was a 'well-known fact' that a senior official was receiving kickbacks from the two companies. None of this appeared in the EFF's letter. Rather than asking why two irregularly appointed and overpaid companies were still being paid, the EFF was demanding to know why they weren't.

At a meeting of parliament's water and sanitation portfolio committee in May, the chairperson, Lulu Johnson, referred to a 'viral letter' demanding that the contractors be paid, and said he suspected that the EFF was conflicted in making that demand. He asked sarcastically if the EFF were themselves contracted by Lepelle, 'as they clearly had a vested interest in the project in Giyani'. He later told amaBhungane that Mokonyane had told the committee she was being 'harassed' by the EFF, and that the party's leaders wanted money for LTE.

LTE and Majola distanced themselves from the allegations that Malema and the EFF had lobbied on behalf of the company and its interests in Giyani, and denied paying Santaclara for political protection. They said that LTE was 'not party' to any engagements between the EFF and government over the Giyani matter. 'No member of LTE ever engaged with the EFF on the Giyani project, either in Giyani or anywhere else.'

Not all EFF leaders were reading from the same script, though. While its two most senior figures tried to keep money flowing to the project, with LTE funnelling money to Malema, the party's representative on parliament's all-important standing committee on public accounts (Scopa) took a firm stance on the Giyani fiasco. Scopa is responsible for overseeing the finances of state entities and has a reputation for its no-nonsense approach. The EFF's Ntombovuyo Veronica Mente was a very active member of the committee and one of the sharpest critics of the Giyani project. During one sitting, she took aim at Majola, saying his name 'kept popping up in a number of fraudulent transactions in the list of irregular expenditure'.

Mente's pointed remarks about everything from double payments and unfinished business to specific legal and regulatory breaches suggest that she possessed a solid grasp of the Giyani matter and wasn't about to let go. More than a year later, she told the committee she was 'not convinced' that the emergency used to justify the project was real. Rather, it was a well-orchestrated 'emergency that paved the way for a bigger project', she said, pointing to the enormous cost overruns. She seemed to have no idea that the person whose name kept popping up was regularly making payments to her party leader. Perhaps Malema thought it was better for the party to speak with dual tongues than to debate the sensitive matter of LTE, with all the awkward questions that might raise. Incoherence, in this case, may have seemed the lesser of two evils.

By 2017, the Public Protector, the SIU and the auditor-general were scrutinising the Giyani project. In a report to parliament later that year, by which time the budget for Giyani was R2,8 billion, with R2,5 billion already paid, the auditor-general's office listed a catalogue of 'failures and red flags', including price-gouging by the contractors, who charged 'excessive project management and professional fees and excessive construction rates' and were double-counting professional hours.

But another year elapsed before the matter finally came to a head. Khato again moved off-site – this time for good. The whole project had become untenable. In October 2018, the minister of finance, Tito Mboweni, stated in parliament: 'The Giyani Water Project is plagued by malfeasance. It is a cesspool of corruption. The challenges range from a complete disregard for supply chain rules to poor contract management, resulting in irregular expenditure.

'It is clear that a new delivery and financing model is required to provide water services to communities. I have requested the National Treasury Director-General Dondo Mogajane to work with the Department of

Water and Sanitation to ensure that appropriate action is taken against all guilty officials implicated in the Auditor-General's report.'

He added: 'The president has informed me that he will go to Giyani to see exactly what has happened and what needs to be done.'[229] Ramaphosa finally visited Giyani years later, in December 2022.

In the meantime, Mokonyane had been relocated to the communications ministry in 2018, when Ramaphosa became national president. She was later implicated in the report of the Zondo Commission of Inquiry into State Capture for not declaring 'gifts', including braai packs, alcohol and money from the controversial politically connected company Bosasa and a R2-million down payment from a family friend for an Aston Martin. She avoided any serious consequences and became deputy secretary-general of the ANC in December 2022.

But the public was a little less forgiving, turning her preferred nickname of 'Mama Action' into 'Mama Aston'. Under Ramaphosa, who had campaigned for the party and national presidency on a ticket of stemming the runaway corruption that had flourished under Zuma, the political will emerged to finally sort out the mess in Giyani.

Having determined that the procurement process leading to the appointment of LTE was deeply flawed, in November 2018 the SIU went to court to have the contract awarded to LTE declared unconstitutional and set aside. In the meantime, it continued its investigations. Just over a week later, on 5 December, Legodi, the Lepelle CEO, was hauled before parliament and grilled by Mente and her colleagues, who demanded answers on the cost overruns, poor planning, irregular appointments and other problems that had hamstrung the project. Wrapping up the meeting, the chair of the committee, Themba Godi, said that 'it was clear that a lot went wrong. It seemed that things were planned in dark corners, and then emerged as well-planned projects, but without money to support it. It was clear from the National Treasury submission that it was made to look like an emergency.'

Not long before, Majola made another payment from another of his companies to an EFF politician. This time, however, he sent the R100 000 not to Malema but to Marshall Dlamini – a little-known EFF MP at the time who would soon rise to prominence in the party and go on to play a key role in Malema's network. But by now the Giyani project was dead in the water, at least as far as LTE's role was concerned. Its contract was finally terminated at the end of the year, by which time the government had spent more than R4 billion on an incomplete project, according to the SIU's findings.

Legodi was eventually removed for his alleged role in maladministration at the water agency. The SIU also sought through litigation to claw back some of the billions misspent on the project. In October 2020, it pursued damage claims to the tune of nearly R2 billion against Legodi and Schmahl, the general manager of operations, and successfully applied to have their pensions frozen pending the outcome of the litigation. Mokonyane, however, appears to have got off the hook.

In November 2023, the SIU told Scopa that its investigation into contracts with LTE had been concluded and that the decision to award the contract to LTE and inflate the price by an order of billions was found to be 'irregular and unlawful'. The SIU alleged that Lepelle had paid more than R4 billion to the contractors through LTE, based on a contract initially worth R90 million. It said there was evidence of price-gouging and corruption involving service providers and officials from Lepelle and the department, and stated that it would hand its report over to the president.

LTE has maintained its innocence. In an interview with the authors in 2020, Majola and his colleague, LTE chief operating officer Sham Maharaj, claimed they were paid fair market rates. The ballooning costs, they argued, were because Giyani was a long-forgotten area, and the water problem was enormous. The portion of the work given to LTE, they said, was just a fraction of what was needed to address the wider problem.

'We spent in the bundus three and a half years, burnt by the sun, building this pipeline,' said Majola.

Majola denied any impropriety or knowingly paying Malema, and he and Maharaj suggested that their company received negative attention because they had 'irked somebody'. As a small black-owned company, they had stepped onto 'hallowed ground' and were seen as upstarts by their bigger and more established rivals. This, they said, had made them a target. They also claimed that most of the work for the project had been completed, and they blamed the department and a lack of funds for the failure to complete all of it.

By 2018, the scale of the failure was apparent from the air. From a helicopter, rows of massive industrial pipes could be seen lying in the veld, slowly decaying in the harsh Limpopo sun. Trenches had been dug along seemingly endless stretches of road, with the occasional deserted construction site along the way. Any infrastructure that was in use seemed to be labouring under growing demand and years of mismanagement.

Some progress followed. In 2019, Construction North, a company owned by the Department of Water and Sanitation, was trying to revive the Giyani project, and its earth movers and trucks were on site laying new pipes.

Although LTE was out of the Giyani picture, and Malema's intervention failed to prevent the collapse of its project there, by this time it had a pile of other government work it could turn its attention to. While it was getting bogged down in Giyani, it had been adding to its list of government contracts.

Back in July 2016, the Ekurhuleni metro advertised a tender for a panel of built environment consultants for the city's real estate department – a lucrative opportunity for the company. Over the next five days LTE made a R2-million payment labelled 'ANC GP' – presumably Gauteng Province, where the metro is located – and a R500 000 payment labelled 'ANC Ekurhuleni'. LTE's appointment to the panel, alongside a handful of other service providers, was confirmed later in the year.

Panels are supposed to offer state bodies a pool of prequalified service providers to choose from, making procurement more efficient and avoiding lengthy open bids for every project of a specific kind, such as large infrastructure projects. Work is supposed to be apportioned fairly to companies on the panel, for instance via rotation or by dividing work in accordance with how well companies scored in their bids to be part of the panel.

The built environment panel was expected to receive roughly R1 billion worth of work which would be divided up among the service providers, but amaBhungane found that LTE received a share of work 'far in excess' of the 'in-principle allocation of around R81 million' it was initially given. It got roughly double that amount, and another R161 million from another panel it was appointed to the following year. Sources from other companies said that they received only scraps, or no work at all. One said that officials made it clear that they would need to pay a bribe to receive work.[230]

The Gauteng metro accounted for over R345 million of LTE's income between 2016 and the end of 2020, mostly through these panels, according to detailed records obtained by amaBhungane. Ekurhuleni – then under the mayorship of the ANC's Masina, whose birthday bash Majola had attended – became an LTE cash cow.

2016 was also a very expensive year for the ANC. Mokonyane, who besides her ministerial role was also the party's head of campaigns, said the ANC had spent 'over R1 billion' in the runup to the local government elections in August. Even allowing for some exaggeration, it was a huge sum, and more than double the R429 million the party was said to have spent in the 2014 elections, which in turn was more than double the amount spent in the 2009 ballot.[231] Elections in South Africa were becoming increasingly big business.

In numerous payments Majola doled out a total of over R10 million to various party structures between the beginning of the year and election day, far outstripping the modest payment of R500 000 to Santaclara for that period.

Most of his donations to the ANC and EFF over the years do not appear to have been tied to specific tenders or political favours and seemed to be more about fostering general goodwill with parties and politicians. But the timing of some payments did coincide with the company's government contracting, like the 'ANC Ekurhuleni' payment, or when Majola made a R1-million payment labelled 'ANC KZN' the day after his company was appointed from a panel of infrastructure and engineering companies by the ANC-run province's cooperative governance and traditional affairs department. That contract, awarded in January 2019 'to undertake the assessment of the state of existing water, sanitation and electricity infrastructure' in KwaZulu-Natal, was worth over R100 million.

If Majola saw his payments to parties and politicians as investments in political capital, they had paid off handsomely.

PART THREE

The Elephant in the Room

CHAPTER 14

The vultures and
the *magwinya* money

W HEN MARGARET CHAUKE needs a few minutes to herself, she drags a chair from the white brick house with the tin roof and the red gutters she shares with her daughter and finds a sunny spot next to an adjacent rondavel. From there, she has a perfect view of her forlorn vegetable patch, which once contained rows of maize standing taller than her.

Spindly mango and pawpaw trees dot the yard, but these are now crowded by weeds. The neatly organised rows are just a memory. The 80-year-old Chauke used to live off the rewards of her hard work, and was proud of it, too – that is, until the vultures took over in Thohoyandou.

Chauke lives in Hasani Dakari, a tiny village in rural Limpopo, about 40 kilometres south of Thohoyandou and eight kilometres northeast of Vuwani in the Vhembe district. Ka-Mahonisi, where Floyd Shivambu grew up, lies 16 kilometres to the east.

The area once formed part of the 'Republic of Venda', the apartheid 'bantustan' that was initially granted 'self-governing' status and supposedly became nominally independent in 1979. When democracy arrived 15 years later, it filled the area's residents with hope. They could not foresee that a new governing elite would continue to pillage the area (and the new province of Limpopo) while failing spectacularly at governing effectively.

The people in Chauke's neighbourhood predominantly speak Tsonga. They find their way along dirt roads scarred with ditches. The plots are more than 2 000 square metres – big enough for a house, a rondavel and patches of maize, potatoes and mangoes.

Nevertheless, life is tough here for ordinary people. Poverty and the searing African sun compete to wither every last blade of grass. 'Tender-preneurs' in shiny cars with seven-figure price tags dodge potholes, and raw sewage is more commonplace than clean water. Trees are scarce, and the taps often run dry.[232]

Despite all of this, Chauke built a good life. She never went to school, never owned a car and never had a salaried job. She built her life with her bare hands – one *magwinya* (fat cake) at a time. When she talks about those early days, her eyes light up. She could spend the whole day on her feet, walking from house to house without any pain. She earned money by selling vegetables from her garden and sometimes even chickens. She also made and sold offal (tripe), but her biggest seller was *magwinya*.[233]

The hardest challenge was getting the ingredients. When Chauke's supplies ran out and the local spaza shops were also out of stock, she had to travel 40 kilometres to Thohoyandou. For city dwellers, this may sound like a 20-minute drive along tarred roads, but in Hasani Dakari, it's a different picture. There were, and still are, no taxi routes in the area, so Chauke and her neighbours have to walk about three kilometres to the main road and wait for a bus. Travelling to Thohoyandou and back takes a full day.

But she had plenty of energy back then, and she was well rewarded for her efforts. At first, she kept her earnings under a mattress, but her children raided her hiding place. She then found other secret spots: a tree trunk in a field a few hundred metres away where her husband grew crops, or her vegetable patch behind the house.

These didn't work either. Her husband convinced her to bank the money at the post office but later withdrew some of it without her permission. When Chauke complained to a neighbour, she advised her to open a savings account at VBS Mutual Bank in Thohoyandou. It seemed like good advice.

After some hesitation, she put her savings in a mealie sack, went into town, found her way around a strange new institution and returned with a passport-sized blue savings book with the symbol of a white elephant on its cover. She was proud when the tellers returned her empty mealie sack, along with a deposit slip for about R8 000.

Initially, she still hid some money in the garden. But the numbers in her 'white elephant' book also crept upwards. 'I would take R1 500 to the bank one month, and R500 the next,' she remembers. 'It was just money I made from selling *magwinya*, sweets, chicken and vegetables.'

For years, she travelled to Thohoyandou once a month and looked at her growing balance with a sense of pride. Towards the end of 2017, it came to a solid R54 035,81.

Chauke planned to expand her business by acquiring pigs and more chickens. But, by early 2018, she started to hear worrying things on the radio, phrases like 'liquidity crisis' and 'possible fraud'. Her neighbours came over and asked, '*Hayi man*, have you heard?'

She recalls: 'We heard the bank didn't have money any more because some of it was given to Zuma, some to Malema and some to Shivambu. The shock . . . I got very sick . . . I didn't know what to do.'

When the VBS bubble burst, so did her dreams. 'I was so broke, I didn't even have money for mealie meal,' she says. 'I was heartbroken. I felt like an orphan.'

In June 2018, Chauke and other VBS clients heard that they could go to Thohoyandou to collect some of their money.[234] Hundreds of people converged on the bank, and long queues formed. She says no one told them what was happening. She spent two nights sleeping on the stoep. 'We took newspapers and put it on the floor to sleep on,' she says. 'It was June and it was very, very cold.'

In the first two years following the scandal, she lost about 20 kilograms. When we visited her again in December 2023, she walked with difficulty and had lost a number of teeth.

'I used to go to Thohoyandou just to check if indeed VBS is closed. And when I realised it is true, I felt very sad,' Chauke said.

Recognising that, for people like Chauke, the stolen funds were a matter of life and death, the National Treasury – using taxpayer money – moved swiftly to reimburse a total of 17 894 individual depositors for their losses, up to an amount of R100 000 each.

The money was placed in accounts they could access at Nedbank. Depositors who'd had more than R100 000 in their VBS accounts lost the balance. Pensioners' savings and money for children's education had all evaporated.

Chauke eventually did receive her savings in full, but the emotional trauma had a devastating effect on her mental and physical health.

When we last spoke to her in 2023, she had little trust left in the banking system. 'I'm no longer working,' she said. 'I am tired. This thing with VBS has caused me many problems. I have no more strength now. I survive on government money [an old-age pension].'

A story that began differently from Chauke's but also ended in tears is that of Nyawasedza Raphunga. The 78-year-old from Tshikombani in Makhado Local Municipality, about 50 kilometres northwest of Chauke's home, started saving with VBS in the 1980s while employed as a general worker and bricklayer's assistant in the Venda homeland's public works department.

Tshikombani is mountainous, green and fertile. Every backyard boasts at least one mango tree heavy with fruit, and maize crops flourish even on unirrigated land. There is no real urban planning to speak of – scrapyards lie right next to residential homes, a legacy of earlier times when tribal leaders sold land without municipal oversight, according to local residents.

Raphunga's community speak mostly Venda.

She said she 'chose VBS because it was a Venda bank created by our Chief [Patrick] Mphephu to keep our savings. It was especially for the elderly, to make things easy for us.'

When you look for Raphunga, chances are you'll find her in the lush orchard next to her house where she grows mangoes, avocados and citrus fruit. She trims her shrubs into perfectly round lollipop shapes and supports her unemployed children and grandchildren on her old-age pension.

When we visited her in December 2023, a toddler was running around the yard, which was strewn with pairs of Crocs in various sizes and shades of pink. Raphunga laughed and pointed to a pair of black, worn, unbranded Pep store sneakers. Those were hers.

'When we heard VBS was no longer functioning, I was crushed . . . I wondered what would happen to our money. We used to sleep outside there in the queue, aiming to be the first to go [into] the bank. We then saw posts outside on the windows saying VBS had been shut down for good. We were scared that we would lose all our money, and there was nothing we could do. Life without VBS was hard . . . We used to keep our stokvel savings at VBS. I had joined two stokvels and both used VBS.'

Bit by bit, she and her friends got the stokvel money back. 'But it was hard to bury loved ones, because we couldn't get the money we needed for burials. We would get the money in instalments, instead of a full figure.'

She also managed to withdraw all the money in her personal account. But when news of the bank's troubles broke, one of her friends suffered a stroke and died.

'So, some people did die without getting their money,' she explained.

Her own health deteriorated, and she couldn't shake thoughts about the bank's demise. 'People who stole our money, stole it and bought clothes,' she said in 2021. 'It hurt us, because these people were rich already. They took the very little we had and bought fancy items. We were trying to save the little we had for our future.'

The early story of VBS Mutual Bank echoes the origin of Volkskas Beperk, now Absa Bank, which was established in 1934 as a cooperative loan bank. Founded in the wake of the Great Depression, Volkskas (literally, the People's Chest) served impoverished Afrikaners for seven years before registering as a commercial bank. Similarly, VBS Mutual Bank was meant to assist Venda people living in the Venda 'homeland'.

As in other 'homelands', land was held in trust by tribal authorities, which made it difficult for people to get housing loans from commercial banks. To address this need, the Venda Building Society was formed in 1982, with some input from the late VhaVenda chief Patrick Mphephu. In 1992, it was converted into a mutual bank, a cooperative financial institution owned by its depositors.

It was still community-centred, focusing on serving people with modest incomes at lower fees than commercial banks. Among other services, it lent small amounts of money to people to allow them to build houses on communal land. Many VBS depositors were burial societies and stokvels.

But problems loomed. Following the transition to democracy, urbanisation picked up pace and many Venda people moved to the cities and towns, where a much broader range of banking products was available. Banks like Capitec, offering affordable banking options, siphoned away VBS Mutual Bank's clientele, and in 2015 the latter's declining fortunes led to a change in ownership, with devastating consequences.

The story of the collapse of VBS Mutual Bank starts with a son of Venda, Tshifhiwa Matodzi. His parents managed a small general-dealer store near the VBS branch in Thohoyandou.[235] As a schoolboy, he made money by selling paper bags. His proud parents opened an account for him at the building society.

From these humble beginnings, Matodzi went on to become a chartered accountant. He was part of the first cohort of black students admitted to the then Rand Afrikaans University in Johannesburg. Coming home for the holidays in the mid-1990s, it did not escape his notice that the queues in front of VBS Mutual Bank were shrinking every year.

In 2012, he heard from a friend that VBS, probably in a last-ditch attempt to survive, had issued more than 600 000 shares and was recruiting investors. The Public Investment Corporation (PIC), a state-owned asset management firm, held 80 percent of the existing stock, and whoever bought the new shares would become the second-biggest shareholder. Matodzi promptly drove to Thohoyandou and bought 10 000 shares for R100 000. He rounded up some friends, and together they registered Dyambeu Investments to buy the rest of the 600 000 shares. Less than two years later, in July 2015, Matodzi was appointed chair of the VBS board.

One early stroke of genius was to involve the Venda king, Toni Mphephu-Ramabulana, whose uncle had played a role in founding VBS.[236] His royal adviser later remarked that the king was 'clueless' about business matters – which must have suited Matodzi just fine. They gave the VhaVenda Trust, representing the royal family, 51 percent of Dyambeu, helping it to gain respect and legitimacy in traditional communities.

Matodzi dictated syrupy letters claiming that he operated 'under the leadership and guidance of His Majesty', but it was just window-dressing.

He was the one pulling the strings, often managing the bank through WhatsApp messages.

From the moment Dyambeu became a minority shareholder in 2012, Matodzi started issuing instructions to VBS staff – sometimes even dictating which suppliers to use. When he became board chair three years later, his power became near-absolute. He regularly requested, and received, 'loans' from VBS. Once granted, they would not be serviced.

He facilitated astronomical overdrafts to his companies and those of his associates. To keep the secret, many people received bribes described as 'commissions' or 'loans', also never to be paid back. At least once, he ordered that all his VBS debt be expunged, after which he continued to rack up even more debt. Matodzi sat on a pot of gold, and for a while the law, credit policies and liquidity were no impediments.[237]

Predictably, though, the large-scale looting eventually created a cash crunch. Matodzi and his acolytes needed to find new sources of money, and the answer lay in municipal funds. The modus operandi was to coax and bribe local government officials to invest large sums of public money (notably grants from central government) in VBS.

To ensure that 'strategic' officials 'remained biased towards VBS', they were 'actively encouraged' to apply for personal loans at the bank, Matodzi admitted in an explosive affidavit signed and submitted to the prosecuting authority in 2024.[238] These were granted indiscriminately without considering policy or adverse credit profiles. By design, the scheme ensured that municipal officials were 'permanently indebted to VBS'.

Within three years, VBS had effectively become a Ponzi scheme financed by unwitting depositors like Chauke and Raphunga as well as a number of municipalities. When investigators and the bank's liquidator started peeling the layers off the proverbial VBS onion in 2018, they found that more than 50 people had conspired to steal and redistribute at least R2,7 billion[239] from the bank through a complex web of private and public institutions. The money belonged to the most vulnerable people in Limpopo and some of the poorest municipalities in the province, and Matodzi was at the centre of it all.

Mutual banks are prohibited from doing business with municipalities. When VBS did, it did not go unnoticed and was tolerated up to a point.

Eventually, vague tip-offs to the Reserve Bank and National Treasury as well as the growing loan book suggested all was not as it seemed. Skirmishes soon ensued between VBS, the National Treasury and the Reserve Bank. A major development came in August 2017, when the Treasury issued a notice to municipalities to say that they were not permitted to place money with VBS and had to call up any investments made with it.

On 11 March 2018, amid a rapidly growing liquidity crisis, the minister of finance, Nhlanhla Nene, placed VBS under curatorship.[240] By April, the curator, Anoosh Rooplal from SizweNtsalubaGobodo Advisory Services, had started to uncover the disastrous state of affairs at VBS, causing the Reserve Bank to appoint Advocate Terry Motau SC and the law firm Werksmans Attorneys to investigate the bank. A month later, on 17 April, investigators launched a search-and-seizure operation at the VBS corporate office in Rivonia, its head office in Makhado and its Thohoyandou branch. Rooplal eventually recommended that VBS be liquidated, which happened on 13 November. Since then, Rooplal and his team have worked to recoup money owed to the bank and to pay out investors and other legitimate creditors.

Motau released his report on 10 October 2018. As its title, 'The Great Bank Heist', suggests, it did not pull any punches. Comparing the events at VBS to 'the most daring heist in South African banking history' about 40 years before, when R400 000 was stolen but no one was arrested, he said his report would reveal that the 'perpetrators of the heist at VBS [had] made away with almost R2 billion'. Rooplal later found this figure to be at least R2,7 billion.

Motau added: 'I trust that, in this case, arrests will be made.'

Indeed, the arrests began in June 2020, starting with Matodzi and eight of his closest accomplices, followed by more than four dozen others. They were charged with 188 counts of corruption, fraud, money laundering, theft and racketeering.[241]

The bank's chief financial officer, Phillip Truter, pleaded guilty to six counts of racketeering, fraud, corruption and money laundering. He accepted a 10-year jail term, with three years suspended in exchange for cooperating with the state. He spent three years and six months behind bars and was released on parole in April 2024.

In the meantime, Matodzi's world came crashing down. In 2018, he became one of the first role players to be sequestrated. His wife divorced him, and he developed health problems.[242] He lost his luxury cars and helicopter and had to exchange his farms and houses for a small flat in his ex-wife's backyard. He was also unemployable.

In the months after VBS was put under curation, Matodzi maintained for a long time that he 'did not steal anything'.

'We had good intentions. If things did not work out our way, we must bow out with pride.'[243] He claimed VBS was the victim of two powerful forces – a white-owned banking establishment that had no appetite for a black-owned competitor, and a large anti-Zuma faction, angry at VBS for giving the former president a home loan for his Nkandla homestead.[244]

He kept up the bravado and denials for four years. In a dramatic about-turn in July 2024, he pleaded guilty to a litany of charges as part of a plea deal with the state. His plea was set out in an explosive 70-page affidavit, signed on 10 July 2024. Poignantly, he started out by saying: 'I am an unemployed adult male of 46 years . . . the former chairperson of the VBS Mutual Bank and executive chairperson of Vele Investments . . .'

He added: 'I take full responsibility for my actions . . . I am co-operating with the police and prosecution in the hope [of rectifying] my wrongdoings and seeking appropriate consequences for my actions . . . I wish to record and offer my sincere and unconditional apologies to all the victims of my activities which include depositors, shareholders, stakeholders, suppliers, staff and members of the public and South African taxpayers at large . . .'[245]

Matodzi was sentenced to a cumulative 495 years in jail after pleading guilty to 33 charges. The sentences are set to run concurrently, and his jail time is an effective 15 years.

But before all this happened, VBS made a last-ditch effort to avoid curatorship in ways that directly relate to our story.

CHAPTER 15

Banking bombshell

IN EARLY 2018, VBS was swimming in a shrinking and increasingly murky pond. By then, the National Treasury had prohibited any further municipal investments, and it had instructed municipalities that had already invested to withdraw their funds. With the spectre of Reserve Bank intervention looming large, panic gripped the VBS top brass. Curatorship, which would entail independent scrutiny of the VBS books, had to be stopped at all costs. It was time to call in some favours.

They did so apparently by leaking news of the impending curatorship to the EFF, which promptly launched a politically charged 'hands off VBS' campaign. Hours before the Reserve Bank was due to announce the curatorship, Floyd Shivambu, then EFF deputy president, fired off cellphone messages to Nhlanhla Nene, the newly appointed minister of finance, and Dondo Mogajane, at the time the director-general of the National Treasury.[246] Nene later read the message into the record during his testimony at the Zondo Commission.

Shivambu wrote: 'Greetings minister, it looks like VBS will be placed under curatorship mainly due to something that National Treasury had not clarified in terms of the accounts of municipalities which were withdrawn due to National Treasury's instruction. It becomes sad when a black-owned bank gets to be placed under curatorship because of things that can be managed differently. Please assist, because it looks like the whole thing will need your final approval. Regards, Floyd.'

Nene, whose final approval was needed for the curatorship to proceed, later told the Zondo Commission that he had refused to succumb to 'this kind of pressure'. In fact, Nene had found Shivambu's resistance odd, because curatorship was aimed at finding a remedy for the bank's precarious situation. 'If we didn't do this,' he testified, 'come Monday that bank would have collapsed.'

Matodzi, too, tried to scupper the curatorship. On 9 March 2018, he sent a 'personal letter' to the then-registrar of banks, Kuben Naidoo, which was leaked to a little-known and now-defunct blog called Un-censored Opinion.

'From day one,' Matodzi wrote, 'the bank's position was clear that we do not want to break the law. All we were asking of Treasury was to withdraw the letter sent to municipalities, as this was causing a run on the bank.'

He added: 'We are not politicians, we were just doing our job and we did it very well. No matter what happens to the bank and its direction going forward, we will leave the space with our heads held high, knowing that we achieved what was considered impossible. In the end, we were faced with a well-organised and powerful system which does not tolerate growing black banks and black excellence.'

To their credit, no one at the Reserve Bank or the National Treasury lent any weight or credence to Matodzi and Shivambu's racially charged gaslighting. According to a Treasury source, the order to municipalities to withdraw their money indeed caused the bank some difficulties. 'But the MFMA [Municipal Finance Management Act] is clear and the Motau investigation proved that this did not cause the bank's liquidity problems. VBS failed because they [its managers] stole the bank into oblivion,' the source said.

On Sunday 11 March 2018, Nene approved Naidoo's recommen-dation and placed VBS under curatorship, initially 'to nurse the bank back to health'.[247] In doing so, Nene finally ran up against a powerful political enemy.

Along with Nene, Ismail Momoniat, a maths whiz and former univer-sity lecturer who was deputy director at the National Treasury at the time, was targeted. Momoniat has had an illustrious Treasury career and is known by insiders as the 'father' of the Public Finance Management Act and the Municipal Finance Management Act. He was one of the Treasury officials who had instructed municipalities to recall their investments from VBS.

The EFF's offensive began on 20 March 2018 at a meeting of parliament's finance standing committee, called to allow officials from the National Treasury, the Reserve Bank and other regulatory authorities to brief members on the unfolding VBS crisis.

Shivambu – a committee member – said he had spoken to the Venda king, who was a shareholder in VBS, and suggested inviting him to brief the committee on a 'more holistic perspective on the bank's situation'. The factors that had led to the bank's collapse should be 'fully interrogated' to restore its 'financial stability'.

He added that the curatorship had not been undertaken with 'due diligence', and that a 'reckless Reserve Bank' had not analysed the consequences of its actions. He asked whether the minister of finance had given the go-ahead for the bank to be placed under curatorship or whether it had been a 'knee-jerk response' by the Reserve Bank.[248]

At a follow-up briefing on 30 May, Shivambu questioned various aspects of the National Treasury's conduct and declared that the curatorship had primarily resulted from the 'negligence of Treasury and lacklustre prudential oversight by the Registrar of Banks'. He also declared: 'If there was any wrongdoing, those involved should be dealt with decisively and be prosecuted if need be.' Given what was to follow, he might well have later regretted saying this.

Shivambu also attacked Momoniat, accusing him of corruption and being anti-African.

During the parliamentary discussions, Momoniat said that, in interactions with the National Treasury, VBS figures had acted as if the bank was 'politically untouchable and enjoyed protection . . . Their arrogance was unbelievable.' To Momoniat, it even appeared as if 'some members within the committee were lobbying to stop the curatorship', he told parliament.

He had clearly touched a nerve. On 5 June, he briefed the finance committee on the unrelated matter of former SARS commissioner Tom Moyane's decimation of the revenue service. In an outburst, Shivambu asked why the National Treasury was always represented by Momoniat when it had an African director-general, adding that it seemed like there were 'deliberate attempts to undermine African leadership in National Treasury'.

In a media interview later the same day, Shivambu said he could not see why Momoniat had to attend all finance committee meetings, whether they dealt with the Reserve Bank, tax matters or the transformation of the financial sector. 'I think he undermines Africans,' Shivambu said. 'He does not take the director-general, finance minister or the deputy finance minister seriously. He thinks he is superior to them. He takes all the decisions, and he is always here in parliament as if he is National Treasury alone.'[249]

Shivambu was sharply rebuked in the meeting, and Momoniat and the director-general of the National Treasury, Dondo Mogajane, also took umbrage to his remarks. Momoniat, who has an illustrious anti-apartheid history, told *Business Day*[250] that he had grown up in a tradition of fighting for nonracialism, and that he rejected any attempt to target people based on race.

Momoniat then lobbed his own grenade, offering to 'take a lifestyle audit from the day I was born' and inviting Shivambu 'to join me in taking a lifestyle audit'.

Shivambu never accepted this offer.

In the days that followed, acting SARS commissioner Mark Kingon suggested that some SARS officials who had been purged during Moyane's horrific reign should be reinstated – and the EFF ramped up their resistance.

Julius Malema had a particular stake in the matter. Some of these purged officials had been directly involved in the 2012 On-Point case.

On 5 July, during a media briefing at EFF headquarters, Malema touched on a range of issues, including the fate of the suspended Moyane.

In a stunning departure from his 2012 stance that blamed Jacob Zuma for his tax woes, Malema redirected his ire towards Pravin Gordhan, at the time the minister of public enterprises, dubbing him the 'real president of South Africa'.[251]

'I became corrupt in this country the day I challenged Pravin's appointment. I said to Zuma, "Why do you keep appointing minorities to the economic cluster to the exclusion of black Africans?" That day, I was declared an enemy, and stupidly enough, I had my own problems with SARS and that's where they got me . . . If you want to die politically, touch Pravin.'

Just two years before this outburst, Malema had energetically defended Gordhan, then serving as minister of finance, against Zuma.

Malema had a fraught history with Gordhan going back to the latter's involvement in cutting off patronage networks in Limpopo. The National Treasury ensured that the cabinet placed the province under partial administration in late 2011, during Gordhan's first stint as finance minister and before he and Zuma fell out. Gordhan was also seen to be Momoniat's close ally. The EFF, reviving old conspiracy theories from the late anti-apartheid era, painted the two men as part of an 'Indian cabal'.

The EFF eventually found a weapon to use against Nene, minister of finance at the time, too. In early October 2018, he acknowledged before the Zondo Commission that he had met the notorious Gupta family multiple times at the height of 'state capture' between 2009 and 2014, including at one of their businesses, Sahara Computers, and at their Saxonwold compound – ground zero for their many corrupt schemes.

The issue was that Nene's testimony contradicted statements that he had made during an eNCA interview in 2016, when he'd said: 'Look, I bumped into them at public gatherings once or twice, but I've never had an engagement and I've never been asked by them to do anything for them.' He also did not tell President Cyril Ramaphosa about the meetings.[252]

The EFF threatened that, unless he resigned, they would expose his son's alleged unlawful dealings with the PIC while Nene had chaired the institution. To this day, the EFF has offered no evidence whatsoever for its claims, and Nene has strongly denied that his family benefited from state money. However, his contradictory statements about the Guptas left him on the defensive. He later told Zondo that the EFF could not afford to have the National Treasury, SARS and the Reserve Bank doing their jobs effectively.[253]

The politics turned against Nene, and Ramaphosa announced the minister's resignation on 9 October 2018.

A day later, the National Treasury released the Motau report. The findings were stunning: the bank managers, directors, auditors and politicians had looted the bank into insolvency. Curator-turned-liquidator Anoosh Rooplal later found that at least R2,7 billion was missing.

But the report contained another bombshell. It listed 27 'persons of interest' who had received 'gratuitous' payments from VBS. Among them, in 17th place, was Brian Shivambu – Floyd's younger brother – who was found to have received at least R16,1 million. The addition of a partial drawdown of a business loan later increased this total to about R18,2 million.

The same evening, the EFF spokesperson Mbuyiseni Ndlozi released an uncharacteristically tame media statement that read: 'The EFF reiterates its position that all who are responsible and illegally benefited from the fraud must be criminally prosecuted immediately . . . The law enforcement agency must do all they can to ensure that all the money that can be recovered must be paid back in full, including attaching properties of the individuals who benefited from the defrauding of VBS . . .'

The next day, on 11 October, *Daily Maverick* reported that the VBS money had gone to a company called Sgameka Projects, owned by Brian but seemingly a conduit for money channelled from VBS to Floyd. Of this, R10 million had gone into the latter's personal account, and R1,3 million had been passed on to the EFF.[254]

In a statement released by Floyd, Brian vehemently denied that he had benefited from the VBS bank heist. He said Sgameka Projects was appointed to provide 'professional consulting services' in mining and insurance to a company called Vele Investments.[255]

He insisted that Sgameka never received any payments from VBS. However, it became evident that he lacked the expertise to consult on mining and insurance and failed to appoint anyone with the necessary qualifications. The statement appears to have been another attempt to obscure the truth.

When the Shivambu brothers released this statement, the Motau report had already found that VBS and Vele were a 'single criminal enterprise, with Matodzi at the helm'. Vele topped Motau's list of the recipients of 'gratuitous payments' at just under R1 billion, followed by Matodzi at R325 million.

Reacting to the *Daily Maverick* report, Floyd vociferously denied ever taking money from VBS, saying 'there's never been any R10 million that came into my account' and that it was 'pure insanity . . . madness of people who want to say that we received R10 million.'[256]

He also challenged *Daily Maverick* to 'bring the proof'.

At an EFF press conference, a relatively subdued Malema said Shivambu had shown his financial statements from as far back as 2014 to party members, and there was no evidence that the party's deputy president had unduly benefited from the scandal. There were exchanges of money between Brian, Floyd, their brother Lucky and their parents, but 'that's how siblings exchange things'. This ignored the glaring fact that most of the money flowing from Brian to Floyd had come from VBS-linked companies.

The party could not act against Shivambu, Malema said, as there was no valid evidence against him. 'There must be prima facie evidence. In the absence of such, there is nothing we can do.'

According to Malema, a preliminary investigation showed that the EFF had not received any money from Brian Shivambu's companies, Sgameka Projects and Grand Azania.

The EFF condemned the VBS looting but added that some of those who had been implicated wanted to challenge the Motau report, and it would be 'premature to judge anyone's guilt'.

Malema blamed the media and factions in the ANC for putting the EFF in the spotlight over the issue. 'Let's be fair. That's what we're asking. Corruption must not be covered up. Corruption must be fought, but please let's be fair,' he said, ignoring the fact that Motau's report was an official, evidence-based investigation. He also appeared to overlook the baseless nature of the EFF's own allegations against Nene's son just days before.

In characteristic Malema fashion, he reframed the allegations against the EFF as a politically motivated attack in which he, Floyd and the party were the victims.

He questioned why the Reserve Bank was not being criticised for not stopping the looting at VBS sooner, why Limpopo ANC officials had not been held to the same level of criticism, and why Brian Shivambu had become the face of the saga while many ANC municipal officials weren't being publicly held to account.

'You leave all the public representatives, you go after one young man who holds no office at all,' he said, adding: 'You want to create the impression that our deputy president was in the Motau report. We see it for what it is. Its intention is to discredit the EFF and make sure the EFF loses support in 2019.'

Next up was a finance standing committee meeting on 7 November. This time, Floyd stayed in the background, and the EFF cudgel was taken up by its spokesperson, MP Mbuyiseni Ndlozi. According to a record of the meeting, he said the Motau report 'did not read like a very good legal document' and contained a 'lot of fiction'.[257]

Again questioning the 'quick decision' to liquidate VBS, he said it was 'very odd that the Reserve Bank did not want to save a black bank' in the way that many others had.

In response, Motau – who was present – said people being named would soon be given the chance to defend themselves in court. Regarding the style, he said events at the bank had affected the 'poorest of the poor', and he had written the report so that it could be understood by people on the street. 'If that constitutes fiction and is a ground for review, again, let the courts decide,' he said.

Ndlozi dismissed Motau's responses as 'patronising and dishonest', describing them as provocative. The poor, he said, knew how to read. Following the lead of Malema and Floyd, Ndlozi asked whether Motau had met Gordhan or Treasury officials, including Momoniat, while working on the report.

Motau denied any undue influence on his findings. In subsequent years, other EFF members joined the fray, trying to shield their leaders from scrutiny and repercussions.

The EFF's vigorous denials, counter-accusations and targeting of journalists, officials and others ultimately backfired. Journalists succeeded in 'bringing the proof', as Floyd Shivambu demanded.

Our data – including bank statements and documents, contracts, WhatsApp messages and the official forensic reports on VBS – show that Matodzi and his accomplices moved VBS money to three captive entities: Vele Investments, Malibongwe Petroleum and Robvet.[258] Matodzi chaired both VBS and Vele and was a majority shareholder in VBS, while

Malibongwe, which was a supposed client of VBS, received at least R40 million in fictitious deposits. Motau identified the Robvet account as a 'slush fund', largely used to bribe municipal officials and conceal questionable payments. All the money disbursed by these three companies was effectively the proceeds of crime, he found.

Central to our story is that these three accounts unlawfully channelled VBS cash to Sgameka Projects, which served as a slush fund for Floyd Shivambu, Malema and the EFF. There was no legitimate business reason for the payments to Sgameka – a fact first established in Matodzi's 2017 WhatsApp messages to VBS treasurer Phophi Mukhodobwane and later reconfirmed in his 2024 affidavit, in which he said the cash was intended to secure the EFF's support and cooperation.

From there, payments were made to Grand Azania, also ostensibly owned by Brian Shivambu but effectively a slush fund for Floyd, and Mahuna Investments, ostensibly owned by Julius Malema's cousin Matsobane Phaleng but in reality a front for Malema. Our financial analysis shows the ultimate beneficiaries of the VBS cash were Floyd and Malema, while the EFF benefited, too.

None of the three companies – Grand Azania, Mahuna and Sgameka – appeared to conduct any legitimate business activities. Despite claims by Brian Shivambu and others that Sgameka was a bona fide consultancy, scrutiny revealed otherwise. It had no business premises, employed no staff, showed no business expenses and failed to pay taxes when due, both our analysis and SARS court documents show. Sgameka was created solely to act as a conduit for funnelling money from VBS.

SARS eventually liquidated Grand Azania and at the time of writing received a court order to wind up Sgameka due to unpaid taxes. Meanwhile, Mahuna – after being exposed by *Daily Maverick* as a front company for Malema – changed its name to Rosario Investment, became defunct a year later and was eventually deregistered.

In the Grand Azania liquidation application, SARS investigators did not mince their words, stating that Sgameka Projects has been 'utilised by its director and only shareholder, Brian Shivambu, as the [vehicle] through which he defrauded the VBS Mutual Bank of approximately R16 million'.

The Reserve Bank's investigations (including the Motau report and supporting analyses by Crowe Forensics) centred on the period from 1 March 2015 – the start of the financial year in which Matodzi assumed control of VBS – to 17 June 2018. These inquiries primarily traced the major outflows of cash from the bank, following the money largely to its initial and sometimes second recipients.

Over time, however, the authors of this book and other investigative journalists continued to follow the money to entities and people further along the chain. The periods of these investigations don't always align with the Motau report, but a coherent picture emerges.

Essentially, between February 2017 and February 2018, Sgameka received R16,1 million from VBS-linked companies. This included a home loan of R1,24 million, used to buy a house for the Shivambus' parents. Additionally, Grand Azania received a R4-million business loan to renovate a restaurant and wine bar in Soweto, of which it managed to draw down R2,1 million before the bank imploded. The total in VBS cash and loans paid out to Brian's companies came to about R18,2 million.

During this period, Sgameka paid R5,16 million to Grand Azania, R4,8 million to Mahuna Investments and R1,3 million directly to the EFF. Smaller payments flowed to EFF service providers.

In what was probably a moment of carelessness, Sgameka also paid R180 000 into Floyd's personal FNB account. Grand Azania, in turn, also sent about R3,6 million to Floyd's personal account.

Bank statements further show that whoever held the Sgameka bank card withdrew R1 000 in cash (the maximum allowed amount at the time on the account) every few days after VBS had been placed under curatorship – up to June 2018, when the account was finally frozen.

While Sgameka's income came entirely from VBS-linked companies, Grand Azania also received funds from other businessmen and companies in Floyd's network. Between November 2016 and August 2018, R15,6 million was paid into Grand Azania's account. This included R5,16 million from Sgameka, at least R700 000 from businessman Lawrence Mulaudzi,[259] and R300 000 from businesswoman Savannah Maziya-Danson, appointed in 2023 as eSwatini's minister of information, communication and technology.

The cash mainly funded Floyd's personal expenses, including his wedding in April 2017, the purchase of luxury vehicles, and construction work and staff salaries at Sud Restaurant and wine bar in Soweto, bank records show.

Between May 2017 and January 2019, Mahuna received an eye-watering R12,2 million, of which R4,8 million came from Sgameka and R500 000 from Grand Azania. The balance came from other people in Malema's network, notably R3,75 million from the Tshwane entrepreneur Hendrick Kganyago[260] and R500 000 from Afrirent, a company linked to a fleet-supply scandal in the City of Johannesburg.

Mahuna's money was spent on the EFF, and covered Malema's personal expenses, including extravagant shopping sprees and real estate investments such as Mekete – his boutique lodge outside Polokwane. We discuss these in Chapter 20.

Despite everything that investigators and journalists had uncovered, an important piece of the puzzle was missing. When and how were the EFF leaders linked to VBS?

It is rare for insiders to speak out against Malema. In April 2019, EFF MP Thembinkosi Rawula – who lost his place on the party's list for the National Assembly – became an exception to the rule when he very publicly criticised the leadership. In an angry Facebook post around the time he resigned, the senior EFF leader wrote that Malema 'in the most recent CCT [central command team] meeting admitted to EFF taking VBS money to finance the revolution'.

With reference to Malema and Shivambu, the post also stated entirely in dramatic capital letters: 'EFF REMAINS A FINANCIAL FISHING NET FOR THE PAIR, AN ANTITHESIS OF EVERYTHING IT [PURPORTS TO BE]. I AM NOW UNLEASHED, WHO CARES?'

Rawula signed off with: 'Bring it on, insult me. Bloody crooks.'

Malema took Rawula to court, demanding a public apology or R1 million in damages. Rawula eventually deleted his Facebook post but stood his ground against Malema in the Eastern Cape Division of the High Court, sitting in Gqeberha. The case became a classic David-versus-Goliath battle. One of Rawula's key advantages was that another EFF MP could corroborate his story.

A week after Rawula's Facebook post went live, EFF MP Zolile Roger Xalisa resigned from the party in a three-page letter starting: 'Dear Julius and your surrogates . . .'

'On 5 to 6 February 2019 the CCT convened its ordinary meeting of the term,' Xalisa wrote. 'The President and the CIC of the EFF during the political overview made an admission that the EFF had received donations from VBS, which is the subject of corruption. He said that no capitalist or government is willing to support a revolutionary movement like EFF, so VBS saw an opportunity that the EFF could be in government, it could assist to ensure that it thrives better. Then . . . the President confirmed that they could not receive the donation with [the] EFF account of theirs but had to devise other means.

'He said sometimes you must kiss dogs or [the] devil to get money. After this . . . CCT members were invited to speak on the impact. All CCT members were present and [some] MPCs, MPs and councillors could also attest [and were] given [an] opportunity.'

Malema lost the defamation case in the High Court. He appealed, but that ended with the Supreme Court of Appeal dismissing his case.

So, when Matodzi finally spilled the beans in July 2024 when he entered into a plea deal with the state, the VBS loot became Malema and Shivambu's recurring nightmare.[261]

As part of the legal process, Matodzi wrote a startling 70-page affidavit that described the gradual hollowing-out of VBS in considerable detail.

The affidavit devoted two pages to Malema and Shivambu. Matodzi admitted that he bought the EFF's silence over a 2016 home loan of R7,8 million to former president Jacob Zuma. Ironically, VBS gave Zuma the loan 'to pay back the money' for upgrades at his Nkandla homestead, as ordered by the Public Protector, Thuli Madonsela, and loudly demanded by Malema and the EFF. In fact, it was the EFF who spearheaded the important constitutional case that found Zuma had breached his duties by failing to implement the Public Protector's report.

Matodzi said he first met Malema and Shivambu after the 'EFF had started a campaign' against VBS over the loan to Zuma. Much of the 'negative publicity' over the Zuma loan had been whipped up by the EFF. As a result, Matodzi asked to meet Malema and was invited to 'the EFF's penthouse' in Sandton around April or May 2017, he wrote. The EFF does not own a penthouse in Sandton, but some of Malema's benefactors do.

Both Malema and Floyd Shivambu were present. Matodzi explained that, as 'black brothers', the constituencies of the EFF and VBS overlapped and had to be supported. To cement this relationship, he proposed that VBS would 'donate R5 million immediately once a bank account has been opened at VBS and [additionally pay] R1 million per month to the EFF'.

After that first meeting, Matodzi and Floyd remained in contact, and the Shivambu brothers opened a VBS business account for Sgameka Projects, linked to Brian Shivambu. Floyd sent him the company details, Matodzi said, and the first payment of R5 million to Sgameka was made on 8 June 2017, followed by several smaller ones.

Matodzi then wrote: 'Myself, Julius and Floyd understood that concept of donation to mean gratification, hence Floyd and Julius did not provide me with [the] EFF's own banking details for these "donations".'

Gratification is a legal term for an improper benefit received in return for a quid pro quo. South Africa's Prevention and Combating of Corrupt Activities Act defines corruption broadly as any instance of a person giving or accepting any 'gratification' that aims to induce someone to act in a manner that is unlawful, dishonest, or amounts to an abuse of authority or breach of trust. Examples of gratification include gifts, cash, loans, the cancellation of debt, a job or property.[262]

Stripped of legalese, Matodzi's statement effectively said that he had bribed Malema and Shivambu into not making a noise about Zuma's Nkandla loan.

In subsequent meetings 'between Julius, Floyd and myself', the politicians wanted even more cash. 'Julius and Floyd informed me that they needed funding to renovate an EFF restaurant called Grand Azania in Soweto,' Matodzi wrote. He told them to apply for a loan.

At VBS, the concept of 'loans' was loosely applied to describe funds flowing out of the bank. Some recipients, like Grand Azania, were hardly expected to repay these loans. Motau characterised these transactions as thinly veiled bribes.

Matodzi further recalled 'several' meetings at Floyd's rented home in Bryanston after the bank had collapsed. It was where he met Brian for the first time. The three men 'agreed amongst [themselves]' to 'regularise the R5 million, plus R1 million monthly donations'.

They drafted and backdated a contract that made it seem like Sgameka did consulting work on petroleum and storage facilities for the VBS-linked company Vele Investments. Matodzi's affidavit directly contradicts Brian's version that he 'consulted' for Vele on mining and insurance.

'The signatories to that contract were myself, representing Vele, and Brian, who was representing Sgameka,' Matodzi's statement read.

The legal word for what Matodzi describes here is 'uttering'. This entails the unlawful and intentional use of a false or forged document to prejudice someone else.[263]

Appearing on pay-TV channel Newzroom Afrika on 14 July 2024, four days after Matodzi's plea deal and affidavit became public, former EFF national chairperson Dali Mpofu suddenly claimed the party had 'never denied' receiving donations from VBS, arguing this was neither irregular nor illegal. 'There is no political party that does not receive donations,' he said.

Mpofu's astonishing statement directly contradicted an earlier denial by Malema, during a radio interview on 18 April 2019 with the late Eusebius McKaiser, when he said that 'no VBS money has flowed into our coffers',[264] while Floyd had asserted 'categorically and clearly, without any fear of contradiction' in parliament on 23 October 2018 that 'the EFF and ourselves as members of parliament never benefited anything from the VBS Mutual Bank looting and the so-called heist that happened there'.[265]

Moreover, Mpofu argued, donations could be made through any vehicle or channel. 'Where is the corruption? Where's the fraud? Where's the money laundering? We are tired of having to say the same thing about this,' he said, claiming that the allegations stemmed from the media's 'political bias'.

Malema himself was confronted with Matodzi's affidavit at a Progressive Caucus briefing a few days later.[266] He adopted a markedly different stance from that of Mpofu, claiming that the affidavit was fraudulent and that he was the target of a political conspiracy.

'There is no Matodzi affidavit,' Malema declared. 'That is sponsored propaganda that is aimed at intimidating and defocusing the EFF . . . No leader of the EFF received VBS money. No EFF received a VBS money. Matodzi never alleges in his affidavit that the money was given to the EFF or the leadership of the EFF.

'In Matodzi's affidavit, which is unbelievable and we dispute . . . is [the claim] that the money was given to a Sgameka. Sgameka money which we never disputed. And Sgameka confirmed he [sic] received the money. To an extent that Sgameka was called by the curators of VBS and Sgameka reached an agreement . . . to pay back the loan they took from VBS . . . that loan has since been paid . . . So there is no one even in Sgameka who has eaten the money of *gogos* [grandmothers].'[267]

Even in Matodzi's version of events, Malema said, Sgameka had not solicited a bribe or asked for a donation. 'He says he offered . . . and he doesn't say the money went to the EFF or EFF leadership, but to Sgameka . . . which had contracts with [Vele and VBS] . . . and it's on the basis of that contract that the curators accepted that settlement of Sgameka.' He added that 'the matter is closed'.

In vintage Malema style, he turned the VBS affair into a demonstration of media bias and a political conspiracy. 'White corruption is not spoken about . . . You are trying to use us in relation to VBS to give corruption a black face . . . which we refuse . . .'

It was a bravura performance – and a profoundly disingenuous one. Among Malema's omissions was the fact that the liquidator of Vele had reached a settlement with Sgameka over R4,55 million, while the liquidator of VBS had clawed back the home and business loans, plus interest. The balance of the R18,2 million was not repaid.

The cash was also not as innocent as Malema portrayed. In an agreement with the Vele liquidator – one that Brian tried to keep secret but which we have since seen – he admitted that there was no legal basis for the cash Sgameka received.[268]

Brian persistently pleaded poverty in his attempts to avoid repayment of his VBS debts. However, just as he faced sequestration – a court procedure that would have triggered a thorough investigation into the destination of the funds – an unknown benefactor settled his debt.

Malema's assertion that money was repaid, which, he seemed to argue, legitimised the money flows, was a fallacy. Under South Africa's anti-corruption legislation, returning stolen money does not erase the original criminal act; at best, it may be considered a mitigating factor during sentencing.

Moreover, his argument overlooks the findings of SARS's liquidation processes, which uncovered fraud and tax evasion.

While Malema acknowledged, perhaps for the first time, that Sgameka had received money from VBS, he continued to ignore the elephant in the room – the issue of where the money went thereafter.

CHAPTER 16

The life of Brian

THE YEAR 2017 was a difficult one for the VBS chair, Tshifhiwa Matodzi. VBS's finances proved to be a perpetual headache, and he was struggling to keep the ship afloat.[269] There were plenty of panicky WhatsApp messages between him and the bank's treasurer, Phophi Mukhodobwane, who often told Matodzi they were running out of money.

A number of factors contributed to the eventual demise of VBS, including the selfishness and greed of its principal actors. The Motau report found that Matodzi himself had looted an astonishing R325,8 million from the bank, using the money to live the high life and to bribe a network of auditors, lawyers, directors, politicians and fixers. Through his company Vele Investments and its affiliates, nearly R1 billion was stolen. Ever larger sums of money were needed to cover the hole in VBS's finances.

This is how Matodzi and Mukhodobwane came to spend 2017 looking for politically connected fixers who could convince large depositors – such as municipalities and state-owned entities – to invest with VBS. The criticism and political turmoil that damaged the bank's reputation only compounded their challenges.

On 8 June 2017, one minute after midday, Matodzi sent the following WhatsApp to Mukhodobwane: 'Please trf R5m into this account from Malibongwe [Petroleum Pty Ltd] and pledge 4m sk that R1m is available. this is an extremely strategic account [sic].'[270] Along with this message, Matodzi sent the bank account number for Sgameka Projects. With his habitual lack of attention to detail, he mistakenly referred to 'Sgameka Trading', but it was in fact the bank account number of Sgameka Projects,

194

with Floyd Shivambu's younger brother, Brian, listed as its sole owner and director.

Later that same day, R5 million reflected in the Sgameka Projects account at VBS Mutual Bank – the first payment it had ever received. It had done no work for VBS and had not provided any invoice.

This was the first of at least seven occasions on which Matodzi became the Shivambus' and Malema's blesser. Up to December 2017, he personally ordered payments totalling R9,55 million to be made to Sgameka – all in slightly cryptic WhatsApp messages. 'Sgameka R1m', Matodzi would text Mukhodobwane. Or 'Pls trf R 600k to sgameka [sic]', 'Pls trf 1m frm malibongwe to sgameka projects [sic]', and 'Pls also do 1m to sgameka [sic]'.

In October 2017, four months after the first payment, a WhatsApp message from Matodzi to Mukhodobwane suggested that the payments were solicited. 'Pls add 600 k to Sgameka they are undr immense pressure [sic],' Matodzi wrote. Seventeen minutes later, Mukhodobwane replied with 'done'.

It is not clear what exactly the 'immense pressure' he referred to entailed, but within 24 hours of Sgameka receiving the R600 000, it sent the entire sum in two payments to Mahuna Investments, Malema's slush fund. Soon after, Mahuna paid at least R100 000 of the VBS cash into the EFF's bank account and spent more than R100 000 on travel costs, which might also have benefited the party.

The last payment Matodzi ordered to Sgameka Projects suggested a quid pro quo. On 28 December 2017, he sent this WhatsApp message to Mukhodobwane: 'Nndaa can we do 350k for sgameka. Those are lobbying fees [sic].'

Given that Matodzi was the chair of the board of VBS Mutual Bank – essentially a non-executive position – he should never have authorised payments to individual banking clients in the first place. Moreover, there is no evidence of a legitimate working relationship between Sgameka Projects and VBS. Instead, he was simply disbursing depositors' money the bank was meant to have ring-fenced.

As recorded before, Sgameka's legal owner, Brian Shivambu, claimed the company did 'consulting work' in mining and insurance linked to

Vele.[271] From the published and confidential forensic material gathered by the Reserve Bank team and SARS, as well as additional research by investigative journalists, key facts about Sgameka have emerged that contradict Brian's claims.

First, Sgameka never seemed to have 'consulted'. There were no records of any company employees doing so. Moreover, Brian seemed to lack the training and expertise to provide consulting services in the highly specialised fields of mining and insurance. His LinkedIn profile suggested his education focused on local government finance,[272] but whether this was true remains unclear.

The company's registered address was Brian's own house – an ordinary face-brick dwelling he rented in the Pretoria suburb of Akasia. This did not seem to fit the picture of a mining and insurance consultancy pocketing millions of rand in fees.

Another oddity is that Brian only mentioned doing 'consulting' work for Vele Investments. But in the eight months between 8 June 2017 and 5 February 2018, Sgameka received R14 262 653,24, mainly from Malibongwe Petroleum and Robvet, in addition to Vele Investments. The Motau/Werksmans report described these as either 'slush funds' or apparently legitimate companies puffed up with 'fictitious deposits'.

Then there was the purpose of the company's loans: a housing loan of R1,46 million, used to buy a house in Krugersdorp for the Shivambus' parents, and a 'business loan' of R4 million, of which R2,1 million was used before VBS imploded.

Sgameka's expenses showed no sign of legitimate business activities one would expect of a functioning company. Specifically, there was no indication of transactions related to salaries, office rent, office equipment, auditing and legal fees, tax payments, vehicles or other travel expenses.

The most indicative factor is that, barring small sums, Brian was not the ultimate beneficiary of the company's riches. Notably, Sgameka paid R5,16 million to Floyd Shivambu's slush fund, Grand Azania, and R4,8 million to Julius Malema's slush fund, Mahuna Investments. Sgameka Projects also paid a total of R1 243 640 into two EFF bank accounts at Standard Bank.

Additionally, Sgameka Projects paid R680 000 towards the purchase of a black Range Rover for Floyd from a dealership in Sandton, and R388 078 'in favour of N.F. Shivambu' to Wesbank as a partial payment for a second vehicle. Only R289 756 of the millions flowing into Sgameka appears to have made it to Brian – from the company he supposedly owned and managed.[273]

As our investigation and the forensic reports made clear, Sgameka was a shell – a conduit for moving money from VBS to Shivambu and Malema. There was no sign of any attempt to build and maintain a viable business. The cash went out as soon as it came in. The funds flowing into Sgameka were the proceeds of crime – as was the money flowing out of it.

In 2017, the Shivambu brothers were swimming in VBS cash. This might have explained why, in a moment of carelessness, R180 000 flowed from Sgameka Projects into Floyd Shivambu's private FNB account in 2017. It was a mistake he would come to regret six years down the line. But more about that later.

Eventually, Brian Shivambu and Sgameka ran into trouble on two fronts: the VBS liquidators and SARS. From March 2018, VBS liquidator Anoosh Rooplal stopped cash flowing out of VBS and set about recovering as much as possible of the looted R2,7 billion and other assets.

He also took steps to recover the two loans made to Sgameka. In a move typical of the VBS scam, the instalments had not been paid and no one at the bank had made a fuss about it. According to court papers, Sgameka had accrued 'significant arrears'.

Brian was held liable for the liquidator's legal costs, too – and his troubles didn't stop there. Around the same time in late 2019, Vele liquidator Richard Pollock started an insolvency inquiry aimed at re-couping some of its irregular disbursements.

Brian and his lawyer, Victor Nkhwashu, were called before a hearing to explain the payments of R4,55 million from Vele to Sgameka Projects. Brian's narrative of doing 'consulting work' unravelled because he could not produce any contracts, invoices or tangible output. Famously, in the course of the hearings, Brian suddenly lost his ability to speak English. A transcript of the proceedings shows he believed he was being denied the right to testify in Xitsonga, while the presiding judge, Brian Southwood, believed he was unduly delaying proceedings in a situation where a 'simple' explanation about the cash flows was required. At the time, Nkhwashu still tried to argue that the R4,55 million was legitimate – a claim that Southwood questioned.

Brian was so riled up by Southwood's scepticism that he applied for the latter's recusal. But he was on a losing ticket. In an about-turn, Brian signed a secret 'acknowledgment of debt' on 23 March 2020 for R4,55 million in favour of Vele Investments. Revealingly, the agreement stated that there was 'no underlying basis' for this payment, and it had to be repaid.[274]

It also included a secrecy clause, inserted at the insistence of Brian's lawyer, to prohibit the parties from disclosing the existence of the agreement and its terms. But, once it had been submitted in court, it became known in any case.

Their efforts were understandable. By admitting that there was 'no underlying basis' for the payments from Vele Investments, Brian effectively acknowledged that the 'consulting' was a ruse and that there had been no legal reason for the payment of R4,55 million.

Brian Shivambu also ran up against the taxman. He had never registered Grand Azania and Sgameka as taxpayers, nor did he pay any tax. So, SARS slapped Brian with a combined income tax and VAT bill of R28,2 million for the 2017 and 2018 tax years, owed by Sgameka Projects and Grand Azania. The total amount included understatement penalties of 200 percent as well as interest. When he failed to pay, SARS applied to have both companies liquidated.

The application to wind up Grand Azania was lodged on 6 August 2021. In a founding affidavit, an official in the SARS unit for criminal and illicit economic activities described Shivambu's conduct as 'obstructive' because he tried to intentionally evade paying tax and then failed to cooperate with the investigation.

He recounted a long process in which Brian had simply ignored SARS and then continued to delay the process in various ways. The company was 'hopelessly insolvent' and unable to pay its debts.

Shivambu used his companies 'as the vehicles through which he defrauded the VBS Mutual Bank', SARS told the court.

Brian Shivambu contested the assessments and how they had been calculated. He claimed Grand Azania had been a 'fully operational events management and catering business' that had run a 'fully fledged' restaurant on Vilakazi Street in Soweto. Establishing and running the restaurant had involved a range of expenses.

He claimed that the company had, in fact, made a loss in 2017 and 2018 and therefore did not owe SARS any taxes.

SARS rejected the invoices and supporting documents because they had no influence on the tax calculations. Some 'invoices were not valid VAT invoices' and did not qualify for deductions, SARS argued in its court documents.

Grand Azania was finally wound up on 24 April 2023.

SARS pursued the liquidation of Sgameka along similar lines but was impeded when Brian unexpectedly submitted income tax and VAT returns in October 2021.

Brian also 'sold' the Krugersdorp house where their parents lived to Floyd Shivambu for R1,46 million, SARS told the court, despite instructions not to trade in the company's assets.

Curiously, the sales agreement between the Shivambu brothers includes no payment schedule and merely states that Floyd should pay Brian within 'a reasonable time'. SARS contended that Brian would have to clarify before the court whether Floyd paid for the property.

Despite the delays, SARS argued that Sgameka remained hopelessly insolvent. In May 2025, Sgameka was provisionally wound up.

Today, Brian Shivambu still seems to be in business in Polokwane, and he appears to maintain two Facebook pages. On one of these pages, he provides no personal or business details but is involved in a series of glitzy commercial events called All Black Parties. A photo shows him dressed in black leather and seemingly lighting a cigar, with a party-goer holding a whisky bottle by the neck in the background. The second Facebook page says he now lives in Pretoria.

If you run into him somewhere, he will vociferously deny ever having been the VBS bagman for his brother Floyd and Julius Malema. He bridles at any suggestion that Grand Azania and Sgameka Projects grew fat on the money of Venda pensioners and local governments serving poor communities in Limpopo and elsewhere – and he might threaten you with legal action.

CHAPTER 17

Loans for show

IN OCTOBER 2017, elderly couple Constance and Elias Shivambu moved into a house in Mindalore, a suburb outside Krugersdorp on the West Rand. The Tuscan-style home had three bedrooms, a study and two bathrooms, a large outside entertainment area and a pool. The 1 000-square-metre plot also housed three garages and additional water tanks, all behind high walls. The security features included an alarm system linked to closed-circuit TV.

Their good fortune, it turns out, came at the expense of VBS clients back home, notably involving the transfer of VBS money to Sgameka Projects.

Company bank statements reflect the first illicit payment of R5 million from VBS-linked Malibongwe Petroleum on 8 June 2017. Soon after, the Shivambus had started house-hunting on the West Rand. They had settled on one of the most desirable houses in the area, which the elder Shivambus 'adored', sources say. In September 2017, Floyd had signed an offer to purchase of R1,46 million to be paid in cash.

But the Shivambu brothers had other expenses. Floyd wanted to start a new business in Soweto, went on expensive shopping sprees and had to send some money to Malema's Mahuna Investments.

So, Brian asked VBS for a home loan instead. He did not qualify for a loan of R1,46 million, even from VBS, and after a credit check, he was classified as 'very high risk', according to documents we have seen. The evidence before the bank's credit committee suggested that he was almost certain to default on the loan agreement.

Luckily for him, Floyd was on hand to iron out the wrinkles in a private conversation with then-VBS bank chairman Tshifhiwa Matodzi. An email between Brian and then-VBS credit manager David Ntlhokwe, dated 19 September 2017, details the discussion.[275]

Brian wrote: 'Please receive the attached documents referred by Matodzi following the discussion Matodzi held with Floyd. It's about the house purchase. It's urgent, and should be registered a mortgage asap [sic].'

The documents attached to Brian's email related to the purchase of the house in Mindalore. Rather surprisingly, they included the credit report labelling him 'very high risk', as well as bank statements. Nevertheless, within two days, on 21 September 2017, a property valuation was finalised. Ntlhokwe then approved the loan.

The bank had every reason not to do so. For starters, Brian was 'very high risk' partly because he already owed Capitec bank R30 000, which he was struggling to repay, the credit report found. VBS documents show the Mindalore bond was approved on condition that Brian settled his debt with Capitec, but, unsurprisingly, he did not do so. In fact, by the end of 2018, the year in which VBS imploded, Brian's debt with Capitec had more than doubled, to about R70 000.

In handwritten notes on the bond approval documents, VBS officials recorded Brian's 'average turnover' as R2,5 million per month, equalling R30 million a year. This figure was misleading, as the money reflected was cash he received for no legal reason, all stemming from the VBS fraud. The inclusion of these numbers shows how far the credit department bent over backwards to accommodate this loan.

As part of the application, Brian had to list a verified home address. Tellingly, he submitted the address of a house that Floyd was renting at the time in the northern Johannesburg suburb of Bryanston, with the help of a Limpopo businessman.[276]

Despite these red flags, the loan was granted. The brothers must have been relieved when the Mindalore house was finally registered under Sgameka Projects on 4 December 2017, ending months of back-and-forth between them and VBS.

Predictably, it didn't take long for Sgameka to start falling behind on the repayments. Between October 2017 and June 2018, it paid more than R100 000 on the loan – but that was over R50 000 less than the bank expected in that period.

There is no evidence that Sgameka faced any repercussions for this failure while VBS still functioned. It appeared to have been overlooked because of the company's strategic importance.

In December 2018, we asked Floyd about the Mindalore house and the circumstances around VBS issuing a loan to the 'very high risk' Brian.

Floyd was dismissive but did not dispute the validity of any of the emails or the banking documents to which the emails referred.

'Fraudulent activities are dealt with by the criminal justice system and not [by] some imaginations of a lousy journalist,' he wrote in reply. 'I think your narrative is bullshit and pure drivel, driven by narrow obsession. Please give me the proof that I received R10-million from VBS.'[277]

Floyd did not deny that he had had private discussions with Matodzi or used his influence with VBS bank managers to get the home loan. He referred questions about the Mindalore house to his brother.

In turn, Brian did not reply to questions about whether Floyd had used his influence to obtain the loan. He simply said: 'I applied for a housing loan, and I was given the loan and I am paying for it.'

When VBS collapsed, Constance and Elias Shivambu – who had nothing to do with the VBS fraud and were most likely unaware of the origins of their sons' wealth – faced the risk of losing their home. But their eldest son came to the rescue. Deed documents show that Floyd 'bought' the property from Sgameka in June 2021 for R1 465 813. Our sources indicate that Sgameka then settled its debt with the liquidator. The payment was made from a lawyer's trust account, but the true source of the money remains unclear. This was a hefty sum, considering that Floyd's parliamentary salary at that time was about R1,1 million a year.[278]

But the Mindalore property was not the only financial matter occupying Floyd's mind in 2017. He also had big business plans and was so eager to get his ventures off the ground that he was willing to set aside politics if it meant getting a little help from members of the white ruling class that he supposedly so despised.

A prominent Afrikaans businessman in the Western Cape – someone Floyd would publicly have labelled a member of the 'Stellenbosch mafia' – tells a revealing story. According to him, Floyd approached wealthy businessmen in the winelands with a pitch. He had the business-savvy Marshall Dlamini, then an EFF MP, in tow.[279]

The timing was telling. Matodzi had ordered the first R5-million payment from VBS to Sgameka to be made on 8 June 2017, and hundreds of thousands of rand started pouring into the Grand Azania account a few days later. Floyd must have felt loaded and a little adventurous.

In late June 2017, Floyd and Dlamini were swirling glasses of award-winning Cabernet with the owner of a prestigious Stellenbosch wine farm, the farm's winemaker and a local businessman who had introduced them. They sat in the cellar, drank a lot of wine and talked about politics.

The men laughed. When billionaires acquired wine farms, they tended to become millionaires soon after, went the cautionary joke. Floyd had set his sights a little lower – a restaurant and wine bar on the historic Vilakazi Street in Orlando West, Soweto. The plan was to call it 'Grand Azania', and he wanted to bottle some of the farm owner's wine under a Grand Azania label. The owner politely turned down the offer. That same evening, Floyd met other members of the 'Stellenbosch mafia' to discuss student housing.

Later that year, in December 2017, having had no luck in Stellenbosch, Floyd and his brother turned to VBS, which still held promise as a reliable source of funding. The bank was willing to cough up the means to realise the restaurant and wine bar. Brian signed a too-good-to-be-true deal with VBS: a R4-million 'business loan' that credit manager David Ntlhokwe effectively gifted to Sgameka Projects.

Granted, the terms weren't great on paper. They included repayment over 24 months at an interest rate of prime plus 300 basis points a year. This translated into monthly instalments of a hefty R190 000. But given what transpired, it seems clear that there was little expectation that Brian would ever repay the loan.

When the implosion of VBS lifted the lid on these backroom deals, the younger Shivambu was also facing other problems. He had, on behalf of Sgameka, ceded a personal investment account supposedly containing R4 million to VBS as collateral for the 'loan'. However, investigators probing the looting of VBS could not find this R4-million 'investment'. The account existed, and there was paperwork to back it up, but sources said neither Sgameka Projects nor anyone else had paid the promised R4 million into the account – a claim bolstered by bank statements.

As building works at Grand Azania progressed, VBS paid a total of R2,1 million of the R4-million loan to service providers, including just over R1,1 million to architects Studio Plus, the designers of the restaurant.

On 2 February 2018, Brian asked VBS managers to release the remainder of the loan. By then, Floyd was already aware that the bank faced serious difficulties and was likely to be placed under curatorship. However, VBS officials never acted on Brian's request. A month later, the Reserve Bank officially placed VBS under curatorship, halting all money flowing from the bank.

At first, the fracas around VBS and the stolen cash appears not to have curbed Floyd's enthusiasm for his Grand Azania dream. The name was simply changed to 'Sud Restaurant'.

In April 2019, Brian still explained all of this as follows: 'I own Grand Azania and applied for a loan of R4-million to build a restaurant business. [I] never received the entirety of the money. The loan amount Grand Azania applied for was paid directly to service providers and suppliers of restaurant equipment, all of which was delivered to the promises [sic]. All the loan amount was paid into the business. Due to the fact that the loan amount was not paid [back] in full and my business was out in strain, progression of the project was delayed.'[280]

Among other things, he had seemingly mislaid the fact that it was not Grand Azania but Sgameka Projects that had applied for the loan.

Floyd, in turn, pretended his cosying up to 'white monopoly capital' and visit to the wine farm had never happened. When we asked him about it, he wrote: 'This is absolute rubissh [sic] and you can continue to humiliate yourself . . . you can continue to drown in confusion, because your masters and handlers are misleading you. I have never been involved in any fraud, and I don't own any business. [. . .] All of this is your imaginary rubissh [sic].'[281]

CHAPTER 18

Wedding worries and big-hearted blessers

WHEN FLOYD SHIVAMBU needed someone to pay for his first wedding, he knew just who to ask. 'Heita,' he wrote to Limpopo business tycoon Lawrence Mulaudzi in a WhatsApp message on 27 March 2017. 'Please don't forget to activate that intervention. Am in great need.'[282] He followed this up with the FNB account details for Grand Azania.

Shivambu lived large and fast but was perpetually short of cash, our sources say. There is some evidence for this in the Grand Azania accounts of November 2016 to August 2018. As noted previously, the company received an astonishing R15,6 million in this period. Shivambu was as diligent in spending the cash as he was in soliciting it. As soon as some benefactor topped up the account, it was promptly bled dry. Expenses included lavish shopping sprees at malls in Sandton and Cape Town. Within days, however, a new source of money would have to be found.

In March 2017, Shivambu's wedding was one month away. Grand Azania had already sponsored his day out to the V&A Waterfront in Cape Town and paid R100 000 marked as 'Fs Wedding' to the events company Be-Sure Events Solutions. There was just R745,41 left in the account; his slush fund was empty. There was no way his parliamentary salary could support his planned wedding expenses, and he had declared no additional income, gifts, shares or businesses.

So, Shivambu started badgering Mulaudzi, a politically connected Limpopo businessman involved in the fuel, gas and oil sectors[283].

Mulaudzi is known for lending a helping hand to politicians. In 2018, he pocketed a R47,5-million advisory fee from a R1,37-billion Public Investment Corporation (PIC) deal. The very next day, he paid close to R6 million towards an expensive townhouse bought by the family trust of ANC leader Zweli Mkhize.[284] Mulaudzi explained this as a legitimate business transaction and denied that it was a kickback related to his dealings with the state-owned investment corporation. Mkhize has never commented on these allegations.

In the same year, the Mpati Commission probed Mulaudzi as a material part of its investigation of the PIC.[285] Judge Lex Mpati found that Mulaudzi had an 'improper' relationship with PIC chair Dr Dan Matjila and that this 'posed a reputational risk for the PIC'.[286]

Investigations at the PIC uncovered a whistleblower's tip-off containing screenshots of text messages between Mulaudzi and several high-profile politicians. Shivambu's 'great need' conversations were captured in these text messages, which the whistleblower also sent to journalist Susan Comrie of amaBhungane, who wrote the first account.[287] At the time, Mulaudzi denied anything untoward in his relationship with Shivambu.

The messages show that in late March 2017, Shivambu sent Mulaudzi multiple messages emphasising his 'great need'. He had to wait about 14 hours for a response. 'Evening DP [deputy president],' Mulaudzi answered at 11.26pm, 'I sent instruction to process outstanding matter. You would be able to sort it out in the morning.'

Shivambu must have been brooding over his phone. Within seconds, he answered with, 'Thanks my brother.' He waited the entire morning of the following day, but no money appeared. At 12.49pm, Shivambu asked: 'Heita . . . Are you winning?'

Mulaudzi answered over an hour later: 'DP, instruction was sent. Let's give them some few hours.'

Again, within a matter of seconds, Shivambu answered: 'Okay cool. Thanks.'

That evening, at 8.47pm, Mulaudzi enquired: 'Did you receive it?' For a third time Shivambu answered immediately: 'Not yet.' And the next morning there was still no movement in the Grand Azania account.

By 12.08pm that Wednesday, Shivambu's patience was wearing thin. 'Heita . . . I still haven't received,' he prompted. He never received an answer.

At the time, *Daily Maverick* obtained access to Grand Azania's bank statements. Correlating the leaked text messages with the bank statements coloured in the emerging picture. On 29 March 2017, the day of this last message from Shivambu, R200 000 landed in Grand Azania's account, marked 'Mulaudzi'.

On 10 April 2017, days before the wedding, Mulaudzi was rewarded with an SMS invitation to the Shivambu wedding in Ka-Mahonisi village in Limpopo.

From the bank statements it appeared that 'Mulaudzi' and 'Lawrence' had sent Shivambu several 'interventions' from as early as 2016 until well into 2018, totalling at least R700 000. When *Daily Maverick* questioned Mulaudzi in 2019 about these and other payments, he declined to comment on what he labelled a 'recycled' article. He maintained he was 'treated very unfairly' and was 'sick and tired of the baseless stories tanking my business deals and tarnishing my image . . . I work with billions, I have lost billions thanks to these stories, I don't care about R500 000. It is my money, I can gift money to whomever I want.'

Mulaudzi ended the phone call at that point but soon followed up with an email stating: 'I also want to put in [sic] record that I never gave any GIFT to Mr. Shivambu.'

Despite these vociferous denials, ourselves and Comrie had different pieces of information that, when put together, provided the clearest picture to date of how Shivambu solicited money from businesspeople. Although Brian was the supposed owner of Grand Azania, the financial records revealed Floyd as the true, ultimate beneficiary of the cash.

Within days of Mulaudzi's R200 000 'intervention', Grand Azania paid R50 000 to Floyd's personal FNB account, with the description 'Repayment Gaw'. While the identities of those with access to Grand Azania's online banking profile remain unclear, the fact that the company's cash was mainly used for Floyd's benefit or deposited into his bank account suggests he was the one pulling the strings. 'Gaw', which seems to be a reference to

Grand Azania Wines, appears in the accounts 51 times, but it is unclear exactly what these payments were for. SARS later cleared up this mystery when investigators attached six months of Shivambu's personal FNB bank statements to its application to liquidate Grand Azania.[288] Grand Azania had made regular payments ranging from R50 000 to R200 000 to Shivambu's private account.

The second big payment funded by Mulaudzi was R80 000, marked 'Fs Wedding' and sent to Be-Sure Events Solutions, followed by R18 450 described as 'Video and Photograph Floyd Wedding'.

Around this time, Shivambu's Grand Azania account was fattened by another R300 000 deposit from 'S. Danson' – businesswoman Savannah Maziya-Danson – and a cash deposit of R190 000 and a R150 000 payment from one 'Levi', whose identity remains a mystery.

Boosted by the cash, Shivambu went on another spending spree between 24 March and 5 May 2017. Grand Azania paid about R50 000 to a photographer from Thohoyandou, R207 000 to Be-Sure Events Solutions and more than R36 000 for accommodation in and around his home town of Malamulele, where the wedding was held. The payments were marked 'Video and Photograph Floyd Wedding', 'Shivambu Wedding', 'Fs Wedding', 'Photography Floyd Wedding', and 'Benny Mayengani Shivambu'. Mayengani is a popular Limpopo singer who performed at the wedding.

The Grand Azania bank card was also used for groceries from stores in Malamulele and to withdraw R14 000 in cash from ATMs in the area between 26 April and 2 May 2017 – the week of the wedding.

Shivambu married Siphesihle Pezi in a traditional ceremony that set Grand Azania back at least R570 000. Guests included Malema, prominent EFF members Dali Mpofu, Godrich Gardee, and Mbuyiseni Ndlozi, then-minister of justice Ronald Lamola, then-deputy minister of finance David Masondo, and the VhaVenda king, Toni Mphephu-Ramabulana, who was also implicated by Motau in the looting of VBS Mutual Bank. Mphephu-Ramabulana later lost a bid to appeal against a court order to pay back R5,6 million to the VBS liquidator.

A day after the wedding, on the evening of 30 April, Shivambu cleared up any doubt about the nature of Mulaudzi's 'intervention'.

'Thank you very much for the assistance towards the success of the wedding,' Shivambu told the latter in another text message. 'We had a very fulfilling event to welcome Makoti [new bride] wa ka Shivambu and all who partook are very happy and satisfied. I really appreciate.'

He attached two photos of himself and Pezi taken on the day of their wedding. Mulaudzi replied: 'You are welcome my brother. Have good time together. [sic] It was so beautiful.'

In an emailed reaction to questions sent to him in 2019, Shivambu said: 'All the assistance I got for my wedding came from close family friends and there was no conflict of interest, none whatsoever.'[289]

However, the illicit cash caused a dual problem: First, Shivambu failed to declare his additional income to parliament. When the authors of this book reported on these financial dealings, complaints from MPs triggered a probe by the Joint Committee on Ethics and Members' Interests, the watchdog responsible for ensuring MPs keep to the rules.

The simplest course for Shivambu would have been to admit that he had neglected to disclose the payments and offer an apology. The fallout would have been minimal. However, this option was not available to him. A belated admission would have required him to acknowledge that Grand Azania – which benefited from the looting of VBS – was linked to him.

His second issue was that SARS, too, seemed to have realised that Shivambu had used Grand Azania as a front to hide behind his younger brother, Brian.

In the six months between May and November 2017, for example, R2,36 million landed in Shivambu's private account. We know this because SARS attached an extract of Floyd Shivambu's FNB bank statement to its Grand Azania liquidation application. Of this, R260 448 was income from his job as an MP. The luxury items he bought in those six months cost about R770 000 – almost three times more than his parliamentary salary for the same period. We understand from our sources that in 2025, SARS initiated procedures to recoup a whopping R24 million in unpaid tax and penalties from Shivambu. That process is ongoing.

So, what did Shivambu do to receive these gifts from Mulaudzi? Another series of text messages suggests a working relationship[290] between the two.

For instance, consider this message, sent from Shivambu to Mulaudzi in January 2017: 'How are you? I was able to talk to [the chairman of a JSE-listed company] and he's committed to talk when he returns from Davos on the 22nd of January. You must remind me of what we have to talk about.'

Mulaudzi replied with: 'Excellent.'

Another example of how Shivambu seemingly solicited cash and favours from businesspeople to support his ambitions and lifestyle is revealed in a legal dispute between a service provider to the Limpopo government and a homeowner in Bryanston, Johannesburg. In this case, Shivambu roped in Limpopo businessman Lufuno Mphaphuli to sign a rental leasing contract and pay the initial fees for an upmarket Bryanston home where he and his family lived for about 16 months.

Mphaphuli owns an engineering company in Limpopo that was in trouble with the Special Investigating Unit (SIU). When the SIU probed corruption and maladministration in the Fetakgomo Tubatse Local Municipality in Limpopo, investigators found a number of problems with a tender to Mphaphuli Consulting to electrify villages.[291] According to the SIU, the municipality had overpaid by R76 million. The matter went to court, and after multiple appeals, the Supreme Court of Appeal and the Constitutional Court dismissed Mphaphuli Consulting's attempt to have the SIU report reviewed.[292]

On 6 October 2016, Mphaphuli signed the rental contract for the Bryanston house on behalf of Shivambu, who had a poor credit record at the time. Court documents show that Mphaphuli also paid the owner R55 360 as a services and damages deposit.[293]

Shivambu's rent was set at R40 000 a month, and after the renewal of the contract, R45 360 a month. Grand Azania paid a total of R583 000 in rent to the owner, including rates and taxes. Three payments – for R280 000, R279 000 and R24 000 – were made between May and November 2017.

This is the same address, incidentally, to which Shivambu invited Lawrence Mulaudzi for a business discussion. It is also the house where VBS chair Tshifhiwa Matodzi later claimed he had met the Shivambu brothers to discuss the fallout from the bank's implosion.

When Shivambu moved out of the house, the owner took Mphaphuli to court and claimed Shivambu owed him R226 970,89 for two months' rent in arrears, items missing from the house and damage to the property. He wanted Mphaphuli to pay up, arguing that he had signed surety for Shivambu and should therefore cover the cost, as Shivambu refused to do so. Mphaphuli denied the claim for a long time, but in 2023 he caved in and paid Shivambu's debts.

When the author asked Mphaphuli about the incident, he recounted the day in 2016 when Shivambu asked him for 'help'. Shivambu visited him at his Johannesburg house to discuss a potential business opportunity, he recalled.

'He came past my house now and then to visit me,' Mphaphuli said in a telephone conversation in 2019. 'During such a visit, we discussed a potential investment opportunity, where Floyd requested my assistance. I spoke to him about my company . . . and he asked me for help.'

Mphaphuli was vague about the type of 'opportunity' he discussed with Shivambu. He said that he 'had no good reason *not* to help the guy' and that they 'speak the same language and come from the same district'. He had decided to help Shivambu as a gesture of goodwill, he said.

He also made it clear that there had been no quid pro quo and that Shivambu hadn't asked for money. He ended the conversation by saying: 'If you look at all the facts, you will see you are talking to an innocent man.' To this day, we have no evidence that Shivambu did Mphaphuli any unlawful favours, although their interactions seem to point to a pattern.

CHAPTER 19

Floyd's travels and the Grand Azania card

FLOYD SHIVAMBU IS a keen Instagrammer, where he describes himself as a 'Pan Africanist. Socialist. Revolution. Marxist Leninist. Focused. Dialectal [sic] Materialism and Labour Theory of Value. Heterodox.'

In 2017, a big theme in his photographic diary was how he, as EFF deputy president, was 'uplifting' the poor and needy. The pictures were almost always accompanied by captions suggesting that the donations were funded by Shivambu and the EFF.

On 12 January,[294] Shivambu donated wheelchairs to an old-age home in the town of Heidelberg in Gauteng. He posted: 'Today, we handed over 15 wheelchairs to Ratanda Old Age home. It's an important mission because we can't postpone the suffering and deprivation of our people [sic].'

Shivambu is in the middle of the photo, flanked by two women and clasping the hand of one of them. He accepts their thanks, wearing an EFF beret. Red and white balloons and a table with a printed EFF tablecloth fill the background.

Six months later, on 9 July 2017, Shivambu posted a picture of himself handing over football kits to a team in his home village of Ka-Mahonisi just outside Malamulele, Limpopo. The caption read: 'Real Fighters FC (Mahonisi Village) defeated Jimmy Jones FS 4-1 today and official

Number 2 in Malamulele SAFA League. Few games and we will gain promotion. Worthy investment!'[295]

The players were blissfully unaware that the kit had been bought by Grand Azania, which got most of its money from VBS – some of it perhaps stolen from the players' parents and neighbours. Similarly, the recipients of the wheelchairs were unaware that the same sort of money would relieve their 'suffering and deprivation'.

The wheelchairs cost Grand Azania R54 000, paid on 6 January 2017. In the Grand Azania bank statements, the payment was described as 'Wheel Chairs Nyiko Shivambu', using Floyd Shivambu's first name.

This was just one indication that Floyd's determined attempts to distance himself from the VBS/Grand Azania scandal did not square with reality.

Prompted by Floyd's denials and the insistence that Grand Azania was Brian's enterprise, we analysed the Grand Azania payments to try to determine the ultimate beneficiary of the account's millions. We found many indications that it had little to do with the younger Shivambu but everything to do with Floyd.

For example, when Floyd married Siphesihle Pezi in 2017, the festivities cost Grand Azania at least half a million rand. Grand Azania also paid the R400 000 deposit on his new wife's Mercedes-Benz less than two months later. Floyd's children's names coupled with words like 'school', 'clothes' and 'child support' appear in the Grand Azania bank statements, too. There were payments for his Range Rover and almost R600 000 in rent for an upmarket house in Bryanston. Added to this is a host of email and SMS payment notifications sent to Floyd's email address and phone.

We analysed 1 041 Grand Azania transactions in the period from November 2016 to August 2018. The word 'Nyiko' appears 50 times, 'Floyd' five times and 'Fs' three times. 'Gaw', presumably short for Grand Azania Wines, 'wedding' and 'EFF' are mentioned 51, 18 and 14 times, respectively. Grosvenor, the name of the street on which Floyd's rental property was located in Bryanston, appears three times. His ID number appears once as a payment reference. In contrast, 'Brian' and his middle name, 'Answer', feature five and eight times, respectively, and no additional payments could be tied to him.

We also analysed about 260 point-of-sale (POS) payments with a Grand Azania card, captured in the company's bank statements.[296] POS payments record information about the store, location and date, all of which is reflected in bank statements.

When we correlated the location data with the Shivambus' social media posts, it showed that these payments were not made by Brian.

The Grand Azania card did, however, follow Floyd around Southern Africa.[297] Using his social media posts and records of events, including the EFF's Twitter/X account, we traced his movements all the way back to December 2016. At the time, before the VBS payments started flowing into Grand Azania, Floyd spent Christmas in his home town, Ka-Mahonisi, in Limpopo. He drove back to Johannesburg on 26 December and swiped the Grand Azania card at the Kranskop and Nyl toll gates.

Between November and December 2016, Grand Azania received R800 000 in 17 payments. One of these was a R100 000 deposit by businessman Lawrence Mulaudzi, who partially funded Shivambu's wedding. The other transactions were amounts of R25 000 or R100 000 – all rounded numbers with none of the rand and cent values usually found on legitimate invoiced payments.

Two days later, the Grand Azania bank card went on a shopping spree at Sandton City. On 28 December 2016, it bought new clothes at Gucci (R20 300), Nike (R3 579,96) and Louis Vuitton (R7 600). The next day, the card made a purchase for R3 495 at Moda Luggage & Leather – just in time for Floyd's birthday trip to Zambia. On 30 December 2016, Floyd posted his crossing of the Kazungula border post between Zambia and Botswana on Instagram.

Floyd spent his birthday on New Year's Day 2017 at the Victoria Falls. The Grand Azania bank card paid R8 429,42 to the Royal Livingstone Hotel, the iconic lodgings overlooking the Zambezi River as it drops down over the falls. On 2 January 2017, Floyd headed back to South Africa, and the card tapped out R1 034,39 at a Zambian airport shop.

Back in South Africa, it appears Floyd hit the ground running. The Grand Azania bank card paid R122 000 towards an apparent National Student Financial Aid Scheme (NSFAS) loan. The transaction is labelled 'NSFAS Repayment', followed by Floyd's identity number. It also bought the wheelchairs for the Ratanda old-age home and paid R50 000 in a transaction described as 'BMW F Shivambu'.

On 9 January 2017, the EFF hosted its first 'war council' meeting of the year at its headquarters in Braamfontein, and Floyd and the Grand Azania bank card apparently stayed over at the Capital Empire Hotel in Sandton. A day later, the Grand Azania card bought groceries at the Hobart Spar in Bryanston, about 400 metres from the home Floyd rented at the time. Between November 2016 and May 2017, the card was used to buy groceries worth R13 635,45 at this shop.

About a month later, on 19 February 2017, the bank card was used to buy a Gautrain ticket from Sandton to OR Tambo Airport (R302). It was also swiped at a café at the airport (R34) and paid for a plane ticket to East London (R1 662) and a hotel in East London (R2 205). The next day, Floyd posted a picture of his view from the East London International Convention Centre.

Next, the card was used for payments to the Premier Hotel (R2 670) and Studio 88 (R249,99), both in East London, and for a return ticket to Johannesburg (R1 944). On 3 March, the EFF celebrated Julius Malema's birthday at its headquarters in Braamfontein. On the same day, the card paid for products worth R8 850 from Louis Vuitton in Sandton.

On 9 March 2017, Floyd was in Cape Town where, during a question-and-answer session in parliament, he lambasted then-Deputy President Cyril Ramaphosa, saying that 'blacks haven't benefited from government intervention [with regard] to economic transformation'. On the same day, the Grand Azania bank card paid for a shopping spree at the Cape Town V&A Waterfront, including R1 999 at Pringle, R7 000 at Replay, R1 670 at The Body Shop and R820 at Bukhara Restaurant.

Grand Azania received its first VBS money on 13 and 22 June 2017 – two payments of R400 000 and R500 000 from Sgameka Projects. Following this cash injection, the card travelled with Floyd to the Eastern Cape to address EFF members at municipalities in the greater East London area. From 23 to 25 June, the card tapped out R2 895 at the Premier Hotel in East London, the OhBrigado Champagne Bar in the same city (R8 000) and the Garden Court Mthatha hotel (R6 932,90).

The card worked hard, and Floyd was apparently having a blast. But he had bigger plans for the company than simply funding his lifestyle: he wanted high flyers from all over to associate the Grand Azania name with luxury living.

At the upper end of Soweto's famous Vilakazi Street, a few metres away from former president Nelson Mandela's Soweto residence and the Hector Pieterson Museum, stands a monument to the VBS bank heist: Sud Restaurant. The 'u' in 'Sud' is represented by a glass of wine.

It is built on the site of the former restaurant and party venue Nambitha, which featured photographs by world-renowned black photographers such as the now deceased Peter Magubane. Magubane's pictures were taken down when the EFF honchos took over and had Nambitha demolished. Tearing it down and replacing the venue with Sud cost at least R3,6 million. The building work was largely financed with Brian Shivambu's 'business loan' from VBS.

The bank statements from Sgameka, Grand Azania and Santaclara suggest Sud Restaurant is equally owned by Floyd Shivambu and Julius Malema. This is supported by stories from insiders as well as Matodzi's 2024 affidavit. Insiders tell stories of Malema 'running the place like it's his own joint' and giving staff cash to buy appliances and cover some of the expenses. According to one employee, 'when Julius comes here, he closes off the VIP section'.

Sud opened in early 2018. For a few months, Malema's cousin Tsholo Malema held a managing position. In an online interview, she described herself as a 'hustler and an entrepreneur', and seemed to claim that she was the owner. People who worked with her, however, described her as clueless about the business and 'just the face' that got celebrities involved. After a few months, she disappeared from Sud and its website.

We understand that by mid-2018, just after VBS had imploded, Sud was perpetually cash-strapped, in part because large amounts were regularly funnelled from the Grand Azania account to Floyd Shivambu's FNB Private Wealth account. He used both accounts to spend large sums on luxury items, clothes and travel expenses, at the expense of the Sud business.

When we visited Sud in 2019, the establishment was surrounded by expensive ClearVu fencing and frequented by all sorts, including ANC branch members from the area.

A company named Sud Restaurant (Pty) Ltd was eventually registered in March 2021, with Brian Shivambu and Malema's close friend Clifford Masinga as directors. The company still exists, but Masinga has subsequently resigned. Wide-eyed business owners and staff working on Vilakazi Street relished in sharing the unsolicited gossip: 'Julius and them' own Sud, they told us. By late 2023, an employee said the restaurant was still 'owned by the EFF boys' but was now 'rented out to other people, while Brian still pretends he is in charge'.

The story of Shivambu's finances would be lacking without a little more detail about his favourite pastime: shopping. From May to November 2017, he spent at least R776 747,73 from his private FNB bank account on clothes and luxury items at Prada, Gucci, Louis Vuitton, Versace and Burberry, and on liquor from fancy wine shops, restaurants and supermarkets. During the same period, his total income from parliament was R260 448,85. All told, he spent almost 300 percent more than his parliamentary salary during this period on clothes and liquor.

Grand Azania's bank statements paint a picture of even greater excess, partly because we have access to a longer period of bank statements – almost two years, from November 2016 to August 2018. The cash inflow for this period was R15 604 730,95, which includes R6 160 000 in VBS loot from the bank and Sgameka Projects. The VBS cash totals just less than 40 percent of all the illicit cash swirling around Grand Azania during this period.

Shivambu previously argued that to question his income was to 'police black wealth'. But it's hard not to think about Margaret Chauke, Nyawasedza Raphunga and their neighbours when reading about his spending sprees fuelled by illicit VBS cash.

On 16 October, Floyd Shivambu dismissed as 'pure insanity' claims that he and other EFF leaders had benefited from VBS funds. A week later, on 23 October 2018, he was due to speak in parliament. Before he began, his fellow MPs chanted: 'Pay back the money', imitating the EFF's notorious parliamentary assaults on Jacob Zuma a few years previously.

Shivambu started by saying that EFF members were 'flattered that people learn from us about demanding accountability from those who do wrong things'.[298]

He then declared that the EFF never benefited from the VBS Mutual Bank looting.

This was a bare-faced lie. In the six months from June to November 2017, when he received R260 448,85 as salaried income, Shivambu's actual (and undeclared) income was R2 315 873,13. Most of the balance came from VBS Mutual Bank and companies linked to it.

He added: 'We as the EFF . . . want to call on the law-enforcement agencies to take decisive action against all the people who did wrong at VBS Mutual Bank.'

By the same token, this call for accountability was an exercise in hypocrisy that backfired on him later and may do so again in the future. In 2024, the parliamentary ethics committee found him guilty of failing to declare additional income from Grand Azania and imposed a penalty. Shivambu tried to challenge the finding in court but failed. In early 2025, the authors were told that SARS was investigating his personal income as well as that of Grand Azania.

CHAPTER 20

Mahuna: The gift that kept on giving

MATSOBANE JOHN PHALENG is a businessman based in Polo-kwane. He calls himself 'Tsubi', a nickname Julius Malema uses for him too. Although he denied it when journalists inquired years ago, Phaleng is, in fact, Malema's cousin.

His Facebook page describes him as CEO and founder of Tsa-Tshidi Trading, and as a 'digital creator'. A photograph posted on 14 December 2024 shows him hugging Malema at a function, with Phaleng in close-fitting black garb and Malema wearing an evening suit with a huge bow tie.

In September 2019, we phoned Phaleng to ask him about Mahuna Investments – the company that had emerged as a slush fund for Julius, but which Phaleng supposedly owned.[299] Specifically, Mahuna Investments had received significant sums of money from Sgameka Projects, which in turn, as we've seen, had received all its revenue from VBS-linked companies.

Mahuna Investments had no website and seemingly did not tender for any state contracts, unlike Phaleng's real company, Tsa-Tshidi Trading. He described Mahuna to us as a small company that was 'doing things right', including paying its taxes. When asked what kind of business his 'small company' did to show a gross income of more than R12 million in 21 months, Phaleng claimed it did consultancy work for Sgameka. It was an odd remark, because by that stage we knew that Sgameka conducted no business, provided no services and received no income apart from the VBS loot. The Mahuna bank statements also reflected no tax or VAT payments in 2017 and 2018.

Phaleng is fond of telling people that he is 'chasing the soft life'. He appears to be less of a showboat than Tshepo Malema – Julius Malema's other cousin and partner in his numerous schemes. But Phaleng and Tshepo do have one thing in common: they are terrible liars.

As said before, from 1 May 2017 to 31 January 2019, our investigation showed the Mahuna bank account received more than R12,2 million, almost half from Sgameka Projects, while Grand Azania contributed R500 000. Much of the rest came from Hendrick Kganyago, implicated in a major Tshwane fuel-tender scandal and Afrirent, the company at the centre of a City of Johannesburg fleet-tender scandal. We will return to Afrirent and Kganyago later.

In this period, Mahuna Investments did not pay any taxes, and its expenses did not reflect any genuine business activity. In this respect, it resembled Sgameka Projects and Grand Azania.

Spending totalled just over R11 million. Only R245 000 of this appeared to have benefited Phaleng. These were regular monthly payments of R10 000, R15 000 and R20 000, described as director's fees and paid into his personal account in 2017 and 2018.

By contrast, Mahuna appears to have paid for Malema's eldest son's school fees, and for rent and pool costs at the house in the affluent Johannesburg suburb of Sandown, where he moved in 2011. It also paid for tailored suits from designer Linda Makhanya, renovations at Malema's Polokwane hospitality venue Mekete Lodge, the EFF's fourth birthday celebrations and Malema's political campaigning.

During the period of our reporting, the Mahuna bank card was Malema's constant companion.[300] As the money flowed into Mahuna from Sgameka, our analysis suggests that Malema – not Phaleng – was the ultimate beneficiary.

These transactions matched Malema's movements as documented in the news and on social media. For example, when Malema attended the Durban July horse race in 2017 and 2018, the Mahuna bank card, too, travelled around Durban and Ballito. The bank card followed Malema to East London on the date of the EFF's fifth birthday celebrations, tagged along for the 2018 land debate in North West, and was in Seshego and

Polokwane, among other things for Malema's grandmother's birthday in 2017, and between Christmas and New Year's Day in 2017, 2018 and 2019. Malema travelled the country, apparently swiping the Mahuna card as he went.

On 12 December 2017, he addressed the EFF 'student command' at the Stay City Hotel in Johannesburg. On the same day, the Mahuna Investments bank card paid for a shopping spree at Sandton City Gucci (R9 900), Louis Vuitton (R11 100), Totalsports (R1 197) and Checkers Hyper (R268,51).

When Malema left for Seshego and Polokwane to celebrate Christmas and New Year in his home town, the card went with him. Between 23 and 28 December 2017, Mahuna paid R13 529,52 for goods bought at Pick n Pay, Truworths, Edgars and Spitz in Polokwane.

In the first half of 2018, the Mahuna bank statements mostly recorded internet payments, but on 1 June 2018, the card went shopping at H&M in Sandton. All seemed to have been forgiven after EFF members, spurred on by their leaders, had months earlier trashed H&M stores over a controversial advertisement.

In July 2018, when Malema, various family members and friends attended the Durban July, the Mahuna bank card joined the party and paid about R45 500 to The Werehouse restaurant (R10 860), the Hampshire Hotel in Ballito (R11 560), Lifestyle Tops in Ballito (R2 090,96) and the Montrose Garage near Harrismith (R990,15) on the way back to Johannesburg. Later in July, Malema used the card on a trip through North West, where he attended the land debate.

In the same month, Margaret Chauke, Nyawasedza Raphunga and other victims of the VBS looting frenzy spent days queuing and sleeping outside the VBS branch in Thohoyandou.

In December 2018, while VBS depositors were facing a bleak Christmas, the Mahuna bank card was used to indulge in a little retail therapy, tapping out R10 200 at Gucci, R29 233 at @Home, R13 905,10 at Mr Price Home, R5 807,81 at Pick n Pay and R59 000 at Linda Makhanya's LM Tailored Suits.

All told, between 2017 and 2018, Mahuna Investments paid an astonishing R415 087 in 10 tranches labelled 'cooperate wear' (sic) to LM

Tailored Suits' Standard Bank account. Some payments were labelled 'JM' or 'JSM'; others were marked as 'cooperate wear'. In September 2019, Makhanya told us his company provided 'personalised image consultations' to clients, including members of royal families and state presidents. Citing client confidentiality, he would not say anything more.[301]

Additionally, Mahuna funded festivities in Polokwane between 20 and 31 December 2018, including a R50 000 internet payment labelled 'Fireworks'.

Mahuna also paid, at least partially, for two properties: Mekete Lodge outside Polokwane, and Malema's house in Sandown, where he had lived while he built his mansion. Today, Malema's Mazimbu Investment Trust owns Mekete Lodge. He, his cousins Ronny and Tshepo, and his wife, Mantoa, are trustees. The house in Sandown is owned by Malema's Munzhedzi Family Trust, with Malema, Ronny and Mantoa as trustees. Malema told parliament he, his wife Mantoa, and their three children are the sole beneficiaries of this trust.

The registration of the properties to these trusts appears to have been finalised after *Daily Maverick* in 2020 exposed Malema's links to the VBS money and spending on Mekete Lodge. Before that, Malema and those around him had long tried to conceal his involvement in the lodge, or his de facto ownership of it. Interviewed in September 2019, Phaleng claimed some sort of ownership, saying: 'We run our hospitality business at Mekete, and we also host public events and bring famous local and national artists and DJs at Mekete, and we charge for entrance and sell food and beverages.'

About the link between Malema and Mekete Lodge, Phaleng said: 'He attended almost all these events . . . he's one of our good patrons, and we really appreciate his support.'[302]

Mekete Boutique and Events is a hospitality venue about 14 kilometres north of Polokwane on the N1. Extensively refurbished and extended in recent years, it is famous for its lavish late-night parties. In 2022, a staff member claimed that Malema had hosted boozy gatherings there at the height of the Covid-19 lockdown and liquor bans – policies that Malema publicly supported. Malema denied the claim.

In 2023, the venue underwent another renovation. A source said Malema had paid out his staff for four months and sent some of them home. Sources also claimed he had spent millions on the upgrades.

When we visited the venue again later that year, staff said the interior had been decorated with trimmings imported from Dubai. The walls and floors were now clad in marble accented with inlaid brass, while elaborate chandeliers hung from the ceiling. Two replica elephants stood guard at the entrance, and the bar featured emerald velvet recliners equipped with USB ports in the armrests.

A night in the presidential suite, whose entrance is decorated with an artwork of former president Nelson Mandela's face, cost R5 500.

The upgrades included two event halls, one of which was named Mahlodi Hall after Malema's late mother, Florah Mahlodi Malema.

Outside, about 150m away from the main lodge, a building site indicated even more activity. Staff said there were plans for about 40 self-catering units.

Who exactly funded these extensive upgrades remained unclear. In December 2023, several hundred thousand rand was spent on a 'soft launch' event that hosted businesspeople, politicians and local celebrities.

Mekete maintains an elaborate website. The 'About us' section describes the venue as 'the epitome of luxury and elegance nestled in the heart of Limpopo . . . a premier destination for those seeking an exceptional event and stay experience'.

Malema's close friend Matome Hlabioa, who died in 2015, once owned Mekete Lodge. The property then passed on to two local companies before Malema officially acquired it in 2020. However, despite the apparent pretence of intervening ownership, Malema had clearly had a directing hand in Mekete for some time. In 2019, following the first reports in *Daily Maverick* about this, he strenuously denied that he had anything to do with Mekete. Soon after, however, he was promoting events at Mekete to his millions of social media followers.

A substantial part of the start-up capital came from Mahuna, extensively funded by Sgameka and ultimately by Vele and VBS. (Some of it also came from his Santaclara fund.) Between late 2017 and December 2018, Mekete seemed to have been Mahuna's single largest expense. Our investigation showed that Malema poured at least R1,9 million from Mahuna into Mekete from as early as October 2017.[303]

In 2017 and 2018, at least 35 online payments apparently related to the Mekete Lodge upgrades were made from the Mahuna account, totalling R2,07 million. These were described as 'Mekete Grading', 'Bar and Kitchen', 'Tent Mekete' and 'Mekete Irrigation'. Payments described as 'Slaysunday' (R654 000) and 'Intimate Sunday' (R28 000) were for events hosted at the venue. Five payments marked as 'buying stretch tent' and totalling R180 000 were also for Mekete Lodge.

Malema's house in Sandown, Johannesburg, was another big-ticket Mahuna item. In the period under review, Mahuna paid a total of R460 000 in four tranches for upgrades to the house, situated on a large plot of more than 2 000 square metres.

Malema moved to this property in 2011 while rebuilding his Silvela Road 'bachelor's pad' – the property that was later auctioned off by SARS – and eventually settled there permanently.

In 2019, the Sandown property was registered as an EFF asset, valued at R5,25 million. At that time, Malema declined to answer any questions about the property, saying 'the EFF will answer that one'. Then EFF spokesperson Mbuyiseni Ndlozi eventually stated on WhatsApp that the party had 'taken a loan from one of the financial institutions'. Yet, the house was unbonded, suggesting that no such loan existed. In 2021, the property was registered to Malema's Munzhedzi Family Trust at an acquisition value of R5,5 million. Since he bought the Sandown property, Malema has knocked it down and rebuilt it twice.

Over the past decade, Malema appears to have accumulated considerable wealth. The opulent Mekete Lodge and the Sandown residence are just two of at least nine properties owned through his trusts and company structures. In his parliamentary disclosures, Malema named himself, his wife, Mantoa, and their three sons as beneficiaries of these trusts, with trusteeships held by Malema, Mantoa and his cousins. While he has declared his interests in these trusts to parliament, he has not disclosed the specific assets held by the trusts and through his company.

Currently, the acquisition value of Malema's property portfolio stands at an astonishing R21,64 million.

This estimate is significantly understated. Over the years, Malema has reportedly spent tens of millions of rand on various upgrades to his properties. Some of these are detailed in these pages.

Some of the properties are bonded, and it is unclear who pays the instalments. Malema cannot afford it all on his parliamentary salary, which was increased to about R1,27 million before tax in the 2024/25 financial year, according to the latest remuneration information.[304] In the 2015/16 financial year, his parliamentary salary was about R1,1 million before tax.

Mekete is the sole property registered under the Mazimbu Investment Trust, yet our sources indicate that this trust plays a pivotal role in Malema's business ventures. Some of these businesses appear connected to Malema's interest in farming. The website of Mgagao Shamba[305] – the only company where Malema currently serves as a director – lists its address as the same land on which Mekete is situated. The site describes Mgagao Shamba farm as 'an oasis of abundance in South Africa's gateway to the north', farming with fruit, vegetables, livestock, game and cotton. The owner is not identified.

Mgagao Shamba company owns a luxury flat in Hyde Park, Johannesburg, a stone's throw from Adriano Mazzotti's properties where Malema's family once lodged. The flat cost R4 million and is bonded for R3,6 million.

Malema's Munzhedzi Family Trust owns seven residential properties, including the Sandown residence. Three adjacent properties in Polokwane's high-security Woodhill estate, right opposite the Mall of the North, cost the trust more than R700 000 each. The erven, which measure about 600 square metres each, are undeveloped and bonded for around R420 000 each.

The trust's fifth property is a house in the Bendor Ridge security estate, Polokwane, allegedly bought for R3,6 million. The family trust of Malema's friend Collins Foromo once owned the house. The sixth is an empty 924-square-metre erf in White River, Mpumalanga, which Malema acquired from EFF member Godrich Gardee and his wife, apparently for R500 000.

The trust owns another undeveloped erf of 2 074 square metres located in a cul de sac in Bendor, Polokwane, with a current value of about R800 000.

The Ratanang Family Trust, in turn, has maintained ownership of the Palmietfontein farm, which has undergone a remarkable transformation. It stands out as the most luxurious property on the smallholding, featuring a large house, a pool and basketball and tennis courts. This is where Malema, according to neighbours, sometimes arrives in a rented helicopter.

CHAPTER 21

Parliament and the 'newspaper junk'

MEMBERS OF PARLIAMENT (MPs) enter into a special relationship with the South African state, acting on behalf of its citizens. The Constitution requires them to swear a 'solemn oath' that they will be 'faithful to the Republic of South Africa and obey, respect and uphold its Constitution and all other Law of the Republic'.

They are also bound by a parliamentary code of conduct, adopted in 2014 and administered by the Joint Committee on Ethics and Members' Interests.[306] In the eyes of the public, the code is associated with disclosures of financial interests, but its scope is actually far wider.

The code aims to promote public trust in representatives, protect the integrity of parliament and hold MPs accountable in their duties and functions. To this end, the code spells out clearly that they must act in the public interest and without regard to their own material interests or those of their family, business partners or friends, avoid potential conflicts of interest, and carry out their duties in a way that is open and accountable.

MPs are expressly prohibited from accepting gifts or benefits intended to corruptly influence them or that would place them in a conflicted position. They may not use their influence in government or privileged information for personal advantage, and are not allowed to benefit from government tenders.

In an attempt to keep them honest and their affairs transparent, MPs must disclose their financial interests to the registrar, including shares in companies, work outside parliament, directorships and partnerships, benefits and interest-free loans, property and other assets.

Anyone may submit a complaint regarding a suspected breach of the code of conduct, but the committee may also consider such a breach on its own initiative. It has a range of powers, including calling the complainant, the MP or any other person to address the committee, instructing the registrar to conduct further investigation, or staging a formal inquiry. The committee can recommend that parliament impose various penalties, from a reprimand to a fine or reduced salary or 'the suspension of a member's right to a seat in parliamentary debates and committees' for an indeterminate period, plus any other penalty the committee 'may deem appropriate in the circumstances'. In theory at least, parliament has wide-ranging powers to act against MPs for broadly defined offences that undermine public trust.

Should parliament accept the committee's recommendations, the committee's determinations become final.

In October 2018, then-DA MP Phumzile van Damme Karlsen lodged a complaint against Floyd Shivambu over the VBS scandal.

A year later, DA leader John Steenhuisen laid another complaint centred on revelations published by *Daily Maverick*. These included that Floyd Shivambu and the EFF had received millions in unlawful VBS cash from his younger brother Brian; that he had benefited from payments made from the companies Sgameka Projects and Grand Azania; that he had failed to disclose the benefits he got from these companies, Brian and his benefactor Lawrence Mulaudzi; and that he had used the savings of 'vulnerable VBS depositors and municipalities, channelled through Sgameka Projects and Grand Azania, to fund his extravagant lifestyle and political aspirations'.

Parliament's ethics committee asked Shivambu to respond to these complaints. In a replying email, he said he had consulted his lawyers and the EFF and was '100% sure that the case you are asking me to respond to is sub judice'.

Shivambu argued that the VBS report – and aspects of it relating to his brother – was being legally challenged, and therefore 'there is no definitive basis to respond to allegations that are subject to judicial review.'

He added: 'I however wish to state categorically that I have had no conflict of interest on any matter that related to VBS as alleged and have not received any payments from VBS.

'I have recently finalized my tax returns and SARS is satisfied with all the submissions on all the issues that relate to revenue collection.

'I therefore write to request that the Ethics Committee wait for the outcome of the judicial review and then restart the whole process of investigations if the committee will still believe that there are issues that still need to be clarified.' This was a bold lie. To this day, there is no judicial review.

Nevertheless, the committee took years to make a finding. In its report released on 2 October 2023, it said the South African Reserve Bank had confirmed no 'judicial review' was in progress, and so the committee had decided to proceed with the complaint.

The committee then summoned the VBS liquidator, who confirmed in an affidavit that Sgameka Projects paid R180 000 to Floyd Shivambu's private account in August 2017.

The liquidator also reported that money was moved from Sgameka to accounts at other banks. He did not have the jurisdiction to obtain information about those accounts and could therefore not give the committee additional information.

The ethics committee consulted the Financial Intelligence Centre (FIC), too. However, the highly secretive FIC, a statutory body tasked with identifying proceeds of crime and money laundering, declined to provide further information about Shivambu, citing restrictions under the FIC Act.

The committee's report continued: 'All other investigative avenues used by the committee to try and trace whether more money was paid to the Member [Floyd Shivambu] via bank accounts to which the liquidator did not have access were unsuccessful. This part of the investigation is therefore inconclusive. The committee decided to finalise the complaint on the evidence that it had before it.'[307]

The committee found that Floyd had breached the code by failing to disclose the R180 000 received from Sgameka. The code prescribed a reduction in salary or allowances for a period not exceeding 30 days, and the committee recommended that parliament impose 'a penalty of a reduction of nine days salary against the Member'.

The National Assembly adopted the report and accepted its findings. So, both the committee and both houses of parliament implicitly acknowledged that some VBS cash found its way to Floyd's private bank account.

This chain of events raised questions. First, given its relatively straightforward findings, it was a mystery why the committee had taken an astounding five years to issue its report. Second, given the gravity of the offence of lying to parliament, it was unclear why such a low penalty was imposed.

Third, and perhaps most seriously, the committee had made no apparent attempt to relate Floyd's conduct to broader (but also punishable) provisions about integrity and honesty. Instead, some of the complaints had simply been ignored.

At any rate, Floyd himself seemed to find the report so potentially damaging that he took immediate legal action against it. In December 2023, he applied to the High Court for an urgent order setting aside the committee report and the National Assembly's decision to adopt it, as well as an order that the findings be suspended while the matter was being considered. The judge dismissed the application and ordered Floyd to pay the costs.

In October 2019, Steenhuisen also lodged a complaint against Julius Malema in respect of the 'VBS scandal'. This complaint, too, was based on *Daily Maverick*'s reports showing that Malema benefited from VBS funds, funnelled through Mahuna Investments that he did not disclose in his declaration of interests; that he used the 'life savings of vulnerable VBS depositors and municipalities to fund his extravagant lifestyle, business interests and political aspirations'; that he 'was involved in a scheme to mask the origin and ultimate beneficiaries of these funds'; and that he misled parliament to believe that he was not connected to Mahuna Investments.

When the registrar of members' interests wrote to Malema later that month requesting a reply, he responded contemptuously on the same day: 'This correspondence serves as both my acknowledgement of your letter

and my official response. [. . .] I think the letter is misdirected because
I've nothing to do with the company in question. Next time come with
something solid and not this newspaper junk. I've nothing to do with
all this nonsense.'

In a second affidavit to the registrar of members' interests, the VBS
liquidator explained that Sgameka Projects had paid R4 803 180 into
an ABSA bank account held by Mahuna Investments. Money from VBS
was paid into the Sgameka account and then 'transferred out into other
bank accounts held by both natural and juristic persons'. The liquidator
could not follow the money any further.

Malema did not hold a bank account with VBS, and no money
was directly transferred to accounts in his name from the Sgameka bank
account. The liquidator had no evidence of 'any account held by the
Member that may implicate him in the VBS scandal'.[308]

The VBS liquidator's probe had reached an impasse, and the FIC
again proved unhelpful. Parliament's ethics committee told the public
it was 'unable to make findings' in the case because it lacked sufficient
information. Unlike Shivambu, who had cash from Sgameka directly
transferred into his personal accounts, there were at least two layers of
separation between Malema and the original source of funds.

As a result, the ethics committee decided to 'close the file in the matter'.

When pushed on the matter, Malema is quick to say the ethics committee found he 'did not receive a cent' from VBS. This, of course, is
untrue – it merely found that it did not have enough information to reach
a conclusion. Despite the mountain of evidence against Malema in the
public domain, he walked away with no sanction or penalty.

PART FOUR

Milking the Metros

CHAPTER 22

An accident of a mayor

THE LOCAL GOVERNMENT elections of 3 August 2016 were a boon for the EFF and a blow to the ANC. Africa's oldest liberation movement continued the electoral slide that had set in under Zuma. Once the smoke cleared and the votes had been counted, the ANC had lost its majority in four of the country's eight metros – Tshwane, Johannesburg, Nelson Mandela Bay and Ekurhuleni. The ANC held on to Ekurhuleni through a power-sharing deal, but Tshwane, Johannesburg and Nelson Mandela Bay fell to the opposition, which cobbled together governing alliances centred on the DA.

The EFF won just over 8 percent of the vote nationally – a decent result for a new party. The 'Red Berets' proclaimed they would not formally join the DA-led coalitions, but the latter would have to rely on their cooperation if they were to survive. This gave the EFF outsized power and influence.

A triumphant Malema and several other leaders, dressed in their signature red overalls and berets, held a media conference in the veld outside Alexandra township, Johannesburg. He could barely conceal his delight in giving the middle finger to the ANC, which had kicked him out only four years earlier. 'Because you all said you were taking collective responsibility [for Zuma], you shall be punished as a collective,' a puffed-up Malema warned his former party. 'The ANC had a choice between Zuma and the metros. Once again, the ANC chose Zuma.'

Immediately after the elections, Malema had in fact entered into negotiations with the ANC and slammed down a laundry list of entirely unrealistic demands. He said the EFF did not seek positions in the metros but demanded the amendment of the Constitution to allow land to be expropriated without compensation; the nationalisation of mines, banks and 'strategic sectors of the economy'; the 'immediate institution of free education'; the abolition of e-tolls (the controversial electronic road toll system around Johannesburg); and the removal of *Die Stem* from the national anthem.

The party also demanded that the controversial nuclear energy deal the Zuma government was reportedly negotiating with the Russians be scrapped, and it wanted a judicial inquiry into the Guptas. But the biggest obstacle was the demand that Zuma be removed as national president. 'We have no power to ask them to remove him as the president of the ANC,' Malema told journalists, 'but as a shareholder of this company called South Africa, we have the right to ask them to recall him as the president of the republic.'

This was typical of the EFF's ostentatious politicking; unsurprisingly, the talks went nowhere. Instead, the EFF – the self-styled pro-black and pro-poor revolutionary party – aligned with the 'liberal' DA against Zuma. But the limits of their relationship of convenience would become clearer as these two parties faced up to the hard realities of governance and coalition politics in the metros. A particularly thorny issue early on was the DA's mayoral candidate for Johannesburg, Herman Mashaba, who the EFF initially refused to work with.

The EFF regarded Mashaba – a businessman and free marketeer who had made a fortune selling hair products to black consumers, and a former chair of the Free Market Foundation – as the embodiment of the most conservative, reactionary side of the DA. It was one thing to work with the DA, but Mashaba was a bridge too far. The EFF branded him a man who 'disdains the poor' and 'hates his blackness', and Malema made it clear that, in exchange for his party's support, he wanted the DA to dump Mashaba.

At the Alexandra briefing, Malema hinted at the Mashaba problem, telling reporters: 'The DA will get our vote in Johannesburg if they meet one condition we put to them, which is between us and them.'

Around the same time, the EFF chair, Advocate Dali Mpofu, told national radio that the party found Mashaba's views objectionable: 'I think he bought too much into the dogma of market fundamentalism, so we do not trust that he will be able to have a favourable look at the poor.' However, he intimated that the Mashaba issue could be overcome, saying that if the latter would clarify his views, he might allay the fears of the EFF.

In the end, though, the DA stood by Mashaba, and Malema and the EFF went along with it. Explaining this decision, Malema said: 'You've got two devils here [the ANC and DA], both of them protecting white capital' – but the difference was that the ANC was 'corrupt to the core'. The ANC was 'extremely arrogant . . . Even when they've performed badly, they still want to pretend like nothing has happened.'

He also spoke of ANC leaders popping champagne despite the party's decline – evidence of a 'party in denial'.

'We are happy to announce there's no deal between the EFF and ANC,' Malema told the gathered media. But he also said there would be 'no deal with the DA'.

What he meant was that the EFF would not enter into a formal co-alition – but there certainly was a deal. The EFF would back the coalitions led by the DA – the 'party of white racists', as Malema called them – from the outside. 'We'll be voting for DA in Tshwane, in Ekurhuleni, in Johannesburg and PE. There is a difference between coalitions and voting for them. We'll vote for them and be in the opposition benches.'

From early on, Mashaba was at pains to demonstrate his willingness to work with 'kingmaker' Malema, and the EFF soon began to exercise a level of control over the mayor's administration that many in the DA found alarming. During Mashaba's three years in office, he went from being an EFF hate figure to moving so close to that party that he was labelled the 'EFF mayor' by some.

Mashaba's chief of staff during his mayoral term was Michael Beaumont, until then a full-time DA staffer. In a later hagiography of his boss titled *The Accidental Mayor: Herman Mashaba and the Battle for Johannesburg*, Beaumont portrays Mashaba as a self-made man and a straight-shooting workaholic who only wanted to get the job done. In this case, the job happened to be cleaning up a city after years of ANC mismanagement and corruption.

For Beaumont, his boss was no politician. He was, rather, an anti-politician who had dared to enter the dragon's lair to reclaim politics from the venal political elite – a man who had loudly declared corruption 'public enemy number one'. Whatever his initial intentions, Mashaba soon learnt that cleaning up corruption in Johannesburg would be a lot trickier than rolled-up sleeves and tough talk, especially with a party like the EFF occupying 30 of the council's 270 seats.

By the end of August 2016, three new DA mayors for the metros had been sworn in – Solly Msimanga in Tshwane, Athol Trollip in Nelson Mandela Bay and Mashaba in Johannesburg.

Mashaba gave 2 of the 10 positions in his mayoral committee – housing and transport – to the Zulu nationalist IFP, with the rest taken up by DA members. Other smaller coalition partners – COPE, the African Christian Democratic Party (ACDP), the United Democratic Movement (UDM) and the Freedom Front Plus – got chairs of council committees.

It was in the IFP-run transport department that early signs emerged of Mashaba's willingness to bend to the whims of other parties – signs that he would ignore the failings of those who kept him in power, just to keep them in line. Specifically, Mashaba was accused of turning a blind eye to malfeasance at the Johannesburg Roads Agency (JRA), which fell under the transport department.

From about March 2017, when a new board was installed at the JRA, the organisation's managing director, Sean Phillips, began raising concerns about potential corruption, directing his appeals at both Mashaba and the IFP member of the mayoral committee (MMC) responsible for transport, Nonhlanhla Makhuba.

Phillips is a veteran civil servant with a doctorate in civil engineering and a faintly perturbed frown. He speaks with dry precision about the labyrinthine laws and regulations of public procurement – a sign of his surefootedness in matters of public governance. This was presumably part of the reason why, after a 'rigorous selection process', he was made managing director of the JRA in May 2016, moving from a similar role at the Municipal Infrastructure Support Agency. He has since become director-general of the national Department of Water and Sanitation.

At the time of his appointment to the JRA, the ANC was still in power in the city. He had applied for the job, he said, as he wanted to be involved in service delivery at the local level. The JRA had a daunting task: developing and maintaining Johannesburg's increasingly potholed and clogged roads, clearing drainage systems, repairing bridges and traffic lights, and generally ensuring that transport in the country's economic hub and largest city functioned as smoothly as possible. One of the entity's flagship projects was the refurbishment of the M1 'double decker' highway – a major artery bisecting the city.

According to Phillips, things started off well for him at the JRA. He had the 'full support' of the board, the ANC's MMC for transport, Christine Walters, and the city manager, Trevor Fowler. Then came the local government elections in August 2016, though it took a while for the change to sink in. In the early days of the new Mashaba administration, Phillips got on well with both the new mayor and Makhuba, the new MMC.

Makhuba supported the service delivery improvements the JRA was trying to achieve. 'I was also impressed by the business-like approach of the new mayor and his expressed commitment to fighting corruption,' Phillips wrote in a note recounting his time as head of the JRA.

By March 2017, things were still moving along nicely, and the JRA had been allocated additional funds to repair potholes and fix traffic lights. The term of the old ANC-appointed board had ended, and a new board was brought in under a colourful new chairperson, Sipho Tshabalala. The owner of a well-known restaurant on Vilakazi Street in Soweto, he had made headlines in the 1990s when he was found guilty of shooting a man dead at a party during an argument allegedly over football and a bottle of brandy. He had turned his court appearance into a spectacle, at one stage appearing in 'a flowing blue and gold robe, matching slippers and designer sunglasses'.[309]

Twenty years later, he was presiding over an important City of Johannesburg agency with a tantalisingly large procurement budget. Not long after being installed as the new chair, Phillips recounts, Tshabalala sat him down and insisted on being involved in the decision-making around JRA tenders. Phillips told him this was not possible as it would contravene the Municipal Finance Management Act – at which point Tshabalala said something like, 'Alright, then you'll have to consult with me informally,' to which Phillips did not agree.

Public entities in South Africa are supposed to procure goods and services from the private sector via an open and competitive tender system. To start with, the Constitution requires that systems for procuring goods or services must be 'fair, equitable, transparent, competitive and cost-effective'. For many years, however, implementation was less clear-cut. Until the adoption of the Public Procurement Act in 2024, public procurement was governed by a plethora of laws and regulations applying to national, provincial and local governments, creating a fragmented regulatory environment that – according to the Zondo Commission – helped to turn it into the 'centrepiece of state capture'.

Nevertheless, in the Johannesburg metro, the process plays out (or is meant to play out) as follows: Tenders are publicly advertised after their specifications have been determined by a committee. Bids are assessed in terms of costs, experience, skills, capacity and, crucially, transformation and affirmative action criteria – specifically, the company's BEE score. Qualifying bids are then evaluated and finally adjudicated by tender committees.

On paper, this is meant to be a systematic and unbiased process, secured by various checks and balances. In reality, however, officials have some level of discretion, and every stage presents opportunities for interference by, say, leaking inside information to a certain bidder, manipulating the scores or disqualifying a bidder on a technicality. The job of an accounting officer like Phillips is to ensure that the tender process remains fair and objective – in other words, compliant with the rules and regulations.

He must stand in the way of politicians, board members, contractors and others who try to influence the process in favour of certain bidders and thus commit tender fraud. This is precisely what he suspected Tshabalala was trying to do. Perhaps most alarming was a proposal from some board members for the creation of a 'Project Management Unit' (PMU), which would entail bringing in consultants to 'manage some of the key procurement processes related to capital works and to manage the implementation of capital works'.

The JRA already had an internal department to do precisely this, headed by an experienced engineer, Mpho Kau. To Phillips, it looked like an attempt to get around the checks and balances built into the

JRA's procurement processes by outsourcing procurement to external and potentially pliant consultants.

According to Phillips, his relationship with Tshabalala soured after he blocked the chairman's attempts to elbow his way into tender processes. 'After one board meeting, the chairperson came to my office, told me that I needed to understand that the new political leadership wants different contractors to be appointed, and then left.'

Board minutes for June and July reflect the chair's increasing interest in one tender in particular: the flagship M1 double-decker highway refurbishment. The contract had been given to a company called White Hazy, which appeared to be struggling to get the job done. As the project fell further and further behind schedule, it became the subject of heated board meetings. JRA management was pushing to remove White Hazy for having failed to deliver, among a host of problems highlighted by Kau. By the time the project was due to be completed, the contractor had only finished about 17 percent of the job, and Joburg's residents had noticed the increasingly dilapidated state of the iconic roadway.

The mounting tension between Phillips and Tshabalala is evident in the minutes, which show that the latter tried to argue, wrongfully, that the board could overrule any decision by management to cancel the contract. Kau was the most vocal in arguing that the contract should be terminated, pointing out that an independent consultant had recommended that multiple times – but management was split.

The JRA's chief financial officer (CFO), Goodwill Mbatha, sided with the chairperson. But Phillips stood firm, insisting that the final decision rested with him. This irritated the chair, who wanted it 'placed on record that the MD had sufficiently stressed his responsibility and it was unnecessary for him to belabour the point further'. It eventually became clear that despite resistance to the idea, the contract would have to be cancelled one way or another.

At this point, says Phillips, Tshabalala was yelling at him in board meetings, accusing him of being a 'failure, both as a manager and a leader'. Exasperated, Phillips decided to approach both the new city manager, Ndivhoniswani Lukhwareni, and Makhuba about his worsening relationship with the chair and his concern about tenders being manipulated.

'They both indicated to me that they thought it was wrong for [Tshabalala] to want to be involved in the awarding of tenders, that they would talk to him, that they were sure he was acting out of ignorance and that the situation would improve once he became better acquainted with his roles and responsibilities.'

It wasn't just Phillips and Kau who were worried about the turn the JRA was taking. Karen Mills, the company secretary, was also concerned about a range of governance issues, including the chair's apparent fixation with tenders. She tried to raise these issues with the board's audit and risk committee.

Instead of dealing with her concerns, the board allegedly tried to muzzle her and warned her not to raise these issues with anyone else. Frustrated, Mills outlined her concerns in a formal submission to the City of Johannesburg's Group Forensics and Investigation Services. She did what she felt she should have done in terms of the Protected Disclosures Act, which is supposed to protect whistleblowers. But the board got hold of a copy of Mills' disclosure, and from then her days at the agency were numbered.

Meanwhile, an increasingly alarmed Phillips had decided to take the 'extraordinary' step of going straight to the mayor. According to him, at a meeting with Mashaba and Lukhwareni, the city manager, 'the mayor indicated that the chairperson should not have anything to do with tenders and that the board should not pursue the establishment of the PMU without addressing my concerns. He indicated that he would set up a further meeting with the MMC, the chairperson and me to address these issues. I was relieved, and felt reassured that the mayor would support me in ensuring good governance at the JRA.'

About 10 days later, the mayor met Phillips, Tshabalala, Lukhwareni and MMC Makhuba. Phillips laid out his concerns in detail – but, he says, the city manager and Makhuba seemed to brush them aside as 'personal relationship issues' between Phillips and the chair. Makhuba made it clear that she was 'disappointed' that Phillips had approached the mayor directly. Phillips claims that both Makhuba and the chairperson also defended the PMU, saying it was necessary to 'address underexpenditure on the capital budget and to improve the management of capital projects', despite the fact that the JRA had spent a decent 87 percent of its 2016/17 capital budget and would have spent over 90 percent had it not been for the City's cash-flow problems, according to Phillips.

He adds that the chairperson was otherwise apologetic – saying he was sorry if he had offended Phillips – and willing to work with him. To Phillips' dismay, Mashaba seemed to buy the apology. He wanted Phillips and Tshabalala to make up and move on, and he seemed intent on avoiding the sticky issues of governance. Phillips felt the underlying problem had not been addressed, and he told the mayor he would have to consider whether he could continue working with the chairperson.

That evening, Phillips received an urgent call from a political advisor to the MMC, asking him to a meeting. He promptly met the advisor, who tried to convince him not to resign, saying that the MMC and the IFP's provincial leader would help Phillips 'manage' the chairperson. Phillips claims, however, that the advisor told him he needed to be aware of two things. The first was that 'all political parties rely on tenders for party political funding [in other words, that they rely on donations from service providers who are awarded tenders]'. The second was that the decision to create a PMU in the JRA was a joint decision of the IFP and the EFF that was taken because it was 'deemed necessary to get around Mpho Kau and his department'. The advisor claimed – incorrectly, according to Phillips – that too many tenders were going to 'established white contractors'.

'When I heard that the decision to establish a [PMU] was a joint decision between the IFP and the EFF, the hair stood up on the back of my neck,' says Phillips. He was immediately reminded of the allegations of corruption involving On-Point Engineers and the PMU at the Limpopo department of roads and transport.

According to Beaumont's biography of Mashaba, 'there was clearly a close relationship' between the EFF and IFP, and though the EFF had said it did not seek any appointments in a coalition government, the party had insisted on having two IFP members in Mashaba's mayoral committee.[310]

After a sleepless night, Phillips submitted his three months' notice of resignation and informed the mayor of his decision. Mashaba did not respond, and when Phillips returned to work, he was told to pack up his belongings and was marched out of the JRA's downtown offices.

The ructions at the JRA sparked a minor exodus. The day Phillips handed in his resignation, the board suspended Mills. Her suspension ran for a year until the board reached a settlement with her. About a week after Phillips' departure, Kau resigned from his post as head of the infrastructure development department.

Although Phillips and Kau were out of the picture, they had already set in motion the removal of the underperforming contractor White Hazy, which reached a settlement with the JRA in December. The company was paid R3,3 million, bringing its total earnings to R16 million. In the meantime, its replacement had been selected the month prior, in November. It was Khato Civils – the company owned by Simbi Phiri that was working hand-in-glove with LTE in Giyani.

The JRA's decision to appoint Khato was also controversial. It was selected through a 'closed' process, meaning there was no competitive bidding. This was an extraordinary move; although it is allowed in law, the circumstances under which it is permissible are tightly circumscribed and include 'emergencies'. The JRA argued that the state of the highway was indeed an emergency, although it was difficult to argue that it was not self-imposed, given the foot-dragging around the cancellation of the White Hazy contract.

But there were also other reasons to be alarmed. The total cost of the project had rocketed from R71 million to R169 million. Added to this, Khato was given upfront payments totalling R22 million – 13 percent of the contract value. Such payments were unheard of during Phillips' time, but he was no longer there to halt these sorts of irregularities. Without the support of Mashaba and the MMC, Phillips had felt that staying on and standing up to the chairperson would have been futile.

Mbatha, the CFO who had consistently sided with the chair, was at first acting in Phillips' position and then permanently appointed. In April 2019, however, he was removed after a rough couple of weeks for the JRA. At the beginning of that month, the investigative TV show *Carte Blanche* aired recordings of a top JRA official negotiating kickbacks with contractors. By mid-month, Mbatha and other 'implicated individuals' were suspended. This followed the long-delayed findings of an investigation by the City that determined that White Hazy had submitted a 'fraudulent' bid for the M1 double-decker bridge project and 'falsified' information about its personnel and experience.

According to a press statement from the mayor's office, a criminal case was opened against the contractor and a submission made to blacklist it. This was scant comfort to residents of Johannesburg. The dysfunction at the JRA was evident in the worsening state of the city's 4 000-kilometre road network, with only 6 percent of the city's 700 bridges deemed to be in good condition.

The agency's poster-child project, the M1 refurbishment, was being botched. Despite the millions sunk into the project, road users were outraged when the rains came in 2020 and the bridge flooded. The customary motions followed: the suspension of a senior official, an apology from the JRA and a half-hearted promise to investigate the matter.

All of this might have brought an unhappy sense of vindication to Phillips and his two purged colleagues, Kau and Mills. Mashaba had fiddled while the JRA burned, and the consequences of his inaction were plain to see. In response to the fallout between Tshabalala and Phillips, the mayor's spokesperson said Mashaba simply could not intervene – his hands were tied until matters were properly investigated.

But that hadn't stopped him from taking a firm position on allegations of corruption at another Joburg entity, City Power. There, Mashaba was all too willing to make his presence felt in ways that some officials felt was overbearing.

At City Power, the EFF's fingerprints were everywhere. With the largest capital budget in the City, the electricity utility was a seemingly endless seam of riches waiting to be tapped, but doing so would first require shaking up its management and board. On that count, if perhaps unwittingly, Mashaba was quick to lend his assistance.

CHAPTER 23

Mashaba comes to the party

IN FEBRUARY 2017, six months into his mayoral term, Herman Mashaba fired Anthony Still, the MMC for infrastructure and environmental services – the first of his executives to be shown the door. At the heart of the dispute was Mashaba's insistence that City Power's managing director, Sicelo Xulu, be removed immediately. Still, whose department was responsible for the utility, antagonised Mashaba when he showed some reluctance to remove Xulu so hastily.

For years, a cloud of allegations had hung over Xulu in connection with a major City Power contract to install smart meters in houses and businesses across Johannesburg. In 2012, the R1,2-billion contract went to a company owned by the well-known businessman Vivian Reddy, an ANC benefactor and supporter of Jacob Zuma. Xulu, too, was said to be close to Zuma.

The following year, in January 2013, amaBhungane ran an article exposing some of the discrepancies in Reddy's tender.[311] The article came days after an ANC gala dinner in Durban where Reddy had reportedly paid R450 000 for a table and Zuma had remarked that 'wise' businessmen who backed the ANC could expect to see their fortunes multiply.

According to the article, evidence suggested that the score sheets for bidders had been adjusted to give Reddy's company, Edison Power, a lead and to push out rivals. A letter informing Edison that it had won the bid was signed before the procurement process was finalised, and the initial recommendation that Edison be given a R600-million share of an R800-million contract was subsequently changed to give it an exclusive contract of R1,25 billion.

However, successive probes had failed to turn up evidence of wrong-doing sufficient to justify sacking the MD, and Still would not act against Xulu without the evidence. In any case, Xulu would have to be removed by the board, not by a political executive. Chaired by the anti-apartheid struggle stalwart Frank Chikane, the board was of the view that Xulu had been cleared. Without new evidence, there were no grounds to remove him.

This was not what Mashaba wanted to hear. From the moment he entered the mayoral office, he had been fixated on the idea that City officials appointed under the previous ANC administration were intent on undermining him. Given the ANC's policy of cadre deployment, his fears were probably not without foundation. But at times, his distrust was such that he suspected that the entire bureaucracy was crawling with agents and sympathisers of the ANC – 'snakes', as he called them – who would stop at nothing to sabotage his government.

In Xulu's case, the mayor's mind was made up. The City Power case must have seemed like a clear opportunity for Mashaba to act against corruption and malfeasance within the city administration. Michael Beaumont writes that he and the mayor believed Still was 'procrastinating' and 'questioning the findings' against Xulu by the City's new forensic unit, headed by General Shadrack Sibiya, the former head of the Hawks in Gauteng. However, there were no 'findings' at the time – or, at least, nothing like the findings Beaumont refers to. Whether down to a failure of memory, sloppy research or sleight of hand, Beaumont had muddled his account.

The fact is that the investigation was only commissioned by the City's forensic unit in early 2017, when Mashaba was determined to have Xulu removed and after City Power's own findings had failed to turn up sufficient evidence for this to occur. The forensic unit subcontracted most of its investigation to an external forensic auditing company called SizweNtsalubaGobodo (SNG), which produced its report only months later, after Still's removal. So, he could not have been removed for refusing to act on the forensic unit's recommendations.

'Mashaba hit the roof when he learnt it was not a former ANC cadre blocking progress on the matter, but his own MMC,' Beaumont writes. 'Mashaba told me that he wanted Still gone. I explained that the party's federal executive had to be involved in such matters. "Brief them, then," he told me, "but do it faster than I can fire him.'"

Still was called into a meeting with the mayor. Half an hour later, he walked out of the office for the last time. Unusually for a political appointee, he went public soon after his dismissal. On national radio, he said it was not in his power, nor in the mayor's, to suspend Xulu summarily. A process had to be followed, and labour law also played a role. In any case, the allegations were not new. Xulu had been investigated many times, and the allegations had not stood up.

Still was followed on radio by the governance expert Professor Ivor Sarakinsky, who said: 'What we're seeing is . . . clear and blatant political interference in the functioning of the board.'

A month after Still's removal, the entire Chikane board was 'retired' at the City Power annual general meeting. Chikane, like Still, was outspoken, telling a radio interviewer: 'We expected it because . . . there were differences about how to handle the MD . . . we were seen as an obstacle, and there was an indication that by the time we go to the AGM, we'll be replaced.'

Chikane was angered by the mayor's implication that his board was soft on corruption. 'We've worked hard to clean up that place,' he said, before shooting off a series of corroborating statistics about cases that were reported to the police and subsequent prosecutions. In the meantime, Xulu, at his own request, had gone on leave while the investigation was ongoing because, Chikane said, 'the environment was so negative'.

At a media briefing around the same time, Chikane said that he had come under pressure to 'act' against the MD, but that the allegations against Xulu had been tested before and he had been cleared. The board had therefore opposed further investigations of the same allegations without new evidence. The City's investigation carried out by SNG nevertheless progressed.

When City Power's new board was appointed, it included two members proposed by the EFF. This was not inherently wrong, and the DA had its own card-carrying members on the board, too – Denis Hunt and Douglas Gibson. But influence at board level could enable influence over appointments, like that of a new MD, and a compromised MD with the support of board members could translate into influence over procurement and afford a degree of cover for schemes for siphoning off money from City Power. For a party desperate for cash, City Power with its massive capital budget was ripe for the taking; the right people just had to be installed. One of the new board members was a familiar figure – Mandla Seopela, who, years before, had helped to mobilise support for Malema after he was expelled from the ANCYL. Seopela had also received a slice of the questionable tenders at the University of Limpopo.[312]

One City Power source described him as competent and professional. But, he said, the other EFF-linked board member was prone to losing his temper and quick to throw around accusations of racism. That individual was Hlayiseka Chewane, a qualified medical doctor and member of the party's central command team. Chewane had been sworn in as an EFF MP in 2015, after Khanyisile Litchfield-Tshabalala was expelled from the party along with two other dissenters, Andile Mngxitama and Mpho Ramakatsa, for criticising the party's leadership.

When the new board was installed, the most pressing item on its agenda was dealing with the sticky matter of Xulu, who was still away from work while being investigated by the City's forensic department and SNG. The latter submitted its report in June, but it was far from the death blow the mayor must have hoped for. The forensic auditors had looked beyond the tender awarded to Reddy's Edison Power to other alleged irregularities in procurement and human resources matters. They found that Xulu, as well as other staff members at City Power, had fallen short on various technical grounds.

The report underscored several governance shortcomings at the City entity. But, on the central issue of the Edison Power contract, SNG concluded that other City Power officials, not Xulu, were mostly to blame for the anomalies in the tender. The report did, however, recommend 'corrective action' against him for failing to notify the City, the auditor-general and the Treasury of the discrepancies in the tender process. Unrelated to that, it also recommended that he be disciplined for having irregularly increased the pay of some staff members based on an un-approved remuneration policy.

Some board members felt that the 'technical infringements' were not what the investigation was really after, and the grounds for removing Xulu were flimsy. But a statement from the mayor's office began with the exaggerated accusation of 'damning' findings at City Power in connection with 'allegations of widespread corruption and mismanagement, costing the public billions of rands'. It was hyperbole. But even before the report was completed, it was clear to everyone involved that, regardless of its findings, it would be untenable for Xulu to remain at City Power – the board would have to remove him somehow. The solution was made easy by the fact that Xulu's term was up for renewal in August, so he was simply told he would not be re-employed.

Xulu cried foul, saying the allegations of corruption and misconduct against him in statements from the City were devoid of evidence and detail. He claimed in a public statement that he had not been provided with a copy of the report and had not had an opportunity to respond to the findings against him. This was despite a legal opinion obtained by City Power in early July that stated explicitly that Xulu was entitled to see the report, and that anyone implicated in it should have an opportunity to respond to findings against them.

The legal opinion also implicitly questioned the premise of the SNG report, cautioning against charging officials for matters that had already been dealt with: 'Where any of the matters have actually been dealt with within City Power and no disciplinary action has been taken, it would in our considered view not be appropriate to institute disciplinary action against those employees involved, unless the decisions not to institute disciplinary action were made irrationally and for an improper purpose.' But that became a moot point, and Xulu moved on without challenging the report in court, even though the City's own legal opinion was that he would have a strong case.

Whereas Mashaba was hands-off at JRA when the MD of that entity felt he needed the mayor's help, he seemed perfectly willing to venture deep into City Power's messy affairs by, among other things, arranging the reappointment of the utility's former internal auditor, Vuyani Singonzo, who had been removed in 2014 under Xulu. In September 2017, Singonzo was reinstalled with three months' salary and annual increases calculated from the time of his termination in 2014.[313] He had been fired after he was found to have abused his position at City Power and broken the code of conduct for internal auditors. An internal City Power report recommended charging him for having 'used confidential information obtained during the course of his duties as manager of internal audit for his personal benefit' during labour arbitration proceedings.

Media reported that Mashaba appeared unmoved by legal opinions from two separate law firms cautioning against reinstating Singonzo, as well as warnings from City Power staff that this would cause reputational harm. The more recent of the two legal opinions, sent to the mayor in March 2017, noted that, based on available evidence, 'it cannot be said that Singonzo's dismissal was procedurally or substantively unfair'. Mashaba was not going to change his mind, saying in a press statement that he was 'pleased to announce . . . the reinstatement of Mr Vuyani Singonzo after being unfairly dismissed'. He apologised to Singonzo 'for the manner in which he was treated' by the previous administration. To some within the utility, it was a worrying sign of the extent to which Mashaba would intervene at City Power.

For the mayor, returning Singonzo to City Power was politically expedient, as the former employee was part of a faction of the largest municipal workers' union that supported him. The South African Municipal Workers' Union (Samwu), an affiliate of Cosatu, was split between the 'legitimate' leadership and a rival grouping, which included Singonzo, that the Labour Court deemed 'illegitimate'. For the new administration, it presented an opportunity to drive a wedge between the factions and widen the rift within organised labour. Here was a powerful union that could, and did, bring Johannesburg to a standstill, now riven with allegations of malfeasance. Playing one side off against the other would help neutralise a troublesome threat. Cultivating links with the grouping that included Singonzo would also strengthen Mashaba's support base. Beaumont – never one for nuance – even came to regard Singonzo as a 'great South African'.

The Citizen quoted sources who said it was important that Singonzo be re-employed 'to enable him to hold a leadership position in a Samwu faction that supports the mayor . . . in order for Singonzo to deal with Mashaba's office as a union representative, the rules dictate that he be a City employee'.

Mashaba's willingness to either wash his hands of a matter and cede control to his political allies, as he was accused of having done at the JRA, or forcefully intervene in City entities when it suited him, made him an increasingly useful ally to the EFF, which had begun lobbying him over City Power. With Xulu out of the way, the next pressing order of business for City Power's board was to find a replacement. In this regard, the EFF board members had a clear favourite among the shortlisted candidates – Lerato Setshedi, a longtime City Power employee who had headed metering services at the utility.

On paper, Setshedi was not a bad choice, although some board members felt there were better ones. Mashaba had interviewed Setshedi – there was nothing improper about that, according to a board member – but was unimpressed. He apparently had another candidate in mind for the MD role. But the two EFF members, according to City Power sources, aligned with another board member in championing Setshedi.

'The trouble with these boards is that the board itself is a bit of theatre, really,' then-board member Denis Hunt told us. 'It's quite difficult to say it's an important decision-making body, but it is important if you want to get the right people in.'

But it was not the support of board members alone that secured Setshedi's lead. Ultimately, high-level political bargaining and the mayor's apparent change of heart likely tipped the balance in his favour. Email correspondence from September 2017 between the mayor and senior EFF leaders – including Malema and Shivambu – suggests that the mayor might have bent to EFF pressure to make Setshedi MD of City Power.

On the morning of 27 September, Mashaba sent a mayoral committee report to his EFF allies, including Malema and Shivambu, writing in a covering email: 'As the Mayoral Committee has approved this document, it is a mere matter of process for the board of City Power to convene a meeting and finalize the appointment process. I have made my request known to the relevant individuals that this meeting must now happen at the earliest opportunity possible in respect of the City of Johannesburg's policies and relevant legislation.'

The document in question was a resolution to appoint Setshedi for a five-year term beginning on 1 October 2017. That he was writing this to the national leaders of a rival party outside his coalition was strange enough. Even more eyebrow-raising was Mashaba's placatory tone. According to Hunt, a DA member, 'it was clear that the mayor had gone with the EFF chaps who wanted Lerato'. Another email suggests there may have been a link between the decision to appoint Setshedi and a walkout by EFF members in the city council. In the email, a senior EFF leader asks Mashaba to contact Shivambu about the Setshedi matter and an earlier 'conversation about EFF PR councillors walking out of your council sitting today'.

Mashaba appears to have backed Setshedi to get the EFF's support in council. He needed Malema's party on side to pass his institutional review – a vital element of his plans for the City, which included introducing broad structural changes and slimming down its bloated management. Pushing the institutional review through the council had already proved impossible, with the previous three sessions collapsing because the ANC walked out and EFF councillors were absent. Mashaba knew that his institutional review was stuck without the EFF's support.

According to a source with direct knowledge of the haggling between Mashaba and the EFF, the latter was holding the mayor's agenda hostage in the hope of extracting quid pro quos, such as influencing the appointment of key officials. And Mashaba's conciliatory message to Malema, Shivambu and others regarding Setshedi's appointment appears to have come just in time. In council the very next day, 28 September, the EFF flipped and voted with the DA-led coalition in support of the institutional review while the ANC's members goaded them from the opposition benches. Mashaba's important policy passed, for the time being, and the EFF would seemingly get its choice as the head of City Power.

Top City Power sources said Setshedi was viewed widely as an EFF appointee. With the new MD ensconced at the utility and EFF members on the entity's board, the stage was set for what was to follow.

In mid-2020, the media began to report on allegations by an anonymous whistleblower about tender-rigging at City Power. At the heart of the controversy was a City Power employee called Percy Mphahlele, a general manager in charge of capital contracts at the utility. Mphahlele, the whistleblower alleged, was manipulating tenders in favour of certain companies. Those contractors – three in total – would allegedly channel kickbacks to Mphahlele via third-party companies.[314]

One of those third parties was Anego Africa Power, owned by Moloshi Seanego, a young businessman and business partner to Mphahlele's 19-year-old son, Prince. Anego's bank statements from March to May 2020 reflect more than R6 million in payments from City Power con-tractors, mostly payments in big round numbers. Some of the money – at least R300 000 – was then passed on to Prince's company, Hlelele Power Projects. In the same period, large sums of cash – tens and even hundreds of thousands of rand at a time – were withdrawn from the Anego account. These included R200 000 withdrawn on the same day that one of the contractors paid in 10 times that amount. At least R2,4 million in the Anego account was channelled into property.

The three contractors had obtained multimillion-rand chunks of a City Power tender for capital expenditure (capex) and maintenance awarded in late 2018. The tender, worth R1,5 billion in total, was split among a pool of service providers and was supposed to run for three years. But it wasn't long before an unsuccessful bidder, Infinite Blue Trading, cried foul and rushed to court, contending that there were 'material irregularities' in the tender that led to it being unfairly excluded.

On 30 May 2019, Judge Roland Sutherland of the Gauteng High Court ruled the tender invalid and set it aside. He agreed that there were 'clear irregularities' that gave rise to 'a reasonable suspicion of deliberate manipulation of the process to improperly exclude the applicant, and perhaps others too'. He ordered a re-evaluation of the bidders while those who held the flawed tender continued to perform their work for up to 90 days. In addition, the matter had to be brought to the attention of the City Power chief executive officer and the mayor.

The judgment then led to a long and grinding court process that included the 'unconscionable dragging of feet on the part of City Power', as a later and far more damning judgment put it in September 2020. By then, the headache had been passed on to Judge AJ Snyckers. This was nearly two years after the tender had been awarded, by which time the case had taken on 'disconcertingly grotesque proportions', as Snyckers put it.

City Power had repeatedly failed to reissue the tender within the pre-scribed deadlines, rushing back to court each time to extend the deadline at the last minute. The terms of the unlawfully appointed contractors were also extended as they continued to profit from what City Power eventually conceded was 'deliberate manipulation' of the bids.

City Power and its head, Lerato Setshedi, had also ignored the initial order to investigate the tender. In response to their attempt to explain their failure, Snyckers wrote: 'It would be difficult to achieve a more minimalist rendition of an account, in the style of Ernest Hemingway, with fewer facts contained in seven sentences.'

Snyckers slammed City Power for conduct that '[bordered] on the contemptuous', but reserved the fiercest criticism for Setshedi. His failure to investigate the alleged fraud was 'either cavalier and brazen disregard' for the order to do so, 'or trepidation at what a proper investigation and report might reveal'. Following Snyckers' 2020 judgment, Setshedi – who was already on special leave as City Power reluctantly investigated him – faced a legal fight to stay out of jail for contempt of court.

Among the numerous companies that got a share of the rigged capex and maintenance tender was F&J Electrical, which was also implicated in Mphahlele's scheme by the whistleblower. City Power became a milch cow for F&J, owned by Freddie Raphahlelo. Just one month after bagging its share of the capex and maintenance tender in November 2018, Raphahlelo's company won another tender of unspecified value, this time for a metering project.

But the big-ticket item came in March, when F&J was awarded a 'turnkey' contract for electrification worth a hefty R229,5 million, much of which was subcontracted to other companies, including the three that paid the apparent kickbacks. An audit conducted years later found that payments by City Power to F&J amounting to nearly R12 million were irregular and should be 'written off', but in the meantime, F&J and the subcontractors were happily feasting at the City Power trough.

On 13 April 2019, less than a month after F&J had received its electri-fication tender, it paid the Malema-linked Santaclara R200 000. Then, just over a month after the company had won a separate tender for LED streetlights in May 2019, a further R400 000 popped into the Santaclara account. This time, however, the money came from Baberwa FC – a third-division soccer club based in Gauteng. What did an obscure soccer club have to do with City Power, its contractors and multimillion-rand electricity tenders?

Journalists at the *Mail & Guardian* linked Baberwa FC to Anego – the company that was reportedly at the heart of Mphahlele's scheme, and which had received the alleged kickbacks from the three contractors. The link was a small payment of R10 000 that Anego made to a staff member of the soccer club. The club's chairman, Joe Seanego, was a City Power employee related to Anego's Moloshi Seanego.

At the time, Joe denied any knowledge of Anego Africa Power but did confirm that he had known Mphahlele senior and junior for a long time. According to the whistleblower, Percy Mphahlele of City Power and F&J's Raphahlelo were 'silent partners' in Joe Seanego's soccer club, and indeed, the club's current and former directors include someone with the surname Mphahlele and a Raphahlelo.

City Power internal records show that while Joe was a City Power employee, he had even approved payments to F&J in relation to older contracts. Not long after his football club had paid Malema, however, Joe was 'challenging his dismissal for gross negligence' in connection with other City Power contracts, the entity's annual report for 2020/21 notes. By that time, City Power's head, Setshedi, had also been removed. To some, it looked like an attempt to clean up the corruption festering within City Power.

But Malema had already seemingly raked in rents. An elaborate racket involving City Power officials colluding with favoured companies had squeezed money out of a vital City entity, with large sums channelled back to those officials along with a cut for Malema, their political protector. Vital to all of this was the unwitting assistance of a mayor who the EFF had not long before said they could never work with.

CHAPTER 24

Cars, trucks and tractors

THE VILLAGE OF Tshakhuma lies about 50 kilometres east of Louis Trichardt, on the road to the old Venda capital of Thohoyandou. It's a picturesque little place, hedged in by verdant hills and centred on a bustling fresh-produce market with piles of bananas, avocados, mangoes and nuts from the surrounding plantations. It was here, of all places, that we ended up searching for a blue Landini Solis tractor and the members of a farming cooperative who were its proud new owners. The tractor was a small, far-flung piece of a puzzle involving a R1,2-billion fleet contract negotiated 500 kilometres away in Johannesburg.

The multi-year contract to provide the City of Johannesburg's so-called 'vanilla fleet' was a huge undertaking, with a price tag to match. It would require a service provider to supply about 2 700 'non-specialised' vehicles – sedans, bakkies and trucks – to Johannesburg's administration and its various entities providing services like water and electricity. These vehicles were the mainstay of the City's fleet, and failure to deliver on the contract would have dire consequences.

The five-year fleet contract, due to end in September 2017, was held by the vehicle rental company Avis. City officials spent months preparing the next five-year tender document. Its sheer magnitude and technical complexity meant that it had to be planned well in advance and would be subject to a rigorous selection process. The successful bidder would not only lease the vehicles to the City but also maintain and service the vehicles and provide support services like call centres. However, the project was bogged down by administrative delays, and the bid was only advertised in September, just as Avis's contract was about to expire.

There were early indications of the EFF's interest in the tender when a company called Afrirent bid as part of a consortium with three other partners. One of them was a company called Mbewu Life, ostensibly a life-insurance company owned by Musa Shibambu. Other members of the consortium claimed he was a cousin of the EFF's deputy president, Floyd Shivambu, although Afrirent denied any knowledge of this. It said Shibambu was introduced to it by one of the other consortium partners.

Shibambu did not deny the link, telling reporters, 'I have my business and Floyd has his,'[315] while adding that they did not do business together. What a life insurer would add to a consortium bidding for a fleet contract was unclear. Floyd Shivambu also did not deny the relationship and, through his party, redirected journalists' questions to his supposed cousin.

By the time the tender closed in November, 16 bids had been submitted. City officials narrowed the list down to five companies, including Afrirent, without its consortium partners, and the incumbent, Avis. These five would enter a final selection process. As the bureaucratic process ground on through early 2018 and Avis's existing fleet contract was extended amid the delays, a man named Sanjay Dubru was parachuted into the position of acting head of the City directorate responsible for the fleet contract: Group Corporate and Shared Services. His arrival would soon cause major turbulence, and eventually the fleet tender would be derailed entirely.

Dubru had been 'seconded' from the Joburg Market, a major distribution hub for fresh produce where, incidentally, Shibambu would take up a position years later. It wasn't long before he ended up in conflict with his new City colleagues. Suleiman Ghanchi, a senior directorate official, claimed Dubru tried to lean on him to manipulate tenders. He told us that Dubru started sidestepping his direct superior and head of fleet compliance, Shaun Ramroop, and approached him (Ghanchi) directly about fleet tenders. Dubru and Ramroop also butted heads.

Ramroop said he had not been consulted about Dubru taking over from the previous acting head, which he found odd, as Dubru came from another institution and was an unknown quantity with 'no prior experience in leading a critical City directorate'. Soon after his arrival, Ramroop accused Dubru of meddling in tenders, including 'requesting confidential tender files from my staff'. When he confronted Dubru, he allegedly responded by saying: 'This is bigger than you and me,' and that Ramroop should not resist. He claims Dubru then started pressuring him into scuppering Avis's chances of getting the fleet contract again, and when he resisted, their relationship worsened to the point where Dubru started excluding him from meetings.

There was no direct evidence that Dubru was acting on behalf of the EFF or Julius Malema. However, if he was attempting to exert pressure on the awarding of a tender to a company linked to the EFF leader, it could suggest Malema's influence might have been at play. Dubru has not responded to our requests for comment. Meanwhile, the Avis contract was extended numerous times while officials managing the fleet contracts tried to finalise the tender. Of the five shortlisted bidders, Afrirent had only just squeezed through, lagging well behind the others in the scoring. Avis had the top score and was the preferred choice of the committee evaluating the tender, with FleetAfrica in second place. Ramroop said he had signed off on a report recommending Avis's reappointment, but Dubru ignored it.

In April, a probity report conducted by a small external consultancy threw a spanner in the works. The report – standard due diligence for large tenders – recommended that the tender be readvertised, primarily due to technical faults in the pricing criteria, as well as concerns about Avis's financial health. Avis's ratios for profit margin, solvency and debt were supposedly below standard and would have exposed the City to risk of failure – a strange conclusion, given that Avis had successfully run the fleet for years. Avis was baffled, saying it had a solid credit rating, 'so we are not sure why the City is concerned about our ability to fulfil tendered obligations. This is all news to Avis. We are the largest fleet company in Southern Africa and have been around for more than 30 years.'

Industry experts were also left scratching their heads. They felt Avis could simply have been asked to post a performance bond, which it had done for another contract, and that the other technical issues identified in the report were inconsequential and could have been rectified after the fact. Regardless, the directorate now had to redo the tender.

As the process started anew, Ramroop was eventually pushed aside – suspended due to what he claimed were 'frivolous and baseless allegations' – and, after five months sitting at home while earning his full salary, he decided to resign before a disciplinary hearing was convened. Shortly after Ramroop's suspension, Ghanchi, the senior official who had also complained about Dubru's interference, left the directorate too.

There was speculation within the City administration that the EFF was keeping a close eye on the tender. One senior executive appointed under Herman Mashaba claimed to have had direct knowledge of the EFF's interest in it. According to his account, local EFF representatives arranged for him to meet the EFF's Marshall Dlamini, then an MP, at a Sandton hotel. This was around the time Afrirent and its consortium partners submitted their bid. At the time, Dlamini was not well known outside the party, but he held the position of the EFF's 'commissar' for economic development. He would soon emerge as a rising star.

'He said to me, there's this tender coming – we want a company that works with us to get it,' said the executive. He claimed to have cut Dlamini short, saying that he had no power to influence the directorate managing the tender. Dlamini denied the account.

Another City official, a deputy director, claimed that a senior manager in the administration had told him that the EFF wanted Afrirent to get the tender – 'the whole thing came from the reds'. It was a claim the manager also denied.

As tensions within the directorate overseeing the fleet tender rose, so did the political temperature within the city. In council, the DA-led coalition was struggling to pass a budget. The EFF was the spoiler; without its support, the coalition was at an impasse. The EFF would not budge, with one party leader saying, with typical EFF bellicosity, that they 'vehemently, unreservedly, unapologetically and ferociously' rejected the planned utility tariff hikes. An article in *Business Day* at the time stated: 'The decision by the metro's kingmakers, the EFF, to abstain from voting on the tariffs led to the collapse of Mashaba's revenue plan and created a huge funding gap in the coming financial year.'

Elsewhere, the EFF was also flaunting its power as a potential disruptor. In Nelson Mandela Bay, it was working hard to unseat the DA mayor, Athol Trollip. 'We are cutting the throat of whiteness,' Malema told EFF supporters in April. After the DA had won 47 percent of the vote in the municipal elections, Trollip's fragile coalition was held in place by small parties, each with one or two seats in the 120-seat council. These parties were fickle allies.

Just how messy the uncharted waters of coalition politics could be was fast being revealed in the metros, where the rules of the coalition game were yet to be written and where local councils were buffeted by the currents of national politics. Parties in councils were often driven by concerns far removed from local issues, as the one-seat African Independent Congress (AIC) demonstrated when it switched allegiance from the ANC and sided with Trollip, effectively giving him a stay of execution in the face of an EFF motion to remove him.

The deciding factor in the AIC's flip was its demand that Matatiele – a small Eastern Cape municipality 650 kilometres from Nelson Mandela Bay – be incorporated within the borders of KwaZulu-Natal. When the ANC failed to deliver this, the AIC switched sides. The EFF, too, was baring its teeth at Trollip most over what were political issues at the national level – it had sworn vengeance for the DA's opposition to expropriation of land without compensation. Unlike in Johannesburg, the DA did not rely on the EFF to govern Nelson Mandela Bay and there was little at stake in that metro for Malema, so the EFF targeted the DA's fragile coalition there.

Trollip survived motions to remove him in March and April, when council sessions ended in chaos, but his opponents finally succeeded in August, when the mayor was pushed out in what the DA called a 'coup', in which his former deputy, the UDM's Mongameli Bobani, was instrumental. After a failed attempt to challenge his ouster in court, Trollip accepted his place in the opposition benches. He reserved his greatest ire for Bobani, who had been removed as his deputy by the council the previous year.

'He represents everything I abhor in government,' Trollip told the Cape Town Press Club about a month after losing the mayoralty. He explained that the DA's attempts to end excessive payments for what it regarded as suspicious contracts had caused friction between him and Bobani.

Ultimately, the EFF, with its six seats, got their way. 'We will remove Trollip as a mayor to communicate, provoke and impress on all DA white members that sensitivity to land loss by black people is a fundamental requirement for leading anywhere in the country,' the EFF's spokesperson, Mbuyiseni Ndlozi, had said months before.

Back in Johannesburg, where the EFF was blocking Mashaba from passing his budget, time was running out. If the budget failed to pass through the council by the end of June, the City risked being placed under administration. That would be a colossal embarrassment for the mayor and the DA. On 12 June, though, the budget passed in time with the support of the EFF. Malema's party had played a game of political brinkmanship and won, as was made clear by headlines like 'Passing of Joburg budget a signal that EFF holds the reins'.

However, according to City sources, this soon raised suspicions. Upon closer examination, it emerged that the EFF had only gained marginal budgetary concessions. Hikes in electricity had been reduced merely from 7,37 percent to 7,17 percent, and hikes in water rates from 14,2 percent to 13,2 percent. The fiery rhetoric in no way matched the EFF's rather lame victory. The ANC noted that the changes were 'cosmetic' and fell far short of a 'pro-poor' budget. So, what was happening behind the scenes, and why did the EFF suddenly seem so content with so little?

Sources in the orbit of Johannesburg's politics surmised that the budget agreement was somehow linked to the fleet deal worth over R1 billion. One source in Mashaba's coalition tipped off amaBhungane in July, the month after the adoption of the budget, speculating that the fleet contract had become a political bargaining chip and that the EFF was holding the budget hostage so that it could influence the tender.

Had the EFF been placated with a quid pro quo granting it influence over the fleet directorate, or perhaps a tacit acknowledgment that if it allowed the budget to pass, there wouldn't be too many awkward questions about its involvement in certain City entities? Beyond speculation and the suggestive timing, however, there was no hard evidence that the fleet deal was tied to the budget negotiations.

The EFF's Ndlozi, when asked by journalists if there was any connection, said: 'None whatsoever'. A spokesperson for the City maintained that the allegation was 'unfounded' and 'without basis', adding that no political figures had been involved in the tender at any point.

However, in his later biography of his boss, Beaumont drew the connection between tricky budget negotiations and concessions to the EFF when he wrote: 'The support of the EFF was secured for every budget and adjustments budget vote in council – six in total by June 2019. They approved senior appointments in the administration. On many occasions, they came to Mashaba with advice on these appointments, either warning us of a potential mistake or guiding us towards more suitable candidates.'[316] Beaumont was probably downplaying the EFF's hardball attitude, but it was still a revealing admission.

Coincidence or not, less than a week after the budget passed, the fleet tender, which would probably have gone to Avis or another equally capable company, was cancelled. It is not clear what, if anything, the directorate did in the following weeks to restart the tender, as the probity report had recommended, but there was now an opportunity to shoehorn in Afrirent without a competitive bid. On 6 July, Johannesburg city manager Ndivhoniswani Lukhwareni wrote to his counterpart at Mogale City municipality, asking permission to 'piggyback' on its fleet contract with Afrirent. On 19 July, Mogale City wrote back granting permission, and the next day Lukhwareni gave Dubru the go-ahead. The fleet directorate could now use an existing contract between Afrirent and another state body in terms of a so-called 'Regulation 32' process, thereby bypassing an open and competitive bid.

Formally, the use of Regulation 32 is tightly circumscribed. Among other prerequisites, the municipality must benefit financially, and it can't later change the terms of the contract. As a result, under Regulation 32, state entities can only bring in existing service providers for jobs that are essentially the same. In reality, however, Regulation 32 has been widely abused to manipulate contracts and reward favoured companies. Every point along complex and bureaucratic procurement processes provided opportunities for manipulation.

On 25 July, as Afrirent's chances of bagging the fleet contract began to look a lot more certain, the company paid R300 000 to Mahuna Investments – Julius Malema's slush fund fronted by his cousin, Matsobane Phaleng.

The very next day, on 26 July, Afrirent's CEO, Senzo Tsabedze, and another company representative sat down for a meeting with City officials. A letter from Tsabedze after the meeting read: 'Foremost, we would like to express our gratitude for the meeting on Thursday 26 July 2018 and the opportunity to quote the City of Johannesburg on the provision of fleet leasing services. Secondly, we are excited to submit our proposal.' The letter proposed what had effectively already been decided: to bypass a competitive bid using Regulation 32 on a tender Afrirent was unlikely to win through a fair, open and competitive process.

A month after the July meeting, Afrirent made another payment to Mahuna – this time for R200 000. On 10 October, the City notified Afrirent that it had been selected as its first fleet provider. The company would begin supplying vehicles in November.

When word of Afrirent's appointment got out, other players in the fleet and vehicle-leasing industry were shocked. While some insiders acknowledged that there was merit in the argument for not awarding the tender to Avis and giving a new company a chance, Afrirent seemed a problematic choice.

In the cancelled bid, Afrirent had scored the lowest among those that met the threshold, and its bid was expensive by comparison. Whereas Avis had bid to provide the fleet at R1,42 billion over the originally specified five years, or R23,7 million a month, Afrirent would now charge R1,26 billion over half that time, or R41,8 million a month. So much for the provisions and rationale of Regulation 32, as Afrirent's appointment made no sense in terms of value for money. It would also need to perform a much bigger and more complex job than at Mogale City, where it was required to provide fewer than 200 vehicles at less than a tenth of the cost of what Johannesburg would pay.

In late November, amaBhungane reported on what looked like kick-backs paid by Afrirent to Mahuna. The two companies, however, had a seemingly plausible alibi. They acknowledged the payments but stuck to the claim that these were entirely unrelated to the Joburg fleet tender.

'It is an insult to an emerging black business to be accused of receiving kickbacks on behalf of a political party or its leadership. We want to put it on record that we never received any bribe on our behalf or on behalf of anyone, and we are not involved in the fleet contract with the [City of Johannesburg],' said Phaleng, Mahuna's ostensible owner, who claimed to have done bona fide work for Afrirent 'from May until August 2018'.

He did not respond to further queries about the nature of the work. Afrirent, via its lawyers, Nicqui Galaktiou Incorporated – whose eponymous founder has also represented Malema and his friend Adriano Mazzotti – denied 'in the strongest terms' that the payments to Mahuna were kickbacks. Rather, the payments were related to a contract Afrirent had with the Limpopo department of rural development and land reform to supply tractors and farming equipment in the province, for which it had legitimately subcontracted Mahuna.

As evidence, Afrirent provided the cover and signature pages of its 'supplier agreement' with Mahuna, dated 2 December 2017. When negative media coverage of the fleet deal later forced the City to investigate, Tsabedze gave his most detailed account yet of the work Mahuna had supposedly done for Afrirent. He told the investigators – who failed to seriously interrogate his version of events – that initially Afrirent's own project managers had provided training on how to use the farming equipment they supplied, but that 'this proved to be counterproductive and costly as there was a language barrier between the project managers and the members of the cooperative at the farms'.

He added: 'The project managers employed by Afrirent were white Afrikaners and the farmers receiving the implements spoke Venda, Tsonga or Pedi. Therefore, Mahuna Investment[s], a company in Limpopo, was contracted to provide logistic and interpretation services to Afrirent at a reduced cost and [Mahuna is] 100 percent black-owned.'

But was this just a ruse to cover up kickbacks? Afrirent claimed it had won its contract with the Limpopo department of rural development and land reform in October 2017, and that the following month – the same month Afrirent submitted its initial bid for the fleet tender – it had engaged Mahuna. Afrirent did indeed have a contract with the department, but it was unclear whether its subcontract with Mahuna was what it purported to be, and Afrirent was cagey about some of the details. For a start, Tsabedze had not signed on the signature page, and his name was simply printed – something Afrirent brushed off, saying through its lawyer that he had in fact signed just by 'completing his name and designation as CEO of Afrirent. I think it would be inaccurate to say that the agreement is not signed.'

Phaleng also listed Mahuna's VAT number as 'N/A' – a red flag for a company receiving such large payments. More significantly, however, the details of the contract remained uncertain, as Afrirent had only provided the cover and signature pages. When amaBhungane requested the full contract, with sensitive information redacted as needed, the company refused, saying 'commercial information must be preserved and cannot be disseminated'.

Afrirent did not provide invoices from Mahuna, nor was it able to provide any other evidence that Mahuna had done any work for it in Limpopo. And there was nothing about Mahuna that suggested it would have provided the services it supposedly had been contracted for. There was no evidence of the company or Phaleng having any logistics, training or translation expertise. Mahuna had no website, and although Tsabedze said he was 'unaware that the CEO of Mahuna was related to Mr Julius Malema', a simple online search would have revealed a 2012 amaBhungane article drawing the link.

Mahuna's banking activity also did not suggest that it was a functioning company. The money it received from Afrirent was in large, round figures of R200 000 and R300 000 – suspicious, because invoices typically contain precise figures, including decimals. Mahuna's largest receipts of around R4,8 million in total were between June 2017 and February from Sgameka Projects, the company owned by Floyd Shivambu's brother Brian – and, as shown previously, Sgameka's income came from VBS. There were no salary payments going out of the Mahuna account aside from 'director's fees' for Phaleng. But there were regular payments for a range of EFF purposes.

To finally disprove Afrirent's alibi and rule out the possibility that it was just pure coincidence – that the payments were in connection with the land-reform project and just happened to coincide with key milestones in the fleet deal – amaBhungane had to get to the beneficiaries of the project. These were the farmers that Mahuna had supposedly interacted with when it provided translation services. To begin with, there was little to go on. The department of rural development and land reform was dragging its feet in response to requests for information and did not disclose who the beneficiaries were.

Afrirent, too, was tight-lipped, referring questions back to the department. And Phaleng, who had been evasive at first, was now totally silent. All amaBhungane had were a few promotional photos, including one of the blue Landini tractor. In one photo, a smiling Afrirent employee hands over keys to a local beneficiary at a farm that, according to the caption, was somewhere near Tshakuma village, with its bustling fresh-produce market and industrious small-scale farmers. A distinctively shaped hill in the background of another picture of the farm allowed amaBhungane to roughly locate the farm. With the tractor's location narrowed down, amaBhungane's reporter (one of the authors of this book) set off to rural Limpopo to find it.

In the area, locals pointed him to the home of a village elder, and it didn't take long before someone was called who knew exactly where the tractor was. It stood, as in the photo, in gleaming baby blue under trees of a dusty yard. Not a single one of the beneficiaries who now owned the Afrirent-supplied vehicle – members of an agricultural cooperative – had ever heard of Mahuna or Phaleng. Afrirent had simply arrived, handed over the hardware, given a brief introduction and moved on. There had been no translator and no evidence whatsoever of Mahuna's involvement, nor had there been any need for it.

When amaBhungane eventually obtained a list of other beneficiary communities from the department, its reporters contacted them as well. Matthews Ledwaba, the founder of the Nsete cooperative near Polokwane, said 'some fleet company' had made the delivery. Staff briefly demonstrated how to use the equipment and took a few photos – and that was it. He gave amaBhungane the number of the fleet company. Unsurprisingly, it belonged to Afrirent. Another farmer told a similar story. He said he had begun receiving goods the year prior and had only engaged with the department and Afrirent. The latter gave a brief demonstration of the equipment, and no translation services were provided. Asked about Mahuna, he said: 'I've never heard of that company.'

Two internal Afrirent sources confirmed what was fast becoming undeniable – that Mahuna had played no role in the Limpopo project. According to the sources, Afrirent had a straightforward supply and delivery contract, and the limited logistical and training elements were performed by staff from Afrirent and Landini – the original supplier of the tractors and farming equipment. 'It was impossible that anyone else had done anything,' said one. A representative of Landini also denied any knowledge of Mahuna.

The records from the department also detailed the equipment Afrirent had delivered, including invoice dates. Between April and August 2018, the period in which Mahuna had supposedly invoiced Afrirent for R500 000, Afrirent had made only two sets of deliveries, both in July. The total of Afrirent's invoices to the department at the time stood at R519 000. The idea that it would have handed over more than 96 percent of that amount to Mahuna for 'translation services' stretched credulity too far.

Malema's mysterious front company was nowhere to be found in rural Limpopo, but the links between Afrirent and the EFF leader were piling up. Again, a humble tractor yielded important clues. Just after Christmas in 2018, as the EFF's campaign for the 2019 national elections gained momentum, media reports showed a grinning Malema in the driver's seat of a brand-new blue Farmtrac FT 6050 tractor, which he was presenting to elderly residents of his hometown, Seshego. The tractor would 'make it possible for them to work the land', Malema was reported to have told the audience.

Just two days later, *The Citizen* ran another story about the EFF donating a tractor – this time to the community of Ward 10 in Blood River, a few kilometres from Seshego. Residents flocked to the sports ground of a local primary school, where photos showed a blue Farmtrac tractor under the EFF's black and red marquee. The report stated: 'The tractor given to the ward was either the same one handed out on Thursday in Seshego, or it's simply the same model of tractor. It's not known how many tractors the EFF has actually purchased.' Indeed, it was the very same tractor, and the EFF had not paid a cent for it – it was given to the party by Afrirent.

AmaBhungane's journalists put to Afrirent the allegation that it had sourced the tractor from a supplier and then provided it to the EFF. It replied: 'We have not made any donation to any political party in exchange for contracts.' When journalists pressed the question, asking specifically if 'Afrirent or Mr Tsabedze has made any donation at all' (not necessarily 'in exchange for contracts') to any political party or politician, the company's response was a straight 'no'. But this was contradicted by the accounts of the supplier, a former Afrirent employee, and another person familiar with the transaction.

At the time, the only official importer that held the marketing and distribution rights for Farmtrac tractors, manufactured by an Indian company, Escorts Agri, was a company called Vukani. A Vukani employee told amaBhungane that 'the tractor was bought from us, and we were asked that we deliver it very urgently just before Christmas. We were told the tractor was a donation to a community in Polokwane. We were given the address where we had to deliver, and the next thing there was an article in the media with Malema on the tractor.' He added that Afrirent had paid for the tractor 'in full'.

Dewald van Bergen, a Vukani manager at the time the tractor was sold to Afrirent, told amaBhungane that 'everything happened through Afrirent'. It ordered the tractor around Christmas, and he was under a 'hell of a lot of pressure' to get it up to Polokwane.

Two other sources confirmed that Afrirent had paid for the tractor and that this was not the first time Afrirent had 'donated' vehicles to the EFF. They claimed Afrirent had supplied over a dozen bakkies for EFF electioneering. Asked to confirm or deny this last allegation, Afrirent told amaBhungane that 'it is incorrect to say that we rented vehicles on behalf of [the] EFF. Vehicles were rented from us, and the client who rented the vehicles from us has paid for the services and we have proof in this regard. We wish to reiterate that we never paid money to the EFF to secure tenders, or in exchange for any favour whatsoever.' Afrirent never provided this sort of proof.

Yet another inconvenient fact emerged to undercut Afrirent's narrative: another payment, this time to Malema's other slush fund, Santaclara. Afrirent sent R150 000 to Santaclara in October 2018, roughly a fortnight after it bagged the fleet contract. Afrirent was mum on why it had paid Santaclara. Presumably, the company, in its attempts to distance itself from Malema and plead ignorance of Mahuna's link to the EFF, had by now painted itself so far into a corner that it figured it was best to say nothing at all. Much like Sgameka Projects, Mahuna's claim to have performed legitimate work for the money it received was a ruse.

Judging by his Facebook page, Matsobane John Phaleng – Tsubi – is leading an active and prosperous life. On 2 January 2025, he posted another picture of him with his cousin Julius and four others, all dressed in black and all with their arms around each other's shoulders. Three of the others are identified but Julius is not mentioned. Tsubi's caption reads: 'We are doing just fine.'

CHAPTER 25

The 'EFF mayor'

IN 1994, 25 years before securing a billion-rand deal with the City of Johannesburg, Senzo Tsabedze was in his final year of high school. It was a time of hope for the country as the green shoots of a new democracy emerged, but his personal circumstances held little promise of a bright and prosperous future. His family was among the poorer residents of his home village in Albert Luthuli municipality, Mpumalanga. His father had worked on an asbestos mine and sought respite from hard labour in even harder drinking. The thought of a similar fate terrified the young Tsabedze, spurring his flight from home as soon as he completed matric.

After fleeing home, he got his first job in Nelspruit at a Chinese restaurant, earning R15 a day. He slept under a tree at a nearby hospital until the manager offered him a space in her garage. He eventually moved into a one-room shack in Pienaar, about 45 kilometres out of town, where local thugs would shake him down and fleece him of his paltry earnings. But the hospitality industry was clearly a good fit for Tsabedze, and he trod a steady path upwards.

After another restaurant job, he became an assistant food and beverage manager at a five-star hotel in Sabie, where he said he was exposed to life's luxuries. A few years later, he took his first step into the business world with a contract to supply linen to hotels in the Kruger National Park, where he worked for a company managing restaurants. 'I was teaching one of the guys at South African National Parks how to play golf and he told me about the opportunity,' Tsabedze was quoted as saying in a media profile. 'They were always looking for black people to provide services, but few companies submitted competitive bids.'[317]

He then acquired a contract to construct classrooms, buying it from another contractor for R150 000. 'Those days you could buy the contract, so I bought the contract and sold it to a construction company for about R500 000,' he said. It was easy money, and he repeated the trick with another construction project, upping his profit margins.

Tsabedze realised just how lucrative the vehicle-rental industry could be when he bought two trucks on an auction and rented them to a fleet company. That was the start of his own budding fleet business, and he got a leg up when the Bushbuckridge Local Municipality gave him his first government contract for fleet management. For that job, he had to rely on a partnership with a larger company because he lacked the financial muscle to put forward a bank loan, but it was just the first of many more government tenders to come.

As his dealings with the government grew, Afrirent, which he founded in 2003, accumulated controversies. In 2017, a media report implicated it in tender irregularities involving a multimillion-rand vehicle-tracking contract it had with the Eastern Cape government. In 2019, a recording of a discussion between a government official and a businessman alleged to be Tsabedze emerged. The businessman could be heard 'bragging about how he gave an MEC R1 million for an ANC Women's League [ANCWL] conference so he could get more contracts with her department', according to an article on the *Sunday Times* website.

The supposed businessman could be heard saying: 'I have been assisting her, even for the ANCWL conference I gave her a million rand to assist her.' He claimed to have worked with the MEC 'from the beginning'. Tsabedze did not deny that it was his voice in the audio clip. He told the *Sunday Times*: 'Political parties raise and receive funds from business so they can implement their programmes [. . .] as a business, we make contributions towards political parties and never to an individual'. However, he added: 'I have never paid or assisted any MEC with funding.'

Though the MEC being referred to was not named, it was clearly Eastern Cape transport MEC Weziwe Tikana, who was also the deputy secretary-general of the ANCWL. She told the paper that people seeking tenders would often 'name-drop', but that she never had anything to do with issuing tenders or raising funds for the ANC, because she had never been the treasurer of either the ANC or its women's league.

When the opportunity to secure the R1,2-billion Johannesburg fleet deal came along, it held the potential to take Tsabedze's growing company to new heights. So, 'investing' a few hundred thousand rand in political capital to secure a tender worth more than a billion rand – while outmanoeuvring an industry giant like Avis in the process – was a no-brainer. Tsabedze reached into his coffers and paid Mahuna Investments – which catapulted him to the next stage of an already impressive business career.

But Afrirent's fleet deal with the City got off to a shaky start. In December, when the contract was only about six weeks old, Absa declined a R1-billion credit facility to Afrirent. The acting city manager, Floyd Brink, rushed to allay Absa's concerns 'about the Afrirent Regulation 32 contract, the recent media article published and the subsequent announcement of the forensic investigation by the City into the procurement process'.

Writing to a senior Absa official, Brink stated that a preliminary investigation by the City had found 'no cause for concern . . . We hope that you find this in order, [and] that this letter will assist you in whatever decision you have to take.'

Absa was unmoved and would not provide the funding – a decision Afrirent and Tsabedze blamed on the negative publicity triggered by amaBhungane's reporting. Absa retorted: 'We do not take financing decisions merely on the basis of newspaper articles.' Meanwhile, the investigation – the preliminary findings of which Brink had cited – continued amid an outcry over the tender.

Brink is an interesting character for anyone tracing Malema's network of influence. In 2013, while employed as a manager at the Limpopo department of roads and transport, he was arrested on charges of fraud. The case against him and another senior official related to a pothole repair project undertaken by the department in early 2011, when On-Point was responsible for managing tenders.

Brink and a co-accused were caught up in a series of sweeping investigations following the cabinet decision of late 2011 to place five Limpopo departments under administration. In October 2013, the two appeared in court in Limpopo, and pleaded not guilty. The state argued they had committed fraud by falsely claiming that flooding had created potholes across the province, thereby creating an emergency requiring urgent patching.

This had allowed them to sidestep an open and competitive tender process. Instead, selected contractors were identified, asked to quote and hurriedly appointed for a total of about R63 million – a tranche of money that otherwise would have been unspent at the end of the financial year and returned to the National Treasury. Among these contractors were TC Foromo Trading Enterprise, owned by Malema's close associate Collins Foromo, and Arandi Trading Enterprises, belonging to Julius Malema's cousin, Tshepo Malema – two familiar faces at Limpopo government departments.

The National Treasury had appointed PricewaterhouseCoopers (PwC) to investigate allegations of irregularities and wrongdoing in the department, and its investigators were alerted to the pothole project by whistleblowers from a local business association, the Forum of Limpopo Entrepreneurs. PwC found that many of the pothole contractors lacked the necessary expertise and merely subcontracted the work to people who could actually do the job, but for significantly less. In some instances, the appointed contractors charged the department despite no work being done at all.

Ultimately, however, the state's case collapsed. There were disputes over the timing of the floods that had created the supposed 'emergency' and whether the need to patch the potholes constituted an emergency intervention. Even more problematic were procedural flaws resulting from changes to the charge sheet and the failure of prosecutors to adequately demonstrate the prejudice caused to the Treasury, the department and their officials by the actions of the accused. The case dragged on into 2015, when Brink and his co-accused were acquitted. The state also lost its case against Tshepo Malema, Foromo and other contractors who were tried separately. For reasons mentioned earlier, the state had bungled its Limpopo corruption cases.

Brink remained at the roads department in Limpopo until, three years later, on 1 August 2018, he was suddenly catapulted into the position of chief operations officer of the City of Johannesburg, with Mashaba as mayor. Brink was an odd pick, rising from relative obscurity to one of the most senior roles in the largest metro in the country. That led some within the City to suspect that his appointment was a concession by Mashaba to the EFF.

'Floyd was pushed through as an unqualified candidate fresh from the On-Point scandal in Limpopo,' said one City source. 'It was a deliberate move by Mashaba to give in to the EFF's demands and prop up his fragile government. Floyd was never up to the job.' Mashaba strenuously denied that Brink's appointment was a political deal with the EFF.

On 10 October, when Afrirent was formally notified of its appointment as the new fleet provider, Brink had been in the job for more than two months, overseeing service-delivery operations and providing strategic leadership.

Like Brink, the mayor defended the fleet contract and denied allegations that it had been manipulated. Mashaba lodged a complaint with the ombud against amaBhungane over what he claimed was its defamatory reporting on the fleet deal. He was furious about the insinuation that he – the self-styled corruption buster – would have anything to do with a fraudulent tender. He took aim at amaBhungane's sources, claiming they were disgruntled employees who were facing disciplinary processes and therefore had an axe to grind.

On 5 March 2019, after scrutinising the reports and hearing arguments from both sides, the media ombud dismissed Mashaba's complaint and agreed with amaBhungane's assertion, 'Just as it is standard practice for politicians to claim credit for the successes of their administration, administrative failures are also often and rightly personalised.'

Mashaba's claim that amaBhungane's allegations were 'patently false' sat uneasily next to the City's decision to investigate the tender. In the same month as the ombud's ruling, the City's investigative unit set up under Mashaba released its own report into the allegations. Seemingly little more than an attempt to go through the motions, it confined itself to the tender's procedural matters.

As later acknowledged by none other than Michael Beaumont, Mashaba's underling and biographer, 'Corrupt elements will always find a loophole to crawl through. Most of the dodgy deals we discovered could never have been proved to have transgressed any supply-chain management processes.'[318]

With such limitations, the investigation was doomed from the start. Investigators could have looked beyond the box-ticking supply-chain documents, but they barely probed witnesses, failed to investigate the alleged kickbacks and largely overlooked key background events. Afrirent and Mahuna were mostly uncooperative when investigators sought to understand their business relationship, and attempts to get contracts from the two companies to clarify matters quickly reached a dead end.

The investigative team was quick to brush aside allegations of political interference while accepting the accounts of those implicated at face value. It paid scant attention to the account of Shaun Ramroop – the head of fleet compliance – stating that his testimony was 'not specific on how this happened or which political party or politician was responsible'.

But this was untrue. In an eight-page document, Ramroop had provided a detailed version of events, referring, among other things, to Sanjay Dubru sidelining him while claiming to be protected by the member of Mashaba's mayoral committee responsible for the fleet directorate. Dubru was interfering in matters he was not supposed to have any involvement in, undermining a tender process intended to be neutral and follow a carefully prescribed path.

'My conclusion regarding the string of events,' wrote Ramroop, 'is that Dubru was brought in to remove me . . . so that he can manipulate the contracts'. He concluded that investigators should try to determine in whose interest Dubru was working. But they showed little interest in doing so, and none of the detail in Ramroop's account made it into the final report. Investigators found no evidence of political interference in the tender, possibly because they did not want to find any.

Afrirent, meanwhile, struggled to fulfil its lucrative new fleet contract and continued relying on Avis to fill the gap. Afrirent had been contracted for 30 months effective from 1 November 2018, by which time Avis's old contract had already been extended due to the bungling of the tender process. When Afrirent missed an initial deadline for a three-month transition at the end of January 2019, Avis's contract was extended to the end of April. When Afrirent remained behind target, Avis's contract was extended again to the end of September, and again after that. In November 2019, a full year after Afrirent's contract began, the City said the company had supplied only about half the required vehicles. The rest were provided by Avis.

It was a costly disaster for the City, and one that could have easily been avoided. To justify bypassing a competitive bid and appointing Afrirent, the City had said it could not extend Avis's previous contract to allow for the rerunning of a competitive bid after the initial one had been cancelled. But according to a legal opinion obtained by the City in April 2019, while the decision to cancel the initial bid was justified, there would have been 'nothing untoward in obtaining further extensions' to Avis's contract. The City could have done that as a temporary measure while preparing a new tender, which would have 'far outweighed the Regulation 32 option' used to circumvent a competitive bid. In any case, Avis's contract had to be extended to make up for Afrirent's poor performance. And not only was Afrirent's performance substandard, but the City was also paying far more per vehicle than if Avis had been allowed to carry on as before.

A City spokesperson acknowledged that Avis's contract could have been extended, but that this would have 'reflected negatively on the City' if it was seen to be 'entrenching' Avis as the service provider 'in perpetuity'. Therefore, the City had opted for a Regulation 32 arrangement, piggybacking on Afrirent's contract with Mogale City – which, the spokesperson said, had gone through a competitive tender process in that municipality. It had received an assurance that Mogale City's supply-chain policies had been followed.

But even this assurance was called into question by a February 2020 report by the National Treasury. It, too, had been probing the Afrirent deal, uncovering a litany of problems. It pointed to the 'huge difference in the size' between Mogale City's requirements and those of Johannesburg, and even found that no valid contract had existed between Mogale City and Afrirent when Johannesburg asked to piggyback on it. The letter from Johannesburg asking to participate in the Mogale City–Afrirent contract, dated 10 July 2018, 'was signed before the contract between [Mogale] and Afrirent was signed on 13 July 2018'.

There were other anomalies. Mogale City, for instance, had a finance lease agreement, meaning it would take ownership of the vehicles at the end of the contract, whereas Joburg would not. This led the Treasury to conclude that the Joburg contract should be 'declared irregular and cancelled', and that the City of Johannesburg 'must commission a forensic investigation within thirty days of receiving this letter and provide National Treasury with progress reports on the forensic investigation'.

After amaBhungane published an article on the findings of the Treasury report, Afrirent said the Treasury had been 'deliberately misled to cast aspersions on Afrirent', and that the company had been subjected to City of Johannesburg investigations that had 'exonerated' it.

By the time Treasury released its report on the fleet contract in early 2020, a new ANC-led administration was overseeing Johannesburg, and Dubru had been suspended in January due to multiple tender irregularities. Geoff Makhubo, Johannesburg's new mayor, declared the 'issues of [the] fleet within the City have proved to be a hotbed of corruption and malfeasance'. Nevertheless, with the help of Avis, Afrirent remained the fleet service provider for a turbulent few years in which control of the city switched back to the DA in late 2021, this time under mayor Mpho Phalatse, then back to the ANC in September 2022, and again back to Phalatse less than a month later as a result of a court order, before she was ousted again in January 2023. She was replaced by a mayoral candidate from the minority Al Jama-ah party agreed to by the ANC and EFF.

In November 2022, after the fleet contract had expired the previous month, Avis and Afrirent began grounding their vehicles. A statement from the DA-run City put the problem down to corruption, stating: 'While the City's own investigation [into the fleet tender] cleared the DA-led coalition government of interference in the contract, amaBhungane uncovered a trail of money that led from Afrirent to senior opposition political leaders. Subsequent forensic investigations by the City implicated a number of senior officials.'

The DA and ANC traded blame for the chaos in the City, accusing each other of obstructing the renewal of the fleet tender and failing to address corruption in the fleet department.

While Mashaba was mayor, from 2016 until his resignation in October 2019, he had come under increasing criticism for capitulating to the EFF. City officials and members of his own DA-led coalition had complained of him turning a blind eye to corruption that centred on the EFF, and of EFF influence spreading under the radar. The EFF was said to be calling the shots on key appointments, feeding on tenders and being handed virtual control over certain departments even though it was not part of the governing coalition.

'The EFF has the DA by the balls,' said one City insider. It wasn't that the businessman-turned-mayor himself benefited from looted funds, or that he necessarily knew exactly what Malema and the EFF were doing, but rather that he didn't want to know. Knowing too much would have invited an awkward reckoning with Malema and his party.

With Mashaba in the mayor's seat, Malema was in an ideal position, exercising power and influence at arm's length, unencumbered by the messy business of formal participation in a coalition. The Red Berets could take to the political stage and loudly claim to have influenced service-delivery successes but just as easily distance themselves from the failures of a coalition they had never formally joined. They reaped the rewards with none of the risk.

Beaumont eventually acknowledged as much, writing: 'So they [the EFF] came up with the voting issue-by-issue arrangement – it allowed them to entrench and maximize their position as kingmakers while being seen forcing their agenda into the government programme without the risk of losing their radical stance. It was a brilliant strategic move on their part. They knew they could reap all the benefits of the coalition, because without their support nothing could happen. Yet if something went wrong, they had the comfort of the distance they derived from being in opposition.'

Malema was so pleased with the arrangement and Mashaba's role in it that he referred to him as 'our EFF mayor' – a label Mashaba's detractors within his own party also adopted. But Mashaba was unmoved. 'As with the coalition partners, and despite criticism from within his own party,

Mashaba insisted that he be accompanied by the EFF at every service delivery event he headlined,' wrote Beaumont.

Mashaba enthusiastically adopted signature EFF talking points and policy, notably the in-sourcing of blue-collar workers like cleaners and security guards – a strange about-turn for a cheerleader of market libertarianism. To Beaumont, this was just another case of his boss expertly navigating the political exigencies of City politics. Here were the 'Capitalist Crusader and Marxist-Leninists' finding 'common ground' and claiming to put the interests of the City first. But to his critics, it was another example of Mashaba's lack of a political backbone and his willingness to sacrifice principle on the altar of expedience.

Mashaba had steadily lost the confidence of otherwise sympathetic voices, even in the business press, which increasingly viewed him as out of his depth. The man given the nickname 'Tiny Trump' was described by some as 'bullish', 'arrogant' and often clueless regarding the procedural obligations of his office, read a *Business Day* editorial in March 2017. It also said he had been an 'unlikely candidate' and 'a man with very little charisma and no experience in government' when he was 'parachuted into the position as the city's number-one citizen. Since then, he has hopped from one foot-in-mouth gaffe to the next. From flip-flopping on policy proposals to his populist comments on immigrants, Mashaba has yet to impress.'

'Like Trump', the editorial added, 'Mashaba likes winning and doesn't like being challenged, say insiders. His advisers, instead of tempering this trait, encourage it – to both his and the city's detriment.'

Perhaps none more so than his chief of staff, Beaumont, who dutifully defended the mayor's every move, including his affair with the EFF, which he described – laughably – as being 'against fraud and corruption'.[319]

Mashaba's signature campaign was an anti-corruption drive that, some of his critics claimed, was more posturing than anything else. Others accused Mashaba of weaponising anti-corruption – of cynically and selectively using his anti-corruption agenda to rid his administration of people he did not want. His apparently very selective approach in how he dealt with allegations of corruption – interventionist at City Power but hands off at the JRA – were signs of a double standard. Mashaba repeatedly claimed his administration had uncovered billions of rand in corruption, but closer scrutiny suggested creative accounting rather than genuine corruption. According to a City insider, he would cherry-pick facts and label a deal or a tender corrupt and count its entire value – not just the bribe or portion alleged to have changed hands illicitly – as tainted money uncovered by the City. In this way, he massively inflated the figures he cited to trumpet his corruption-busting successes.

'Forensic investigations are complex,' said the insider. 'You're looking into so many people involved in multiple processes and so many legal technicalities, which makes proving fraud and corruption down to an individual tricky. But you can't say that to someone like Herman, who needed soundbites and quick political wins.'

The 2019 national elections were a turning point for Mashaba and the DA. Following the party's disappointing performance, a review panel made up of former party leader Tony Leon, former party CEO Ryan Coetzee and Michiel le Roux, the former chairperson of Capitec Bank and a major donor, investigated the reasons for the party's backslide. They zoomed in on the DA's internal dynamics and the 'indiscipline and factionalism' afflicting it. By October 2019, when the panel released its report, many within the party believed that Mashaba's dalliance with the EFF had gone too far – a concern highlighted in the report. In Johannesburg and Tshwane, the strategy of forming coalition governments with the support of the EFF had been a 'mistake', it concluded.

'First, our governments in those cities are unable to prosecute a properly DA agenda because we are overly beholden to the EFF [. . .] Second, it is corrosive of the DA's brand to rely on the EFF's support to govern given that party's political philosophy, policy agenda and general behaviour.'

The report criticised DA leader Mmusi Maimane for what it said was his indecision and inconsistency. Among its recommendations was that Maimane resign as leader, along with the chairperson of the DA federal council, James Selfe, who had earlier announced his retirement, and its chief executive, Paul Boughey, who had already decided to resign.

There were other casualties of the fallout, notably Mashaba. Although it stopped short of specifically mentioning Mashaba or his role in courting Malema, the report had in effect launched a broadside against the mayor and what had become a defining feature of his administration – appeasement of the EFF. Mashaba resigned shortly after the report came out.

Announcing his departure from the mayoralty and the party at a media briefing on 21 October 2019, Mashaba thanked the EFF 'for their dedication to the work of delivering the dignity of change to our residents'. Maimane, who had stood beside Mashaba as he took aim at the DA, resigned soon afterwards.

Amid the DA's internal struggles, the EFF had lost 'its' dependable mayor in Johannesburg. When elections for a new mayor came in December, they put forward one of their own – caucus leader Musa Novela, who received 30 votes. But it was the ANC that successfully exploited the moment and installed its candidate, Geoff Makhubo.

As the smoke cleared, some within the City administration felt that they were crawling out of a three-year nightmare during which the EFF had effectively been given licence to gorge on City budgets and its deployees in the bureaucracy worked against their colleagues, undercutting existing procurement systems and acting with virtual impunity.

Afrirent remains the fleet provider. In December 2024, it again grounded its vehicles due to the City's outstanding debt.

CHAPTER 26

Tender comrades

PERHAPS THE CLEAREST case of Julius Malema directly benefiting from corrupt tenders in the metros was in the administrative capital of Tshwane, where a contractor aligned with the EFF won part of a massive fuel contract. The contractor, a company called Balimi Barui Trading (BBT), started scooping up tenders in the city well before the 2016 municipal elections that brought another fragile DA-led coalition to power.

From about 2014, when the ANC ran Tshwane, BBT won various contracts – for debt collection as well as the supply of cement, chemicals and cables. But the big win came in 2015 with a three-year tender to supply the city with fuel for its fleet of cars, bakkies and trucks. And so began the boom years for BBT. From 2016, the company started to feature among the City of Tshwane's top service providers, raking in an average of more than R10 million a month. In the same year, a man named Abram 'Stanley' Kganyago was employed as the City's director of fleet performance, monitoring and compliance in the corporate and shared services department – the department that issued fuel tenders.

Kganyago's newly created position came with a R1-million salary and oversight over 36 members of staff. But he was wholly unsuited for the job, with almost no relevant experience. He was an external candidate, with a law degree and, according to his application, the only time he had spent in a related field was as a trainee at AFS Group, a fleet and fuel management company. But even that seemed to have been falsified – AFS told amaBhungane that it had 'no record of him being employed by AFS' or having had 'any relationship' with the company.

As part of his application, Stanley Kganyago provided two references. One was Sidwell Phutheho, a senior executive at BBT and a related company, Bertobrite. The other was Hendrick Kganyago, the owner of BBT. Their surname aside, Stanley and Hendrick had much in common. In 2005, they and one other person had formed a close corporation called Buzzabee Global Networks, registered at Hendrick's residential address in Ormonde, Johannesburg – the same address where BBT was registered. When Stanley registered another close corporation a few years later, he used the same address. He was also, until March 2017, listed as a director, alongside Hendrick, of a company called Mmaseroka Holdings.

The two Kganyagos were probably related and were said to be brothers by those who knew them. Hendrick had Stanley on the inside over-seeing tenders, contracts and payments to his companies. Stanley would probably have overseen the work of Bertobrite – where Hendrick's wife was a director – after it secured a tender in April 2016 to fit glass to City vehicles. Then, in February 2017, Hendrick's company Bulldozers Trading scored another contract, this time for maintaining the City's vehicles for a year.

The contract, with a maximum value of R32,9 million, should have worried City officials. Bulldozers had contracted with the City ostensibly as part of a joint venture with an older, more established company called Transit Solutions. But strangely, in the agreement with the City, Hendrick signed as the 'duly authorised' representative of both parties. Moreover, he used only his first and middle names. There was no signature from a representative of the other joint-venture partner, because there was no partner – in other words, it appeared to be a fraud.

When Transit Solutions was approached by amaBhungane, it said it had no knowledge of the agreement. 'Transit Solutions never consented to be part of any joint venture with Bulldozers, and we never gave any party permission to use the company's name in the context referred to,' it said. The dodgy deal went unnoticed and unpunished because the official handling the contract was none other than Hendrick's man on the inside. Furthermore, the City continued paying the company well after the contract had expired, at least until mid-2018.

By that time, Bulldozers had squeezed R43 million out of the City for work that one official claimed the City could have done itself. The money, said the official, was 'just given away'. The City's chief financial officer seemed to concur when – according to a record of discussions about the City's fleet – he said that outsourcing maintenance was not necessary as it would simply replicate what the City could do itself.

And even if the City could not, an industry insider said it was common practice for fleet providers – of which there were three in Tshwane – to maintain the vehicles they supplied to the City. Regardless, in 2018, a contract to track vehicle fuel consumption and movements that was held by Afrirent – the company that scored the City of Johannesburg fleet contract and paid Malema's Mahuna Trading – was handed to Bertobrite.

The baton passed to Bertobrite after Afrirent had underperformed on the tracking contract. Two sources – one a City official and another a fuel-industry insider – said independently of each other that Hendrick had presented himself as a representative of Afrirent. It was never entirely clear why. The City official claimed that Afrirent employees working on the tracking contract simply switched to Bertobrite, which then added a contract worth tens of millions of rand to its portfolio.

Quietly, Stanley did the Kganyago family's bidding, ensuring that more and more money flowed to their companies while concealing any potential concerns about Hendrick's dealings. If some City employees knew about his conflicted position, they did nothing to stop him – and the most egregious looting was yet to come.

Midway through 2018, the fuel-supply contract held by BBT was coming up for renewal, and the City began the tender afresh. To start with, that meant convening a committee of City officials to determine the specifications of the new tender. Among them was none other than Stanley Kganyago. When the committee members had to declare potential conflicts of interest, Stanley said, using his given name: 'I'm Abram Kganyago. I declare I don't have interest in the matters to be discussed in the meeting.' Nobody seemed to pick up on his lie, or if they did, they said nothing.

As this was a huge tender and there was a lot of money to go around, some committee members argued in favour of giving other companies a slice. The committee's chairperson voiced concern over the fact that BBT controlled the fuel supply for the entire City fleet, and that, in the interests of 'empowerment' and 'sharing the cake', the new fuel deal should be split. One member who was less enthusiastic about this idea was Stanley, who clearly wanted to protect Hendrick's interests. He argued against giving the tender to more than one company. For Hendrick, there was much to lose – other vultures were circling his lucrative turf, and he needed to protect what was 'his'. Ultimately, however, Stanley lost the argument. The tender would be split among different companies.

At the time, Tshwane's politics were in turmoil. The DA was nominally in charge, but by late 2018 there was a growing rift between the mayor, Solly Msimanga, and the city manager, Moeketsi Mosola – a power struggle that threatened to cripple the administration.

Amid the drawn-out political fight, the renewal of the fuel tender stalled. Hendrick Kganyago's original three-year fuel contract had already been extended and was due to expire at the end of January 2019. On Friday 25 January, with the clock ticking, Mosola hurriedly appointed a committee of five officials who would have to work through the weekend to evaluate the bids. They compiled a shortlist of 10 bidders ranked by price, with BBT coming out on top. The committee recommended the appointment of BBT and two other companies, Rheinland Investments and MDZ Fleet Solutions.

But BBT was not the most cost-effective choice – far from it. In fact, the City was about to be fleeced, because BBT had successfully gamed the system: City officials had somehow overlooked a glaring anomaly in its pricing. It was a remarkable oversight – one that the veteran investigative journalist and amaBhungane founder Stefaans Brümmer picked up almost immediately as he began scanning through tender documents at amaBhungane's offices in Salt River, Cape Town, two small, spartan rooms littered with boxes of documents and the occasional framed front-page story mounted on the wall.

Brümmer's eye for forensic detail, honed by decades in investigative journalism, led him straight to the fuel prices, which appeared totally out of kilter. BBT had provided wildly extortionate rates for two categories of fuel – unleaded 95 and high-grade diesel – but absurdly low rates for the four remaining categories.

This was because BBT appeared to know something the other bidders did not – that the City only really used two grades of fuel, the same grades for which BBT had quoted astronomically high prices. Indeed, the City's own figures for several months over 2019 showed that it used these two grades of fuel exclusively. But the officials evaluating the bids did not take actual consumption into account and failed to weigh the bidders' prices accordingly. For each bidder, they simply added together the quoted prices for the categories of fuel – the lower the total, the better the pricing score.

This crude and inappropriate method of determining affordability allowed BBT to make its bid appear the most affordable overall. Where other shortlisted bidders offered between R14,05 and R16,13 for un-leaded 93, BBT's offer came in at an improbably low R9,93. And where others quoted between R14,03 and R14,82 for low-grade diesel, BBT only quoted R7,45 – almost half as cheap, and below the basic price of imported fuel. It knew it would never have to supply these categories of fuel.

It was a similar story for two other grades of fuel that the City did not use. By undercutting on these items, BBT secured its share of the tender, from which it could reap obscene profits by supplying the fuel grades the City did use at hugely inflated prices.

To have scored the bids fairly, the City would only have had to weigh the various fuel categories in proportion to consumption. Had it done so, BBT's bid would have been prohibitively expensive, placing it a distant last. Instead, having won its share of the tender, the company would now be in a position to reap exorbitant profits on high-grade diesel and unleaded 95. BBT expected to be paid R18,65 for unleaded 95 – considerably more than the second-most-expensive offer of R16,35, and vastly more than the cheapest offer of R13,85. No other bidder did what BBT did, not because the others were playing a gentleman's game, but because they simply were not privy to inside information.

The procurement documents reflect a degree of unease among City officials about BBT's bid, with at least one having 'expressed his concern about the discrepancy in prices of the respective service providers', according to the minutes of a meeting. But instead of demanding that bidders be reranked according to a fair pricing system, the committee adjudicating the bid simply endorsed BBT and the other two winners, and recommended that the City negotiate with the higher bidders to lower their prices – a recommendation that was largely ignored.

By early 2019, BBT was in the money once again, having secured the roughly R500-million tender alongside MDZ and Rheinland. When amaBhungane received a tip-off from within the City administration about corruption surrounding the fuel tender, it was alleged that the process had been manipulated by and divvied up among politicians. MDZ was said to be linked to Floyd Shivambu, Rheinland to Julius Malema, and BBT to the ANC. The source was on to something, but the picture that emerged was more complex. Rheinland was indeed linked to Malema through his friend and Rheinland's owner, Theo Mphosi – but so was BBT. And there was evidence that BBT was greasing the EFF leader's palm for a leg up in the fuel tender.

On 31 January 2019, the DA and its mayor, Solly Msimanga, tried to bring down Mosola, the city manager, in council. An earlier attempt to get rid of him had failed, but Msimanga was determined to remove Mosola, who was embroiled in controversy over his appointment of the consulting firm GladAfrica to manage R12 billion worth of City projects.

The GladAfrica contract had been criticised in preliminary reports by a law firm and the auditor-general. But Mosola had gone to court and interdicted the lawyers' report, preventing an investigation. It was what he'd done after the court case – attacking the mayor and the City's political leadership – that was the stated reason for the latest motion in council to have him removed.

On the day, Mosola was booked off on leave. The motion to suspend him was tabled in the morning. According to someone close to these events, the EFF – together with the ANC, which swung from calling for his head to protecting him in council – began playing for time and filibustering. Simultaneously, there was a mad rush to get the fuel tender signed off.

Despite being away from work, Mosola approved the tender, and the council voted on his suspension immediately after. In the event, the motion was kicked down. Some within the City speculated that last-minute backroom deals had been struck and that the EFF had held Mosola hostage, saying that if he refused to sign the tender, they would side with the DA and have him removed.

There was no other reason for Mosola to have signed then and there. Finalising the fuel tender was urgent, but not that urgent. It had already been extended amid procedural delays, and the City had fuel reserves. When *News24* asked why this was done in such a rush, given that the tender had been on the metro's agenda for more than six months, Mosola responded: 'Supply-chain processes differ in the City, and each appointment is dealt with on its merits.'[320]

Hendrick Kganyago could now breathe a sigh of relief – he had the crooked tender in the bag and stood to make a mint from it. On the very same day Mosola signed the award to BBT and the two other bidders, Hendrick deposited R501 400 in Mahuna Investments' bank account.

Hendrick Kganyago's 31 January payment was not the first to Malema's front company Mahuna, nor would it be the last. Malema also wasn't the only senior EFF figure benefiting from the BBT owner's largesse.

On the morning of Thursday 5 July 2018, about seven months before the tender was awarded, representatives of about 70 hopeful companies, including BBT, piled into boardroom A19 of the city's fleet department offices in downtown Pretoria. They were there for a compulsory briefing on the fuel tender by City officials. Aspirant bidders who did not attend the briefing were automatically disqualified.

The very next day, Mahuna's Absa bank statement reflected a R250 000 payment with a two-letter reference, 'HK' – the initials of Hendrick Kganyago. Later payments to Mahuna were labelled 'Mmaseroka', the name of some of Kganyago's companies and his family trust, or just 'fuel payment', leaving little doubt about what the payments were for.

Eighteen days after the briefing, on 23 July, the bid window closed. It would now be up to City officials to evaluate the large stack of submissions, weed out noncompliant bidders and begin the laborious selection process that would end only the following year.

Throughout that time, the money from Kganyago to Mahuna kept flowing. On Friday 27 July, at the end of the week of the briefing session, he paid R500 000 into the Mahuna account. He also paid R1 million to a company linked to EFF MP and central command member Marshall Dlamini who, the year before, had allegedly tried to lean on a senior Joburg metro executive to influence the fleet tender. While he was not publicly well known, he was starting to gain a reputation in City circles as an EFF 'fixer'.

Dlamini's association with Malema went back years. He was said to have been close to the murdered ANCYL secretary-general Sindiso Magaqa, who, like him, was from Umzimkhulu in KwaZulu-Natal. He joined the EFF early on but mostly flew under the radar as a businessman with strong political ties and, increasingly, a party backroom operator. Those who knew him said he owned a security company and had at some stage provided security services to the party and its leadership.

Malema saw him as efficient and hard-working, and he quickly won the favour of the EFF commander-in-chief. Perhaps more importantly, according to those who got to know him, he was someone with money and could rake in a lot more of it for the party. That made him valuable and catapulted him into senior leadership.

In 2015, Dlamini made it into parliament – which the EFF treated as a carousel, constantly replacing MPs either as reward or punishment. He was also appointed – fittingly for someone with his business acumen – as the party's commissar for economic development. According to a former EFF MP, Dlamini was initially reluctant to take up a parliamentary position as it meant letting go of business interests. But he nevertheless ended up in the legislature and, rather than leaving business behind for a career in politics, began to mix the two.

Dlamini was said to always be willing to fund EFF activities, including clandestine ones. A *City Press* article about EFF members jockeying for positions claimed he had tried to bribe members with inducements like phones, which he furiously denied. He was credited with growing the party's support in KwaZulu-Natal, where EFF votes quadrupled from around 70 000 in the 2014 elections to well over 300 000 in 2019, so party insiders were not surprised when Malema earmarked him for advancement. At the EFF's elective conference in 2019, he replaced the lacklustre Godrich Gardee as secretary-general.[321]

At times, Dlamini's hustle was on display. Messages show him throwing his weight around the metros, in one case ordering officials to intervene in an internal legal matter in which he, as an MP with no political position in any metro, should not have had any involvement in. Sources say he always knew much more than he should have about the administrative affairs of the metros.

Dlamini was a director of a long list of companies, including more than a dozen with 'DMM' in their name – his initials in reverse – although DMM Media and Entertainment was not one of them. This was the company that Kganyago paid, and its sole director was one Wesley Dlamini, who was 30 years old at the time. But beyond the 'DMM' label and their shared surnames, there was a lot more connecting the EFF and Marshall to Wesley.

According to information in our possession, Wesley had listed one of Marshall's companies – Eyethu Translodge & Plant Hire – as his employer. In 2016, in response to subcontractors who accused Eyethu of not paying them, Marshall claimed he had sold the company the previous year when he became an MP. Company records also showed that Wesley was a director of separate companies together with Floyd Shivambu's brothers, Lucky and Brian. DMM Media even had the same logo on social media as DMM Holdings, which Marshall had established in 2014 'as a black-owned enterprise providing diversified services and products'.

By the time the fuel tender was awarded on 31 January 2019, Kganyago had paid Malema and Dlamini R10,8 million in 17 payments. But it didn't end there. Kganyago was enjoying an enormous windfall, and despite the recommendation by tender adjudicators that the City negotiate the winning bidders down, the City failed to mitigate the damage. This is where the figures become more intricate.

To begin with, the government regulates a 'basic fuel price' based on the imported cost of fuel, which fluctuates monthly. Next, taxes and levies, costs and allowable margins are piled on to yield wholesale and retail prices. Fuel-tender bidders were providing quotes tied to a regulated wholesale price, and their quoted prices should have risen or fallen monthly in relation to that price. So, if a bidder quoted 50 cents cheaper than the wholesale price for a litre of fuel in, say, June 2018, come February 2019 it would receive the wholesale price for that month less the 50 cents – the difference in this case expressed as a discount to the City on the wholesale cost of fuel.

Quotes provided by bidders should have been adjusted every month, in line with variations in the fuel price, and the margin between the quoted and wholesale prices should have remained the same. But this did not happen. By the time the tender was awarded, six months after the bid window had closed, the regulated fuel price had fallen by more than a rand per litre of diesel and more than two rand per litre of petrol. The City should have reduced the amount it was paying the fuel suppliers, but its own financial records showed that it did the opposite.

When the contract started in February 2019, the City was overpaying for the two types of fuel it used, unleaded 95 and high-grade diesel, by R4,74 and R2,51, respectively. The fact that these costs were higher than pump prices completely defeated the point of the tender to source low-cost fuel for the City.

Despite its intention to negotiate fairer prices, the City appeared to be a willing victim of BBT's rip-off. It put the overpayment down to an 'honest mistake', but one that, as amaBhungane reported, was 'replicated faithfully, month after month'. And as Kganyago's profits accumulated, he kept pumping cash into DMM and Mahuna, which was renamed Rosario Investment in 2018 after being exposed as a Malema front. He also began making payments to the Malema front company Santaclara.

There was an intriguing allusion to revolutionary history in the names of Malema's two slush funds. In 2016, the year Malema visited Cuba to pay his respects to Fidel Castro, he changed the name of Voorsprong Trading and Projects, as it was then known, to Santaclara Trading. Santaclara is the town in Cuba that houses Che Guevara's mausoleum. Rosario Investment refers to the city of Rosario – Guevara's birthplace in Argentina. Naming companies used to fund a life of extravagance and greed in honour of a famously selfless and ascetic revolutionary was a strange paradox, and a fitting testament to Malema's contradictory politics.

By August 2019, Kganyago had stuffed a total of R15 million into the slush funds of his political friends. It was perhaps owing to the political protection he enjoyed that he was able to swindle the City with such reckless abandon.

In June 2020, in a case brought by one of the losing bidders for the fuel tender, the North Gauteng High Court set aside the tender, ruling it 'irrational' and 'unfair'. The judge noted that the overpayments had 'only ceased after September 2019, coincidentally after an article appeared on the amaBhungane website'.

In October 2021, reports emerged that the Hawks were investigating the tender and had requested information from the City relating to 'allegations of fraud and corruption committed against the City of Tshwane relating to the [tender], which was awarded to Balimi Barui Trading, MDZ Holdings and Rheinland Investment CC'. Like so many other Hawks investigations, nothing has been heard of this since.

PART FIVE
New Departures

CHAPTER 27

Shock troops

'WE DON'T NEED a street named after Theo,' Julius Malema told the audience. 'Once you've impacted the lives of human beings, your name will forever be called. Why would I forget Theo when Theo came into my life when everybody walked out of my life? [. . .] Theo is engraved in our hearts . . . If it was not for Theo, some of us wouldn't be where we are.'

Malema was speaking at the funeral of Theophilus Mphosi, who had died suddenly on 5 June 2022, reportedly from Covid-19. Some members of the family, however, believing he was poisoned, arranged for the exhumation of his body, and obtained independent pathology reports that they said showed evidence of poisoning.

He was a year younger than Malema, and the two had known each other for years. The second of four children, Mphosi came from a prominent business family based in Bochum, Limpopo – a nondescript, dust-blown town north of Polokwane now known as Senwabarwana. His parents were hard workers who started the town's first supermarket in the 1990s. It soon became a thriving business.

After obtaining a Bachelor of Commerce degree from the University of Pretoria in 2002, Mphosi joined the family business and became the driving force behind its expansion and diversification. New ventures included construction, logistics, restaurants and sporting sponsorships, but the family's most notable achievement came with the establishment of a fuel franchise called Global Oil.

Mphosi initially had something Malema did not – money. And he was generous with it. As Global filling stations popped up across Limpopo and the country and Mphosi's wealth only seemed to grow, he became a dependable friend who was always willing to open his wallet for the aspiring politician from Seshego, whose family had struggled to put food on the table during his childhood. When Malema was kicked out of the ANC, Mphosi was there to break his fall.

The Mphosi family's wealth grew and grew, 'to the point where, at the time when Julius was kicked out of ANC, Theo would help him start the EFF, even though Theo maintained strong links with people in the ANC,' said a source who knew the family. Malema acknowledged as much in his speech at his friend's funeral.

'Theo formed this EFF with his money and made it work,' Malema said. 'When an account is given [of Theo], you cannot delete the name EFF . . . Who are the people who formed this organisation? You're going to find Theo's name in there. So, we don't need anyone to remind us of who Theo is.'

Before handing the microphone to Cassel Mathale, Malema made a point of mentioning tenders, saying out loud what might have been sitting uneasily in his own mind – that 'many people in this hall had this or that appointment or arrangement with Theo which needed to be fulfilled . . . many are asking themselves what's going to happen about that construction tender we have, about this or that opportunity we were pursuing together. But sitting here, you've got an assurance that Theo was not just an individual but an institution – a CEO with a well-established executive that has got a chairman who's still alive.' It might have been a hint to the said chairman not to mess with a relationship that had served Malema well.

But it had not always been smooth and uncomplicated. Mphosi and Malema often fell out, as they did a few years before Mphosi's death. They would fight over trivial things, and sometimes disagreements over money would fuel the problem, say those close to the family. And when the EFF began harassing the Mphosi businesses it was a sure sign that all was not well between the two men.

The latest rupture began around 2019. Though it's not clear what triggered it, it coincided with the Tshwane fuel tender. Rheinland Investments – an important company in the Rheinland stable owned by Mphosi – was one of the trio of companies that scored the tender.

As amaBhungane's source in Tshwane had speculated (correctly, as it turned out), Rheinland was linked to Malema. However, there was no evidence suggesting that either Rheinland or Mphosi had made any payments to Malema related to the fuel tender.

According to the source who knew the family, 'He said it's not us this time.'

In 2019, Mphosi's life changed significantly. Having long struggled with addiction, he had left his wife but was getting sober. At the same time, his elder sister was assuming a more hands-on role in running the business. A chartered accountant by training, she is said to have tightened the purse strings.

In January 2020, Jossey Buthane, then the EFF chair in Limpopo, posted the following on social media: 'I am not scared of an *Inkabi* [hitman] hired by a blood thirsty owner of multiple Global garage owner [sic]. Stop with the warnings come and do it once. Let's see . . .'

The fight appeared to have spiralled out of control.

A few weeks before, in the early hours of 30 December 2019, an associate of Malema's, George 'Blacks' Maluleka, was shot in what looked like an attempted hit. The incident happened while Maluleka was driving away from Malema's Mekete Lodge outside Polokwane after an end-of-year party. He was hit in the legs but survived, and a passenger was unscathed. According to a police report, Maluleka suspected that Mphosi was involved. The report stated: '30 dec 2019 at 04h00 from Mekete Lodge along N1 road when he [complainant] and passenger heard some gun shots and suddenly realized he was being shot at. He was shot in his legs by unknown people, but his passenger saw the person who was shooting. He is suspecting Theo Mphosi because he always threatened to kill him.'

Buthane claimed that Mphosi had called him at around seven o'clock that morning and said, 'I've dealt with that boy [Maluleka] – my boys have shot him left and right.'

According to Buthane's version, the shooting was in revenge for Maluleka informing Mphosi's wife that her husband was supposedly having an affair. Whether or not Mphosi was actually involved in the shooting is unclear, but the incident escalated the tensions that had been brewing between Mphosi, on the one hand, and Malema and his cronies on the other.

Malema allegedly allowed Buthane to lead a campaign against Global garages, the family's flagship enterprise. The perfect pretext for an all-out offensive on Global presented itself when two of its security guards shot and killed two local men at a Global filling station in Ga-Masemola, Limpopo, in the early hours of 3 July 2020. Community members denied allegations that the two men were armed robbers and said one was a pensioner. They said they had come to collect social grants from a building next door to the garage and had arrived early to beat the queues.

Days after the incident, Buthane sprang into action. Claiming to champion the rights of residents, he rallied a crowd that temporarily shut down the fuel station. He kept relentlessly attacking the company throughout the year, stating on social media that Global was selling fake fuel and that Mphosi family companies were exploiting their workers and corruptly obtaining tenders. The specifics of these claims were unclear, but it was evident that there was a back story to Buthane's very public and narrowly targeted outrage.

Buthane had a long history with Malema and provincial politics. He had been a senior manager in Pinky Kekana's office when she was MEC for roads and transport, the epicentre of the On-Point saga. He had been active in local ANC politics and was a close ally of Malema's before joining the EFF in late 2013. By then, he had already gained a reputation for thuggery, and his political career was consistently marred by instances of violence. These included allegedly beating up members of a rival ANCYL faction who had challenged Malema in 2011, his arrest the following year for another instance of alleged assault on a league member, and his second arrest the same year after he and his mother were accused of disrupting a political meeting, chasing comrades while wielding a spade, and throwing stones at people. Buthane and his mother spent Mother's Day behind bars, but were then set free.

In September 2014, the media reported: 'As EFF members staged an all-night vigil in Polokwane on Monday night ahead of their commander-in-chief's court date on corruption charges, police went looking for his trusted lieutenant, Jossey Buthane'[322] – this time in connection with a charge of assault with intent to do grievous bodily harm after he had reportedly beaten up a fellow EFF member. By now, Buthane was a senior EFF leader, having been 'parachuted' into the position of Limpopo coordinator.

Then, in 2015, he appeared in court yet again after allegedly beating a student with a stick. In 2017, he faced charges for assault in a domestic dispute, and in 2020 he was granted bail in connection with a separate case in which he was alleged to have had a hand in a vigilante attack. The man nicknamed 'Stalin', was in and out of court for much of his political career.[323] Nothing ever came of any of these cases.

In 2018, he and other EFF members were caught on camera assaulting members of a local business association calling itself the Radical Economic Transformation Forum (RETF). The RETF's spokesperson, Thabo Mabotja, said the organisation was fighting for a stake in big tenders – they wanted local businesspeople to be given a 30 percent share of all tenders over R30 million. He labelled Buthane a 'provincial bully'. Buthane defended his actions, saying the EFF was defending black businesses against threats and harassment from the RETF. He said the forum had already shut down black businesses. A short video clip showed a mob in EFF attire viciously assaulting RETF members with sticks outside the Fusion Boutique Hotel in Polokwane, where the RETF had been set to meet officials about a major road-construction project. At least one member of the forum was hospitalised.

A former senior EFF leader who worked closely with Buthane claimed that, like Marshall Dlamini, Buthane's prominence in the party owed much to his ability 'to go get money'. Buthane, the source claimed, was not afraid to weaponise the local EFF. He was a larger-than-life figure, zooming around Polokwane in a luxury red Porsche Cayenne to rally a crowd for this or that political intervention.

The blood-red Porsche was another link between Buthane and Malema's 'tenderpreneurial' network, because although he appears to have had free use of it, Buthane was not the formal owner. On paper, it belonged to a company called Mmamode Trading Enterprise, registered to an address in a village outside Tzaneen. Its sole director, credit records show, was an employee of Selby Manthata's Selby Construction and his wife's Oceanside Trading.

Buthane appears to have been a loyal Malema supporter in Limpopo, but he would soon mobilise provincial EFF members for a much bigger fight on behalf of Malema's business allies.

In mid-2018, angry residents poured into the crumbling streets of Ga-Mphahlele in rural Limpopo to protest against Dithabeng Mining, which they claimed was an 'illegal' chrome mining operation run by Malema's friend Mazzotti and his business partners.

Ga-Mphahlele is a dusty little dorp consigned to poverty. There is an emptiness to the place, and it is a world away from leafy Hyde Park, Johannesburg, where it was revealed later that same year that Malema and his family resided in a high-security complex owned by Mazzotti. Mazzotti claimed at the time that Malema's wife, Mantoa, rented the property at market rates.[324]

In Ga-Mphahlele, the most active members of society go elsewhere in search of work, and the more successful among them send money home to fund roomy villas with columned entrances that look strangely ostentatious amid the meagreness of their surroundings.

On the southern outskirts of the village, surrounded by mostly barren fields, Mazzotti's open-cast mine had continued to expand despite resistance from many in the community who were so fed up they were blockading roads and demanding a halt to mining. The mine itself had the air of a fly-by-night operation – a giant pit and a couple of prefabricated offices surrounded by scrubby fields and emaciated cows.

At the entrance, a group of dishevelled men hid from the sun under a lone tree. These were the '1 000 Madoda', so-called for supposedly accepting R1 000 each to act as the company's security guards. The men – ex-convicts and the homeless among them – allegedly helped Dithabeng and the local chiefly authority stamp out opposition to the mine and were much feared in the area. The community was split between those who felt they had not been consulted about the mine that was encroaching on their land and those who supported the mine, including the chief.

Further complicating the messy affair was a power struggle over the chieftaincy that Dithabeng was accused of exploiting. The young chief, Malekutu Phatudi-Mphahlele – whose flashy lifestyle and aloofness earned him little respect among his impoverished subjects – was accused by a rival faction of usurping power and selling out the community.

That faction, calling itself the Royal Council, claimed that Mazzotti and his partners, in collusion with Chief Phatudi-Mphahlele, had simply gone over the heads of the community to strike a mining deal and bypass meaningful consultation with the villagers whose livelihoods would be affected by the mine and who relied on the land the mine was now taking over.

Dithabeng strenuously denied having done anything improper, saying it had engaged extensively with the community ahead of a meeting in February 2017. At the meeting, which was attended by more than 800 community members, 'consensus was reached to sign an agreement in public as a sign of a broader buy-in'. It was followed by a 'signing ceremony' held later that month at a run-down local school, where a beaming Mazzotti and his business partner showed up in black suits and sunglasses to seal the deal.

The Royal Council painted a rather different picture of the consultation, claiming that the meeting was nothing more than a rubber-stamping exercise – a way to give the appearance of community consensus. The people of Ga-Mphahlele, the rival faction claimed, were presented with a fait accompli after Chief Phatudi-Mphahlele had 'hijacked' the community trust formed on behalf of the community to control and administer its assets. There was ample evidence to support the allegation that the trust had been manipulated. AmaBhungane found glaring discrepancies in the trust's records, and some trustees themselves complained about having had information withheld from them and being kept in the dark about the running of the trust and its dealings with the mine.[325] The chief, it appeared, had unilaterally struck a deal with Dithabeng on behalf of the trust and the community. It was, the Royal Council charged, a complete violation of customary rights.

At some point in early 2017, angry community members had called on a group of local EFF 'fighters' to support them during a meeting with mine bosses, including Mazzotti. When they arrived, Mazzotti allegedly phoned his old buddy Malema and asked him to intervene. According to Topa Mphahlele, a local EFF leader who would later join the African Transformation Movement (ATM), Mazzotti then handed him the phone, at which point Malema ordered him and his EFF comrades to stand down. Several former EFF members, all of whom later joined the ATM, claimed to have been present and confirmed the story. Both Malema and Mazzotti denied that the phone call had taken place.

In September that year, the Royal Council sent a letter to Buthane in which they accused his party of 'meddling' in Ga-Mphahlele's affairs and intimidating striking workers at the mine. The letter claimed that Topa had led a group of EFF members to the mine on 13 September and 'bullied the workers', warning them that 'they should resume duty whether they like it or not because Mr Malema will not like the delay in production'.

Asked by amaBhungane to respond to the allegations, Buthane said the claims that he had meddled in the community's dispute with the mine were being peddled by 'disgruntled' former members who were 'playing dirty politics with the EFF'. When asked if he had met Mazzotti, Buthane said: 'I don't remember.' Pressed further, he said: 'Look, if I meet Mazzotti, there is nothing wrong with that.'

Ga-Mphahlele resembles, in some respects, a story that has played out across the rural former Bantustans, where self-interested traditional leaders remain trapped in a colonial time warp and continue to act with scant concern for the people they are supposed to represent. In dusty, impoverished Ga-Mphahlele, where – as in many other places – the long arm of the state barely reaches, a chief was allegedly acting with impunity and selling out the community by pawning off communal assets. Yet, in democratic South Africa, the institution of chieftaincy was supposed to democratised and brought in line with the ideals of the Constitution.

New laws and regulations were written to transform traditional councils into democratic and representative bodies, safeguard the rights of those living under traditional authorities and prevent chiefs from signing away land rights without the consent of the community. But this vision remains unrealised, and poor governance is partly to blame. Both the government and mining interests have found it convenient to maintain the status quo, as it is ultimately much simpler to deal with a few easily swayed traditional leaders than to negotiate with fractious communities in the hope of achieving some form of consensus.

The fight for change, however, has progressed in court. Ironically, in the same year the community of Ga-Mphahlele began revolting against the mine, the High Court and Constitutional Court issued rulings affirming communities' rights over their land.

The Constitutional Court judgment began with a citation from Franz Fanon: 'For a colonised people the most essential value, because the most concrete, is first and foremost the land: the land which will bring them bread and, above all, dignity.'

Yet, in Ga-Mphahlele, a party that professed to be 'Fanonist', having energetically championed justice for the Marikana massacre victims, now stood accused of playing for the other side.

CHAPTER 28

The charge of the Red Berets

I T'S A MUGGY Durban day in the summer of 2021. Sitting in a garden café, former EFF MP Sipho Mbatha nurses a beer as he reaches deep into his past, recounting the turbulent 1980s.

He has an encyclopaedic memory of the politics from that time, which he recalls with careful consideration. He grew up not far away, in Umlazi, and his first taste of politics came in 1983 during the school boycotts. He had only just entered his teens and, like many of his peers, was swept up in political forces he did not fully understand. But it was the beginning of a long involvement with the ANC, which ended after the 2012 Mangaung conference and Jacob Zuma's re-election as party president. For him, the ANC had 'proclaimed its own death' after the victory of a faction of talentless crooks. They could have had Kgalema Motlanthe but chose Zuma and his dodgy courtiers instead.

The next year, on 26 July 2013, Mbatha was at Uncle Tom's Hall in Soweto for the birth of the EFF, following frenzied attempts to mobilise supporters and scrape together the money needed to enter national politics. Malema had become a beacon for a bunch of angry former ANCYL members, community activists, intellectuals and disaffected ex-ANC members like Mbatha.

For Mbatha, Malema inspired hope: 'He had said he was leaving the ANC, and he was not leaving it lying down.' He did not know Malema well but had worked with him and the ANCYL over the years in various youth development initiatives. Mbatha saw him as a 'comrade who was upright and frank'.

As one of Zuma's sharpest critics, Malema's popularity rose as the president's fell – his scandals momentarily forgotten by those who now looked to him and the EFF as an alternative to the ANC. But there were warning signs that he was far from reformed.

'I had picked up those stories about influencing tenders,' Mbatha says, 'and then there was the conspicuous consumption.' Malema had not shed his taste for expensive watches, fancy clothes and a lifestyle that seemed beyond his means.

Mpho Ramakatsa, another ANC member to join the EFF, recalls Adriano Mazzotti often appearing alongside Malema in those early years, which raised some eyebrows within the party. At the time, though, they thought it was best to look the other way. The EFF was desperate for funds, and if Malema's backers in the business world were willing to chip in, then so be it. Years later, Malema would say to party members: 'For us to get where we are going, fighters, we are going to have to kiss a lot of frogs on the way.'

'Some of us had to dig deep into our pockets,' says Ramakatsa, who drove all over the country to drum up support for the new party. He was unemployed at the time after a legal battle in which he and five other Free State ANC members had dared to challenge key Zuma ally, premier Ace Magashule. They had won, obtaining an order nullifying the province's elective conference, but by then Ramakatsa was fed up with the ANC, which had been his political home since the 1980s.

During apartheid, he had joined the party's student wing, gone into exile, trained with uMkhonto weSizwe in Angola and returned to South Africa to fight the struggle from within. He was arrested and sent to Robben Island. Now this struggle veteran was in a new party led mostly by people who, like Malema, were too young to have earned their stripes in the fight against apartheid.

As a political elder and former Robben Islander, Ramakatsa had the pedigree for the EFF's interim leadership. He was effectively Malema's second-in-command, tasked with building the party at ground level ahead of the national elections in mid-2014 and a year-end 'people's assembly' to elect new EFF leaders. With the assembly came the first open conflict within the barely one-year-old party.

On Sunday 15 December 2014, the second day of the event in Mangaung, delegates from EFF branches across the country got down to the delicate business of electing a new leadership. To Lucky Twala, by then an EFF MP, the whole thing seemed staged. 'You had Julius sitting on the stage and people being deployed strategically across the hall. They nominate a name, Julius raises his hand in support of that name, and the whole hall raises their hands too.'

Any nomination that did not have Malema's approval fell flat. The candidate would be nominated by someone on the floor, Malema would stare coldly into the crowd, hands folded, and only a handful of delegates would dare raise theirs. It was like a Stalinesque pantomime, until a group of Gauteng rebels got up and began chanting anti-Malema songs. They complained of being sidelined while delegates from the North West were given every opportunity to nominate. They stormed out and burned a list of candidates for the party's central command team (CCT) that they claimed had been pre-approved by Malema and his faction. A 'visibly angry' Malema tried to contain the situation, declaring: 'People are allowed to lobby in conferences. They can do that without fear or favour.'[326]

Andile Mngxitama – the extremist EFF MP who later founded the Black First Land First movement before joining Zuma's uMkhonto weSizwe Party (MK Party) – rejected his own nomination to the CCT in protest against Malema. Realising that he lacked the numbers, he also declined his nomination for the position of deputy secretary-general. 'My revolutionary conscience will not allow me to accept,' he told reporters at the time.[327]

Malema's faction swept the floor, packing the CCT with loyalists and leaving a bunch of bitter EFF members – including Ramakatsa and his supporters – in its wake. Ramakatsa hadn't even secured a spot on the CCT. 'Part of what we were pushing for was that Floyd [Shivambu] cannot deputise Julius – you can't have a party of friends,' he says today.

In February 2015, two months after the people's assembly, separate attempts by Mngxitama and his allies to address the media ended in brawls between his supporters and rival EFF members. For some, like

Khanyisile Litchfield-Tshabalala, it was a Damascus moment. She said of Malema: 'A leader who steals from the poor to feed his lifestyle can't be a revolutionary.'[328]

Litchfield-Tshabalala, Ramakatsa and Mngxitama were suspended from the party, alongside Twala, for criticising the party leadership and bringing the party into disrepute. Mngxitama was accused of having leaked information to the media, some of which related to a car bought by the EFF and registered in the name of a third party – Voorsprong Trading, as Malema's front company Santaclara was then named.

By April, it was all over for Ramakatsa, Mngxitama and Litchfield-Tshabalala. The disciplinary process concluded, and the three were frog-marched out of the EFF for good.[329] Twala – another former Robben Island prisoner – remained suspended but left soon after. The party he walked away from, he said, had become a 'private company – a vehicle for the interests of a clique. When an organisation has a president for life, that's a problem in itself.'

While Malema's critics in the wake of the people's assembly might have been dismissed as bitter losers, driven by personal vendettas, and as 'egomaniacs'[330], they did at least have a point – their erstwhile leader's rise to power was paved with fraught and disputed elections. Notably, these included his 2008 election as ANCYL president, also in Mangaung. At the time, Malema was the preferred choice of the incumbent president, Fikile Mbalula, but his opponent, Saki Mofokeng, had most of the provinces behind him. The lobbying machine went into overdrive.

'We met delegates secretly, offering assistance to delegates and giving them money' to 'sell the name of Julius as president', says Mbatha, as he recounts the days before the ANCYL election. It was a 'highly divisive' event marked by suspicion, prolonged delays, allegations that delegates' credentials had been manipulated, and rowdy exchanges that even led to fist fights.

Back then, ANC deputy president Kgalema Motlanthe publicly con-demned the 'state of disorder', while Mbalula apologised to the country for the actions of 'disruptive elements' that had marred the event.[331] Malema was pronounced ANCYL president by a narrow margin, but the results were disputed as soon as they were released, and the conference had to be postponed. However, in June 2008, Mofokeng surprised many when he conceded defeat and called for unity.

By the next elective conference in Midrand in the winter of 2011, Malema's position was even stronger. Lebogang Maile opposed Malema, but lacked provincial backing, so he needed to be nominated from the floor with the support of at least 30 percent of the delegates to meet the nomination threshold and pose a significant challenge to Malema.

This required a show of hands in front of the incumbent – and getting enough delegates to do that was 'near impossible'. Some complained of 'fear and intimidation'.[332] Malema was relatively secure in his presidency, but the whiff of dissent at a pre-conference meeting, where Maile supporters had stood up in Malema's presence and chanted for their man, seemed to have infuriated him. 'We must agree to be led,' Malema declared. 'As long as you don't agree to be led, you are an anarchist.'[333]

For Mbatha, who attended the Midrand conference, the EFF's first people's assembly years later evoked a strong sense of déjà vu. Malema cemented his control of the new party, and Mbatha believes that the EFF then began its slide into authoritarianism. He remained in the party until he and another EFF MP, Mmabatho Mokause, were forced to resign from parliament for alleged 'laziness and underperformance' in 2017. This no doubt coloured his view of Malema, but he claims that he had mounting concerns about the party and its leader long before he was replaced. He was alarmed by Malema's power over the party and how he arbitrarily wielded it. 'I saw a different picture [among] the leaders – they were purging, and purging,' he says.

The 'arrogance' and 'disdain' shown towards some comrades shocked him. In his view, 'a lot of good people were expelled between 2016 and 2017 for no reason, and a lot of good people who were there from the beginning of the EFF took it upon themselves to leave.'

The churn among EFF MPs was indeed remarkable. By February 2018, over 60 percent of the 31 EFF parliamentarians in both houses of parliament had resigned or been expelled. Some resigned strategically and were redeployed 'laterally' (rather than being redeployed to a lower sphere of government – in effect, demoted). Nevertheless, the startling figures could not be attributed to healthy internal competition. Not even the

ANC, 'riddled with factional acrimony', as a report from the Institute of Race Relations (IRR) put it, came close to the EFF's turnover rate.[334]

The anomaly was partly attributed to the EFF being a fledgling party struggling to find skilled and competent officials. But this alone could not account for the turnover. The IRR ascribed it to a 'silent revolution' inside the EFF – a 'systematic purge' of its parliamentary caucus.[335] The claim might have been exaggerated but was not without basis. The ongoing instability and uncertainty created by the party's 'highly autocratic disciplinary machine' was a way of preserving Malema's power. Nobody under him could feel safe or secure in their positions. It was a strategy that Zuma had also employed, the IRR noted.

According to Mbatha, EFF leaders in parliament and elsewhere 'were being set up for failure' and could be removed on a whim. EFF MPs were not only expected to pay 15 percent of their salaries to the party as a kind of tithe and cover their own party organising costs, but also had faced other unreasonable demands. At least, that's how Mbatha felt. Councillors in impoverished rural areas had to pay for buses to send party supporters to rallies, which was a tall order for EFF leaders without wealthy patrons willing to fork out.

'What are you thinking when you demand that low-level leaders raise R800 000 for EFF events?' Mbatha asks. 'A councillor in some impoverished area – how do you think they would pay for 20 buses? Do you want them to be corrupt?'

After the EFF's 10th anniversary celebration in July 2023, the CCT culled dozens of leaders for failing to arrange buses to transport supporters to the event – including its KwaZulu-Natal chairperson, the MP Vusi Khoza. Malema had lashed out and shamed 'lazy people', warning that 'your stay in the EFF depends on your contribution'.[336]

Even Malema's confidant and strongman in Limpopo, Jossey Buthane, was not safe. In the November 2021 local government elections, EFF support in Limpopo dropped by more than two percentage points, from 16,8 percent in 2016 to 14,5 percent. For the party, it was a worrying portent of what was to come. And for Buthane, it sealed his fate.

In January 2022, he and his Limpopo comrades attended a CCT meeting in Johannesburg where a report on the elections was discussed.

Buthane got word that national leadership might move against his Limpopo team. 'Businesspeople knew before we knew – they said, "We know you're going to be disbanded,"' Buthane told us. He wouldn't say who those businesspeople were.

During the meeting, some CCT members criticised Buthane's team, but if Malema supported their views, he didn't show it. Nevertheless, a dip in the party's stronghold province was hard to swallow, and something needed to be done. The next day Malema's tone had changed completely, and the CIC announced that the Limpopo leadership would be disbanded.

Buthane was incensed. He and his team were removed, and the former national spokesperson, 'commissar' Mbuyiseni Ndlozi, was deployed to rebuild party structures in the province ahead of a provincial people's assembly to elect new leaders – an event that Buthane did not bother to attend. According to a former senior EFF source who knew Buthane well, it was an EFF principle that members of a disbanded structure should not contest the elections to reconstitute the same structure. Buthane was not even elected at branch level to attend the people's assembly.

Buthane himself holds a more conspiratorial view, claiming that the drop in voter share was just a pretext and that Malema himself recognised how hard the provincial leadership had worked before the elections. According to Buthane, Malema removed him and instructed other comrades not to let him contest at the people's assembly because the EFF leader backed the Limpopo faction of his old friend Jacob Lebogo.

Buthane says he heard 'rumours on the ground' that Lebogo wanted to oust him. 'I even went to Mekete, Julius's plot, to confront him about why he was backing these guys.' He claimed that staffers from the national office led by Ndlozi ensured that Lebogo and one other were elected to attend the people's assembly, and that he was excluded. He could still have run against Lebogo, but says: 'I chose not to contest – I was fed up already.' Buthane went on to start a local union, and then took the path of many former EFF members and rejoined the ANC before the 2024 national elections.

One thing Buthane and many others agree on is that the CCT tends to act as a rubber stamp for Malema's decisions. A former senior EFF leader in Limpopo says that although there might have been grounds for disbanding the provincial leadership, Malema did want to shoehorn Lebogo into a leadership position. 'Julius calls the shots, though on some points he has allowed some democracy. But when he really wants something, he gets it.'

Mbatha concurs, saying the nature of the organisation is 'quasi-democratic' and that Malema has packed the CCT with loyalists and 'friends' who are quick to stamp out the first sign of any real dissent.

Over time, the EFF has increasingly bent to the whims of its leader – a leader who has become ever more mercurial since Ramaphosa became president. Again and again, Malema has brazenly contradicted himself.

In February 2017, Malema lauded then finance minister Pravin Gordhan for his firm stance on corruption while the two of them were fighting Zuma. 'If there is only one person who's giving some form of hope for our people, we must be able to support that person, and Pravin comes across as such an individual who's a unifier, who's seeking good for our country,' he declared.[337]

The next year, as the VBS Mutual Bank scandal cast a shadow, Gordhan was labelled 'corrupt' and a 'dog of white monopoly capital', while Floyd Shivambu railed against an imaginary 'Indian cabal', said to include Gordhan and the long-standing Treasury official Ismail Momoniat.[338]

Also in 2017, Malema blamed disgraced former Eskom CEO Brian Molefe for the Gupta-linked corruption that had brought the company to its knees.[339] But in 2023, he called for Molefe to be returned to Eskom once again to fix the ailing utility.[340]

The same thing happened with axed Western Cape judge president John Hlophe. In 2021, Malema supported this 'man of integrity' for the position of chief justice; but in 2017, he had described Hlophe as a 'rotten potato' who should be removed from the judiciary.[341]

The EFF had erred in their support for former Public Protector Busisiwe Mkhwebane, Malema said in 2017: 'We just took a puppet from [the] Guptas' kitchen and said, "Let's give her a chance"'.[342] A few years later, when Mkhwebane came under fire for yet another incompetent report – this time on a pension matter involving Gordhan – the EFF rushed to her defence.[343] Mkhwebane's political usefulness appeared to endear her to the EFF leader, who was facing heightened scrutiny of his affairs and growing trouble related to VBS. In 2023, after Mkhwebane was finally impeached, the EFF welcomed her with open arms and deployed her to parliament, calling her a 'servant of the people' and 'one of the most successful public protectors of our democracy'.[344]

Anyone, it seemed, who was an enemy of Ramaphosa at the time was a friend of the EFF. Not long after, there was a rapprochement between Malema and Zuma. Having gone from Zuma's staunchest defender to his fiercest critic, suggesting he should 'rot in jail', he flip-flopped once more in 2021 and flew in a helicopter to Zuma's Nkandla home for tea – then changed his mind again three years later.

The tea party at Nkandla, months before Zuma began his brief stint in prison for contempt of court, was the culmination of a de facto alliance between anti-Ramaphosa groups within and outside the ANC, which coalesced into a sort of 'radical economic transformation' or RET faction. In Malema's eyes, Zuma was suddenly rehabilitated. Two of Zuma's most vocal, and comical, backers – Carl Niehaus and the ATM's Mzwanele Manyi – even crossed over to the EFF in 2023. Politics may demand a degree of flexibility, but, as Malema's critics pointed out, the only consistency in his views on others was their inconsistency. By now, his eye-rolling 'flip-flops' were a staple of pithy comment pieces.[345]

He tried to brush off the criticism in 2023, saying: 'Flip-flopper is a title given to me by my enemies, and why should I worry about what my enemies think of me?'[346] It didn't change the fact that his contradictions and contortions were dizzying, even for some of his most ardent followers.[347]

There was a ruthless logic beneath it all. Malema's backtracking on Zuma revealed a cold expediency. Having been removed from the presidency, Zuma was no longer the EFF's public enemy number one. Now, Ramaphosa and his government's efforts to clean up the state and criminal justice system, which had been decimated under his predecessor, posed a direct threat to Malema. Zuma, Malema and many of their closest associates must have seen storm clouds gathering – unwanted scrutiny, ruined careers and possibly even time in jail.

But Ramaphosa's reforms were overly cautious and painfully slow, as the president – renowned for his deliberate, consensus-building approach – sought to navigate an ANC riven by deep divisions and vested interests. Good intentions faced heavy constraints, and excising the cancer of corruption required utmost delicacy – if Ramaphosa cut too deep, he risked slicing into an artery. Many in the ANC found the corruption of the Zuma era just a little too mercenary – and damaging to the party's image. Yet, many of these critics were hardly unblemished themselves. As the State Capture Commission made clear, corruption had become a structural problem within the ANC. It was at the core of its funding model, and turning off the taps of patronage too quickly could have cost Ramaphosa dearly.

Ramaphosa's own controversies were bogging down his anti-corruption drive. First public protector Mkhwebane looked into Ramaphosa's 'CR 17' campaign for ANC party president, accusing him of misleading parliament and possible money-laundering. Her report was excoriated in court, where judges added to the long list of unflattering adjectives used to describe her work as public protector – 'reckless', 'confused', 'irrational'.

Then, in 2020, came Farmgate. Zuma ally Arthur Fraser blew the lid off the theft of what he claimed were millions in undeclared dollars stashed in a couch at Ramaphosa's Phala Phala ranch. Fraser, a former state security boss, was commissioner of correctional services at the time and would go on to unconstitutionally release Zuma on medical parole from his 15-month sentence for contempt of court.

The EFF seized on these scandals. To the EFF, Ramaphosa had always been a natural bogeyman – the billionaire 'butcher of Marikana' and the man who, as chair of the ANC's disciplinary appeals committee, helped to seal Malema's fate as ANCYL leader.

But the president was popular – much more so than his party. And his efforts to clamp down on sleaze, as limp wristed as they would come to be seen, were backed by collective goodwill from a populace fed up with the corruption of the Zuma years. Every day on live TV, the wide-ranging Commission into State Capture exposed, in granular detail, the rot in South African politics.

Zuma had demonstrated the speed with which a world-leading insti-tution like SARS could be gutted of its investigative capacity, and it was always going to be easier to destroy than to rebuild. However, if the overall picture was one in which reform was hindered, the appointment of competent officials in some instances began to yield improvements in ways that threatened Malema. SARS, in particular, was slowly being turned around.

The past was catching up with Malema and Zuma. As the latter faced revived corruption charges related to the 1990s arms deal, the VBS-related trials and investigations continued, and a resuscitated SARS was again sniffing around Malema and Floyd Shivambu's affairs. We understand that so far Malema may have been more successful at evading SARS than Shivambu. In the meantime though, Malema faces the prospect of additional corruption investigations, and even the possible reinstatement of the On-Point case.

In response to the looming threats, Malema and Zuma loyalists parroted their leaders' conspiracy theories about murky cabals and shadowy plots, lobbed the same baseless criticisms at the NPA and SARS, and denounced judges as 'captured'.[348] It was as shameless as it was transparent, and it had everything to do with self-preservation. History had come full circle. Here was Malema making common cause again with the person he once said he would die for, who then became his sworn enemy and who, like him, was now a victim. But, like before, Malema's relationship with Zuma was double-edged. The former president ended up severely harming the EFF's electoral prospects when, in December 2023, just six months before the 2024 national elections, he publicly endorsed the newly formed MK Party. He was soon after suspended from the ANC.

The MK Party, named after the ANC's armed wing in the liberation era, was the latest ANC breakaway claiming to be the authentic custodian of the ruling party's legacy – and the ANC tried to thwart it from the outset by embroiling it in litigation.

The new party's leadership displayed glaring signs of incompetence and was soon beset by power struggles that included murky intelligence reports and allegations of a plot to poison Zuma. The cloak-and-dagger politics was classic Zuma, the former ANC intelligence honcho, and he quickly cemented control of the party. But just days before the May election, the Constitutional Court ruled that he was ineligible for a seat in parliament because of the 15-month jail sentence handed to him in 2021 (of which he served only two months). However, he remained the leader of the MK Party.

Like the EFF, the party was challenging the ruling ANC on its own turf and drew heavily on ANC tradition. Both the EFF and the MK Party have employed the anti-capitalist vocabulary of the liberation struggle, and both have claimed to be the true heirs of the ANC's legacy. Ideologically, however, the differences between the EFF and MK Party are profound. In claiming the mantle of progressivism, the MK Party only masks its deeply reactionary politics.

In contrast, Malema genuinely believes in the core progressive ideals he espouses. As head of the EFF, he has consistently supported gay rights and gender equality, decried tribalism, and opposed the death penalty. For all his opportunism and contradiction, his political world view is anchored by a strong and consistent adherence to pan-Africanism. This is evident in his willingness to take a firm stance against xenophobia – an unpopular position in a country where foreigners are easy fodder for populist politicking.

There have been times when he has wavered and given in to the anti-foreigner impulses of some of his supporters, like when the EFF went from restaurant to restaurant to aggressively inspect how many foreigners each employed. But he has mostly shunned the chorus of xenophobia, demonstrated sympathy for black foreigners, and spoken out against their victimisation. The electoral costs of this stance have presumably not been lost on someone as politically intuitive as Malema.

The same cannot be said of Zuma, who has stamped his backward-looking, chauvinistic politics on his new party. With its progressive-sounding demand for 'radical economic transformation' and constant references to 'white monopoly capital', the MK Party conceals its real intentions. For Zuma, radical economic transformation is synonymous with the continued looting of the state under the guise of redistribution. It signals to power brokers and party benefactors that under him the taps of patronage would keep flowing. At the same time, espousing radical economic transformation aids Zuma in his self-depiction as a political martyr. In his world he is, and always has been, the target of countless conspiracies by outside forces, including unnamed foreign intelligence agencies, because he dares to challenge the status quo. But his radicalism is hollow.

The MK Party's claim to spearhead progressive politics sits uneasily with its leader's embrace of a staunch traditionalism and xenophobia in party ranks, like when the party's women's league in eThekwini demanded the mass deportations of foreigners.[349] On the campaign trail, Zuma was a knee-jerk conservative on social issues such as gay rights, corporal punishment and parenting, which led him to bizarre ideas like his proposal that teenage parents be forced to complete their studies on Robben Island. He stoked discontent over the slow pace of transformation, rampant poverty, the lack of services and jobs, and myriad social ills by tapping into the most reactionary sentiments of his supporters.

His message was as simple as it was enticing. It harked back to a romanticised, uncomplicated African past when the youth respected their elders, patriarchal authority was unchallenged, and subjects deferred to chiefs. And it appears to have resonated in the traditionalist Zulu hinterland of KwaZulu-Natal, where Zulu ethnic identity remained deeply etched in society and chiefly authority had long been a powerful mobilising force, nurtured for decades by the apartheid state and its collaborators. This was the bedrock of ethnic nationalism that sustained the IFP, but it was also familiar territory for Zuma, having been a source of his political strength during his battle for supremacy in the ANC.

Back then, armed with his '100% Zulu Boy' slogan, Zuma had broken a sacrosanct ANC rule – a prohibition on tribalism and ethnic exclusivism – in a deliberate effort to whip up support among Zulus. The subtext of his narrative was that a leader of the Zulu nation was under attack by external forces, as were all proud Zulus by extension. It worked, and it would continue to define Zuma's political strategy. As his sleaze was exposed, with his popularity waning and the law closing in on him, Zuma would again fall back on his ethnic identity and perceived victimhood. And by conflating his own plight with collective grievances, he helped lay the groundwork for the 2021 riots – a wave of unrest sparked by Zuma's imprisonment for contempt of court – and then built a party devoted to his self-preservation.

At the MK Party's manifesto launch at Orlando Stadium in May 2024, Zuma made it clear to the packed crowds that the party would embrace Zulu nationalism as well as the institutional custodians of Zulu ethnic identity – chiefs. The symbolism of Zuma being ushered into the stadium by Zulu regiments and giving his speech entirely in isiZulu was obvious enough. More significant was his promise to restore the powers of traditional rulers to 'allow them to make decisions about their community without the involvement of the government' and his argument in favour of traditional courts 'as a better platform to resolve issues instead of the biased courts of today'.

It was indicative of his contempt for South Africa's Constitution, which he and the MK Party view merely as a foreign imposition and which they seek to abolish. In place of 'Roman-Dutch law' would be a legal system embedded in what the MK Party deems to be African custom, with a prominent place in government for unelected chiefs. The support for traditional institutions is directed at one group of tribal leaders in particular – the Zulu royal elite, with whom the party retains close ties through personalities like Zuma himself and Chief Phathisizwe Chiliza, the deputy traditional prime minister of the Zulu kingdom who is also an MK Party member.

Unlike the MK Party, the EFF has steered clear of tribalist politics. And unlike the former party's outright rejection of constitutional democracy, Malema's attitude to the country's founding document has been ambivalent. The EFF has wielded it to great effect in its legal battles against Zuma, championing precedent-setting cases. The EFF's counsel in the Nkandla case, Tembeka Ngcukaitobi, captivated the nation with his strident defence of the Constitution and the Office of the Public Protector. The EFF's incessant demand that Zuma 'pay back the money' for publicly funded upgrades to his Nkandla compound reached the highest court in the land, which ruled that the president had failed to uphold his oath of office by defying Public Protector Thuli Madonsela's binding remedial action.

Through its creative use of litigation and the tools of democracy, the EFF has proven that it is not merely a disruptor. The shouting matches and punch-ups in parliament have been only one part of a bigger, multi-pronged strategy. On the other hand, the EFF's subsequent attacks on the judiciary, the media and other key institutions of democracy, driven by a combination of conspiracy theories and the naked self-interest of its leaders, suggest a cynical and instrumental approach to the Constitution – to be used when it suits them and ignored when it doesn't. Increasingly, the latter holds true.

Regardless of their differences, however, the EFF and MK Party focused on the same disgruntled voters ahead of the elections. The polls showed strong support for Zuma's new upstart, despite it being plagued by chaos and infighting. Only the most blindly overconfident EFF leader would not have been worried about the MK Party threat.

The day of reckoning came on 29 May. The results trickled in, the markets trembled, and voters waited anxiously for the outcome of what everyone knew would be a watershed moment in South African politics. Despite the high stakes, turnout was at a record low, and Zuma's new party benefited from the widespread disillusionment of the electorate. It did even better than most pollsters predicted, winning over 14,5 percent of the national vote. The MK Party's votes were heavily concentrated in KwaZulu-Natal (where it was said to have systematically captured ANC branches, ultimately getting 46 percent of the vote) and other regions with large proportions of Zulu speakers, including southern Mpumalanga.

Though the MK Party's share of the vote fell far short of the majority its leaders laughably claimed they would get, Zuma had slammed down a wild card. The MK Party eroded the ANC's voter base, leaving the party that would 'rule until Jesus comes back' down to only 40 percent of the vote. Zuma had effectively leveraged grievances and ethnic nostalgia to achieve this major shift.

It was hardly surprising – coming as it did from a party given to conspiracy theories and contemptuous of constitutional democracy – that the MK Party proffered baseless claims of vote rigging in the election. Shortly before the vote was announced, Zuma had made a dramatic entrance at the IEC's election centre and issued an ominous warning to postpone the results announcement, failing which 'trouble' would ensue.[350]

The results, however, were announced without incident. The MK Party did launch an appeal in the Electoral Court, demanding a new election.

But eventually it quietly withdrew its application.[351] In the meantime, its MPs initially stayed away from parliament in protest, despite what to everyone else looked like somewhat of an electoral triumph for the MK Party.

Unlike Zuma and his party, Malema accepted what was ultimately an embarrassing election result for the EFF. Left with less than 10 percent of the vote, the EFF was perhaps the hardest-hit party in the elections. The ANC remained in government, but the EFF had to concede its place as third-largest party to the MK Party. The latter's 14,5 percent – considerably more than the EFF had ever won – was achieved by taking a chunk out of both the ANC and EFF support bases, stunting the slow but steady growth of Malema's party.

For the EFF the damage was worst in KwaZulu-Natal – the second most populous province after Gauteng. The province that had drama-tically boosted the EFF's numbers in the previous election, in what was seen as a protest vote against Ramaphosa, had now become the spoiler of EFF fortunes. There, the party fell from just short of 10 percent in 2019 to a meagre 2,6 percent in 2024, while the MK Party raked up 46 percent of the vote.

As the final results came in, Malema appeared visibly defeated – a far cry from the person who, in a carefully choreographed performance the year before in front of an FNB Stadium packed with his adoring supporters, was lifted into the sky on a mechanical concertina platform, fist in the air, as confetti and pyrotechnics added to the cultish fanfare of the moment.

Addressing the crowd at the EFF's 10th anniversary celebrations in 2023, Malema had reminisced about the founding of the party at Uncle Tom's Hall in Soweto, when 'fighters came from all over South Africa from Cape Town to Musina'.

'We did not even have money to pay for the hall,' he went on. 'Those fighters who came, came for a mission. They were very patient. They never fought the leadership. They knew that this is the beginning of a journey, and that journey will produce a giant, and that giant will represent our people.'

But even in that euphoric moment, Malema had not been able to ignore the scandal catching up with him. 'No leader of the EFF is arrested for VBS, no leader of the EFF is in court because of VBS. They wanted to use the VBS to destroy the EFF once more. They failed,' he said.

A year later, the party that claimed to be a 'government in waiting' would have to keep waiting. The ANC, meanwhile, would have to negotiate to remain in government. Along with the DA and a bunch of smaller parties making up more than two-thirds of the seats in parliament, the ANC agreed to co-govern. And, after half-hearted overtures were made to the MK Party and the EFF, those two were ultimately excluded from the new 'government of national unity' (GNU).

As the leaders of the opposition to Ramaphosa's GNU, Zuma and Malema were forced into an awkward embrace. Two men who not long before had been bitter enemies now looked like they could create a formidable alliance – the so-called 'progressive caucus' in parliament. But the cracks in that entente were quick to show.

Uneasy bedfellows to begin with, both parties were led by megalomaniacal leaders who had every reason to be suspicious of each other. Even more so than the EFF, the MK Party was subject to the whims and machinations of a volatile, corruption-plagued individual, and at times infighting threatened to tear the nascent party apart. Its poor performance in key KwaZulu-Natal by-elections soon after the national vote in May pointed to an uncertain future.

But none of the MK Party's setbacks came close to the bloodbath the EFF was about to experience after the national elections. On Monday 2 August 2024, Mzwanele Manyi announced that he was quitting his short-lived career in the EFF to join the MK Party, continuing a game of musical chairs. He had only joined the EFF the year before and was quickly made an MP, having come from the ATM and before that the ANC. His departure from the EFF was hardly surprising, as he remained a staunch Zuma-ite and spokesperson for Zuma's foundation.

But a far bigger loss awaited the party. On Thursday 15 August, Malema's deputy and confidant, EFF co-founder Floyd Shivambu, publicly announced his departure. It was a devastating loss that laid bare just how vulnerable the party was.

At a hastily convened press conference at party headquarters, Malema spoke about Shivambu's resignation in very personal terms. 'To me he is not just a comrade but a brother, and he will remain a brother, even when he pursues his political career differently. We formed this organisation together . . . When he sent me a letter yesterday I felt the same pain when I received the news of the passing of my mother,' he said.

The mood at the media briefing was sombre, but Malema and Shivambu were at pains to portray respect in front of the cameras. Malema denied there had been plans to replace Shivambu as his deputy. Shivambu did not give reasons for his departure but spun it, rather implausibly, as a move that would strengthen the left – a 'revolutionary gesture that will unite progressive forces'.

Anticipating the criticism that awaited him, he said: 'My sincere plea is that the [EFF] should also avoid slander and mischaracterisation of an otherwise revolutionary and disciplined decision'.

The MK Party made much of Shivambu's defection, announcing his appointment as national organiser a week later. Observers spoke – over-optimistically, as it turned out – of Shivambu's strategic and organisational brilliance, and how he would build political structures and turn the party into a lasting political force.

Rumours about the reasons for Shivambu's defection quickly started circulating. According to some reports, there were cumulative differences between Malema and Shivambu, but the breaking point came when they disagreed over a possible deal to join the ANC in government. According to this version of events, the party had been close to reaching an agreement with the ANC – a plan that Shivambu supported but which was unilaterally vetoed by Malema. Other reports claimed that Malema and his 'brother' Shivambu had been locked in a power struggle within the EFF for two years, that Shivambu had apparently planned to challenge Malema for the party presidency in December 2024, and that Malema had been determined to thwart those ambitions at any cost.

Our information suggests that Shivambu also took personal circumstances into account. Court documents lodged in the Pretoria High Court in early 2025 reveal that SARS is trying to recoup about R24 million in unpaid taxes from Shivambu, some linked to the looting of VBS. Our sources report that Shivambu was notified of his tax debt around 7 August 2024, just a week before his resignation. A week later, witnesses saw him with Zuma at the luxury Oyster Box hotel in Umhlanga.[352] Zuma is said to have offered 'assistance' of an unspecified nature if Shivambu defected to the MK Party. Hours after this meeting, Shivambu informed Malema of his decision to leave the EFF.

Evidently, tension and distrust had started to grow between the two men well before the turning point of the 29 May elections. The signs were there in July 2023, at a plush gala dinner at Emperors Palace casino in Gauteng to commemorate the EFF's 10th anniversary where it cost R1,2 million to book a table of 10 to share with the EFF's 'commander-in-chief'. At the event, Malema spoke glowingly about his deputy and the bond between them. He praised Shivambu as a thinker with big ideas. But then the speech took a foreboding turn. Noting that they were 'not in a competition with each other', Malema said that should Shivambu get tired of him, he shouldn't organise against him. 'Just tell me, "I think you have served your term, it is time to go."'

Malema added that he had no mercy for those who plotted against him. 'The problem starts when you start organising against me, and I hear it in the corners. I'm ruthless against people who do such things to me, so never try that with me. And he [Shivambu] knows that, because I've never lost a conference in my life, and no one I supported has lost a conference in my life.' These were not empty threats. Malema's political track record showed how cruelly calculating he could be, especially at elective conferences.

Ultimately, Shivambu did not last long in Zuma's fractious new party. He fell out very publicly with Zuma's daughter Duduzile Zuma-Sambudla, and in June 2025 Shivambu was removed as the party's secretary general, less than six months after his appointment. The ostensible reason for sacking him was his unauthorised visit to fugitive and self-proclaimed prophet Shepard Bushiri in Malawi. Shivambu, however, claimed that he was removed on the basis of a fake internal intelligence report that accused him of conspiring to take over the party, and said Zuma was surrounded by 'political scoundrels'. Soon after he announced plans for a process to consult on the possibility of launching a new party. His touted plan of strengthening the supposed 'progressive forces' by moving to the MK Party seems to have ended in a shambles.

The second most prominent EFF figure after Shivambu to leave was advocate and former chairperson Dali Mpofu, who announced in November 2024 that he had joined Zuma's party. In an SABC interview, he said he had helped to set up the MK Party while he was still in the EFF.

Following Mpofu's departure, Malema posted a cryptic message on social media: 'Only two more of your favourites remain, and the list will be finalised. They sing beautifully and are always willing to pose for pictures and sign roll calls, but remember, their souls are long gone.'

Disgraced former public protector and EFF MP Busisiwe Mkhwebane also resigned, as did prominent actor and long-time EFF member Fana Mokoena.

As the December elective conference approached, Malema's paranoia was increasingly apparent. He and his supporters constantly referred to 'infiltrators', 'deserters', 'betrayal', 'sabotage' and attempts to destabilise the EFF. At the party's Gauteng general assembly in November, Malema warned that the EFF 'has most recently experienced most dangerous levels of infiltration', perpetuated by 'founders of the movement who have been converted into sleeper agents and double agents who sat among us but reported elsewhere'.

Malema was especially hostile to veteran EFF MP and former spokesperson Mbuyiseni Ndlozi, whom he treated with open contempt. The charismatic Ndlozi was close to Shivambu and was said to have known in advance of the latter's decision to leave the EFF. He had a small but vocal following in the EFF and was a contender for a position in the party's top six, which Malema aimed to pack with loyalists. In the lead-up to the elective conference, the acrimony towards Ndlozi intensified. In November, journalists reported that he was barred from attending the conference the following month, but Malema dismissed the claims as 'shebeen gossip'.

On 13 December, nearly 2 500 delegates from across the country convened at Nasrec in Johannesburg for the party's national people's assembly – a three-day affair that Malema called the 'highest demonstration of democracy within the EFF'. He began his three-and-a-half-hour opening speech by warning of the 'coordinated and deliberate efforts to destroy us'. Adopting a defensive stance, he told delegates that 'since our inception, despite the negative caricature of our movement characterised by dictatorship, we have remained committed to this internal democratic process without failure'.

He then plunged into a wide-ranging discourse on Marxist-Leninist orthodoxy, reading from his prepared speech. 'Fighters, the unity and struggle of the opposite helps us understand the nature of struggle and conflict between social groups, such as class struggle between the bourgeoisie and the proletariat,' he droned as bored fighters fanned themselves in the Johannesburg heat.

'All things in the universe exist in a constant state of change and development. Conflict, therefore, through the Marxist lens of dialectics, is not only negative, as it can be a necessary part of the process of revolutionary change and development.' It was unusual to hear Malema elaborating on the finer points of scientific socialism and dialectical materialism – a role usually reserved for the party 'ideologue', Shivambu.

Malema then turned to the party leaders who remained by his side and heaped praise on one of his closest loyalists, secretary-general Marshall Dlamini. In a jab at EFF defectors, Malema hailed Dlamini as 'one of the most reliable comrades I've encountered'. He also singled out treasurer Omphile Maotwe for flattery, but said nothing about chairperson Veronica Mente, seen as close to Shivambu. Malema ended his address in tears, thanking his family for their support and love and finishing with a quote from Martin Luther King Jr: 'In the end, we will remember not the words of our enemies but the silence of our friends.'

Conspicuous by his absence – and silence – was Ndlozi. He had, after all, been banned. At a press conference during the assembly, Malema couldn't conceal his irritation at questions about Ndlozi. 'We are not going to answer the question about Mbuyiseni Ndlozi . . . whoever is not here was not supposed to be here from the beginning. So, you are not going to reduce this organisation to some individual . . . We're dealing with political issues here, not egotism, not people who think they are bigger than this organisation.'

Once again, the result of the vote for the top six on 15 December was a foregone conclusion. Malema's slate won uncontested. He would lead the party for a third term, with Godrich Gardee as deputy. Dlamini and Maotwe retained their positions, EFF MP Nontando Nolutshungu replaced Mente, and Leigh-Ann Mathys succeeded Poppy Mailola as deputy secretary-general. Ndlozi was not even in the 60-person CCT. Malema had maintained his stranglehold on the much-diminished party machinery. But for the moment, with everything else collapsing around him, it looked like a pyrrhic victory.

The wave of defections was not only down to the allure of the new MK Party. It was in large part due to factors within the EFF, most notably Malema's stifling rule – people had as much incentive to leave the EFF as they did to join Zuma's party. Malema's unwillingness to accommodate dissent had turned, after the elections, to unalloyed paranoia. He spoke like a dictator desperate to cling to his last vestige of power. Shivambu, meanwhile, seemed somewhat more at ease after having crawled out of Malema's shadow.

In an echo of a decade ago, many among the commentariat are ready to dismiss Malema as a spent force. Ultimately, those prepared to write Malema's obituary in 2012 were proven wrong. Whether he can rebuild the EFF and revive his political career after this latest juncture, however, is far from certain.

The political reality looks a lot different now than over a decade ago, when the mass unrest on the mines in the wake of the Marikana massacre provided a richly symbolic backdrop to the EFF's first few months. In the following years, Zuma's popularity plummeted, and for an increasing number of voters the EFF became the only credible radical alternative to the ANC.

Now Zuma and his party lay claim to being the new voice of the left. According to Malema, the MK Party is progressive in name only. There is nothing of substance that makes them genuinely left-wing. He isn't wrong.

Nevertheless, they have appropriated the metaphors of the ANC's long struggle history and will present themselves as a left alternative to both the ANC and the EFF in future elections. The EFF may also have to compete with the ANC's long-standing alliance partner, the South African Communist Party, which announced at its national congress in December 2024 that it would contest future elections independently.

In short, Malema now faces a very different set of electoral challenges than when the EFF first fought for the vote.

Meanwhile, Malema's tax woes continue to dog him, in addition to lingering threats of criminal prosecution relating to VBS and other corruption allegations. In a typically preemptive move, Malema claimed in July 2023 that SARS had resorted to 'bullying and intimidating' members of his family as part of a sustained campaign against him.[353]

On top of that, he is concerned about how he will continue to fund his party. The thought of EFF support plateauing or even declining at a national level worries Malema, because he is aware of how fickle his backers in the business world are. Their horizons are short term. It's pay to play – money attached to expectations of reward, whether in the form of tenders or political favours – and his benefactors will only risk betting on the EFF if they perceive it to be a serious power broker.

During his opening address at the national people's assembly, Malema did not miss the opportunity to thank the 'businesspeople who have stood with us . . . We commend their contributions, even as they have declined in recent times due to challenges we have faced. Support for the EFF from the business sector has diminished because many of those who initially supported us were opportunistic and possibly corrupt.'

It was a frank admission of the EFF's financial difficulties, on the one hand, but a disingenuous statement on the other, given that he and the EFF had thrived on what were plainly opportunistic and dubious arrangements with businesspeople, as we have seen.

For all his many setbacks, however, Malema will not quietly disappear. Nor will the root conditions that push people towards radical alternatives to the ANC. At a structural level, the problems of unemployment and inequality will continue to feed radical politics and populist politicians. South Africa has entered a new era of coalitions, which will provide windows of opportunity for Malema to pry open, as he did in the metros. As the negotiations leading to the formation of the GNU revealed, much of the ANC leans instinctively more towards their former comrades in the EFF and the MK Party than towards the liberal DA. Malema is quick to exploit divisions, and his relatively short but remarkable career shows that these are precisely the chaotic conditions in which he has thrived.

Endnotes

1   Julius Malema, EFF media conference in response to the Motau report on the VBS scandal, 16 October 2018, video on YouTube.

2   Nyambeni Mandiwana, "Juju slams ANC over ex-cadre", *Polokwane Observer*, 27 June 2015, https://www.citizen.co.za/review-online/news-headlines/2015/05/27/anc-is-quiet-juju/

3   Bill Freund, "South Africa: The end of apartheid & the emergence of the 'BEE elite'", *Review of African Political Economy*, 34, 2007, https://www.scienceopen.com/hosted-document?doi=10.1080/03056240701819533

4   Junior Khumalo and Pule Letshwiti-Jones, "Zuma lawyers write to ANC, claiming ruling party benefitted from arms deal, not him", *News24*, 18 August 2021, https://www.news24.com/news24/zuma-lawyers-write-to-anc-claiming-ruling-party-benefitted-from-arms-deal-not-him-20210818

5   Phillip de Wet and Mmanaledi Mataboge, "Chancellor House: R266m for nine years of lies by ANC partner", *Mail & Guardian*, 29 September 2015, https://mg.co.za/article/2015-09-29-chancellor-house-r266-million-for-9-years-of-lies-by-anc-partner/

6   Ibid.

7   Dewald van Rensburg, "The ANC's manganese 'gold' mine", amaBhungane, 9 May 2022, https://amabhungane.org/220510-the-ancs-manganese-gold-mine/

8   Ibid.

9   Ibid.

10 Susan Booysen, *The African National Congress and the Regeneration of Political Power*, Wits University Press, 2011, p. 13.

11 Pravin Gordhan, Budget speech in the South African National Assembly, 2013, cited in Ryan Brunette et al, "Reform in the contract state: Embedded directions in public procurement regulation in South Africa", Development Southern Africa, 36(4), 2019, https://www.researchgate.net/publication/332487047_Reform_in_the_contract_state_Embedded_directions_in_public_procurement_regulation_in_South_Africa

12 For more on procurement and the 'contract state', see: PARI, "The Contract State: Outsourcing & Decentralisation in Contemporary South Africa", 2014, https://pari.org.za/wp-content/uploads/2017/05/PARI-The-Contract-State-01082014-1.pdf; Jonathan Klaaren et al, "Public Procurement and Corruption in South Africa", PARI working paper, 2021, https://osf.io/bej9z/download

13 ANC, "Strategy and tactics of the ANC", December 2012, as adopted by the 53rd National Conference, 16–20 December 2012, Mangaung, Free State. https://www.anc1912.org.za/wp-content/uploads/2021/01/Strategy-Tactics-2012.pdf

14 Booysen, *The African National Congress and the Regeneration of Political Power*, p. 375.

15 Karl von Holdt, "The political economy of corruption: elite formation, factions and violence", in Mbongiseni Buthelezi and Peter Vale and (eds), *State Capture in South Africa: How and Why It Happened*, Cambridge University Press, 2019.

16 Ronnie Donaldson, "Intro/retrospection on a provincial capital: Pietersburg/Polokwane revisited", Urban Forum, Vol 16, October 2005, https://www.researchgate.net/publication/225435181_Introretrospection_on_a_provincial_capital_PietersburgPolokwane_revisited

17 South African History Online, "Polokwane: the segregated city", 4 July 2011. After the end of World War Two, apartheid and the Bantustans dramatically reshaped the town, which was growing rapidly

in the post-war boom years. The white population doubled in the decade following the end of the war, making up 8 000 of a total population of 20 500.

18 Fiona Forde, *An Inconvenient Youth: Julius Malema and the 'New' ANC*, Jonathan Ball, 2011.

19 Ibid, pp. 31-32.

20 South African History Online, "Polokwane: the segregated city".

21 Forde, *An Inconvenient Youth: Julius Malema and the 'New' ANC*, p. 55.

22 *IOL*, "Cosas leader was a 'real dunce' at school", 27 May 2002, https://www.iol.co.za/news/south-africa/cosas-leader-was-a-real-dunce-at-school-87261

23 Ibid; also see: *IOL*, "Cosas has lost it, say former leaders", 6 May 2001, https://www.iol.co.za/news/politics/cosas-has-lost-it-say-former-leaders-65294

24 Commissioner for the South African Revenue Service against Julius Sello Malema in the High Court of South Africa, sequestration application, case number 5455/2013, 2013.

25 Ibid.

26 Malema, JS v Commissioner for the South African Revenue Service, compromise agreement, case number 76306/2015, 2015.

27 Ibid.

28 Mandy Rossouw and Adriaan Basson, "Malema's new tax dodge", *Mail & Guardian*, 9 July 2010, https://mg.co.za/article/2010-07-09-malemas-new-tax-dodge/

29 Forde, *An Inconvenient Youth: Julius Malema and the 'New' ANC*, 2010; *City Press*, "Malema linked to dirty firm", 18 July 2010, https://www.news24.com/news24/malema-linked-to-dirty-firm-20150429

30 Millennium Waste Management v Chairperson Tender Board (2007), Supreme Court of Appeal, 165 (RSA), 2007.

31 Malema, JS v Commissioner for the South African Revenue Service, compromise agreement.

32 Ibid.

33 Ibid.

34 Piet Rampedi, "Malema linked to 'wrecked' taxi rank", *News24*, 4 March 2011. https://www.news24.com/news24/malema-linked-to-wrecked-taxi-rank-20110403

35 Ibid.

36 Commissioner for the South African Revenue Service against Julius Sello Malema in the High Court of South Africa, sequestration application.

37 Moffet Mofokeng, "Malema faces arrest", *IOL*, 30 October 2011. https://www.iol.co.za/news/malema-faces-arrest-1167518

38 Malema, JS v Commissioner for the South African Revenue Service, compromise agreement.

39 Ibid.

40 Makhudu Sefara, " 'Ex-premier' in Scorpions probe", *News24*, 9 January 2005, https://www.news24.com/news24/ex-premier-in-scorpions-probe-20050109; *Mail & Guardian*, "Ramatlhodi's lucky escape", 7 February 2009, https://mg.co.za/article/2009-02-07-ramatlhodis-lucky-escape/; *Mail & Guardian*, "Tender rewards overturned", 22 July 2005, https://mg.co.za/article/2005-07-22-tender-award-overturned/; *Mail & Guardian*, "Cabinet to study ANC's Scorpions decision", 22 January 2008, https://mg.co.za/article/2008-01-22-cabinet-to-study-ancs-scorpions-decision/; *News24*, "The rise of a R500m empire", 30 April 2015, https://www.news24.com/news24/the-rise-of-a-r500m-empire-20150430

41 Moolman Group, "Manaka tackles property market", *Waterpas/Spirit-level*, No. 25, January 2009, https://moolmangroup.co.za/wp-content/uploads/2020/10/NewsletterNo.25Jan2009.pdf; *Mail & Guardian*, "Major increase in Home Affairs building rental", 5 March 2012, https://mg.co.za/article/2012-03-05-major-increase-in-home-affairs-building-rental/

42 Commissioner for the South African Revenue Service against Julius Sello Malema in the High Court of South Africa, sequestration application.

43 Malema, JS v Commissioner for the South African Revenue Service, compromise agreement.

44 Lionel Faull, "Malema's 'list' of pals feed on school meals", *Mail & Guardian*, 26 October 2012, https://mg.co.za/article/2012-10-26-00-malemas-list-of-pals-feed-on-school-meals/

45 Craig McKune, "How Julius Malema pulls tender strings", *Mail & Guardian*, 5 August 2011, https://mg.co.za/article/2011-08-05-how-julius-malema-pulls-tender-strings/

46 Malema, JS v Commissioner for the South African Revenue Service, compromise agreement

47 Supreme Court of Appeal, "Judgment: National Director of Public Prosecutions (appellant) and Jacob Gedleyihlekisa Zuma (respondent)", case number 573/08, 12 January 2009. https://www.saflii.org/za/cases/ZASCA/2009/1.pdf

48 McKune, "How Julius Malema pulls tender strings".

49 Malema, JS v Commissioner for the South African Revenue Service, compromise agreement.

50 Ibid.

51 Ibid.

52 *City Press*, "ANCYL lands a lucrative contract", 2 May 2010, https://www.news24.com/news24/ancyl-lands-a-lucrative-contract-20150429

53 Dumisane Lubisi, "ANCYL leaders coining it – claim", *News24*, 2 May 2010, https://www.news24.com/fin24/ancyl-leaders-coining-it-claim-20100502

54 Commissioner for the South African Revenue Service against Julius Sello Malema in the High Court of South Africa, sequestration application.

55 Adriaan Basson and Piet Rampedi, "Malema's sugar daddy", *City Press*, 6 November 2011, https://www.news24.com/citypress/politics/news/malemas-sugar-daddy-20111105

56 Thabiso Thakali, "No panic, but Juju's house shoots up", *IOL*, 11 February 2012. https://www.iol.co.za/news/politics/no-panic-but-jujus-house-shoots-up-1232070

57 Malema, JS v Commissioner for the South African Revenue Service, compromise agreement.

58 Ibid.

59 Selby Construction, "Infrastructure development solutions", brochure. https://www.selbyconstruction.co.za/our_profile.pdf

60 McKune, "How Julius Malema pulls tender strings".

61 Nelly Shamase and Lungile Dube, "Malema's allies milked millions from dodgy water projects", *Mail & Guardian*, 8 June 2012, https://mg.co.za/article/2012-06-08-malemas-allies-milked-millions-from-dodgy-water-projects/; Piet Rampedi, "Tender tampering scam uncovered", *IOL*, 4 February 2013, https://www.iol.co.za/news/politics/tender-tampering-scam-uncovered-1463835

62 State v Moreroa and Others, ZAGPPHC, North Gauteng High Court, Pretoria, 22 January 2016, https://www.saflii.org/za/cases/ZAGPPHC/2016/20.html

63 *Sunday Times*, "Who is Steve Bosch?", 14 August 2011, https://www.timeslive.co.za/politics/2011-08-14-who-is-steve-bosch/

64 Malema, JS v Commissioner for the South African Revenue Service, compromise agreement.

65 Ibid.

66 Ibid.

67 Ibid.

68 TS White, "Supporting affidavit in the case of ex party preservation order application of National Director of Public Prosecutions in re: The remaining extent of the farm Schuilkraal", 623, 2012.

69 White, supporting affidavit (Schuilkraal).

70 PS Bothma, "The significance of trustee independence for the validity and administration of a trust", dissertation presented for the degree of Doctor of Laws in the Faculty of Law at Stellenbosch University, 2020.

71 Absa bank statements for Mazimbu Investment Trust for the period 23 April 2013 to 18 January 2014. Attached to court documents in *JS Malema v SARS* in the compromise agreement challenge.

72 Malema, JS v Commissioner for the South African Revenue Service, compromise agreement.

73 Forde, *An Inconvenient Youth: Julius Malema and the 'New' ANC*, p. 41.

74 AmaBhungane, "Limpopo varsity fuels Malema's mining revolution", 21 September 2012, https://amabhungane.org/limpopo-varsity-fuels-malemas-mining-revolution/

75 Lionel Faull, "DA wants probe into varsity funding", 24 September 2012, *Mail & Guardian*, https://mg.co.za/article/2012-09-24-da-wants-probe-into-varsity-funding/

76 Sapa, "IFP calls for answers on FYL Limpopo university tenders", *TimesLIVE*, 21 September 2012, https://www.timeslive.co.za/news/south-africa/2012-09-21-ifp-calls-for-answers-on-fyl-limpopo-university-tenders/

77 Faull, "DA wants probe into varsity funding".

78 Mandy Rossouw, "Juju's cousin lands multimillion-rand govt deals", *Mail & Guardian*, 3 June 2011, https://mg.co.za/article/2011-06-03-malema-brother-lands-multimillionrand-govt-deals/

79 Fiona Forde, "Malema 'pushed' for payment for cronies", *Mail & Guardian*, 16 September 2011, https://mg.co.za/article/2011-09-16-malema-pushed-for-payment-cronies/

80 Ibid.

81 Rossouw, "Juju's cousin lands multimillion-rand govt deals".

82 Forde, "Malema 'pushed' for payment for cronies".

83 *Sunday Independent*, 2 September 2013, "R700m feeding scheme probe"

84 Lionel Faull, "Malema's 'list' of pals feed on school meals", *Mail & Guardian*, 26 October 2012, https://mg.co.za/article/2012-10-26-00-malemas-list-of-pals-feed-on-school-meals/

85 Commissioner for the South African Revenue Service against Julius Sello Malema in the High Court of South Africa, sequestration application.

86 Carien du Plessis and Adriaan Basson, "Malema 'stole my land'", *City Press*, 8 January 2012, https://www.news24.com/citypress/politics/news/malema-stole-my-land-20120107/

87 AmaBhungane, "Polokwane's landed gentry", 19 August 2011, https://amabhungane.org/polokwanes-landed-gentry/

88 AmaBhungane, "How Juju's Mauritius wedding host made his millions", 4 November 2011, https://amabhungane.org/how-jujus-mauritius-wedding-host-made-his-millions/

89 AmaBhungane, "How Juju's Mauritius wedding host made his millions".

90 *City Press*, "This is how Juju rolls!", 24 July 2011, https://www.news24.com/news24/archives/city-press/this-is-how-juju-rolls-20150429

91 Mzilikazi Wa Afrika, Rob Rose and Stephan Hofstatter, "Friend who gave him R1.2m car is in tender trouble", *Sunday Times*, 7 August 2011, https://www.timeslive.co.za/politics/2011-08-07-friend-who-gave-him-r12m-car-is-in-tender-trouble/

92 eNCA, "R16m Limpopo school stands vacant and vandalized", 23 December 2014.

93 Public Protector South Africa (PPSA), *On the Point of Tenders: Report of the Public Protector on an Investigation into Allegations of Impropriety and Corrupt Practices Relating to the Awarding of Contracts for Goods and Services by the Limpopo Department of Roads and Transport*, Report no 10 of 2012/13, https://www.dailymaverick.co.za/wp-content/uploads/121010_PP-Report_On-the-point-of-tenders.pdf

94 McKune, "How Julius Malema pulls tender strings".

95 PPSA, *On the Point of Tenders*.

96 White, supporting affidavit (Schuilkraal).

97 PPSA, *On the Point of Tenders*.

98 S Ravat, "Affidavit in the case of The Commissioner of the South African Revenue Service against Julius Sello Malema", 2012.

99 McKune, "How Julius Malema pulls tender strings".

100 PPSA, *On the Point of Tenders*.

101 White, supporting affidavit (Schuilkraal).

102 Ibid.

103 Ibid.

104 Ibid.

105 Despite Kekana's questionable record as MEC for roads and transport in Limpopo at the time when this department and the province were robbed of hundreds of millions of rand, she is now deputy minister

in the Presidency for planning, monitoring and evaluation. In November 2022, Kekana was found to have received R170 000 from the 'tenderpreneur' Edwin Sodi, but claimed it wasn't a kickback or bribe, and that she had not meant to mislead parliament. See Jan Gerber, "Deputy minister Pinky Kekana to be reprimanded for taking R170 000 from Edwin Sodi for reasons kept secret", *News24*, 16 November 2022, https://www.news24.com/news24/politics/parliament/deputy-minister-pinky-kekana-to-be-reprimanded-for-taking-r170-000-from-edwin-sodi-for-reasons-kept-secret-20221116

106 PPSA, *On the Point of Tenders*.

107 Ibid.

108 Malema, JS v Commissioner for the South African Revenue Service, compromise agreement.

109 Frank Maponya, "Malema back in the dock", *Sowetan*, 30 November 2012, https://www.sowetanlive.co.za/news/2012-11-30-malema-back-in-the-dock-again/

110 AmaBhungane, "Joburg council set for showdown over city manager appointment", 10 March 2022, https://amabhungane.org/220310-joburg-council-set-for-showdown/

111 Malema, JS v Commissioner for the South African Revenue Service, compromise agreement.

112 Ibid.

113 Mzilikazi Wa Afrika, Rob Rose and Stephan Hofstatter, "Tender boss paid Malema", *TimesLIVE*, 14 August 2011, https://www.timeslive.co.za/politics/2011-08-14-tender-boss-paid-malema/

114 Ibid.

115 White, supporting affidavit (Schuilkraal).

116 PPSA, *On the Point of Tenders*.

117 White, supporting affidavit (Schuilkraal).

118 State v Moreroa and Others.

119 "National Director of Public Prosecutions, Ex Parte, In re: The remaining Extent of the farm Schuilkraal 623", Registration Division LS, Polokwane, Limpopo. North Gauteng High Court, Pretoria.

120 White, supporting affidavit (Schuilkraal).

121 PPSA, *On the Point of Tenders*.

122 Nicolette Honeycomb, "Affidavit in the case of The Commissioner of the South African Revenue Service against Julius Sello Malema", 11 July 2012.

123 McKune, "How Julius Malema pulls tender strings".

124 PPSA, *On the Point of Tenders*; White, supporting affidavit (Schuilkraal); Honeycomb, affidavit.

125 McKune, "How Julius Malema pulls tender strings".

126 Adjusted for inflation, this would amount to almost R195 million in April 2024, calculated between 30 January 2012 and 1 April 2024.

127 *The Citizen*, "Former HOD of Limpopo Roads and Transport sentenced to 8 years in prison for kidnapping", 21 July 2017, https://www.citizen.co.za/review-online/news-headlines/2017/07/21/former-hod-limpopo-roads-transport-sentenced-8-years-prison-kidnapping/

128 Desiree van der Walt, "Pinky Kekana must go – DA Limpopo", *Politicsweb*, 11 October 2012, https://www.politicsweb.co.za/politics/pinky-kekana-must-go--da-limpopo

129 Barry Bearak, "ANC issues caution in singing polarizing songs", *New York Times*, 7 April 2010, https://www.nytimes.com/2010/04/08/world/africa/08safrica.html

130 Forde, *An Inconvenient Youth: Julius Malema and the 'New' ANC*, p. 185.

131 ANCYL press statement, "We must follow the Zimbabwe model", 8 April 2010, https://www.politicsweb.co.za/politics/we-must-follow-zimbabwe-model--ancyl

132 Russel Molefe and Frank Maponya, "Limpopo sabotaging Zuma administration – Gordhan", *Sowetan*, 20 January 2012, https://www.sowetanlive.co.za/news/2012-01-20-limpopo-sabotaging-zuma-administration-gordhan/

133 State Capacity Research Project, "Betrayal of the promise: how South Africa is being stolen", May 2017, https://pari.org.za/betrayal-promise-report/

134 Piet Rampedi, "Malema allies' housing tenders readvertised", *The Star*, 8 May 2013, https://www.iol.co.za/news/politics/malema-allies-housing-tenders-readvertised-1512387/

135 Staff reporter and Sapa-AFP, "Guilty: Julius Malema suspended from ANC", *Mail & Guardian*, 10 November 2011, https://mg.co.za/article/2011-11-10-guilty-julius-malema-suspended-from-anc/

136 *Legalbrief Today*, "Media storm over Malema's tender excesses", Issue number 2505, 22 February 2010, https://legalbrief.co.za/diary/legalbrief-today/story/media-storm-over-malemas-tender-excesses-2/pdf/

137 Piet Rampedi and Dumisane Lubisi, "Malema's R140m tender riches", *City Press*, 21 February 2010, https://www.news24.com/citypress/southafrica/news/malemas-r140m-tender-riches-20100221

138 Anna Majavu, "Cosatu dares Zuma", *Sowetan*, 10 February 2010, https://www.sowetanlive.co.za/news/2010-02-10-cosatu-dares-zuma/

139 Julius Malema, "Media peddling lies about me – Julius Malema", *Politicsweb*, 22 February 2010, https://www.politicsweb.co.za/party/media-peddling-lies-about-me--julius-malema

140 *News24*, "Malema 'still firm's director' ", 23 February 2010, https://www.news24.com/fin24/malema-still-firms-director-20100222/

141 *News24*, "Juju's dodgy R27m bridges", 28 February 2010, https://www.news24.com/news24/jujus-dodgy-r27m-bridges-20150429

142 Karabo Keepile and Sapa-AFP, "Malema fracas: Blame the 'forces of darkness' ", *Mail & Guardian*, 23 February 2010, https://mg.co.za/article/2010-02-23-malema-fracas-blame-the-forces-of-darkness/

143 *News24*, "Tumi Mokoena's statement on Malema", 2 March 2010, https://www.news24.com/news24/tumi-mokoenas-statement-on-malema-20100302

144 Sapa, "De Lille blasts Malema over tax evasion allegations", *TimesLIVE*, 7 March 2010, https://www.timeslive.co.za/news/south-africa/2010-03-07-de-lille-blasts-malema-over-tax-evasion-allegations/

145 Sapa, "De Lille blasts Malema over tax evasion allegations".

146 *Sowetan*, "Juju throws lavish birthday party", 4 March 2010, https://www.sowetanlive.co.za/news/2010-03-04-juju-throws-lavish-birthday-party/

147 Public Protector, *Report on an Investigation into Complaints Relating to Improper Awarding of Tenders by Municipalities in Limpopo and North West*, 13 August 2010, https://www.pprotect.org/?q=content/report-investigation-complaints-relating-improper-awarding-tenders-municipalities-limpopo

148 Rampedi and Lubisi, "Malema's R140m tender riches".

149 Nkululeko Ncana, "Fortress Malema will replace Juju's old home", *Sunday Times*, 10 July 2011, https://www.timeslive.co.za/sunday-times/lifestyle/2011-07-10-fortress-malema-will-replace-jujus-old-home/

150 Sapa, " 'Malema building a R16 million mansion' ", *Sowetan*, 18 July 2011, https://www.sowetanlive.co.za/news/2011-07-18-malema-building-a-r16-million-mansion-/

151 *Mail & Guardian*, "Malema probe: Hawks start digging", 21 August 2011, https://mg.co.za/article/2011-08-21-malema-probe-hawks-start-digging/

152 https://newafricanmagazine.com/3606/

153 State v On-Point Engineers, Cuthbert Lesiba Gwangwa, Gwama Properties, Julius Sello Malema and Kagisho Dichabe, racketeering charge sheet signed by 25 November 2012.

154 Lionel Faull, "Everything but on point", *Mail & Guardian*, 12 October 2012, https://mg.co.za/article/2012-10-12-00-everything-but-on-point/

155 Ibid.

156 *IOL*, "Cops ready for Malema and Co", 26 September 2012, https://www.iol.co.za/news/cops-ready-for-malema-and-co-1389625

157 David Smith, "Julius Malema 'unshaken' after money laundering charge", *The Guardian*, 26 September 2012, https://www.theguardian.com/world/2012/sep/26/julius-malema-unshaken-money-laundering/

158 State v Moreroa and Others.

159 Moloko Moloto, "Juju buoyed by associates' acquittal", *IOL*, 2014, https://www.iol.co.za/news/south-africa/limpopo/juju-buoyed-by-associates-acquittal-1667054

160 Moloto, "Juju buoyed by associates' acquittal".

161 John Steenhuisen, post on Twitter/X, 17 October 2016, https://x.com/jsteenhuisen/status/788047282306514948

162 State v Moreroa and Others.

163 Mpho Raborife and Naledi Shange, "Malema off the hook – for now", *News24*, 4 August 2015, https://www.news24.com/news24/malema-off-the-hook-for-now-20150804

164 South African Parliament, Justice and Correctional Services Committee, "National Prosecuting Authority on its Annual Report 2012/13; DoJCD audit outcomes", Parliamentary Monitoring Group, 2013, https://pmg.org.za/committee-meeting/16434/

165 State v On-Point Engineers, Cuthbert Lesiba Gwangwa, Gwama Properties, Julius Sello Malema and Kagisho Dichabe.

166 National Prosecuting Authority, "Proceeds of alleged Malema farm paid to the state", media statement, 26 August 2015, https://www.npa.gov.za/sites/default/files/media-releases/2015%20August%2026%20-%20Proceeds%20Of%20Alleged%20Malema%20Farm%20Paid%20To%20The%20State.pdf

167 United States Attorney's Office: Middle District of Florida, "International fugitive sentenced in drug conspiracy", 7 December 2020, https://www.justice.gov/usao-mdfl/pr/international-fugitive-sentenced-drug-conspiracy; Ronel van Wyk, "Affidavit in the SARS Commission of Inquiry", 2018.

168 United States Attorney's Office, "International fugitive sentenced in drug conspiracy".

169 Johann van Loggerenberg, *Tobacco Wars: Inside the Spy Games and Dirty Tricks of Southern Africa's Cigarette Trade*, 2019, Tafelberg.

170 Van Wyk, "Affidavit in the SARS Commission of Inquiry".

171 United States Attorney's Office, "International fugitive sentenced in drug conspiracy".

172 Mbuyisi Mgibisa, Zukile Majova, Stefaans Brümmer, Sam Sole and Nic Dawes, "Agliotti and the Cuban 'drug lord'", *Mail & Guardian*, 29 June 2007, https://mg.co.za/article/2007-06-29-agliotti-and-the-cuban-drug-lord/

173 Ibid.

174 Van Wyk, "Affidavit in the SARS Commission of Inquiry".

175 Mgibisa, Majova, Brümmer, Sole and Dawes, "Agliotti and the Cuban 'drug lord'".

176 Van Loggerenberg, *Tobacco Wars: Inside the Spy Games and Dirty Tricks of Southern Africa's Cigarette Trade*.

177 Adriano Sauro Lorenzo Mazzotti affidavit to SARS in his personal capacity, 6 May 2014.

178 Alex Patrick, "Tobacco tycoons, politicians bid farewell to Carnilinx director, Kyle Phillips absent after girlfriend's death", *News24*, 10 December 2022, https://www.news24.com/news24/southafrica/news/tobacco-tycoons-politicians-bid-farewell-to-carnilinx-director-kyle-phillips-absent-after-girlfriends-death-20221210

179 Nkosana Lekotjolo and Business Day Online, "Malema: I live a life of poverty", *TimesLIVE*, 9 March 2010, https://www.timeslive.co.za/sport/2010-03-09-malema-i-live-a-life-of-poverty/

180 Commissioner for the South African Revenue Service against Julius Sello Malema in the High Court of South Africa, sequestration application.

181 Richard Poplak, "Hannibal Elector: The white EFF guy decodes the future", *Daily Maverick*, 6 February 2014, https://www.dailymaverick.co.za/article/2014-02-06-hannibal-elector-the-white-eff-guy-decodes-the-future/

182 Wiekus Kotze on X, https://x.com/WiekusK/status/536952055215443968?s=20

183 Lebogang Seale, "'This is how Malema pays his tax'", *IOL*, 8 April 2015, https://www.iol.co.za/news/politics/this-is-how-malema-pays-his-tax-1841894

184 Malema, JS v Commissioner for the South African Revenue Service, compromise agreement.

185 Commission of Inquiry into State Capture, testimony by Nhlanhla Nene, 14 March 2019, https://www.statecapture.org.za/site/files/transcript/69/14_March_2019_Sessions.pdf Last accessed 7 January 2024

186 Greg Nicolson, "Free from sequestration threat, Julius Malema looks forward to 2016", *Daily Maverick*, 2 June 2015, https://www.dailymaverick.co.za/article/2015-06-02-free-from-sequestration-threat-julius-malema-looks-forward-to-2016/

187 Nicolson, "Free from sequestration threat, Julius Malema looks forward to 2016".

188 Qaanitah Hunter, "SARS retreat is a victory for SA – Juju", *Mail & Guardian*, 2 June 2015, https://mg.co.za/article/2015-06-02-malema-this-is-a-victory-for-sas-democracyan-end-to-my-tax-woes-is-a-victory-for-sa-juju/

189 South African Judiciary, "Judgment, Malema v Commissioner for the South African Revenue Service, North Gauteng High Court", case number 76306/2015, 29 April 2016, https://www.saflii.org/za/cases/ZAGPPHC/2016/263.html

190 Matuma Letsoalo, "Malema's millions: Juju ally resists tax probe", *Mail & Guardian*, 18 May 2012, https://mg.co.za/article/2012-05-18-malemas-millions-juju-ally-resists-tax-probe; *News24*, "Malema's business partner drops tax fight", 7 August 2012, https://www.news24.com/news24/malemas-business-partner-drops-tax-fight-20150429

191 The only other reference to the affidavit was a report by Kyle Cowan headlined "The damning evidence against Julius Malema the NPA chose to ignore", *News24*, 1 December 2019, https://www.news24.com/news24/exclusive-the-damning-evidence-against-julius-malema-the-npa-chose-to-ignore-20191201. Cowan refers to "explosive allegations . . . in a never seen before affidavit deposed to by one of Gwangwa's employees", setting out in great detail how "Malema's lifestyle was funded by Gwangwa with money from Limpopo's public coffers". However, Honeycomb's name is not mentioned.

192 Commissioner for the South African Revenue Service against Julius Sello Malema in the High Court of South Africa, sequestration application.

193 SARS court documents.

194 Eleanor Momberg and Matthew Savides, "Uproar over Malema's R16 playboy mansion", *Sunday Independent*, 18 July 2011, https://www.iol.co.za/sundayindependent/news/uproar-over-malemas-r16m-playboy-mansion-1100826

195 PPSA, *On the Point of Tenders*; Honeycomb, affidavit; Letter from SARS to JM and Brian Kahn Inc, in "Presentation by Financial Investigations team".

196 Wa Afrika, Rose and Hofstatter, "Tender boss paid Malema".

197 White, supporting affidavit (Schuilkraal).

198 Ibid.

199 Ibid; Honeycomb, affidavit.

200 White, supporting affidavit (Schuilkraal).

201 Ravat, affidavit.

202 Adriaan Basson and Piet Rampedi, "Malema's secret fund", *City Press*, 24 July 2011, https://www.news24.com/news24/malemas-secret-fund-20110724

203 PPSA, *On the Point of Tenders*.

204 WA Hofmeyr, "Founding affidavit in the ex parte application of National Director of Public Prosecutions In re: The remaining extent of farm Schuilkraal 623", 2012.

205 *News24*, "Malema: First the house, now the farm", 12 May 2013, https://www.news24.com/news24/malema-first-the-house-now-the-farm-20150429

206 Ferial Haffajee, "Young Malema had a farm – is this why he wants to expropriate land without compensation?", *HuffPost*, 8 March 2018, https://www.huffingtonpost.co.uk/entry/young-malema-had-a-farm-is-this-why-he-wants-to-expropriate-land-without-compensation_uk_5c7e886ae4b06e0d4c233164

207 Sapa, "Malema arrested for speeding at 215km/h", *Mail & Guardian*,19 December 2013, https://mg.co.za/article/2013-12-19-malema-arrested-for-215kmh-speeding/

208 Honeycomb, affidavit.

209 *News24*, "'Malema can solve corruption at Aurora'", 30 August 2012, https://www.news24.com/news24/malema-can-solve-corruption-at-aurora-20120830/

210 Honeycomb, affidavit.

211 "ANCYL: Malema: Address by the president of the ANCYL, at the 1st National General Council, Midrand", Polity.org.za, 26 August 2010, http://www.polity.org.za/article/ancyl-malema-address-by-the-president-of-the-ancyl-at-the-1st-national-general-council-midrand-25082010-2010-08-26

212 Stephen Grootes, "The fall of Malema – game gone wrong or long-term gamble?", *Daily Maverick*, 5 March 2012, https://www.dailymaverick.co.za/article/2012-03-05-the-fall-of-malema-a-game-gone-wrong-or-a-long-term-gamble/

213 Azad Essa, "Will Marikana resurrect Julius Malema?", Al Jazeera, 10 September 2012, https://www.aljazeera.com/features/2012/9/10/will-marikana-resurrect-julius-malema

214 *Daily Maverick*, "Ten revelations from the #GuptaLeaks that changed the course of SA", 1 June 2022, https://www.dailymaverick.co.za/article/2022-06-01-ten-revelations-made-by-the-guptaleaks-that-changed-the-course-of-sa/

215 Sizwe Sama Yende, "Court frees Malawian tycoon's millions", News24, 10 September 2017, https://www.news24.com/fin24/court-frees-malawian-tycoons-millions-20170908

216 Serah Makondetsa, "Facts around Malawi water scheme don't wash", AmaBhungane. 29 March 2017, https://amabhungane.org/facts-around-malawi-water-scheme-dont-wash/

217 8 June 2017, amaBhungane, "New Malawi water scheme is in the interests of a few, not the country", https://amabhungane.org/new-malawi-water-scheme-is-in-the-interest-of-a-few-not-the-country/

218 The Times Group, 25 March 2017, "Demystifying Simbi Phiri", https://archive.times.mw/index.php/2017/03/25/demystifying-simbi-phiri/

219 *City Press*, 'How Mokonyane paved the way for a consulting firm to earn billions', 18 March 2018, https://www.news24.com/news24/how-mokonyane-paved-the-way-for-a-construction-firm-to-earn-billions-20180317

220 Public Protector South Africa, "Report on an Investigation into allegations of maladministration by the Department of Water and Sanitation in the awarding of various tenders", Report no 14 of 2020/21, https://www.pprotect.org/sites/default/files/legislation_report/FINAL%20BASSON%20v%20DWS%2022%20Dec%202020%20final.pdf

221 *City Press*, 14 March 2016, 'R170m and still no water', https://www.news24.com/citypress/news/r170m-and-still-no-water-20160314#:~:text=R170%20million%20was%20paid%20to,fortunate%20enough%20to%20have%20boreholes .

222 Rorisang Kgosana, "Malema's version on discharging firearm filled with contradictions, state argues", TimesLIVE, 9 December 2024, https://www.timeslive.co.za/news/south-africa/2024-12-09-malemas-version-on-discharging-firearm-filled-with-contradictions-state-argues/ (Malema was charged with unlawful possession of a firearm and ammunition, discharging a firearm in a built-up area or public place, reckless endangerment of people and property, and failing to take reasonable precautions to avoid danger to people or property. Snyman was charged with failing to take reasonable precautions to avoid danger to people or property and providing a firearm or ammunition to someone not allowed to possess it. After various delays, the trial resumed in December 2024. Evidence – including a video of the incident that went viral – showed that Malema fired 14 to 15 shots from a 9mm Glock pistol, followed by seven shots from an assault rifle. He admitted that he had fired shots 'in order to excite the crowd' but claimed the cartridges were blanks, and 'anything without ammunition is not a gun'. The state prosecutor, Joel Cesar, said that Malema had 'lied about obvious things' in his evidence and was evasive about others. At the time of writing, judgment had not been delivered.)

223 *Sunday Times*, 13 October 2019, "Julius Malema's 'slush fund' exposed", https://www.timeslive.co.za/sunday-times/news/2019-10-13-julius-malemas-slush-fund-exposed/

224 *City Press*, "Nomvula Mokonyane's Watergate", 10 July 2016, https://www.news24.com/citypress/news/nomvulas-watergate-20160710

225 Public Protector South Africa, "Settlement agreement between Dr Zodwa Dlamini and Department of Water and Sanitation represented by Minister NP Mokonyane", 14 October 2016.

226 *The Citizen*, 17 November 2016, "Fraud and corruption cause delay in Limpopo water project", https://www.citizen.co.za/lowvelder/lnn/article/fraud-and-corruption-cause-delay-in-limpopo-water-project/ *News24*, 12 February 2017, "Nomvula Mokonyane's water department is bankrupt", https://www.news24.com/news24/nomvula-mokonyanes-water-department-is-bankrupt-20170211

227 EFF Statement, "The EFF Condemn The Termination of Water Project in Giyani By The National Treasury", 27 October 2016.

228 Letter from EFF deputy president and chief whip Nyiko Floyd Shivambu to minister of Finance Pravin Gordhan, 27 October 2016.

229 Bizcommunity, "Corrupt officials in Giyani Water Project to feel the heat", 25 October 2018, https://www.bizcommunity.com/Article/196/604/183506.html

230 AmaBhungane Centre for Investigative Journalism, 4 May 2021, "Millions Out, Billions In (Part Two): Company that bankrolled the ANC and Malema scored big in Ekurhuleni".

231 *Daily Maverick*, 20 August 2019, "SA Politics 101: The Chosen One (a.k.a. the one with the most money)", https://www.dailymaverick.co.za/article/2019-08-20-sa-politics-101-the-chosen-one-a-k-a-the-one-with-the-most-money/

232 Marcia Zali, "'No one is campaigning to us' – Vuwani residents on municipal elections", *Mail & Guardian*, 24 October 2021, https://mg.co.za/article/2021-10-24-no-one-is-campaigning-to-us-vuwani-residents-on-municipal-elections/

233 Lucas Ledwaba, "VBS scandal: 'They took the very little we had and bought fancy items", *Daily Maverick*, 21 August 2021, https://www.dailymaverick.co.za/article/2021-08-21-vbs-scandal-they-took-the-very-little-we-had-and-bought-fancy-items/

234 On 11 June, the curator issued a notice asking customers with less than R1 000 in their VBS accounts to visit their nearest branch and close their accounts. They would receive all their money. Individual depositors with larger balances could continue to withdraw R1 000 per day, and burial societies up to R7 000 per burial. Despite the curators' best intentions, this seemed to cause a lot of confusion, and people with deposits of more than R1 000 also converged on the bank. See VBS Mutual Bank notice to customers, 11 June 2018, https://www.vbsmutualbank.co.za/curatorship.php/

235 Tshifhiwa Matodzi, affidavit, signed 10 July 2024; Neesa Moodley and Pauli van Wyk, "Corruption Central – VBS chairperson Tshifhiwa Matodzi's canary song, Part One", *Daily Maverick*, 30 July 2024, https://www.dailymaverick.co.za/article/2024-07-30-watch-the-pillaging-of-vbs-mutual-bank-daily-maverick-journalists-unpack-the-fraud-at-the-heart-of-the-banks-failure/

236 T Motau, assisted by Werksmans Attorneys, "The Great Bank Heist: Investigator's Report to the Prudential Authority", 28 September 2018.

237 Tshifhiwa Matodzi, affidavit; Moodley and Van Wyk, "Corruption Central – VBS chairperson Tshifhiwa Matodzi's canary song, Part One".

238 Ibid.

239 Pauli van Wyk, "Five VBS robbers-in-chief – R2,7bn gone (R800m more than previously thought) – still zero criminal prosecutions", *Daily Maverick*, 7 November 2019, https://www.dailymaverick.co.za/article/2019-11-07-five-vbs-robbers-in-chief-r2-7-bn-gone-r800-million-more-than-previously-thought-still-zero-criminal-prosecutions/

240 National Treasury, "Treasury's response to the VBS Mutual Bank matter", 14 March 2018, https://www.treasury.gov.za/comm_media/press/2018/2018031401%20TREASURYS%20RESPONSE%20TO%20THE%20VBS%20MUTUAL%20BANK%20MATTER.pdf

241 State versus Matodzi and Others (CC11/2021) [2024] ZAGPPHC 399, North Gauteng High Court, Pretoria, 26 April 2024, Southern African Legal Information Institute, https://www.saflii.org/za/cases/ZAGPPHC/2024/399.html

242 Alex Mitchley, "Inside Matodzi's plea agreement: Who VBS looting kingpin will testify against", *News24*, 13 July 2024, https://www.news24.com/news24/southafrica/news/inside-matodzis-plea-agreement-who-vbs-looting-kingpin-will-testify-against-20240713

243 Dewald van Rensburg, "'We must bow out with pride,' says VBS boss Tshifhiwa Matodzi", *Daily Maverick*, 6 July 2020, https://www.dailymaverick.co.za/article/2020-07-06-we-must-bow-out-with-pride-says-vbs-boss-tshifhiwa-matodzi/

244 Ibid.

245 Tshifhiwa Matodzi, affidavit; Moodley and Van Wyk, "Corruption Central – VBS chairperson Tshifhiwa Matodzi's canary song, Part One".

246 Zondo Commission testimony by Nhlanhla Nene, 14 March 2019, https://www.statecapture.org.za/site/files/transcript/69/14_March_2019_Sessions.pdf

247 National Treasury, "Treasury's response to the VBS Mutual Bank matter".

248 Parliamentary Monitoring Group, "Capitec and VBS Mutual Bank briefing", Finance Standing Committee, 20 March 2018, https://pmg.org.za/committee-meeting/26045/

249 Linda Ensor, "Floyd Shivambu objects to non-African Ismail Momoniat's repeated presence in meetings", *Business Day*, 5 June 2018, https://www.businesslive.co.za/bd/national/2018-06-05-floyd-shivambu-objects-to-non-african-ismail-momoniats-repeated-presence-in-meetings/

250 Ibid.

251 Tshidi Madia, "Gordhan, media and Moyane – Malema lashes out", *News24*, 5 July 2018, https://www.news24.com/news24/gordhan-media-and-moyane-malema-lashes-out-20180705

252 Greg Nicolson, "Ramaphosa accepts Nene resignation, appoints Tito Mboweni as finance minister", *Daily Maverick*, 9 October 2018, https://www.dailymaverick.co.za/article/2018-10-09-ramaphosa-accepts-nene-resignation-appoints-tito-mboweni-as-finance-minister/

253 Zondo Commission, testimony by Nhlanhla Nene.

254 Pauli van Wyk, "The Shivambu Brothers and the Great VBS Heist", *Daily Maverick*, 11 October 2018, https://www.dailymaverick.co.za/article/2018-10-11-the-shivambu-brothers-and-the-great-vbs-heist/

255 Ibid.

256 Greg Nicolson, " 'Pure insanity', 'madness': Floyd Shivambu dismisses VBS claims", *Daily Maverick*, 16 October 2018, https://www.dailymaverick.co.za/article/2018-10-16-pure-insanity-madness-floyd-shivambu-dismisses-vbs-claims/

257 Parliamentary Monitoring Group, "VBS Mutual Bank", 7 November 2018, https://pmg.org.za/committee-meeting/27444/

258 Tshifhiwa Matodzi, affidavit; Moodley and Van Wyk, "Corruption Central – VBS chairperson Tshifhiwa Matodzi's canary song, Part One".

259 Luvano Ntuli and Michael Marchant, "Unaccountable 00045: Lawrence Mulaudzi – potential partner or perpetual pick-me?", *Daily Maverick*, 20 November 2024, https://www.dailymaverick.co.za/article/2024-11-20-unaccountable-00045-lawrence-mulaudzi-potential-partner-or-perpetual-pick-me/

260 Micah Reddy and Stefaans Brümmer, "Tender comrades part 2: Tshwane tenderpreneur's R15m 'EFF tithe' ", amaBhungane, 30 September 2019, https://amabhungane.org/tender-comrades-part-2-tshwane-tenderpreneurs-r15m-eff-tithe/

261 Ibid.

262 Pinsent Masons, "New South African 'failure to prevent' corruption offence takes effect", *Out-Law News*, 5 April 2024, https://www.pinsentmasons.com/out-law/news/south-african-failure-prevent-corruption-offence

263 Tshifhiwa Matodzi, affidavit; Moodley and Van Wyk, "Corruption Central – VBS chairperson Tshifhiwa Matodzi's canary song, Part One".

264 Pauli van Wyk, " 'Cruising nicely' on VBS: EFF's Parties, Lies and Looted Money", *Daily Maverick*, 27 May 2019, https://www.dailymaverick.co.za/article/2019-05-27-cruising-nicely-on-vbs-effs-parties-lies-and-looted-money/

265 eNCA, "Floyd Shivambu addresses parliament", YouTube, 23 October 2018, https://www.youtube.com/watch?v=TJe8Oe2GF_g

266 '#EFFInParliament', Facebook, Economic Freedom Fighters, 18 July 2024, https://www.facebook.com/watch/?v=1904335520039071; "Julius Malema finally responds to VBS affidavit matter", YouTube, Daily Updates ZA, 18 July 2024, https://www.youtube.com/watch?v=vu4L7A5Tubk

267 '#EFFInParliament', Facebook.

268 Pauli van Wyk, "Floyd Shivambu's brother quietly pays back R4.55m, admits he received the VBS money gratuitously", *Daily Maverick*, 6 June 2021, https://www.dailymaverick.co.za/article/2021-06-06-floyd-shivambus-brother-quietly-pays-back-r4-55m-admits-he-received-the-vbs-money-gratuitously/

269 T Motau and Werksmans Attorneys, "The Great Bank Heist: Investigator's Report to the Prudential Authority".

270 Pauli van Wyk, "The other side of the VBS puzzle – Matodzi's WhatsApps reveal purpose and payments to Malema and Shivambu's slush funds", *Daily Maverick*, 7 June 2020, https://www.dailymaverick.co.za/article/2020-06-07-the-other-side-of-the-vbs-puzzle-matodzis-whatsapps-reveal-purpose-and-payments-to-malema-and-shivambus-slush-funds/

271 Pauli van Wyk, "The Shivambu Brothers and the Great VBS Heist".

272 Brian Answer Shivambu, LinkedIn, https://www.linkedin.com/in/brian-answer-shivambu-90a04733/?originalSubdomain=za

273 Pauli van Wyk, "VBS scandal: Sars demands R28.2m from Brian Shivambu, displays clear connection to Floyd", *Daily Maverick*, 15 August 2021, https://dailymaverick.co.za/article/2021-08-15-vbs-scandal-sars-demands-r28-2m-from-brian-shivambu-displays-clear-connection-to-floyd/

274 Pauli van Wyk, "Floyd Shivambu's brother quietly pays back R4.55m, admits he received the VBS money gratuitously", *Daily Maverick*, 6 June 2021, https://www.dailymaverick.co.za/article/2021-06-06-floyd-shivambu's-brother-quietly-pays-back-r4-55m-admits-he-received-the-vbs-money-gratuitously/

275 Dewald van Rensburg, *VBS: A Dream Defrauded*, Penguin Books: Cape Town, 2020.

276 Pauli van Wyk, "The Chronicles of Grand Azania, Part Three: Floyd Shivambu's four strikes", *Daily Maverick*, 26 November 2019, https://www.dailymaverick.co.za/article/2019-11-26-the-chronicles-of-grand-azania-part-three-floyd-shivambus-four-strikes/

277 Pauli van Wyk, "Along with the R16.1-million in illicit payments, VBS approved Brian Shivambu's R1.46-million home loan with a little help from uBhuti ka Brian", *Daily Maverick*, 9 December 2018, https://www.dailymaverick.co.za/article/2018-12-09-along-with-the-r16-1m-in-illicit-payments-vbs-approved-brian-shivambus-1-46m-home-loan-with-a-little-help-from-ubhuti-ka-brian/

278 President of the Republic of South Africa, 'Determination of salaries and allowances of members of the National Assembly and permanent delegates to the National Council of Provinces', Proclamation Notice 66 of 2022, *Government Gazette*, 14 June 2022, https://www.gov.za/sites/default/files/gcis_document/202206/46545proc66.pdf

279 Pauli van Wyk, "The Great VBS Heist: How the Shivambu brothers benefited even more", *Daily Maverick*, 3 April 2019, https://www.dailymaverick.co.za/article/2019-04-03-the-great-vbs-heist-how-the-shivambu-brothers-benefited-even-more/

280 Ibid.

281 Ibid.

282 Pauli van Wyk, "The Chronicles of Grand Azania, Part One: How a slush fund paid for Floyd Shivambu's wedding", *Daily Maverick*, 6 October 2019, https://www.dailymaverick.co.za/article/2019-10-06-the-chronicles-of-grand-azania-part-one-how-a-slush-fund-paid-for-floyd-shivambus-wedding/

283 Susan Comrie, "PetroSA Taps notorious political operator for massive offshore gas deal", amaBhungane, 24 January 2024, https://amabhungane.org/petrosa-taps-notorious-political-operator-for-massive-offshore-gas-deal/

284 Pieter-Louis Myburgh, "Exposed: Zweli Mkhize's R6m 'cut' from PIC's R1.4bn deal using Unemployment Insurance Fund money", *Daily Maverick*, 13 February 2022, https://www.dailymaverick.co.za/article/2022-02-13-exposed-zweli-mkhizes-r6m-cut-from-pics-r1-4bn-deal-using-unemployment-insurance-fund-money/

285 "Report of the Judicial Commission of Inquiry into Allegations of Impropriety at the Public Investment Corporation", 12 October 2018, https://www.treasury.gov.za/Report%20of%20the%20PIC%20Commission.pdf

286 Ibid.

287 Susan Comrie, "WhatsApps expose Floyd and the 'Red Boys'", *Daily Maverick*, 5 May 2019, https://www.dailymaverick.co.za/article/2019-05-05-whatsapps-expose-floyd-shivambu-and-the-red-boys/

288 Liquidation, "The Commissioner for the South African Revenue Service v Grand Azania Pty Ltd.", High Court, Pretoria, case number 33257/21, 7 July 2021

289 Van Wyk, "The Chronicles of Grand Azania, Part One: How a slush fund paid for Floyd Shivambu's wedding".

290 Susan Comrie, "WhatsApps expose Floyd and the 'Red Boys'".

291 South African Government, "Special Investigating Unit welcomes decision of Supreme Court of Appeal on electrification of Limpopo villages", 7 September 2023, https://www.gov.za/news/media-statements/special-investigating-unit-welcomes-decision-supreme-court-appeal/

292 Special Investigating Unit, "SIU welcomes the Constitutional Court dismissal of Mphaphuli Consulting's bid to review the SIU report on Operation Mabone", 6 June 2024, https://www.siu.org.za/siu-welcomes-the-constitutional-court-dismissal-of-mphaphuli-consultings-bid-to-review-the-siu-report-on-operation-mabone/

293 Van Wyk, "The Chronicles of Grand Azania, Part Three: Floyd Shivambu's four strikes".

294 Van Wyk, "The Chronicles of Grand Azania, Part Two: Floyd Shivambu's time of spending dangerously", *Daily Maverick*, 13 October 2019, https://www.dailymaverick.co.za/article/2019-10-13-the-chronicles-of-grand-azania-part-two-floyd-shivambus-time-of-spending-dangerously/, last accessed 9 January 2024

295 Van Wyk, "The Chronicles of Grand Azania, Part One: How a slush fund paid for Floyd Shivambu's wedding".

296 Van Wyk, "The Great VBS Heist: How the Shivambu brothers benefited even more".

297 Van Wyk, "The Chronicles of Grand Azania, Part Two: Floyd Shivambu's time of spending dangerously".

298 eNCA, "Floyd Shivambu addresses parliament", YouTube, 23 October 2018, https://www.youtube.com/watch?v=TJe8Oe2GF_g

299 Pauli van Wyk, "VBS Theft & Money Laundering: Julius Malema's time of spending dangerously", *Daily Maverick*, 8 September 2019, https://www.dailymaverick.co.za/article/2019-09-08-vbs-theft-money-laundering-lifes-little-luxuries-julius-malemas-time-of-spending-dangerously/

300 Ibid.

301 Ibid.

302 Ibid.

303 Ibid.

304 *BusinessTech*, "Ramaphosa approves salary hikes for ministers, MPs and premiers", 6 June 2024, https://businesstech.co.za/news/government/775579/ramaphosa-approves-salary-hikes-for-ministers-mps-and-premiers/

305 Mgagao Shamba, website, https://mgagaoshamba.co.za/

306 Its full title is "The Code of Ethical Conduct and Disclosure of Members' Interest for Assembly and Permanent Council Members", https://www.parliament.gov.za/storage/app/media/Ethics/Code%20of%20Ethical%20Conduct/Code_of_Ethical_conduct_V2.pdf

307 Parliament of the Republic of South Africa, "Media Statement: Ethics Committee Finds Hon Shivambu Breached Code of Conduct on VBS Complaint", 2 October 2023, https://www.parliament.gov.za/press-releases/media-statement-ethics-committee-finds-hon-shivambu-breached-code-conduct-vbs-complaint.

308 Parliament of the Republic of South Africa, "Media Statement: Ethics Committee Unable to Make Finding on Allegations of Breach of Code Against Hon Malema MP", 2 October 2023, https://www.parliament.gov.za/press-releases/media-statement-ethics-committee-unable-make-finding-allegations-breach-code-against-hon-malema-mp/

309 Mungo Soggot, "Was the murderer really a student?", *Mail & Guardian*, 4 October 1996, https://mg.co.za/article/1996-10-04-was-the-murderer-really-a-student/

310 Michael Beaumont, *The Accidental Mayor: Herman Mashaba and the Battle for Johannesburg*, Zebra Press, 2020.

311 Lionel Faull and Sam Sole, "Jo'burg's R1bn 'present' to Zuma benefactor", *Mail & Guardian*, 18 January 2013.

312 AmaBhungane, "Limpopo varsity fuels Malema's mining revolution", 21 September 2012, https://amabhungane.org/limpopo-varsity-fuels-malemas-mining-revolution/

313 Gosebo Mathope, "Mashaba reinstates axed internal auditor despite two legal opinions", *The Citizen*, 27 September 2017.

314 Thanduxolo Jika, Sabelo Skiti and M&G Data Desk, "Allegations of corruption at City Power", *Mail & Guardian*, 11 June 2020.

315 Micah Reddy and Stefaans Brümmer, "Firm that won R1bn Jo'burg fleet contract paid Malema-EFF 'slush-fund'", amaBhungane, 29 November 2018, https://amabhungane.org/firm-that-won-r1bn-joburg-fleet-contract-paid-malema-eff-slush-fund/

316 Beaumont, *The Accidental Mayor*, p. 101.

317 Leseja Malope, "Making sense of cents: From sleeping under a tree to churning billions", *City Press*, 1 February 2019.

318 Beaumont, *The Accidental Mayor*, p. 213.

319 Ibid, p. 127.

320 Pelane Phakgadi and Alex Mitchley, "Tshwane City manager survives late-night motion to suspend", *News24*, 31 January 2019.

321 Micah Reddy, "Analysis: At EFF congress, keep an eye on money man Marshall Dlamini", *Daily Maverick*, 11 December 2019.

322 Moloko Moloto, "Malema ally sought", *IOL*, 30 September 2014, https://www.iol.co.za/news/malema-ally-sought-1757669

323 Frank Maponya, "Residents beat up Juju's men", *Sowetan*, 14 December 2011, https://www.sowetanlive.co.za/news/2011-12-14-residents-beat-up-jujus-men/; *News24*, "Juju's friend arrested after 'chasing comrades with spade'", 14 May 2012, https://www.news24.com/news24/jujus-friend-arrested-after-chasing-comrades-with-spade-20150429; Jenni Evans, "Senior EFF member in court on assault charge", *News24*, 27 August 2015, https://www.news24.com/news24/senior-eff-member-in-court-on-assault-

charge-20150827; Moloto, "Malema ally sought"; *IOL*, "EFF bad boy taken into custody", 6 September 2015, https://iol.co.za/news/politics/eff-bad-boy-taken-into-custody-1911374/; Peter Ramothwala, "ANC MP, EFF provincial chairman out on bail for malicious damage to property and theft", *Sowetan*, 14 January 2020, https://www.sowetanlive.co.za/news/south-africa/2020-01-14-anc-mp-eff-provincial-chairman-out-on-bail-for-malicious-damage-to-property-and-theft/; Polokwane Review, "EFF's Jossey Buthane in court for assault", 31 August 2017, https://www.citizen.co.za/review-online/news-headlines/2017/08/31/effs-jossey-buthane-in-court-for-assault/

324 *News24*, "Malema's wife, kids live in house owned by 'tobacco smuggler'", 3 December 2018, https://www.news24.com/news24/malemas-wife-kids-live-in-house-owned-by-tobacco-smuggler-20181203

325 Micah Reddy, "Malema Buddy's Mine Leaves Community Reeling", amaBhungane, 28 July 2019, https://amabhungane.org/malema-buddys-mine-leaves-community-reeling/

326 Thuletho Zwane and Matuma Letsoalo, "EFF's national assembly disrupted by anti-Malema group", *Mail & Guardian*, 15 December 2014, https://mg.co.za/article/2014-12-15-effs-national-assembly-disrupted-by-anti-malema-group/

327 Richard Poplak, "Burning berets: the EFF People's Assembly takes a turn", *Daily Maverick*, 15 December 2014, https://www.dailymaverick.co.za/article/2014-12-15-burning-berets-the-eff-peoples-assembly-takes-a-turn/

328 Sapa, "EFF suspends MPs Mpho Ramakatsa and Lucky Twala", *Mail & Guardian*, 19 February 2015, https://mg.co.za/article/2015-02-19-eff-suspends-mps-mpho-ramakatsa-and-lucky-twala/

329 *Politicsweb*, "The EFF NDC's ruling against Andile Mngxitama & co", 13 April 2015, https://www.politicsweb.co.za/documents/the-eff-ndcs-ruling-against-andile-mngxitama--co

330 *Politicsweb*, "Our response to Andile Mngxitama – EFF", 5 February 2015, https://www.politicsweb.co.za/politics/our-response-to-andile-mngxitama--eff

331 Sapa, Sapa-AFP and *Mail & Guardian* online reporter, "Motlanthe criticises ANCYL congress chaos", *Mail & Guardian*, 7 April 2008, https://mg.co.za/article/2008-04-07-motlanthe-criticises-ancyl-congress-chaos/

332 Forde, *An Inconvenient Youth: Julius Malema and the 'New' ANC*, p. 203.

333 Ibid, p. 204.

334 Institute of Race Relations, "The EFF's internal revolution", 8 February 2018, https://irr.org.za/reports/occasional-reports/the-effs-internal-revolution

335 Ibid.

336 Unathi Nkanjeni, "'If I were them I would resign' – Malema on 428 EFF representatives banned from anniversary bash", *TimesLIVE*, 3 August 2023, https://www.timeslive.co.za/politics/2023-08-03-if-i-were-them-i-would-resign-malema-on-428-eff-representatives-banned-from-anniversary-bash/

337 Thapelo Lekabe, "Malema says Gordhan deserves a standing ovation", *The Citizen*, 22 February 2017, https://www.citizen.co.za/news/south-africa/malema-says-gordhan-deserves-standing-ovation/

338 *Politicsweb*, "Dismantle the Pravin Gordhan cabal! – Floyd Shivambu", 19 October 2018, https://www.politicsweb.co.za/documents/dismantle-the-pravin-gordhan-cabal--floyd-shivambu; News24, EFF hits back at Gordhan with charges of their own, 26 November 2018.

339 Vhahangwele Nemakonde, "Brian Molefe is not black, says Malema", *The Citizen*, 25 May 2017, https://www.citizen.co.za/news/south-africa/brian-molefe-not-black-says-malema/

340 Kailene Pillay, "EFF's Julius Malema calls for Brian Molefe's return to Eskom and Ramaphosa to step down immediately", *IOL*, 15 May 2023, https://www.iol.co.za/news/politics/effs-julius-malema-calls-for-brian-molefes-return-to-eskom-and-ramaphosa-to-step-down-immediately-b68676fc-9ee5-43b8-b137-12878d772d95

341 Unathi Nkanjeni, "'Flip-flop' or change of mind? SA reacts to Malema supporting Hlophe to become next chief justice", *TimesLIVE*, 8 October 2021, https://www.timeslive.co.za/news/south-africa/2021-10-08-flip-flop-or-change-of-mind-sa-reacts-to-malema-supporting-hlophe-to-become-next-chief-justice/

342 Tshidi Madia, "We regret supporting Mkhwebane – Malema", *News24*, 23 January 2017, https://www.news24.com/News24/we-regret-supporting-mkhwebane-malema-20170123

343 Jenni Evans, "EFF stands by Public Protector after earlier misgivings", *Mail & Guardian*, 28 May 2019, https://mg.co.za/article/2019-05-28-eff-stands-by-public-protector-after-earlier-misgivings/

344 Nonkululeko Njilo, "Impeached Busisiwe Mkhwebane joins EFF 'to protect the poor and marginalised' (NB not satire)", *Daily Maverick*, 16 October 2023, https://www.dailymaverick.co.za/article/2023-10-16-impeached-busisiwe-mkhwebane-joins-eff-to-protect-the-poor-and-marginalised/

345 *Mail & Guardian*, "The hypocrisies of the EFF and the twists of our prejudice", 4 July 2019, https://mg.co.za/article/2019-07-04-the-hypocrisies-of-the-eff-and-the-twists-of-our-prejudice/

346 Unathi Nkanjeni, "Malema: 'Flip-flopper is a title given to me by my enemies' ", *TimesLIVE*, 19 May 2023, https://www.timeslive.co.za/politics/2023-05-19-malema-flip-flopper-is-a-title-given-to-me-by-my-enemies/

347 *News24*, "TIMELINE | Flip-flops or standing on principle? The EFF's ever-changing position on Mkhwebane", 17 March 2021, https://www.news24.com/news24/opinions/analysis/timeline-flip-flops-or-standing-on-principle-the-effs-ever-changing-position-on-mkhwebane-20210317

348 Karyn Maughan, "Malema attacks Batohi for being 'too close' to his nemesis Gordhan", *Business Day*, 3 February 2019; Zintle Mahlati, "Malema claims judiciary captured in favour of Ramaphosa and ANC", *News24*, 21 March 2021, https://www.news24.com/News24/malema-claims-judiciary-captured-in-favour-of-ramaphosa-and-anc-20220321c

349 Nhlanhla Mabaso, "MK Party's Women's League demands mass deportation of undocumented foreign nationals", *Eyewitness News*, 22 November 2024, https://www.ewn.co.za/2024/11/22/mk-partys-women-s-league-demands-mass-deportation-of-undocumented-foreign-nationals

350 Stephen Grootes, "Violence & Threats, Inc: Zuma may have overplayed his violent hand", *Daily Maverick*, 2 June 2024, https://www.dailymaverick.co.za/article/2024-06-02-violence-threats-inc-zuma-may-have-overplayed-his-violent-hand/

351 Rorisang Kgosana, "MK party withdraws electoral court challenge disputing election results", *Business Day*, 3 July 2024, https://www.businesslive.co.za/bd/politics/2024-07-03-mk-party-withdraws-electoral-court-challenge-disputing-election-results/

352 Confidential interview with Pauli van Wyk.

353 Norman Masungwini, "Malema claims SARS terrorised and intimidated his family", *City Press*, 29 July 2023, https://www.news24.com/citypress/politics/malema-claims-sars-still-baying-for-his-blood-and-intimidating-his-family-20230729

Index

Acknowledgments

MICAH REDDY

The idea for this book goes back years, with bursts of writing punctuated by long gaps – our enthusiasm waxing and waning with changing personal and political circumstances.

The encouragement and gentle persuasion of Na'eemah Masoet, Maryna Lamprecht, and Erika Oosthuysen at NB Publishers got us writing. They also kept us focused. My thanks to Maggie Davey, too, for her support. The rest of the team at Tafelberg made this book what it is: Albert Weideman, Mike Cruywagen, Anna Tanneberger, Marthie Steenkamp, Sadé Walter, Jean Pieters and Tracey Hawthorne. Riaan Wolmarans and Riaan de Villiers provided rigorous editing. Thank you to our lawyers, Charl du Plessis, Willem de Klerk and Sanet de Lange. And to my co-author, Pauli, my immense gratitude. Without your contribution this would have only been half a book.

Sam Sole and Stefaans Brümmer gave me my first break in investigative journalism and taught me most of what I know about the trade. Their voices were in the back of my head while writing this book. The book draws heavily on the work of other journalists, too. There's competition in the world of South African journalism, but also a true spirit of camaraderie, and colleagues were always ready to assist. Fiona Forde deserves special mention. I must also thank my colleagues at amaBhungane for helping with the investigations that made up much of this book – especially Susan Comrie, Karabo Rajuili, Caroline James, and Cherese Thakur for helping make sense of the EFF and Malema's network. And to colleagues elsewhere, notably Thanduxolo Jika, Sabelo

Skiti, and Karyn Maughan, I owe a great deal for their insights and help on important aspects of the book.

Our work would not be possible without our sources, some of whom are named in the book and many of whom cannot be named. Thank you for your information and your willingness to accept the risks in sharing it.

Laura Phillips, Luke Spiropoulos, and Liam Minné took an interest in this project and were always willing to share their valuable thoughts.

I owe a special thanks to my family. To Nicole, for her political insight, her abundant patience, and her willingness to sacrifice so much of her own time so I could get this done. To Tessa, for her eternal encouragement and generosity. To Niall, for his incisive political research and ideas on the EFF and other aspects of South African politics, and for being a reliable drinking companion. And to Sofia, for making the last couple years infinitely more joyful, if a little more challenging at times.

To Sudeshan, Vasu, Priya, Andrew, Eila, and Louise, you have all, in some way or another, made this process both lighter and more rewarding.

And, lastly, to two people who are no longer with me but who taught me to be curious – Anne and Govin.

PAULI VAN WYK

Trying to tell a story about Malema is a complicated exercise. We focused the book therefore on a single theme, that of the ecosystem Julius Malema built and operates in. The book is not a conclusive view on this ecosystem, either. There is much we don't know, or only suspect and cannot prove – those stories were left out. These pages do, however, offer the benefit of hindsight, with multiple stories that, when put together, paint a certain picture. In this storytelling endeavour, our names may be on the cover, but we stand on strong shoulders.

The writing of this book was a team sport. It would not exist without our sources. It takes immense courage to be an honest public and corporate official these days. There is a long list of people who risked retribution to tell us what they knew. Their names will never be displayed on a plaque honouring their commitment to our country. Only trauma, bullying and the loss of their livelihoods would follow if any suspicion of lending a helping hand fell on them. And yet, many decided to do the right thing. I honour your commitment to justice and to South Africa.

Fortunately, there are friends and colleagues I can name and thank.

To Maryna Lamprecht, who commissioned this book six years ago and still believes in its message – your friendship is life's gift. To Na'eemah Masoet and Erika Oosthuysen, who were kind and patient, particularly in the face of too many missed deadlines and last-minute changes. To Albert Weideman, Riaan de Villiers, Riaan Wolmarans, Tracey Hawthorne and Sadé Walter, who worked under extreme pressure – we could not have done it without you.

To our lawyers, the shield between us and trouble – thank you Charl du Plessis, Willem de Klerk and Sanet de Lange.

To Fiona Forde, who wrote the definitive story on Malema's youth and his early political business career – your insights were invaluable to us and to the country.

To my colleagues and friends in the media who doggedly tracked Malema's walk and talk over two decades – much of what we recount here has your fingerprints all over it: Susan Comrie, Sam Sole, Stefaans Brümmer, Craig McKune, Adriaan Basson, Piet Rampedi, Thanduxolo Jika, Sabelo Skiti, Rob Rose and Karyn Maughan.

Branko Brkic, without your support I may not have survived to tell the tale. We will continue to shine a light on the truth.

To my co-author and friend, Micah Reddy – a big thank you. I honour your integrity and the resolve it takes to refuse to stand by as a spectator to wrongdoing.

To my parents, who still remind me that you cannot debate a wrong into a right. And to The Husband, who monitors my struggle, who makes me laugh when I am too serious, who pulls me up when the water washes over my head and who always brings the fairy lights.

About the authors

Micah Reddy is a journalist and Africa coordinator at the International Consortium of Investigative Journalists (ICIJ). Previously, he was an investigative journalist at the amaBhungane Centre for Investigative Journalism in South Africa, and before that, the national coordinator for media freedom and diversity at the Right2Know Campaign. Reddy holds a master's degree in African studies from Oxford University and a bachelor's in history from Wits University. He was managing editor at the *Yemen Times* in Sana'a. He has also worked as an editor in Egypt and on a range of freelance research and reporting projects, most recently in Ukraine for Al Jazeera and *Daily Maverick*. He lives in Johannesburg.

Pauli van Wyk is a financial crime investigator and former investigative journalist at Scorpio, *Daily Maverick*. She holds an MBA and a master's degree in communication (journalism). Previously, Van Wyk worked at *Mail & Guardian*, Netwerk24 and *Beeld*. She has won the Standard Bank Sikuvile Award for Journalist of the Year and for Investigative Story of the Year, and was the runner-up for the Taco Kuiper Award for her work on VBS Mutual Bank and the decimation at the South African Revenue Service.